If you're wondering why you should buy this new edition of *Understanding Ethnic Conflict*, here are five good reasons!

1. Part I includes the **most recent studies and theories** to help you learn about the study of ethnic conflict and its connections to international relations and comparative politics.

2. Chapter 5, "Nationalism and the Collapse of Empire: The Russian–Chechen Conflict," now includes the conflict between **Russia and Georgia** to update you on political instability in the region. In turn, Chapter 7, **"Intractable Ethnic War?: The Tamil-Sinhalese Conflict In Sri Lanka"** explains why government forces were finally able to defeat Tamil separatists on the battlefield.

3. Chapter 8, "Weak States and Ethnic Conflict: State Collapse and Reconstruction in Africa," includes new cases to help you understand the complex conflicts in the **Democratic Republic of Congo** and **Sudan**.

4. Chapter 9, "Western Military Intervention and Ethno-religious Conflicts: Iraq, Afghanistan, and Former Yugoslavia," analyzes **U.S. involvement in Iraq and Afghanistan** and provides you with a better understanding of these complex ongoing conflicts.

5. Every case study in Chapters 5 through 9 contains a box that shows you how to **apply theory** to different ethnic conflicts. We also include new maps for all our case studies.

PEARSON

*Fourth Edition*

# UNDERSTANDING ETHNIC CONFLICT

**Raymond C. Taras**
*Stanford University*

**Rajat Ganguly**
*Murdoch University*

**Longman**

Boston  Columbus  Indianapolis  New York  San Francisco  Upper Saddle River
Amsterdam  Cape Town  Dubai  London  Madrid  Milan  Munich  Paris  Montreal  Toronto
Delhi  Mexico City  Sao Paulo  Sydney  Hong Kong  Seoul  Singapore  Taipei  Tokyo

**Acquisitions Editor:** Vikram Mukhija
**Editorial Assistant:** Toni Magyar
**Marketing Manager:** Lindsey Prudhomme
**Production Manager:** Fran Russello
**Project Coordination, Text Design, and Electronic Page Makeup:** Swapnil Vaidya,
  GGS Higher Education Resources, A division of PreMedia Global, Inc.
**Cover Design Manager:** Jayne Conte
**Cover Illustration/Photo:** epa/Corbis
**Printer and Binder:** RR Donnelley & Sons, Inc.

**Library of Congress Cataloging-in-Publication Data**

Taras, Ray
  Understanding ethnic conflict/Raymond Taras, Rajat Ganguly.—4th ed.
    p.  cm.
  Rev. ed. of: Understanding ethnic conflict, ©2006.
  Includes bibliographical references and index.
  ISBN 978-0-205-74230-1
  1. Ethnic conflict—Political aspects.   2. Ethnic conflict—International cooperation.   3. World
politics.   4. Nationalism.   5. Conflict management—Political aspects.   6. Conflict management—
International cooperation.   I. Ganguly, Rajat.   II. Taras, Ray, 1946- Understanding ethnic conflict.
III. Title.

  GN496.T37 2010
  327.109'04—dc22

                                                                          2009025180

1 2 3 4 5 6 7 8 9 10—DOH—12   11   10   09

**Longman**
is an imprint of

www.pearsonhighered.com
ISBN-13: 978-0-205-74230-1
ISBN-10:     0-205-74230-0

# BRIEF CONTENTS

# CONTENTS

# PREFACE

Ethnicity, religion, and nationalism are some of the most powerful forces shaping contemporary politics. They may become even more relevant to a world working its way out of a financial crisis. When good times are over, people frequently retreat into the security of traditional identities, which, they believe, have successfully withstood the test of time. Having been victimized by the failure of economic globalization, people in various parts of the world are once again drawn to simple communitarian structures based on shared language, culture, religion, history, and economic fortunes.

The value of economic interdependence may have been called into question, but that of democracy has not. In 2007, about two-thirds of the 192 countries in the United Nations met the standards for being termed an electoral democracy, and there have been few signs of a pushback since. Given widespread consensus about democracy, variance in the domestic stability of countries is accounted for, whether competition between ethnic or religious movements exists in them or not. The spread of such movements across borders can determine whether entire regions of the world are stable and at peace, or not.

Some experts have speculated that violent conflict *between* regions—and even between entire civilizations—may occur because of cultural differences rooted in ethnicity and religion. The most notable academic work advancing this thesis was Harvard political scientist Samuel Huntington's controversial book *The Clash of Civilizations and the Making of World Order*, published in 1996. It contended that culture matters so much in international politics that future conflicts and alliance systems would be based primarily on them—not on the type of ideological competition that marked the cold war era. Huntington's thesis was not novel: the belief that religious differences between cultures engender conflict can be traced as far back as the Christian crusades against Islam beginning in the eleventh century, described by Ibn Al-Qalanisi in his *Damascus Chronicle*. Even earlier, the clash between Hellenistic civilization and the Persian empire in the fourth century B.C. became the subject of one of the western world's first historical texts, Thucydides' *The Peloponnesian War*. The significance of *The Clash of Civilizations* lay in Huntington mapping the nature of international conflicts in a postbipolar world and highlighting the centrality of ethno-nationalist and religious identities to it.

After the collapse of the Soviet Union and the independence of many new states after 1991, political scientists with expertise in area studies turned their attention to nationalism's renewed salience to state building. The comparative politics of nationalist movements, their strategies, and their objectives became a mainstream part of political science research. The ethnic conflicts and cleansings that resulted from majority and minority groups struggling for power in a country—the Balkan states in the 1990s furnish a clear example—drew the attention of area specialists.

It was only toward the end of that decade that a paradigm shift—a change in the prevailing analytic framework for examining nationalism and conflict—took place. Recognition of the phenomenon of the internationalization of ethnic conflict signified that a strictly comparative approach focused on a country's domestic politics now contained incomplete explanatory power. To take into account all the key variables in the making of an ethnic conflict, the comparative politics bias had to be jettisoned in favor of a framework capturing the dynamics between states, regions, and even civilizations. It had become clear that, in the anarchic postbipolar world in which superpower rivalry had ended and commanding unity of an ideological-military bloc had lost its importance, ethnic or religious conflict in one country could lead to involvement of many outside actors—without the fear that a core conflict involving global superpowers would result.

The first edition of this volume was published two years after *The Clash of Civilizations* appeared. It reflected the shift to examining ethnic conflicts from an international relations perspective but, unlike Huntington, we decided to adopt a micro rather than macro approach to conflict. In this fourth edition, we highlight the discrete variables, in place of civilizations, shaping ethnic conflicts in different parts of the globe. These variables include the role of seemingly contradictory international norms asserting the principles of self-determination and territorial integrity, international organizations (like the United Nations [UN] or the North Atlantic Treaty Organization [NATO]), regional powers and brokers, ethnic entrepreneurs, ethnic kin in neighboring states, and ethnic resources. The conflict management and conflict resolution process, and the peace-making and peace-keeping dimension to ethnic conflict, are central to our international relations framework. Since the late 1990s, new international relations approaches—which we have incorporated into our volume—have added voting, arms trafficking, resource grabbing, and xenophobia as factors that may internationalize a domestic conflict.

In short, resurgent nationalisms and religious fundamentalisms have contributed to the fractious nature of international politics. These forces have not triggered an all-out world war, but they have set off worldwide conflict—a subject this book addresses in detail.

We should not be surprised by the staying power of nationalism. It was the most influential political idea throughout most of the nineteenth and all of the twentieth centuries. Beginning with the French Revolution in 1789, the ideology of nationalism—citizens' consciousness of and loyalty to the nation before anything else—transformed the basis of political legitimacy from a dynastic principle to *la patrie,* that is, legitimacy grounded in a *nation*'s will to exercise self-determination. Early in the nineteenth century, this notion spread from Europe to Latin America and served to undermine Simon Bolivar's quest for a *continental* nationalism that would embrace all liberated countries of South America. From its ideological roots in the 1850s, Marxism had to make the case—most often unsuccessfully—why the working class of all nations deserved to be emancipated and empowered before subjected nations were. In the twentieth century, both anticommunist and anticolonial movements were built around the principle of nationalism—overthrowing imperial rule in order to achieve national self-determination. Peoples' need to affirm a collective self, to embrace a collective identity, to rationalize their attachments and sense of belonging to a community, and to construct images of the *other* who does not belong, all explain the continuing appeal of nationalism into the twenty-first century.

Nationalism's negative effects have invariably overshadowed its constructive quality. Some of the worst crimes against humanity have been committed in the name of nationalism. In the last century, the horrors of Nazism and fascism—extremist, exclusionary ideologies bent on a "Final Solution" for undesirable minority groups who supposedly did not fit—left an enduring imprint on human memory. Although the world promised "never again," the rise of ultranationalism in various parts of the globe a half-century after Nazism's defeat raised new concerns about the prevalence of racism, xenophobia, and even new genocides (as in the case of Central Africa in the 1990s).

The response to the terrorist attacks of September 11, 2001, was to produce an unusual strain of nationalism having global implications: an edgy American patriotism regarded by many non-Americans as an enterprise in U.S. hegemony. For those critical of President George W. Bush's foreign policy, the United States decided to substitute its interpretation of otherwise widely shared values such as democracy (equated by the Bush administration with electoralism), globalization (asserting the extraterritorial rights of multinational corporations), freedom for women (which postcolonial studies summarized as "white men saving brown women from brown men"), and international humanitarian norms (American-spearheaded "human rights imperialism"). The spread of anti-Americanism all over the globe represented a backlash against the "civilizational chauvinism" underlying U.S. values promotion. In the end, the majority of U.S. citizens, too, found the balance sheet of such foreign policy behavior to be negative, and in 2008, they elected one of the most improbable candidates for the presidency, Barack Obama, to change course.

Nationalism can have many positive attributes, of course. They include reinforcing a sense of shared identity among people living in an increasingly atomistic, materialist, and fast-changing world. The dehumanizing and exploitative colonial and communist empires were overthrown in great part by the rise of nationalist movements. Nationalist movements of minority peoples have produced newfound protection for cultures and languages in peril. In the United States, the quest to restore national pride was a large part of the reason for electing Obama. It is as important as ever to study nationalism and its political consequences—bad and good.

## FEATURES

The traditional approach to studying nationalism and ethnic conflict has been to give greater attention to the domestic factors triggering conflict and pay less attention to the international dynamics that make conflict escalate and cause regional instability. This book redresses the balance in favor of the international perspective. We begin with five fundamental questions about nationalism and ethnic and religious conflict: (1) Why does it occur? (2) How does the international system—that is, the community of states, its international organizations, and individual countries—react to ethnic conflict? (3) Why do some ethnic and religious conflicts become internationalized while others do not? (4) What can be done to resolve such conflicts? (5) Should external parties intervene or not?

The book is organized in the following way. Part I provides the conceptual tools for understanding nationalism and ethnic conflict; Part II applies these tools and presents case studies of recent conflicts. Chapter 1 examines what ethnic conflict is, what its sources—including cultural values and religious belief systems—are, and how it differs from other types of strife. It inquires into the reasons why this type of conflict developed into an international phenomenon after the cold war. Chapter 2 explores the connection between ethnic conflict and international relations. It describes the normative context framing ethnic conflict. For example, in some cases, the international community invokes doctrines of sovereignty and nonintervention in the internal affairs of states to withhold recognition of breakaway movements (like Catalonia in southern Europe or Kurdistan in the Middle East); on other occasions, an international norm like national self-determination is invoked by a group of states to recognize the independence of an implausible and unviable state (like the United States and the European Union (EU) backing the formation of a Kosovo state).

Chapter 2 also evaluates the moral arguments advanced in support of an ethnic group's right to separate from an existing state and form a separate one.

Chapter 3 looks at the factors that lead to the internationalization of ethnic conflict. Humanitarian emergencies brought on by genocidal actions; an explosion in refugee numbers; the systematic killing, torture, and rape of noncombatants; and deployment of child soldiers can produce external intervention in an ethnic conflict. State collapse following the disintegration of a central government can lead to the rise of ethno-terrorism, political and economic instability, and guns-for-drugs trade, thus provoking outside involvement.

Partisan intervention and counterintervention in ethnic conflicts may produce different outcomes in different countries. Chapter 4 considers conflict resolution and suggests how ethnic strife can be managed through international action. It weighs the different roles that third parties, such as states, international governmental organizations (IGOs), and international (INGOs) and other nongovernmental organizations (NGOs) can play in settling ethnic disputes, for example, through peace keeping, peace making, and peace building.

Case studies make up Part II of the book. Each case explains why an ethnic and/or religious conflict has occurred, how the international system has reacted, why the conflict has or has not been internationalized, and the reasons for intervention or nonintervention by external parties. We used several criteria to select cases: their contemporary importance, the different lessons that can be learned from them, and their geographical mix—they are taken from different parts of the globe, ranging from the Europe-Asia borderland to Asia, Africa, Europe, and North America. We recognize that other cases of internationalized ethnic conflict may be just as important. Among those not included in this volume are the Israeli–Palestinian conflict, the standoff over Kashmir, China's rule over Tibet, the movement to unite Kurdistan, and the successful independence struggles of East Timor and Eritrea. We hope that, after exploring the fourth edition of *Understanding Ethnic Conflict,* readers will ask questions about these and other cases of ethnic and religious conflict similar to the ones posed here.

We include three full case studies of separatist challenges that have been unable to engineer the legal breakup of a state: the Chechens' struggle to secede from Russia, the Quebec sovereignty movement's efforts to separate from Canada, and the Sri Lankan Tamils' fight for an independent Tamil homeland (Eelam) separate from Sri Lanka. We also examine the special circumstances that allowed seven sovereign states, including Kosovo, to emerge from the disintegration of Yugoslavia, and two additional entities, Abkhazia and South Ossetia, to gain limited international recognition following the breakup of Georgia. The unsuccessful breakup bids (Chechnya, Quebec, Tamil Eelam) were characterized by little to no third-party military intervention in support of the separatists. By contrast, two of the post-Yugoslav states (Bosnia Herzegovina and Kosovo) became independent as a direct result of U.S. and EU military and political support. Abkhazia and South Ossetia's independence were a mirror image of these, with Russian military and political support being advanced in the place of that of the West.

Chapter 5 focuses on the Caucasus, in particular, the Russian–Chechen conflict. It considers why, despite the lack of international support and systematic Russian repression, Chechen rebels continue to fight a war of attrition against Russian forces deployed in the region. Our argument is that the dismantling of an empire—the former Soviet Union—precipitated a wave of nationalist movements—some *under*

Russia's tutelage (Abkhazia and South Ossetia in the Republic of Georgia), others directed *at* the hegemonic nation (Chechnya and Ingushetia). Georgia itself has been described as a little empire, and it, too, has experienced centrifugal forces. The ethnic and religious complexity of the Caucasus invites interest on the part of many neighboring countries, thereby furnishing an illuminating case of the nexus between ethnic identities and international security.

By contrast, Chapter 6 assesses the constitutional crisis in Canada brought on by the Quebec sovereignty movement. Despite recent electoral setbacks, Quebec nationalism is only a national crisis away from becoming fully mobilized. This case raises the issue of whether the use of constitutional methods of secession, like a referendum, is an effective way to break away from a western liberal democratic state.

Chapter 7 deals with the Tamil–Sinhalese conflict in Sri Lanka. This protracted ethnic conflict ebbed and flowed and, for a time, engaged India in it. It proved nearly impossible to resolve through third-party action, even though ceasefires had at times been negotiated. In recent years, Tamil secessionists increasingly became stigmatized as terrorists, and they became isolated in the international arena as a result. This outcome gave the Sri Lankan government a free reign to use massive military power to win this ethnic conflict on the battlefield; this outcome has now been achieved with the complete destruction of the Liberation Tigers of Tamil Eelam (LTTE), the main Sri Lankan Tamil insurgent group, and the killing of its top leaders including Velupillai Prabhakaran, the group's supreme leader.

Chapter 8 examines the various outcomes of ethnic conflicts that may result from the existence of a weak state. Drawing on cases from the African continent, we consider instability originating in the ethnic divisions and resource struggles in Central Africa. Beginning with genocidal acts in Rwanda, ethnic conflict spilled over to the neighboring Democratic Republic of Congo. It engendered so much outside intervention, especially in its northeastern and eastern regions, that the Congo conflict has been described as Africa's first world war. In Sudan, a longstanding conflict about political power between north and south took on a religious dimension and also eventually a racial one. In the absence of a strong state, the Christian versus Muslim battle lines attracted international attention; soon a dispute with similar contours broke out in Darfur, in western Sudan. Again, third parties became embroiled over control of the region's energy resources; these third parties included major international players like Europe, the United States, China, and the African Union. In contrast, successful construction of a strong state and effective management of ethnic diversity are illustrated by postapartheid South Africa (topics also discussed in Chapter 8).

Chapter 9 addresses the key question of what impact western military intervention in various countries since the 1990s has had on preexisting ethnic and religious cleavages. The cases of U.S.-led military engagement—at times supported by NATO or makeshift multinational coalitions—in former Yugoslavia, Afghanistan, and Iraq has produced differing results. In the first case, two independent Muslim-led states—Bosnia Herzegovina and Kosovo—were created in the Balkans at the expense of eastern Orthodoxy, specifically, Serbia. In Afghanistan, western military forces, as well as the Islamic fundamentalist Taliban, competed for the support of major ethnic groups, often led by warlords, The so-called war on terror fought in that country helped turn political divisions into ethnic ones. In Iraq, too, ethnosectarian divisions were worsened by U.S. military occupation. It is unclear whether these divisions will be exacerbated or be overcome when U.S. forces withdraw completely. The more general question we address is, Why have there been such different political outcomes when western military forces have intervened?

Finally, Part III considers the dilemma of whether or not international organizations and independent states should intervene in ethnic and religious conflicts in the world today. In Chapter 10 we tackle the ideas of liberal internationalism, international security, fighting a just war, and functional integration as reasons to intervene in ethnic and religious disputes. But we also identify the parameters within which such intervention, whether by an international organization or a great power, will do good and not harm.

We need to emphasize that nationalism is neither the sole explanation for most of what happens in politics, nor is it the mobilizing potential constant over time and place. In fact, we are drawn to the conclusion that only certain types of nationalism endure for a long time. In international politics, power, security, and economic well-being are the factors that determine what is in a state's national interest. Nationalist ideology is usually a much smaller factor in the calculation. To be sure, *national interest* is a misnomer because we are usually talking about the "interests of *state*" (a more precise term comes from French: *raisons d'état*). After all, about 90 percent of the world's states are multinational (that is, made up of several nations), so the interests of state may really mean the interests of the dominant nation in a multinational country.

Nationalism has been an appealing ideology because it promises power, security, and economic well-being for a nation while declaring that it will not bow to pragmatic concerns that could compromise these goals. Should not a great nation, nationalists say, also be a great power? The moment that two ethnic or religious groups within one state, or two states in proximity to each other with different dominant nations, define their interests in this way—literally as their national interest—ethnic conflict is in the making. We hope that the focus of this fourth edition of *Understanding Ethnic Conflict*, a focus on the interstices of nationalism, ethnic conflict, religious differences, and international politics, provides an innovative perspective on some of the principal sources of contemporary international fractiousness.

## NEW TO THIS EDITION

The fourth edition of *Understanding Ethnic Conflict* introduces recent theorizing about ethnic conflict and about new forms of conflict resolution measures that may work. It expands analysis of post–cold war theories about the internationalization of ethnic conflict. The more interventionist role played by international organizations like United Nations peace-keeping missions and International Criminal Court (ICC) investigations is emphasized. Our case studies have been updated, and new ones have been added. Our concluding chapter (Chapter 10) now focuses exclusively on the question that world powers and international organizations ask themselves: Should we intervene or not in an ethnic conflict?

- Chapter 1 provides the conceptual tools for analyzing ethnic conflict. In addition to reviewing longstanding schools of thought, we provide a separate section that looks at the most recent theorizing, from the 1990s to the present.
- Chapter 2 describes international norms on domestic ethnic conflict and the moral arguments used by ethno-separatist groups to break away from what they view is an oppressive state. This fourth edition identifies what we call the emerging global regime on ethnic minorities.

- Chapter 3, on the factors leading to the internationalization of ethnic conflict, gives added coverage to migration and refugee flows—much of them risky and "illegal"—as cases of humanitarian crises requiring international attention.
- Chapter 4, on peace keeping, peace making, and peace building, spotlights the more ambitious role played by the UN in managing ethnic conflicts.
- Chapter 5 is organized in a new way to include up-to-date analysis of Russia's intervention in ethnic disputes in the Caucasus, in particular, in Georgia.
- Chapter 6, on Canada, adds coverage of the reasonable accommodation debate in Quebec, as well as of other issues that can trigger a revitalized sovereignty movement there.
- Chapter 7, on Sri Lanka, has a new section explaining the reasons for the government's military defeat of the Tamil rebels and the political options for restructuring Sri Lanka.
- Chapter 8 contains new sections on the complex conflicts in the Democratic Republic of Congo, including its northern (Ituri) and eastern (Kivu) regions, and in Sudan, in particular, Darfur.
- Chapter 9 has extended analysis of the political efforts to remake Iraq following the U.S. military drawdown. It updates coverage of the intensified war in Afghanistan. It adds a new section on Kosovo's independence and its consequences.
- Chapter 10 has a new theme: when should international actors intervene in an ethnic conflict? It considers the implications for managing contemporary ethnic conflict of the Obama administration's re-assessment of the United States' global role, as well as of the increased activism of international organizations like the United Nations and the International Criminal Court. It examines how the notions of just war, smart power, preemption of security threats, imperial impartiality, and multilateralism apply to the future of ethnic conflict resolution.

## SUPPLEMENTS

Longman is pleased to offer several resources to qualified adopters of *Understanding Ethnic Conflict* and their students that will make teaching and learning from this book even more effective and enjoyable.

### For Instructors

**MyPoliSciKit Video Case Studies for International Relations and Comparative Politics**
Featuring video from major news sources and providing reporting and insight on recent world affairs, this DVD series helps instructors integrate current events into their courses by letting them use the clips as lecture launchers or discussion starters.

### For Students

***Longman Atlas of World Issues (0-321-22465-5)*** Introduced and selected by Robert J. Art of Brandeis University and excerpted from the acclaimed Penguin Atlas Series, the *Longman Atlas of World Issues* is designed to help students understand the geography and major issues, such as terrorism, debt, and HIV/AIDS, facing the world today. These thematic, full-color maps examine forces shaping politics today at a global level. Explanatory information accompanies each map to help students better grasp the concepts being shown and how they affect our world today. This supplement is available at no additional charge when packaged with this book.

***Research and Writing in International Relations (0-321-27766-X)*** Written by Laura Roselle and Sharon Spray of Elon University, this brief and affordable guide provides the basic step-by-step process and essential resources that are needed to write political science papers that go beyond simple description and into more systematic and sophisticated inquiry. This guide focuses on the key areas in which students need the most help: finding a topic, developing a question, reviewing literature, designing research, analyzing findings, and actually writing the paper. This supplement is available at a discount when packaged with this book.

## ACKNOWLEDGMENTS

In the effort to examine ethnic, cultural, and religious conflicts affecting international politics in a comprehensive and comparative way, we have incurred intellectual debts that we would very much like to acknowledge. We are grateful for the constructive comments on various sections of the book made by Robert Charles Angel (University of South Carolina), Jacob Bercovitch (University of Canterbury, New Zealand), Maya Chadda (William Paterson University), Earl Conteh-Morgan (University of Southfield), Osama Fatim (Tulane University), François Grin (University of Geneva), Ulf Hedetoft (Copenhagen University), Cecile Jackson (University of East Anglia, United Kingsom), Guy Lachapelle (Concordia University), Ian Macduff (Victoria University of Wellington), Bryan Maddox (University of East Anglia, United Kingdom), Sam Makinda (Murdoch University), Bo Petersson (Lund University), Garry Rodan (Murdoch University), Bill Safran (University of Colorado), Muhammad Siddiq (University of California, Berkeley), Donna Lee Van Cott (University of Connecticut), Jerold Waltman (Baylor University), and Stephen White (University of Glasgow).

We would like to thank the reviewers, a list as long as it is distinguished, who offered critiques of various iterations of the book: Tine Bertran (McMurry University), David Carment (Carleton University), Sharyl N. Cross (San Jose State University), Larry Elowitz (Georgia College and State University), V. P. Gagnon (Cornell University), Sumit Ganguly (Indiana University), Michael P. Gerace (Northeastern University), Greg Gleason (University of New Mexico), Aref Hassan (St. Cloud State University), Chaim D. Kaufmann (Lehigh University), Steve J. Mazurana (University of Northern Colorado), Getachew Metaferia (Morgan State University), Andrew A. Michta (Rhodes College), Alexander J. Motyl (The Harriman Institute, Columbia University), Stephen Saideman (McGill University), Jaroslav Tir (University of Georgia), Gabriel Topor (Columbia University), Crawford Young (University of Wisconsin). We learned from all of them.

To Marjorie Castle (University of Utah), very special thanks for exacting a high level of writing, argumentation, and political science. In appreciation of the thoughtful, meticulous work performed by this edition's copy editor, Marianne L'Abbate. It was a pleasure to work with Swapnil K. Vaidya, our production editor. And to Vikram Mukhija, our New York editor, our gratitude for constructively brainstorming about and embracing this fourth edition.

*Raymond Taras*

*Rajat Ganguly*

# CHAPTER 1

# Ethnic Conflict on the World Stage

## INTRODUCTION

**Ethnic conflict** is not a new phenomenon. From the very beginning of human history, "communities organized on putative common descent, culture, and destiny have coexisted, competed, and clashed."[1] Yet the novelty of ethnic conflict in the late twentieth and early twenty-first centuries lies not in the existence of conflict among ethnic groups but in the intensity and global manifestation of that conflict. The adverse effects of such conflicts are felt in equal measure in the developed and developing worlds. Even as globalization theorists insist on the primacy of economic factors in shaping a new twenty-first-century global order, cultural divisions seem to have a greater impact on the state of world politics.

## DEFINITIONS

An **ethnic group**, or **ethnic community**, can be defined as a large or small group of people, in either traditional or advanced societies, who are united by a common inherited culture (including language, music, food, dress, and customs and practices), racial similarity, common religion, and belief in a common history and ancestry and who exhibit a strong psychological sentiment of belonging to the group. Ethnic groups can be of two distinct types: **homelands societies** and **diaspora communities**. Homelands societies include long-time residents of a given territory and thereby claim exclusive legal and moral rights of ownership over that land; such claims are usually backed up by historical (factual and mythical) and archaeological evidence. Ethnic diaspora communities are found in foreign countries and are mainly caused by population migrations, induced either by oppression in their home state or by the attraction of better economic prospects and opportunities. Ethnic diasporas do not normally seek territorial rights in a foreign state but usually demand

1

"nondiscriminatory participation as individuals in public affairs—voting, office holding, access to justice—plus nondiscriminatory access to education, employment, housing, business opportunities, and public services; and official recognition of their right to maintain institutions that perpetuate elements of their inherited culture."[2]

An ethnic group's transformation into an **ethnic nation** occurs when, as Ernest Barker has noted, political and statist ideas develop within the group:

> A **nation** is a body of [people], inhabiting a definite territory, who normally are drawn from different races, but possess a common stock of thoughts and feelings acquired and transmitted during the course of a common history; who on the whole and in the main, though more in the past than in the present, include in that common stock a common religious belief; who generally and as a rule use a common language as the vehicle of their thoughts and feelings; and who, besides common thoughts and feelings, also cherish a common will, and accordingly form, or tend to form, *a separate state* for the expression and realization of that will.[3]

As long as an ethnic nation is coterminous with a **state**,[4] it can be termed a **nation-state**. However, out of the approximately 192 states in the world roughly, 90 percent are **multiethnic** or **multinational** because they incorporate two or more ethnic groups or nations. Theoretically, Barker's definition of the nation implies that the state is the natural outgrowth of **national self-determination**—a nation's desire and ambition to maintain and govern itself independently of other nations. Hence, it would be logical to assume that the formation of nations preceded the formation of states. As far as Europe and North America is concerned, the formation of nations seems to have occurred first, which then provided the incentive and momentum for the formation of modern states. In the developing world, however, the process mostly occurred the other way round. In Latin America, Africa, and Asia, Western conquest and colonization led to the creation of multiethnic and multiracial administrative entities. These administrative entities were converted, by and large, to sovereign states during decolonization (mostly in the first half of the nineteenth century in Latin America and in the second half of the twentieth century in Asia and Africa) without first ascertaining, in most cases, the political aspirations of the constituent ethnic and racial groups, thereby creating artificial multiethnic and multiracial states. Hence, **state building**, usually occurred first in the postcolonial states, to be followed by the more difficult task of building a national identity (that is, nation building) that would supersede hundreds of ethnic identities within their borders.

**Nation building** is a complex task that could proceed along one of two tracks. First, a nation could be conceived in purely ethnic terms. If so conceived, the nation would define an individual's membership in and loyalty to the nation in terms of lineage and vernacular culture[5]; in such a schema, minority ethnic group members could not hope to "become part of the [majority or dominant] national grouping."[6] Clearly, ethnic nation building in multiethnic states, by keeping out minority ethnic groups from the dominant or core national group, could hardly be expected to promote interethnic harmony and peace. By contrast, a nation could be conceived in political or civic terms. Thus conceived, an individual's membership in and loyalty to the nation is defined in terms of citizenship, common laws, and political participation, regardless of ethnicity and lineage.[7] In the complex multiethnic postcolonial states of the developing world, only civic nation building could foster an inclusive nationalism that would supersede hundreds of ethnic identities within their borders.

Whether it is conceived in ethnic or civic forms, a nation that expresses sentiments of loyalty toward the nation-state can be said to demonstrate the spirit of **nationalism**. Conceptual problems have bedeviled the term *nationalism* ever since it made its appearance after the French Revolution, yet most scholars concur that nationalism incorporates two important characteristics: first, nationalism is an emotion or a sentiment, and second, it is a political doctrine. Hans Kohn, for instance, stressed the emotional or sentimental nature of nationalism when he wrote that nationalism "is first and foremost a state of mind, an act of consciousness."[8] Boyd Shafer, too, viewed nationalism as a sentiment or emotion that binds a group of people with a real or imagined historical experience and common aspirations and prompts them to live as a separate and distinct community.[9] Ernest Gellner, however, emphasized that nationalism is a political doctrine that requires the congruence of political and national units.[10] Similarly, Anthony Smith argued that "[n]ations are distinguished by the fact that the objective of their social action can only be the 'autonomous polity,' a sovereign state of their own. . . ."[11]

The transformation of an ethnic group into an **ethnic political movement** occurs when an ethnic community is converted "into a political competitor that seeks to combat ethnic antagonists or to impress ethnically defined interests on the agenda of the state."[12] Theoretically, an ethnic political movement may try to represent "the collective consciousness and aspirations of the entire community," but in practice, ethnic political movements often "split into several tendencies or concrete organizations, each competing for the allegiance of the community and for the right to be its exclusive representative."[13] But on the whole, the strength of an ethnic political movement depends on the strength of **ethnic solidarity**—the duties and responsibilities of members toward their ethnic group. Finally, an **ethno-religious group** can be defined as one where ethnic and religious identities are inseparable in the making of community. Because this seems to encompass so many groups, ranging from Irish Catholics to Serb Orthodox, to Arab Muslims, and to Indian Hindus, and because there are important exceptions to each case, the ethno-religious category seems analytically unhelpful, except, arguably, to explain **ethno-religious conflict**— a clash of cultures rooted in both objective and psychological factors that fuse lineage with a religious belief system.

## HOW IS ETHNIC IDENTITY FORMED?

*Ethnic identity* can be defined as "the set of meanings that individuals impute to their membership in an ethnic community, including those attributes that bind them to that collectivity and that distinguish it from others in their relevant environment."[14] Generally, one may speak of three main schools of thought on the questions of how ethnic identity is formed and why it persists: the **primordialist**, the **instrumentalist**, and the **constructivist**.

Primordialists regard ethnic identity as essentially a biologically given or "natural phenomenon."[15] Understood in this sense, ethnic groups "constitute the network into which human individuals are born" and where "every human infant or young child finds itself a member of a kinship group and of a neighborhood," and therefore comes to share with other group members certain common objective cultural attributes.[16]

Some of these common objective cultural attributes are language, religion, customs, tradition, food, dress, and music.[17] Along with objective cultural markers, primordialists also stress the subjective or psychological aspects of self- and group-related feelings of identity distinctiveness and their recognition by others as a crucial determinant of ethnic identity formation and its persistence.[18] The exact nature of these psychological feelings is not very clear, although three requirements seem important for group creation: emotional satisfaction or warmth that one receives from belonging to a group; a shared belief in the common origin and history of the group, however mythical or fictive, that helps to set up the boundaries of the group; and the feeling among group members that "the social relations, within which they live, [are] 'sacred' and [include] not merely the living but [also] the dead."[19]

Ethnic identity from the primordialist perspective, therefore, is a "subjectively held sense of shared identity based on objective cultural . . . criteria."[20] Anthony Smith exemplified this approach when referring to six "bases," or "foundations" of ethnic identity: the existence of a group name in order to be recognized as a distinct community by both group members and outsiders; belief in common ancestry; presence of historical memories (as interpreted and diffused over generations, often verbally) among group members; shared objective cultural attributes (such as dress, food, music, crafts and architecture, laws, customs and institutions, religion, and language); attachment to a specific territory as an ancestral and traditional group homeland; and feelings of common solidarity with other group members.[21] Discussing the conditions that promote the formation and survival of ethnic groups, Smith argued that, in medieval times, four factors favored ethnic crystallization and survival: the acquisition (or later the loss) of a territorial homeland, a history of struggle with various enemies, the existence of some form of organized religion, and the development of a strong belief in the myth of "ethnic chosenness."[22] Smith concluded that, in modern times, the most important developments that have promoted peoples' sense of their ethnic identity include the increasing cultural and civic activities of the modern state, the intellectual production of an intelligentsia within ethnic groups, and the development of the ideology of nationalism, particularly its ethnic (as opposed to civic) forms.[23]

In contrast to primordialism, the instrumentalists simply view ethnicity as "a tool used by individuals, groups, or elites to obtain some larger, typically material end."[24] From this perspective, ethnic identity, one among several alternative bases of identity, gains social and political significance when ethnic entrepreneurs—either for offensive or defensive purposes or in response to threats or opportunities for themselves and/or their groups—invoke and manipulate selected ethnic symbols to create political movements in which collective ends are sought.[25] At such moments, ethnicity can be a device as much as a focus for group mobilization through the select use of ethnic symbols. Politicized ethnicity is thus the creation "of elites, who draw upon, distort, and sometimes fabricate materials from the cultures of the groups they wish to represent in order to protect their well-being or existence or to gain political and economic advantage for their groups as well as for themselves."[26]

In turn, constructivists categorically reject the notion that ethnic identity is either a natural phenomenon or that it is simply a tool that is invoked and manipulated by ethnic entrepreneurs for individual and collective political ends. Pointing out that the presumption of naturalness of ethnicity obscures the human hand and motivations behind its formation, constructivists contend that ethnic and national identities are enduring social constructions. That is, they are the products of human actions and choices "rather than biologically given ideas whose meaning is dictated by nature."[27]

Max Weber, one of the earlier writers who stressed the social construction of ethnic identity, viewed ethnic groups as "human groups" whose belief in a common ancestry, in spite of its origins being mostly fictitious, is so strong that it leads to the creation of a community.[28] This led Weber to conclude that ethnic membership by itself "does not necessarily result in ethnic group formation but only provides the resources that may, under the right circumstances, be mobilized into a group by appropriate political action."[29]

In his seminal study on nationalism, *Imagined Communities*, Benedict Anderson, following in Weber's footsteps, argued that the "nation" (including its ethnic variant) is essentially "an imagined political community."[30] In this sense, the nation is a cultural "invention" or "construction" simply because most members of a nation will never know, meet or hear their fellow members, but in their minds they will retain the strongest emotion for and image of their shared national membership. Anderson further argued that this national imagination operated at three levels. First, the boundaries of the nation are imagined to be finite in the sense that beyond the imagined national boundaries lie other nations; in this way, the imagination of the nation is *limited*. Second, the nation is imagined to be *sovereign*, in the sense that "nations dream of being free" and the "gage and emblem of this freedom is the sovereign state."[31] Third, the nation "is imagined as a community" in the sense that irrespective of differences and conflicts that may exist within the group, "the nation is always conceived as a deep, horizontal comradeship."[32] It is the imagined bond of community and fraternity, which, in Anderson's opinion, has influenced members of nations over centuries to lay down their lives for their own nations.

In his study of ethnic identity formation, Charles Keyes drew a distinction between social descent, which is a form of kin selection through which human beings seek to create solidarity with those whom they recognize as being "of the same people," and genetic descent, which involves the transmission of biological characteristics through genetic inheritance. Keyes argued that it is the cultural construction of social descent that leads to the formation of ethnic identity because it determines the characteristics that indicate who does or does not "belong to the same people as oneself."[33] He cautioned, however, that there "is no invariable pattern as to which cultural differences will be seized upon by groups as emblematic of their ethnic differences."[34] Instead, the type of cultural markers that are put forward "as emblematic of ethnic identity depends upon the interpretations of the experiences and actions of mythical ancestors and/or historical forebears."[35] These interpretations often take the form of historically symbolic myths or legends that can be found in stories, music, artistic depictions, dramas, and rituals.[36] But no matter how these myths and legends are created and presented, "the symbols of ethnic identity must be appropriated and internalized by individuals before they can serve as the basis for orienting people to social action."[37]

Constructivists, however, acknowledge that the social construction of ethnic identity and its internalization by individuals do not necessarily lead to its politicization. Rather, ethnic identity gets politicized and becomes a variable of sociopolitical action "only if access to the means of production, means of expropriation of the products of labor, or means of exchange between groups is determined by membership in groups defined in terms of nongenealogical descent."[38]

From the preceding discussion, it becomes clear that one of the most contentious issues among the primordialists, instrumentalists, and constructivists concerns the role of culture in the formation of ethnic identity. Earlier primordialists (such as

Geertz, Isaacs, Naroll, Gordon, Mitchell, Epstein, and Furnivall) considered ethnicity to be a biologically given phenomenon organized around objective markers such as common cultural attributes.[39] This viewpoint—of assigning primacy to culture in the formation of ethnic identity—came under attack in the late 1960s, and scholars (Kuper was one of the first) increasingly questioned the primordialists' basic assumption that a dependency relationship exists between cultural and sociopolitical groupings, including ethnic groups.[40] Subsequently, some scholars (Barth, Glazer, and Moynihan) analytically distinguished between the objective and the subjective bases of ethnicity.[41] Social constructivists relegated culture to a secondary position in the formation and persistence of ethnic identity, while instrumentalists went much further and suggested that cultural markers can even be manipulated to rationalize the identity and existence of an ethnic group.

## WHY DOES ETHNIC CONFLICT OCCUR?

Scholars and practitioners have been preoccupied with the question of why ethnic polarization and conflict occur for a long time. In a general sense, however, theorization about ethnic polarization and conflict can be divided into several chronologically defined episodes or waves. In post–Medieval Europe, for instance, the new ideas of nation, nationalism, and national self-determination, products of the Enlightenment, came together powerfully to destroy the Medieval order and usher in the era of the modern nation-state. By the beginning of the twentieth century, these ideas had spread around the globe due to the dual impact of the Industrial Revolution and European colonialism. Anticolonial movements started to gather steam and nationalist conflicts broke out in Europe in the first half of the twentieth century, and these events led to the beginning of the first wave of theorizing about nationalism and ethnic conflict, which many experts linked strongly with the process of modernization.

### The First Wave: Modernization, Nationalism, and Ethnic Conflict

Sociologist Emile Durkheim was one of the earliest writers who explored the link between modernization and nationalism. Durkheim argued that, due to the division of labor brought about by modernization, societies transform from a "mechanically integrated" state to an "organically integrated" one. In a mechanically integrated society, primordial ethnic identities of that society's members help to create and maintain social structure, cohesion, and unity. But as society modernizes and division of labor takes place, "every citizen becomes dependent on every other citizen," and each person becomes "a small piece in a huge puzzle that can only be completed when each performs his or her particular role."[42] This creates the foundation for the rise of nationalism in modernizing societies. Durkheim argued that, to survive and meet the challenging needs of modernization, "modern societies need the cohesive force of the reconstituted collective norms of the 'mechanical' type of society [and therefore] must reorganize themselves as modifications of the old communitas, or disintegrate."[43] Therefore, reorganization of traditional society into a cohesive nation is both a requirement as well as a consequence of modernization. Ironically, however, in Durkheim's view, as nationalism gains ground in a modernizing multiethnic society, it reduces the significance of the parochial ethnic identities, thereby making such identities disappear altogether over time.

Other scholars followed Durkheim's lead in regarding the breakdown of traditional society due to modernization as the root cause for the rise of nationalism. Writing in the mid-sixties, Eisenstadt argued that, in a modernizing society, nationalism forms the bridge between a community's tradition and the modernizing process by creating new roles incorporating the parochial and universal orientations of individuals.[44] Smelser highlighted the disruptive effects of modernization in traditional societies and the role of nationalism in maintaining order. By triggering rapid change in society, modernization inevitably produces conflict and violence. In such chaotic conditions, people who are most adversely affected by the destruction of traditional society may be attracted to collective movements such as nationalism. Hence, nationalism is a by-product of industrialization, and it provides people whose lives have been disrupted with a relatively easy way to accept painful changes.[45]

Arguably, the most ambitious theory linking the development of modern industrial society to the rise of nationalism came from Ernest Gellner. In *Thought and Change,* Gellner established that modernization required the remolding of any traditional society that experienced it into a standardized, homogeneous, centrally sustained "high cultural type" with which the population could identify. The modern nation-state, with its laws, institutions, symbols, and political culture, was this new society.[46] In *Nations and Nationalism,* Gellner further emphasized that the key objective requirement for rapid industrialization is the development of the modern nation-state, with a strong and centralized sovereign authority.[47] Because states in Medieval Europe lacked strong central governments, they were unsuited for the tasks that industrialization demanded. It was only with the breakdown of the feudal states and the gradual development of modern nation-states, with centralized sovereign authority, that Europe made rapid industrial progress. However, the "breakdown of the feudal state, and the emergence of centralized 'sovereign' authority was [also] important for the development of nationalism, for it provided a strong state structure from which a homogeneous nation could be shaped."[48]

Although Gellner offered one of the most influential theories of nationalism employing a modernization paradigm, his critics pointed out several weaknesses in his analysis. For instance, in an influential essay published in 1972, Walker Connor argued that a fundamental reality of the post–World War II international state system, particularly in the developing world, was that an overwhelming majority of these states were multiethnic. The most dominant form of nationalism found in these states was not the state-centric civic type (signaling the failure of political nation-building enterprises) but the more particular and parochial ethnic kind, which Gellner's theory certainly did not account for.[49] Gellner's theory also offered little explanation for the rise of ethnic nationalism in the "post-industrial" societies of the West: "Contemporary nationalisms have arisen in long-industrialized countries such as Britain, Belgium, and Spain, which Gellner might have called 'nation-states.' Something new seems to have happened there, outside Gellner's theory."[50] Other critics argued that Gellner's theory failed to shed any light on the question of why nationalism had such a powerful emotional appeal for people: "Why should people be prepared to die for what is in [Gellner's] analysis an imperative of a rational economic and social system of industrialization? Nationalist behavior in its contemporary form is hardly explained in this theory. It deals instead with the reasons why industrializing states adopted a national form in order to prosper, and the nationalism which was associated with that."[51]

Because modernization theories of nationalism were unable to explain the rise of ethnic nationalism in many developing as well as developed states in the immediate post–World War II period, they gradually came to be discredited. In their place arose a range of theories that linked the modernization process with the emergence and rapid diffusion of ethno-nationalist and religious sentiments. These theories accounted for political fragmentation, instability, and antidemocratic developments by pointing to the side effects of state modernization. For example, in their analyses of the growth of ethnic, religious, and political extremism in the Middle East, Halpern, Berger, and Binder alluded to the destruction of traditional elites, elite culture, and peoples' sense of security caused by the disruption of traditional ways of life that accompanied modernization, democratization, and urbanization.[52] Ethnic nationalism was one way the new urban middle and lower-middle classes responded to the cultural disorientation and physical disruption of the traditional way of life. Thus, the rise of ethnic nationalism in societies experiencing urban anomie, elite permeability, and mass extremism was inevitable, the argument went, and would undermine democracy. However, ethnic nationalism could itself be superseded by totalitarianism.[53]

Writing within the framework of the modernization paradigm, Karl Deutsch, in his *Nationalism and Social Communication*, developed the concepts of mobilization and **assimilation** to argue that modernization, by producing greater sociopolitical mobilization and increasing assimilation of those mobilized, was the primary cause for the development of state nationalism. To Deutsch, mobilization did not simply mean the entrance of large numbers of people into the arena of social, economic, and political competition but was also a process that allowed people, through intensive communication (especially through the mass media), to create a "public," or nation; the desire to belong to a group and create a nation stemmed from the economic and psychological insecurity caused by the disruptions of modernization.[54] Deutsch, however, signaled the dangers of disruption of this integrative process by arguing that parochialism, or regionalism (including ethnic forms), with its concomitant instability and disorder, could result in situations in which mobilization outpaces assimilation. Thus, for Deutsch, the "mobilization–assimilation gap" that is created when mobilization outpaces assimilation in a modernizing society is at the root of the rise of ethnic nationalism that can lead to conflict, instability, and state fragmentation.

Samuel Huntington and Daniel Lerner referred to the tension between the **"revolution of rising expectations"** and the **"revolution of rising frustrations"** caused by modernization in accounting for the rise of ethnic nationalism and disintegrative tendencies in developing states. According to Huntington and Lerner, the process of modernization in developing societies caused rapid social and political mobilization by breaking down the traditional order and expanding the communications and transportation networks. This, in turn, led to a sharp increase in the number of political participants who were politically conscious, socially aware, and sensitive to the poverty in which they lived. Consequently, the volume and intensity of socioeconomic demands on the political system markedly increased as more and more newly mobilized groups entered the arena of political competition. However, the capacity of the political system to respond to all these demands in an equitable way was restricted because economic growth was modest, and state elites feared that an equitable distributive response to popular demands would further slow down economic growth. As a result, the euphoria after independence caused by a "revolution of rising expectations" was soon replaced by the despair of a "revolution of rising frustrations." The failure of the state to meet the rapidly growing demands and needs of a modernizing and expectant society led to political fragmentation and decay and to the rise of parochial and regional ethno-nationalist sentiments.[55]

Strain theorist Clifford Geertz accounted for the rise of ethnic nationalism by referring to the disorienting process, or "strain," of modernization and the failure of the state to draw different ethnic groups into the national mainstream. This increased the economic, cultural, and political divergence of these groups from the rest of the state. But strain theorists added the qualification that the politicization of ethnic identity and the rise of ethnic nationalism were temporary aberrations that would gradually disappear as the process of structural differentiation produced a reintegrated society.[56] Stein Rokkan further highlighted the salience of three factors that he contended could prevent states from integrating ethnic groups into the national life: territorial concentration and remoteness of the ethnic groups, their social isolation, and their economic isolation.[57]

In the 1970s, a growing dissatisfaction with the explanatory value of the theories that linked modernization to ethnic nationalism emerged. Two shortcomings of these theories were viewed as particularly crucial. First, these theories regarded ethnic nationalism negatively, as undemocratic and extremist, a viewpoint that came to be challenged. Second, the theories that linked modernization and ethno-nationalism offered insights about the causes of ethno-nationalism mainly through inference and induction because their focus was primarily on the process of modernization and its associated problems, such as democratic instability, violence, and revolution. But with ethno-nationalist movements proliferating in the 1970s, the need for more analytically rigorous and robust explanations became pressing. Scholars who were not prepared to discard the salience of the modernization process to the rise of ethno-nationalism developed two new theories dealing directly with ethnic political mobilization: the developmental approach and the reactive ethnicity approach.

The central argument of the developmental approach is that "ethnic identity" forms "the essential independent variable that leads to [ethnic] political assertiveness and militant separatism, regardless of the existence of inequality or dominance."[58] The developmental approach thus assigned primacy to cultural identity and argued that distinct ethnic communities prefer to be governed poorly by their ethnic brethren than wisely by aliens. Foreign rule, this approach contended, is degrading for the community. Also, the developmental approach recognized the salience of the modernization process behind the rise of ethno-nationalist sentiments. Walker Connor, an early exponent of the developmental perspective, contended that the process of modernization helped to sharpen ethnic identity and spark ethno-nationalist sentiments in several ways. First, the spread of social communication and mobilization, by extending the political and administrative reach of governments into peripheral ethnic homelands previously enjoying substantial **autonomy**, helped to increase outlying ethnic groups' awareness of their own distinct culture, their contempt for alien rule, and their desire to preserve their autonomous lifestyles. Second, improvements in communications and transportation, by bringing members of different ethnic groups into contact with each other, further helped to increase ethnic minorities' cultural awareness by highlighting the cultural distinctions between members belonging to different groups, as well as by underscoring the cultural affinity among members belonging to the same group. Third, by widely disseminating the message of the right of national self-determination, political mobilization played a key role in the formation of militant ethno-nationalist consciousness in many parts of the developed as well as developing world. Finally, post–World War II global political developments such as the onset of the cold war and the nuclear standoff between the **superpowers** made it more unlikely that a militarily weak power would be annexed by a larger power. As a result, many smaller ethnic groups could consider the option of political independence, which in turn raised ethno-nationalist consciousness, sentiments, and aspirations.[59]

The main theorist elaborating the reactive ethnicity approach was Michael Hechter, although the original idea was derived from Marxist social theories developed by Lenin and Gramsci. Based on his study of the Celtic minority in the United Kingdom, Hechter argued that exploitation characterized the relationship between members of dominant cultural groups and members of peripheral ethnic groups in advanced industrial states. Such exploitation usually results in a cultural division of labor in which valued roles and resources are allocated to the members of the dominant ethnic group. This in turn creates resentment among the peripheral and subordinate groups and increases their consciousness about their ethnic identity to the point of politicizing it. In other words, faced with the pressure of infiltration of their ethnic homeland by members of the dominant group, the stunted development of their region due to its treatment as an appendage of the national economy, and the destruction of the social fabric of their society due to economic exploitation caused by the cultural division of labor, peripheral ethnic groups may politically mobilize for collective action. One way that dominant ethnic groups can dampen or weaken such political mobilization by peripheral groups and ensure the continuity of the cultural division of labor is by selectively co-opting potentially destructive or divisive leaders from the peripheral ethnic groups.[60]

By combining economic and cultural factors, Hechter added an important dimension to the analysis of ethnic political mobilization. But the independent variable—the cultural division of labor—was in Hechter's own opinion only a necessary and not sufficient condition for the formation of ethnic political movements.[61] Although applied to the study of the Celtic minority in the United Kingdom, the reactive ethnicity approach could be used to explain political and nationalist mobilization among peripheral ethnic minorities in many parts of the developing world that followed from their economic exploitation and infiltration by core or dominant ethnic groups. What the model could not explain, however, was political mobilization by economically privileged and prosperous ethnic groups.

## The Second Wave: Multiethnic States and Democratic Instability

The inability of the modernization paradigm to satisfactorily explain the rise of ethnic conflict and the undermining of democracy in multiethnic societies led to the formulation of a new group of theories that essentially believed that multiethnic states could not be both democratic-capitalist and politically stable. The plural society approach developed initially by the British economist J. S. Furnivall and later expanded and modified by the West Indian anthropologist M. G. Smith was an early example of such thinking.[62] The main premise of the approach was that, in democratic-capitalist plural societies, interethnic relations are marked by fierce competition in the marketplace; hence, these societies fail to develop a sense of common political identity that could overcome the ethnic differences among the various constituent groups. As a corollary, unrestrained economic competition may actually generate competing ethnic nationalisms that, in turn, may lead to violent conflict and political instability. Furnivall believed that the only way plural societies could be held together is through the application of the external force of colonialism.[63]

Smith further developed the plural society approach even while expressing pessimism about the chances of achieving democratic stability in a pluralist state. He argued that, in multiethnic states, the different ethnic groups could be politically incorporated in one of three ways, each generating a different set of problems for stability and democracy. First, members of different ethnic groups could be "uniformly" incorporated as equal citizens with equal civil and political rights and liberties, regardless of ethnic affiliation. While this type of incorporation would lead to the creation of a civic nation-state, in reality it would also result in assimilative policies being pursued by the dominant ethnic group, which could then lead to resentment and even revolt among minority ethnic groups. Second, different ethnic groups could be "equivalently" incorporated with equal or complimentary public rights and status, thereby creating a consociational democratic polity. But while the **consociational democracy** model held out the most hope for multiethnic states, in practice it was unlikely to produce democratic stability because most often, "the components of a consociation are unequal in numbers, territory, and economic potential."[64] Consequently, real or perceived grievances could lead to ethnic conflict and political instability. Finally, ethnic groups could be "differentially" incorporated to create a system in which a dominant ethnic group monopolizes political power and maintains its hegemonic position by excluding other groups from power. But differential incorporation would lead to dominant–subordinate relations among ethnic groups and exclude subordinate groups from real power; hence, this type of setup would also not create stable and democratic multiethnic states.

Even though the plural society approach painted a bleak picture of the prospects for stable and democratic multiethnic states, some scholars continued to express doubts about "the incompatibility view of ethnic relations within a single sovereign [democratic] state."[65] This led to the development of the consociational democracy approach that readdressed the issue of stability and democracy in multiethnic states. In his seminal work *Democracy in Plural Societies,* Arend Lijphart argued that in multiethnic societies, the traditional Westminster majoritarian model of democracy (found in Britain) favoring one-party cabinets, two main political parties, a "first past the post" electoral system, a unitary and centralized form of government, and an unwritten constitution would not be able to ensure stability and democracy. Rather, stability and democracy could be maintained in multiethnic states by creating a consociational democratic polity with the following key features:

- Cooperation among political elites, leading to the formation of coalition governments and executive power sharing
- Formal and informal separation of powers and checks and balances among the various branches and levels of government
- Balanced bicameralism through special minority representation in the upper chamber of parliament
- The existence of multiple political parties representing different ethnic groups
- Proportional representation in parliament
- Territorial and nonterritorial federalism and decentralization of power
- Allowance for ethnic groups to veto legislation affecting their vital interests
- A high degree of autonomy for each ethnic community to run its own affairs
- A written constitution with elaborate and difficult procedures for amendment and that explicitly laid down certain fundamental rights that cannot be violated by the government[66]

The empirical evidence suggests that the record of consociational democracy has been mixed. While it has produced relatively stable multiethnic democratic states (such as Switzerland, Holland, Belgium, and Canada), it has failed to prevent the outbreak of ethnic conflict elsewhere (such as in Sri Lanka, Cyprus, and Lebanon).

Eric Nordlinger attempted to build on the consociational democracy model by underscoring how elite cooperation and "structured elite predominance" is necessary to preserve democratic stability and prevent conflict in mutliethnic societies. In *Conflict Regulation in Divided Societies,* Nordlinger suggested that elite cooperation through compromise and concessions may be motivated by some combination of the following conditions: existence of stable coalitions, proportional representation, depoliticization, mutual veto power, desire to thwart external threats to the state, pressure from the business class for political stability, inability of any one group to acquire political power and office without support from other groups, and the threat of civil violence in the event of noncooperation. However, Nordlinger was skeptical about the positive impact on elite cooperation of crosscutting ties between ethnic groups or of the geographical isolation of ethnic groups. He argued that there simply was not enough evidence to suggest that crosscutting ties between ethnic groups reduces conflict in multiethnic societies; similarly, geographical isolation of ethnic groups, instead of promoting elite cooperation, may actually lead to unequal development of ethnic groups, thereby increasing sentiments for autonomy or separation.[67]

A theoretical approach that fell between the pessimistic plural society approach (which believed that political stability in multiethnic states could be maintained only by coercion and control) and the overly optimistic consociational democracy approach (which believed that political stability could be provided in multiethnic states by the right type of democracy) was the **hegemonic-exchange** model. It attempted to blend consociational democratic ideas with theories of control and dominance to advance a different perspective. Donald Rothchild, an exponent of the hegemonic-exchange approach, found from a study of several African states that most of their governments could impose only a limited amount of hegemony on ethnic groups within their borders because these governments lacked the necessary coercive capability (as the plural society approach would require) and political legitimacy (as the consociational democracy approach would entail). Therefore, the governments of these so-called soft states had to continuously engage in a process of "exchange" (or bargain) with the various ethnic groups within their borders in order to maintain political stability and thus preserve the sovereignty and territorial integrity of the state. The result was a hegemonic-exchange system of state-group relations that, as an ideal type, "is a form of state-facilitated co-ordination in which a somewhat autonomous central-state actor and a number of considerably less autonomous ethno-regional interests engage, on the basis of commonly accepted procedural norms, rules, or understandings, in a process of mutual accommodation."[68] The hegemonic-exchange system thus did not regard ethnic politics within a state as a clash of primordial identities. Instead, it believed "that ethnic groups have overt, tangible interests that can be pursued in a rational, utility maximizing manner," which meant that "tradeoffs and bargaining are possible, and ethnic violence can be ended by changes in policies of allocation of power and wealth."[69] The role of the state under this scheme is not that of an "oppressor, but as a mediator and facilitator; and in order to play this role it must reject an exclusivist approach to access to power in favor of an inclusive strategy based on ethnic balancing."[70] Rothchild found that national governments in many postcolonial African states such as Nigeria, Mauritius,

Togo, Ivory Coast, Zambia, Kenya, and Zimbabwe were often a hegemonic coalition of representatives belonging to various ethnic groups and regions.

## The Third Wave: Resource Competition and Ethnic Nationalism

A more instrumentalist explanation for the politicization of ethnic identity and outbreak of ethnic conflict was developed in the late 1970s and early 1980s by the resource competition approach. It posits that in multiethnic societies, large-scale ethnic identity formation and politicization is promoted when various ethnic groups are forced to compete with each other for scarce resources and rewards.[71] Such competition may lead to the rise of ethnic political movements if a group's "previously acquired privileges are threatened or alternatively when underprivileged groups realize that the moment has come to redress inequality."[72] At such moments, ethnic groups may come to develop a perception of **relative deprivation**, which can be defined as "the perceived discrepancy between value expectations and value expectancies in a society"; in other words, ethnic groups are more likely to mobilize politically for collective action if they come to believe that they have received less (their expectations) than what they deserve (their expectancies).[73] The perception of relative deprivation builds gradually over several stages. In the first stage, an ethnic group comes to recognize that deprivation in society exists. Then, in the second phase, the group develops the understanding that not all groups in society experience deprivation uniformly and that some other groups enjoy what they lack. This is followed, in the third stage, by the generation of feelings among the group members that the situation of deprivation in which they find themselves is not just inequitable but also unfair. Such sentiments eventually crystallize, in the final stage, into firm conviction that the inequitable and unfair situation of deprivation in which the group finds itself can be rectified only through collective political action.

A key feature of the resource competition approach is the dynamics of intense inter- and intragroup elite interaction and competition over the politicization of ethnic identity. This phenomenon is more pronounced in modern states, particularly those in the middle ranks of economic development, because the process of modernization leads to rapid social mobilization. However, these states usually lack the large economic and financial resources needed to cope with and satisfy the increased aspirations that rapid social mobilization creates. Hence, these states are particularly vulnerable to intense competition and conflict between ethno-political elites. For instance, in his study of ethnic and communal conflicts in India, the former Soviet Union, and Eastern Europe, Paul Brass has shown how altered conditions of elite competition, the emergence of new elites, resource scarcity, and centralizing tendencies worked together to generate intense elite competition and ethnic polarization in these states.[74] The resource competition approach has been criticized, however, for overemphasizing the role "of greedy elites and manipulative, power-seeking regional leaders who take advantage of the communal spirit for their own ends."[75]

## The Fourth Wave: Theories of Ethnic Conflict in the Post–Cold War Era

With the collapse of communist ideology and the Soviet empire in the early 1990s, which brought to an end the cold war era, a number of violent ethnic conflicts broke out in the former Soviet Union, in eastern and southeastern Europe, and in parts of Africa and Asia. Many of these conflicts centered on the status of ethnic minorities in newly independent states, minorities' aspirations and demands for political autonomy and/or secession, and irredentist claims and counterclaims involving neighboring states. The existing theories of ethnic conflict (which we have alluded to previously in this chapter) often could not fully explain the reasons behind the outbreak of violent ethnic conflict in places like Chechnya, Nagorno-Karabakh, Slovenia, Croatia, Bosnia-Herzegovina, Somalia, Rwanda, Burundi, Congo, Sierra Leone, Liberia, Indonesia, Kashmir, and Afghanistan. This led to the development of a new wave of theory building, particularly by international relations experts who had hitherto been reluctant to see ethnic conflict as an international issue.

**ANCIENT HATREDS AND ETHNIC CONFLICT**   One of the earlier explanations for the outbreak of violent ethnic conflicts in the aftermath of the end of the cold war was the idea of "ancient hatreds," a concept that was mainly the creation of journalists and media personnel covering the Balkan ethnic conflicts and the various ethnic civil wars in sub-Saharan Africa. The core argument put forward here was that the ethnic groups locked in violent combat had a lengthy history of bellicose intergroup relations. Periods of relative peace in intergroup relations prevailed when strong central authority managed to keep a tenuous ethnic peace through the use of rewards and sanctions. Whenever central authority weakened, though, intergroup relations became hostile and violent. From this, it followed that under communist rule in countries such as Yugoslavia, ethnic relations were kept in check by strong central elites (for example, President Tito). But when the center itself became weak and crumbled, as in the early 1990s, the relations between the constituent ethnic groups, such as Serbs, Croats, Slovenes, Kosovars, Macedonians, and Bosnian Muslims, "naturally" regressed to violence.[76]

A variant of the "ancient hatred" argument was that the end of the cold war, by inducing the superpowers to gradually disengage from costly commitments in faraway places that did not immediately affect their national interest, allowed old ethnic animosities to resurface and old scores to be settled once and for all. This argument presupposed that during the cold war, bipolar politics between the superpowers managed to suppress local ethnic conflicts. One reason for this was that both superpowers regarded confrontation through the support of rival proxy ethnic groups as inherently dangerous. Hence they generally stayed out of local ethnic politics unless the costs and risks of partisan intervention were perceived to be reasonably low.[77] Another reason why superpowers were able to suppress local ethnic conflicts was because of the structure of the global bipolar alliance system that allowed the superpowers to maintain firm control over their respective allies' behavior. With the end of the cold war, this checks-and-balances system collapsed, and various types of internal conflicts came to the forefront in many parts of the world.

A case in point was postcommunist Afghanistan. After the withdrawal of Soviet forces and the collapse of the Soviet-backed Nazibullah government in 1992, Afghanistan was de facto partitioned into semiautonomous territories. The absence of strong central authority enticed regional states such as Pakistan, Saudi Arabia, and Iran to expand their influence in Afghanistan and the west Asian region by exploiting ethnic and religious divisions.[78] The resultant ethnic civil war created conditions for the rapid proliferation of Islamic fundamentalist ideology and religious warriors (*jihadis*). Even before the Taliban (Muslim seminarians) takeover of the country in 1997, Islamic warriors trained in Afghanistan had started joining *jihads* (holy wars) in

Kashmir, Tajikistan, Algeria, Egypt, Yemen, and Chechnya.[79] Therefore, Afghanistan became a much larger, newer version of Lebanon (hit by a long-lasting civil war beginning in 1975): the Afghan government could not assert its sovereign authority over the profusion of fighting forces in the country, and the country became a haven for ethnic warlords, drug traffickers, and illicit-arms dealers.

Central Asian politics in the early 1990s also exemplified the problems associated with the end of the cold war. An upsurge in Islamic sentiments and rivalry between foreign powers for influence was apparent in Uzbekistan and Tajikistan. In the former, Saudi Arabia helped finance the construction of more than 600 mosques in the Ferghana Valley alone. In neighboring Farsi-(Persian-) speaking Tajikistan, Iran invested large sums to support Islamic insurgents fighting the central government in a protracted civil war. The potential for a Tajik–Uzbek conflict also increased after the end of the cold war. The origins of the Tajik–Uzbek conflict went back to 1925, when Stalin dismembered Turkestan and the republics of Bukhara and Khorezm to create the Soviet republics of Tajikistan and Uzbekistan. Khozhent, an ethnically Uzbek city, was placed in Tajikistan, whereas Samarkand and Bukhara, two predominantly Tajik cities, were incorporated into Uzbekistan. With the Soviet Union's disintegration, some radical Tajik nationalists demanded the return of Bukhara and Samarkand from Uzbekistan, increasing tensions between these two states.[80] Thus, the emergence of newly independent Muslim states in Central Asia introduced unpredictable new dynamics into regional politics. The ethnic turmoil in Afghanistan further posed a real danger that it could spill over into Central Asia. Newly independent Uzbekistan and Tajikistan naturally preferred Afghanistan to be governed by their own respective ethnic kinfolk than by Pashtun fundamentalists. Hence, they threw their support behind the Northern Alliance led by Ahmed Shah Masood, an ethnic Tajik leader, and Abdul Rashid Dostum, an ethnic Uzbek warlord. The predominantly Pashtun *mujahideen* (and later the Pashtun-dominated Taliban regime) vilified this threatening alliance and invoked the specter of a greater Uzbekistan or a greater Tajikistan that would carve up Afghanistan. This specter instilled a sense of fear among the Pashtuns and thus stoked their ethnic nationalism vis-à-vis the Tajik, Uzbek, and other ethnic minorities in Afghanistan. A wider confrontation involving Afghanistan, Tajikistan, and Uzbekistan was, therefore, always a possibility.

**IRREDENTIST–ANTI-IRREDENTIST CONFLICT AND FOREIGN INTERVENTION IN ETHNIC DISPUTES** Due to the outbreak of several irredentist–anti-irredentist ethnic conflicts in the Balkans (for example, conflicts between Serbia/Montenegro and Croatia, between Serbia/Montenegro and Bosnia-Herzegovina, between Serbia/Montenegro and Kosovo in the former Yugoslavia) and in the former Soviet territories (for example, between Armenia and Azerbaijan over the enclave of Nagorno-Karabakh, and between Russia and Georgia over Abkhazia and South Ossetia) in the early 1990s, and the intensification of several existing ones in Asia (conflict between India and Pakistan over Kashmir) and Africa (conflict between Ethiopia and Somalia over the Ogaden), there was renewed interest among experts in analyzing **irredentism** (territorial claims made by one state against a neighboring state on the basis of shared ethnic ties with a minority ethnic population residing within the neighboring state) as a source of inter- and intrastate ethnic conflicts. Experts were also eager to learn the reasons that may induce foreign states to intervene in ethnic disputes occurring in neighboring states, thereby sparking a wider and more intense conflict.

Myron Weiner had previously noted why and how irredentist–anti-irredentist conflicts involving international border-straddling ethnic groups could have serious repercussions for interethnic relations and national integration in both the revisionist (that is, irredentist) and status-quo (anti-irredentist) states. In the status-quo state, the onset of an irredentist–anti-irredentist struggle with a neighboring state may create tensions in interethnic relations in several ways. First, as the neighboring irredentist power presses its claim and expresses concern for the plight of its ethnic kin, usually a minority in the status-quo state, it could raise expectations among that ethnic minority that it will either be incorporated into the revisionist state or at least will be able to form an independent state of its own with support from the revisionist state. Having developed such expectations, the minority ethnic group in the status-quo state will resist attempts by that state to integrate the group more firmly within the state, thereby leading to strained relations and even conflict. Second, as demands for revising boundaries persist on the part of the irredentist state, the status-quo state is likely to view the minority ethnic group as a grave risk to the territorial integrity of the state. The status-quo state then may try to accelerate programs to "nationalize" schoolchildren belonging to the minority ethnic group, demand expressions of loyalty from group members to the national government and the state, and increase police surveillance and repression of the minority ethnic group, all of which may further inflame the situation. Finally, as a result of the status-quo state's crackdown, significant numbers within the minority ethnic group may come to regard the status-quo state as the oppressor and an obstacle in the path to its merger with the revisionist state or to its full independence. In such situations, the minority ethnic group may be forced to choose among three alternatives: it could accept the existing boundary and strive to improve its status within the status-quo state; it could support the irredentist claim of the revisionist state, thus making clear its preference for merger with that state; or if the ethnic group happens to be a minority in both the revisionist and status-quo states, it could choose to join its conationals in a struggle to break free of both states. Which option it selects depends on the outcome of debates within the ethnic group. Unless the minority ethnic group chooses the first option, its repression at the hands of the status-quo state is likely to increase. In that event, segments within the ethnic group (especially youth and students) may organize an insurgency movement against the status-quo state, with help from the revisionist state. Faced with a mounting insurgency, the status-quo state may have no choice but to respond with severe repression. This may induce the revisionist state to intervene militarily to protect its ethnic kin from slaughter, leading to a full-fledged interstate ethnic war.[81]

The irredentist–anti-irredentist conflict between two neighboring states with an overlapping ethnic group may also lead to internal ethnic fragmentation in the revisionist state. Faced with persecution of its conationals in the status-quo state, a revisionist state may become fixated with boundary modification. The country's economic development may then suffer, the political culture and public mood may turn militant, and the regime's tolerance level for disagreements may fall so low that it would most likely respond with repression toward those who disagreed with its policies. If the status-quo power stands firm on the boundary issue, frustration may eventually overwhelm both the leaders and the public of the revisionist state. The government of the revisionist state could then start arming its conationals across the disputed border and may even launch an attack on the status-quo state. If the military campaign fails to change the territorial status quo in its favor, public discontent could grow in the revisionist state and spill over into domestic politics. Frustrated irredentist claims and growing domestic political instability may even produce regime change in the revisionist state. The conationals across the disputed border may also vent their anger and frustration at the government of the revisionist state.[82]

In their more recent study, *For Kin or Country: Xenophobia, Nationalism, and War*, Saideman and Ayers argued that the collapse of empires (such as the collapse of the Austro-Hungarian and Ottoman empires after World War I, the collapse of the British empire after World War II, and the collapse of the Soviet empire after the cold war) inevitably redraws geographical borders and divides populations and families. This sets the stage for the emergence of irredentist–anti-irredentist conflicts and interstate ethnic wars. Sensing the public mood in the aftermath of a traumatic empire collapse and the associated hardships that it brings, new leaders who emerge on the political scene often promise their citizens that they will actively seek the return of conationals and territories that may have been lost in the empire's collapse. This may lead them to advocate aggressive foreign policies that could in turn result in costly and devastating interstate ethnic wars. Saideman and Ayers acknowledged, however, that not all states undergoing transitions in the wake of an empire's collapse would automatically follow irredentist foreign policy. For instance, despite facing tremendous political and economic difficulties during their transition from communism to a market democracy, only Armenia, Croatia, and Serbia followed an aggressive irredentist foreign policy against their neighbors, leading to severe ethnic conflict, while Hungary, Romania, and Russia practiced much more restrained foreign policy. They concluded that ultimately it is internal forces and the imperatives of domestic politics that drive irredentist foreign policy, even if following such a policy risks a country's self-destruction. Ironically, they also concluded that xenophobia may have actually worked to stabilize many postcommunist states in eastern Europe and dampen irredentist sentiments and designs.[83]

In the post–cold war era, it was a common assumption of scholars and practitioners that international crises would be more easily managed through the cooperation of states. As the ethnic wars in the former Yugoslavia unfolded, however, the assumption of crisis management through state cooperation proved to be false. Instead, the evidence from former Yugoslavia and from several other cases from Asia and Africa showed that partisan intervention and support by foreign states were not only often responsible for the onset of ethnic conflicts but also significantly affected a conflict's scope, intensity, and eventual outcome. But why do states continue to provide partisan support to either ethnic insurgents or governments of states experiencing ethnic conflict, especially because conventional wisdom suggests that states' mutual vulnerability to ethnic conflicts and secessionist insurgencies ought to make them extremely cautious about pursuing such aggressive foreign policy? Rejecting both the realist and neoliberal answers to this question, Saideman has argued that states' foreign policies toward ethnic conflict in another state is determined mainly by domestic politics. Assuming that politicians are mainly interested in gaining and maintaining office, he argues that leaders are likely to accord the highest importance to the interests of their supporters and constituents. It follows, therefore, that if these supporters and constituents have strong ethnic ties with one of the parties involved in ethnic conflict in another state, then politicians and decision makers would be inclined to keep their constituents happy by backing that side in the conflict. Saideman adds that this inclination of politicians to keep their supporters and constituents happy is stronger if the leaders face strong domestic competitors.[84]

**STATE COLLAPSE, ANARCHY, AND ETHNIC CONFLICT**   A growing phenomenon of the post–cold war world is **state collapse**, which can be described as "a situation where the structure, authority (legitimate power), law and political order [within a state] have fallen apart and must be reconstituted in some form, old or new."[85] The most dramatic example of this took place in December 1991 when the Soviet Union collapsed into fifteen new independent states. Since then, some of the new states that emerged out of the wreckage of the Soviet Union have also been threatened with collapse—Georgia, Moldova, even Ukraine. Elsewhere, notably in sub-Saharan Africa, states such as Somalia, Sudan, Liberia, Angola, Sierra Leone, and the Democratic Republic of Congo (formerly Zaire) suffered various degrees of collapse and have since grappled with the problems of reconstruction. Several other states in West Asia and the Middle East, notably Afghanistan and Iraq after the 2003 U.S. invasion, have faced similar crises. A common feature of these collapsed states is the onset of violent ethnic civil wars of varying degrees of intensity. This raises the obvious question: Is there a link between state collapse and the outbreak of violent ethnic conflict? In other words, does state collapse create an environment that is conducive to violent conflict among the ethnic groups that emerge from the wreckage of these states?

Using the realist concept of the **security dilemma**, Barry Posen argued that intense military conflict among ethnic groups in collapsed states is highly probable. His main contention was that, in a situation of emerging domestic anarchy caused by state collapse (which resembles the anarchical environment of the international states system), the primary concern of the fearful successor entities (states as well as the ethnic groups aspiring for autonomy or statehood) is for physical security and well-being. And because the key to security and well-being is power, these successor entities are pushed into a natural competition for power. But this competition for power, in turn, creates a security dilemma for all actors; encourages them to indulge in worst-case-scenario analysis; and triggers violent conflict among them by stoking their sense of opportunity or vulnerability.[86] Posen added a caveat to the model—nuclear weapons: "nationalism is less important from a military standpoint in a nuclear relationship."[87]

Posen's model has been criticized for not being able to fully explain the outbreak of ethnic conflict in situations where the ideal state monopolizing the use of violence does not exist, but state authority has not completely collapsed. In such **halfway-house states**, political authority is usually "biased towards or against particular ethnicities, so competition is waged among different ethnic groups for control of the state."[88] Because the state could be an ethnic group's greatest ally or its greatest adversary due to the resources it possesses, an ethnic group will typically come to believe that if it fails to capture state power, then it could find itself at the mercy of the state controlled by another group and thus find itself in an extremely vulnerable situation. This forms the core of the security dilemma confronting ethnic groups in halfway-house states, a dilemma whose resolution depends on the preferences and strategies of ethnic politicians: "If politicians take radical stands favoring some ethnic groups at the expense of others, the security climate will deteriorate. On the other hand, if politicians downplay ethnic identities, building multiethnic constituencies and developing civic or other non-ethnic ideologies, then ethnic groups will feel more secure."[89] Thus, the interaction of two processes—ethnic insecurity and ethnic politics—determines ethnic political outcomes in halfway-house states. If insecurity among ethnic groups is high and politicians opt for ethnic-oriented policies (as they may do under pressure from their supporters), violent ethnic conflict may result.[90]

Both Posen and Saideman's models presume that in difficult circumstances, ethnic groups may find it hard to make credible commitments toward peace. But why does this commitment problem occur? After all, the decision to fight (as opposed to a decision to seek peaceful outcomes) is usually a costly choice that ethnic groups decide to make. James Fearon has argued that this commitment problem, which leads ethnic groups along the path of costly war, occurs when three conditions are met: first, when ethnic groups interact under conditions of anarchy and in the absence of a third party who can guarantee and enforce any agreements worked out among the groups; second, when at least one of the groups is convinced that its ability to opt out of joint arrangements would lessen in the near future; and third when the same group calculates that choosing to fight in the present would be a far better option compared to the scenario it would face in the near future if it chose to cooperate.[91] Logically, it then follows that if ethnic war is to be avoided, three things need to happen. First, the early involvement of a third party, who can persuade and/or coerce the adversaries into a peace arrangement and who can then enforce the provisions of that arrangement, would be conducive for peace (this is, however, easier said than done). Second, the nature of the peace arrangement itself—for instance, consociational type of arrangements where ethnic groups would retain the right to block future moves deemed injurious to their interests, or constitutional arrangements that would provide ethnic groups a guaranteed right to withdraw or secede from the joint arrangement—would be crucial to get ethnic groups to credibly commit to peace. Third, the cost to ethnic groups for choosing war over peace in the present must be increased substantially for them to make credible commitments toward peace—this could be done by injecting an international peace-keeping force into the region and/or creating a hurting military stalemate through international support to the weaker sides in the dispute.

**HUMAN EMOTIONS AND ETHNIC CONFLICT**   Unlike rational choice explanations of ethnic conflict, which view ethnic groups as rational actors making calculated choices to either fight or seek peace, theories that emphasize the emotional nature of ethnic conflicts regard "the motivation to participate in or support ethnic violence and discrimination as inherent in human nature."[92] More specifically, four inherent human emotions—fear, hatred, rage, and resentment—form the core motivation for individuals and groups to indulge in ethnic violence (which may include various kinds of atrocities such as rape, murder, ethnic cleansing, and genocide). Petersen defines emotion as "a mechanism that triggers action to satisfy a pressing concern" and suggests that it helps individuals and groups to meet situational challenges in two ways: by raising "the saliency of one desire/concern over others" and by heightening "both cognitive and physical capabilities necessary to respond to the situational challenge."[93] Of the four emotions identified above, fear, hatred, and resentment allow individuals and groups to address identified desires and/or concerns: for instance, fear increases the desire for security, and it helps individuals and groups to meet security challenges; hatred allows individuals and groups to identify historical grievances and injustices, and it provides a way to redress them; and resentment prepares individuals and groups to address status and self-esteem shortcomings. Rage, on the other hand, is an emotion that can often lead individuals and groups toward a course of action than can prove to be self-destructive. By offering a release for pent-up frustrations and personality disorders, rage can lead to cognitive distortions that justify murderous violence and other kinds of atrocities during ethnic conflict.[94]

Lake and Rothchild have also stressed the emotional side of ethnic conflict by noting that "collective fears of the future" faced by an ethnic group often motivate it toward conflict with other groups in a multiethnic society. In particular, two fears appear to be more salient than other types of fears: (1) fear of being assimilated into the dominant culture as a result of policies pursued by a hegemonic state, and (2) fear of physical safety and survival, especially in multiethnic settings where the various groups are largely of equal strength and therefore cannot absorb the others politically, economically, or culturally. When these two fears coalesce, ethnic conflict usually results.[95]

**POVERTY, RESOURCES, AND ETHNIC CONFLICT**    In recent years, a substantial body of literature has developed that links poverty and inequality with ethnic conflict and civil war. In his seminal study, *Minorities at Risk*, political scientist Ted Gurr found that economic differences (measured in terms of inequalities in income; in land and property holdings; in access to higher or technical education; and in a presence in business, the professions, and official positions) between majorities and minorities in multiethnic societies as well as outright economic discrimination of minorities (that is, the systematic exclusion of minorities from access to desirable economic goods, conditions, and positions that are open to other groups in society) were the main factors behind the onset of ethnic conflict. Gurr's study also found that in most multiethnic states, economic differences between majority and minority communities and economic discrimination of minorities were often the result of deliberate social practice and public policy. As Gurr put it, "policies of neglect and deliberate exclusion are substantially responsible for the persistence of contemporary inequalities."[96]

Development theorist Frances Stewart hypothesized that the existence of "horizontal inequalities" among different ethnic groups in multiethnic states were at the root of civil unrest. Stewart viewed horizontal inequalities as multidimensional, incorporating political, economic, and social elements, and argued that ethnic groups' unequal access to political, economic, and social resources can seriously affect individual and group well-being and social stability. Additionally, when inequalities in resource access and outcomes coincide with cultural differences, culture can become a powerful mobilizing agent leading to political disturbances and ethnic civil wars.[97]

Fearon and Laitin have found that, in the post-1945 period, ethnic conflict and civil war more generally were more prevalent in countries with a low per capita income and high levels of poverty, a large population, rough terrain, and large deposits of natural resources such as oil. Poor states are more likely to be financially and bureaucratically weak states, which makes them more likely to witness bouts of political instability. Large population and endemic poverty also favor rebel recruitment and the formation of insurgent outfits. Rough terrain and weak state capacity reduces the chances of rebel capture, thereby lowering the risks associated with armed insurgencies. Oil exports favor civil war by increasing the "prize" value of capturing the state or region, and because (conditional on income level) oil producers tend to have less developed state administrative apparatuses and capabilities.[98] Fearon and Leitin's findings are also largely replicated by Theisen's recent study, which found that poverty and dysfunctional institutions are robustly related to ethnic conflict.[99]

While most studies of poverty and inequality tend to highlight grievance-based motivations for ethnic conflict and civil unrest, economists such as Grossman have offered what has now come to be known as the greed hypothesis. Put in simple terms, proponents of the greed hypothesis argue that rebellion (including ethnic ones) is like an industry that generates profits for the participants. These profits accrue mainly from criminal activities such as looting; extortion; imposition of "taxes" on populations in areas that rebels control; weapons and contraband smuggling; drugs and human trafficking; and extraction and sale of easy-to-loot natural resources such as oil and gas, precious metals, and other primary products. The bottom line is that rebellions are formed and sustained as long as the profits from the rebellion far outstrip the costs associated with it.[100]

Oxford economists Paul Collier and Anke Hoeffler have argued, however, that the best way of understanding why rebellions and civil wars happen is to look at them from an opportunity or feasibility perspective. The perspective includes five different criteria of opportunity. The first factor is the availability of finances: cases where would-be rebels could extort money or obtain it from diaspora communities or foreign powers increase the probability of rebellion. A second factor that influences opportunity is the cost of rebellion: in states that have high human capital, per capita income, and growth rates, the cost of rebellion tend to be high, thus creating a disincentive for civil war; conversely, in states with low human capital, per capita income, and growth, the cost of rebellion is much smaller and the potential for profits is high, thus creating an incentive for rebellion. The third factor is military advantage: in this context, Collier and Hoeffler found that a dispersed population increases the risk of rebellion and civil war. A fourth factor is the ethnic diversity of the population: the risk of rebellion and civil war in heterogeneous societies was far less (because rebel cohesion is harder to maintain), provided no ethnic group tried to dominate the other groups. The last factor is the size of the country's population: Collier and Hoeffler argued that the risk of conflict is proportional to a country's population because both opportunities and grievances increase with an increasing population.[101] In a later study, the authors again reiterated that there is enough evidence to support their original hypothesis that, where a rebellion is financially and militarily feasible, it will occur.[102]

Since the late 1990s, there has been a flood of research exploring the possibilities of a link between natural resources and the onset of civil and interstate wars.[103] In this context, territory, oil, and water are frequently mentioned as resources likely to promote conflict.[104] Demographic and environmental factors have also been highlighted in post–cold war security discourses.[105] One quantitative, cross-national time-series study covering the 1950–2000 period that tested the neo-Malthusian proposition that population pressure on natural renewable resources makes societies more prone to low-intensity conflict found that where land scarcity combines with high rates of population growth, the risk of armed conflict increases somewhat.[106] Another empirical study based on a large dataset found the following patterns: first, the presence of oil in a state increases the likelihood of conflict, particularly separatist conflict; second, the availability of easy-to-loot commodities like gemstones and drugs do not necessarily provide an incentive for new conflict, but they tend to lengthen existing conflicts; third, no apparent link exists between legal agricultural commodities and civil war; and fourth, the association between primary commodities (a broad category that includes both oil and agricultural goods) and the onset of civil war is not robust.[107]

In recent years, particularly with regard to ethnic civil wars in several sub-Saharan African states, diamonds have been reported to have played a significant role behind such conflicts. In their study of African "blood diamonds," Lujala, Gleditsch, and Gilmore found evidence that the production of secondary diamonds does increase the risk of the onset of ethnic civil war, especially in countries divided along ethnic lines. Primary diamonds, on the other hand, make ethnic war onset and incidence less likely.[108] Snyder and Bhavnani have taken a slightly different view regarding the link between the availability of easy-to-loot natural resources in a state and its propensity for rebellion and civil war. The question they address in their study is what explains why easy-to-loot natural resources like alluvial diamonds produce civil war in some states (such as in Sierra Leone) but not in others. But instead of focusing on the rebels, Snyder and Bhavnani focus on the political leaders to argue that, in countries that have an abundance of easy-to-loot natural resources, whether political leaders are able to keep peace and political order depends on the availability of resources that are not easy to loot; the mode of extraction of easy-to-loot resources, especially whether they are extracted by hard-to-tax artisans or, alternatively, by large, taxable industrial firms; and patterns of state spending.[109] In a later study, Snyder argues further that states can build different types of institutions of extraction on easy-to-loot natural resources with differential effects on political stability. If rulers are able to forge institutions of extraction that give them control of revenues generated by easy-to-loot resources, then these resources can contribute to political order by providing the income with which to govern. Conversely, the breakdown or absence of such institutions increases the risk of civil war by making it easier for rebels to organize. Snyder concludes by noting that a focus on institutions of extraction provides a stronger understanding of the wide range of political outcomes—from chaos to dictatorship, to democracy—in resource-rich countries.[110]

**ELITES, MASSES, AND ETHNIC CONFLICT**    A radically different explanation for the outbreak of ethnic conflict in the immediate post–cold war period stressed intense intragroup elite competition. For instance, Gagnon made the case that violent ethnic conflict like the one in former Yugoslavia resulted mainly from "the dynamics of within-group conflict."[111] The main role in fomenting conflict along ethnic cleavages or fault lines is usually played by elites within an ethnic group who wish to mobilize their own supporters and fend off domestic political challengers. "Such a strategy is a response by ruling elites to shifts in the structure of domestic political and economic power: by constructing individual interest in terms of the threat to the group, endangered elites can fend off domestic challengers who seek to mobilize the population against the status quo, and can better position themselves to deal with future challenges."[112] Hence, a conflict with other groups, "although justified and described in terms of relations with other ethnic groups and taking place within that context, has its main goal within the state, among members of the same ethnicity."[113]

A similar but more synthetic explanation for ethnic civil war was put forward by Stuart Kaufman, who borrowed Kenneth Waltz's classic three levels of analysis in international relations to argue that ethnic conflict is best understood by looking at the interaction of three causal factors: mass preferences (first-level factor), ethnic elites' behavior (second-level factor), and the rules of the international system within which groups interact (third-level factor).[114] Using the example of the ethnic civil war in Moldova, one of the fifteen successor states to the former Soviet Union, Kaufman demonstrated that ethnic wars are usually caused by the combined presence of mass hostility within ethnic groups, ethnic outbidding and outflanking by political elites within the groups, and a security dilemma that increases collective fears for the future. When all three factors are present, each helps to exacerbate the other two, leading to an increasing spiral of ethnic violence: "belligerent leaders stoke mass hostility; hostile masses support belligerent leaders; and both together threaten other groups, creating a security dilemma which in turn encourages even more mass hostility and leadership belligerence."[115] This escalation in violence can be either mass-led or elite-led.

**GLOBALIZATION AND ETHNIC CONFLICT**   Using globalization theories of competition for trade and investment among states, international political economists have also attempted to explain the clamor for statehood by many nonstate ethnic nations in existing multiethnic states. For instance, Alberto Alesina and Enrico Spolaore suggested that globalization offered economic incentives to nonstate ethnic nations residing within existing multiethnic states to seek independence. In the early years of the General Agreement on Tariffs and Trade (GATT) regime, when trade barriers between countries were still high, it made economic sense for nonstate ethnic nations and regions to remain within large multiethnic states, with their large markets. But with the World Trade Organization (WTO) regime (created in 1995) providing for freer trade, small ethnic nations and geographical regions could hope to become politically independent and economically viable. The single European market, for example, provides incentives for the Catalans in Spain, the Scots in Great Britain, and the Ladin speakers in South Tyrol in Italy to demand greater autonomy. Quebec's desire for independence from Canada is also predicated on Quebecers joining the North American Free Trade Agreement (NAFTA).[116]

Nobel laureate economist Gary Becker made a more detailed but similar argument. He contended that, due to the rapid growth in international trade under the Bretton Woods system, the economic prosperity and viability of states is no longer dependent on having a large domestic economy. On the contrary, in a globalized world, small states enjoy four distinct economic advantages. First, for reasons of economic efficiency and competition for markets, small states can concentrate on only a few products and services, thus filling a niche that is too small for large states. Second, the national economies of small states are more homogeneous and therefore can avoid or minimize internal clashes among special interests. Third, the goods and services that small states specialize in tend to be less exposed to trade quotas and other tariff and nontariff restrictions because their volume and amount is often not enough to affect producers in large countries. And fourth, small states are more likely to be accepted as members by economic blocs and alliances, such as the European Union, because the volume of their production would not pose a competitive threat to the other members.[117] Becker further argued that the economic success enjoyed by small entities such as Hong Kong, Singapore, Monaco, and Mauritius have provided a powerful "demonstration effect" on ethno-nationalists in many parts of the world: "Many of these groups concluded that they can do better economically by becoming separate nations and concentrating on producing specialized goods and services for the world economy."[118] Becker's examples included the Czech Republic, where (after its split from Slovakia) economic growth was rapid, unemployment significantly lowered, and exports reoriented toward the West. Becker was equally optimistic about the economic viability of Quebec if it seceded from Canada: "After perhaps a severe adjustment period, Quebec could find a prosperous place in the world economy by trading with Canada, the U.S., and Mexico as well as the rest of Latin America."[119]

## GOALS OF ETHNIC POLITICAL MOVEMENTS

From the preceding discussion, it is clear that the basis of ethnic identity and the causes of ethnic conflict are complex and vary across time and space. Similarly, the goals and objectives pursued by politically mobilized ethnic groups can be wide-ranging and not susceptible to easy generalizations. However, in his *Minorities at Risk* project, Ted Gurr provided a typology of the various types of ethnic political movements in the second half of the twentieth century and the kinds of demands that each type of movement has tended to make.

Gurr used the term *nonstate communal groups* to refer to peoples sharing language, ethnicity, region of residence, and history but who do not necessarily constitute nations or states.[120] A politically salient nonstate communal group is one that either collectively suffers or benefits from systematic discrimination vis-à-vis other groups in a state and/or engages in political mobilization and action in defense or promotion of its self-defined interests.[121] Gurr further subdivided politicized nonstate communal groups into national peoples and minority peoples: national peoples are "regionally concentrated groups that have lost their autonomy to expansionist states but still preserve some of their cultural and linguistic distinctiveness and want to protect or reestablish some degree of politically separate existence," whereas minority peoples "have a defined socioeconomic or political status within a larger society—based on some combination of their ethnicity, immigrant origin, economic roles, and religion—and are concerned about protecting or improving their status."[122] Gurr further subdivided national peoples into two types: ethno-nationalist groups that are regionally concentrated peoples with a history of organized political movement for autonomy and/or separation; and indigenous peoples who are mostly peripheral groups with sharp cultural differences from the dominant groups who controlled the state and are concerned mainly about issues of group autonomy. Similarly, he grouped minority peoples into three distinct types: ethno-classes that are ethnically distinct minorities mostly descended from slaves or immigrants and specialize in distinctive low-status economic activities; militant sects that are groups primarily concerned with the defense of their religious beliefs;[123] and communal contenders that are culturally, linguistically, and geographically and/or regionally distinct groups aspiring to a share of state power. Communal contenders may be of three further subtypes: dominant, advantaged, or disadvantaged. Often, communal contenders, if they find themselves in a losing position in a coalition within the state, transform into ethno-nationalists and "opt for exit in the form of separatist movements."[124]

Of the 233 nonstate communal groups identified by Gurr as being in existence between 1945 and 1989, over two-thirds were national groups, 81 were ethno-nationalist (such as Croatians and Quebeçois), and 83 were indigenous peoples (such as Native Americans and Australian aboriginals). There were 45 ethno-classes, ranging from African Americans in the United States and in nine Latin American societies to Muslims in France and Koreans in Japan. Most of the 49 militant sects consisted of Muslim minorities (Turks in Germany, Muslim Albanians in Yugoslavia, Malay Muslims in Thailand, Kashmiris in India). There were 25 advantaged communal contenders (such as the Tutsis of Burundi and the Sunnis of Iraq) and 41 disadvantaged communal contenders (many of the tribal groups in sub-Saharan Africa).[125]

Gurr's cross-national empirical data indicated a pattern of group demand for full political autonomy and independence and for an expansion of political, economic, and social rights. Predictably, grievances about economic rights were greatest among indigenous peoples and ethno-classes, both of which suffered the greatest economic disadvantages. Militant sects usually demanded social rights. Demands for political autonomy, in turn, were most often put forward by ethno-nationalists. Disaggregating autonomy demands further, Gurr concluded that the "common denominator of almost all autonomy demands is the historical fact or belief that the group once governed its own affairs."[126] In contrast, he discovered "no global or regional correlation between the severity of [political and economic] discrimination and the intensity of separatist sentiments."[127] Paradoxically, little correlation was found between minority separatism and political or economic differentials. On the contrary, where differentials were relatively small, as between Quebecers and English Canadians, Basques and Castilians, or Ukrainians and Russians, minority separatism was often at its strongest. The contemporary condition that most strongly intensified the demand for political autonomy and independence was ecological stress (on group lands and resources): "It is the single strongest correlate of separatism among most of the regionally concentrated minorities, including ethno-nationalists, militant sects, and indigenous peoples, but not communal contenders."[128] Demographic stress and cultural differentials also intensified "separatism among ethno-nationalists, though not among any other types of groups."[129]

The *Minorities at Risk* project contended, in short, that a lack of congruence exists between a group's political-economic status in society and its demand for separation. Thus, it has not been "the wretched of the earth," to employ Frantz Fanon's term, that have, by and large, made independence claims, but rather large, relatively privileged, regionally based national peoples that remain rueful over the loss of the political autonomy they once had, probably suffer some degree of ecological and demographic stress, and demonstrate significant cultural differences from the dominant groups.

## Conclusion

Until the end of the cold war, ethnic movements and conflicts were not given much attention by international relations specialists. There were several reasons for this. First, influenced by the modernization paradigm, international relations scholars assumed (incorrectly, as we now know) that the process of modernization would eventually lead to the assimilation of minority ethnic groups within the dominant culture, thereby creating a common identity uniting all inhabitants of the state and eliminating the sources of ethnic conflict. Hence, they regarded ethnic and religious conflicts as nothing more than an "ephemeral nuisance." Second, during the early 1970s, those international relations scholars interested in examining ethnic revival organized their research differently from developmental theorists. They focused on issues such as the impact of international capitalism on politics (dependency theories), the impact of class structure on society (neo-Marxist theories), and the decision-making processes within the governing elite structure (the policy studies or domestic structures approach).[130] Third, operating within the East–West ideological battle, both western liberals and Soviet Marxists tended to be dismissive about the power of ethnic sentiments in the contemporary world.[131] A fourth reason for the neglect of ethnic conflict by international relations experts stemmed from their preoccupation with other issues: the East–West and North–South disputes, interstate conflicts, nuclear proliferation, disarmament, left-wing revolutionary movements, regional integration, and the global economy.[132] Finally, epistemological and methodological divergence between the English and American traditions in international relations studies was also partly responsible for the neglect of ethnicity and nationalism: whereas American scholars focused their attention on issues of integration and interdependence, the English tradition made interstate relations the main focus of the discipline.

Due to the explosion of ethnic conflict in the post–cold war period, international relations scholars were compelled to become fully engaged with this phenomenon. Because ethnic conflict is ultimately connected with issues of war and peace, human rights, democratization, and the global order, it has become a core subject of study and analysis within the international relations discipline.

In *Understanding Ethnic Conflict*, we argue that the outbreak of ethnic conflict poses three challenges before the international community. Each of these challenges is discussed in more detail in the next three chapters; here we briefly sketch what these dilemmas entail. The first challenge is normative: as more and more nonstate ethnic groups seek to enter the international community as sovereign states, how should the international community respond to secessionist claims in the absence of any clear guidelines? To date, the international community has generally sided with states and not with ethnic insurgents. In those rare cases, such as the conferral of state status on the Palestine Liberation Organization (PLO), where the international community went against the interest of one of its member states and supported the state's domestic ethnic challenger, special political circumstances and considerations—and not the application of any uniform legal criteria—guided that decision. But this bias favoring existing states and existing international norms can be unfair (and hence unjustifiable) to those ethnic groups whose reasons for protest and rebellion seem justified from a moral standpoint. This is the crux of the normative challenge associated with ethnic movements that the international community needs to address in order to protect ethnic minorities at risk. We explore these issues in more detail in Chapter 2.

The second challenge concerns security: the outbreak of ethnic conflict may produce consequences or outcomes that pose grave risks for the international community. The formation of international terrorist networks, the perpetration of genocidal massacres and other forms of human rights abuses, the explosion in the number of refugees and the creation of complex humanitarian emergencies may all be connected with the outbreak of ethnic conflict and may threaten international order and peace. In Chapter 3, we discuss some of the more serious consequences of violent ethnic conflict and the difficult choices that the international community has to face in dealing with these situations.

The final challenge is crisis management: because ethnic conflicts are usually costly in human security terms, what would be the most effective way to prevent, manage, and resolve such conflicts? Would unilateral military actions, like those under the Bush administration, remove the source of these conflicts? Or would they in fact exacerbate them? Because disputants are unlikely to be the agents of conflict resolution, would international third-party intervention be an effective alternative? But under what conditions should third parties intervene in ethnic conflict? Chapter 4 examines the case for international intervention and suggests when it may prove beneficial and when it may be ill-advised.

## Discussion Questions

**1.** Discuss the different manifestations of ethnic conflict in the world today. Are some more dangerous than others?

**2.** What are the main differences between a civic nation and an ethnic nation? Why is the civic nation more conducive to building stable multiethnic societies?

**3.** Identify the main schools of thought regarding the formation and persistence of ethnic identity, and point out their central arguments. In your opinion, which school of thought can better predict the rise of ethno-nationalism in the world today?

**4.** Discuss the assumptions of various theories of ethnic political mobilization. Compare the explanatory power of theories based on factors such as ancient hatreds, modernization, insecurity, elite competition, and globalization.

**5.** Describe the linkage between the nature of an ethnic group and the goals it pursues. Under what conditions is an ethnic group likely to pursue statehood? What are the consequences when it does pursue the goal of statehood?

## Key Terms

assimilation
autonomy
consociational democracy
constructivist
diaspora communities
ethnic community
ethnic conflict
ethnic group
ethnic nation
ethnic political movement
ethnic solidarity
ethno-religious conflict

ethno-religious group
halfway-house states
hegemonic exchange
homelands societies
instrumentalist
irredentism
multiethnic
multinational
nation
nationalism
national self-determination
nation building

nation-state
primordialist
relative deprivation
"revolution of rising expectations"
"revolution of rising frustrations"
security dilemma
state
state building
state collapse
superpowers

## Notes

1. Milton J. Esman, *Ethnic Politics* (Ithaca, N.Y.: Cornell University Press, 1994), p. 1.
2. Ibid., p. 9.
3. Ernest Baker, *National Character and the Factors in Its Formation* (London, 1927), p. 17 (emphasis added). Quoted in Norman D. Palmer and Howard C. Perkins, *International Relations: The World*

*Community in Transition,* 3rd ed. (New Delhi: CBS Publishers, 1985), p. 19.
4. The state is a legal concept describing a social group that occupies a defined territory and is organized under common political institutions and an effective government; additionally, the state exercises sovereign power within its borders and

is recognized as sovereign by other states.

5. Anthony D. Smith, "The Ethnic Sources of Nationalism," *Survival,* 35, no. 1, Spring 1993, p. 55.

6. Charles A. Kupchan, "Introduction: Nationalism Resurgent," in Charles A. Kupchan, ed., *Nationalism and Nationalities in the New Europe* (Ithaca, N.Y.: Cornell University Press, 1995), p. 4.

7. Ibid.

8. Hans Kohn, *The Idea of Nationalism: A Study in its Origins and Background* (New York: Macmillan, 1951), p. 8. See also Hans Kohn, *Nationalism: Its Meaning and History* (Princeton, N.J.: D. Van Nostrand, 1955), p. 9.

9. Boyd C. Shafer, *Nationalism: Myth and Reality* (New York: Harcourt, Brace and World, 1955), p. 10.

10. Ernest Gellner, *Nations and Nationalism* (Ithaca, N.Y.: Cornell University Press, 1983), p. 11.

11. Anthony D. Smith, *Theories of Nationalism,* 2nd ed. (New York: Holmes & Meier, 1983), pp. 19–20.

12. Esman, *Ethnic Politics,* p. 27.

13. Ibid.

14. Ibid.

15. See Clifford Geertz, *Old Societies and New States: The Quest for Modernity in Asia and Africa* (Glencoe, Ill.: Free Press, 1963); and Harold Isaacs, "Basic Group Identity: The Idols of the Tribe," *Ethnicity,* 1, 1974, pp. 15–42.

16. John Rex, "Ethnic Identity and the Nation State: The Political Sociology of Multi-Cultural Societies," *Social Identities,* 1, no. 1, 1995, pp. 24–25. See also Judith Nagata, "In Defense of Ethnic Boundaries: The Changing Myths and Charters of Malay Identity," in Charles F. Keyes, ed., *Ethnic Change* (Seattle: University of Washington Press, 1981), p. 89.

17. See Anthony H. Richmond, "Migration, and Race Relations," *Ethnic and Racial Studies,* 1, January 1978, p. 60; and Smith, *Theories of Nationalism,* p. 180. For a stimulating discussion on the role of food in the formation and, more important, the stereotyping of ethnic identity, see Uma Narayan, "Eating Cultures: Incorporation, Identity and Indian Food," *Social Identities,* 1, no. 1, 1995, pp. 63–86.

18. Nathan Glazer and Daniel P. Moynihan, *Beyond the Melting Pot: The Negroes, Puerto Ricans, Jews, Italians and Irish of New York* (Cambridge, Mass.: MIT and Harvard University Presses, 1963), pp. 13–14.

19. Rex, "Ethnic Identity and the Nation-State," p. 25.

20. Timothy M. Frye, "Ethnicity, Sovereignty and Transitions from Non-Democratic Rule," *Journal of International Affairs,* 45, no. 2, Winter 1992, p. 602.

21. Smith, "The Ethnic Sources of Nationalism," pp. 50–51.

22. Ibid., pp. 52–53.

23. Ibid., pp. 53–55.

24. David Lake and Donald Rothchild, "Spreading Fear: The Genesis of Transnational Ethnic Conflict," in Lake and Rothchild, eds., *The International Spread of Ethnic Conflict: Fear, Diffusion, and Escalation* (Princeton, N.J.: Princeton University Press, 1998), p. 5.

25. Ibid., p. 6; Ted Robert Gurr, *Peoples Versus States: Minorities at Risk in the New Century* (Washington, D.C.: United States Institute of Peace Press, 2000), p. 4.

26. Paul R. Brass, *Ethnicity and Nationalism: Theory and Comparison* (Newbury Park, Calif.: Sage, 1991), p. 8.

27. Peter Jackson and Jan Penrose, "Introduction: Placing 'Race' and

Nation," in Jackson and Penrose, eds., *Constructions of Race, Place and Nation* (London: UCL Press, 1993), p. 1. See also Jan Penrose, "Reification in the Name of Change: The Impact of Nationalism on Social Constructions of Nations, People and Place in Scotland and the United Kingdom," in Jackson and Penrose, eds., *Constructions of Race, Place and Nation,* p. 28.

28. John Stone, "Race, Ethnicity, and the Weberian Legacy," *American Behavioral Scientist,* 38, no. 3, January 1995, p. 396.

29. Ibid.

30. Benedict Anderson, *Imagined Communities: Reflections on the Origin and Spread of Nationalism,* Revised Edition, (London and New York: Verso, 1991), p. 6.

31. Ibid., p. 7.

32. Ibid.

33. Charles F. Keyes, "The Dialectics of Ethnic Change," in Keyes, ed., *Ethnic Change,* p. 6.

34. Ibid., p. 7.

35. Ibid.

36. Ibid., p. 9.

37. Ibid.

38. Ibid., p. 11.

39. See Geertz, *Old Societies and New States;* Isaacs, "Basic Group Identity," pp. 15–42; Raoul Naroll, "On Ethnic Unit Classification," *Current Anthropology,* 5, October 1964, pp. 283–312; Milton Gordon, *Assimilation in American Life: The Role of Race, Religion and National Origins* (New York: Oxford University Press, 1964); J. Clyde Mitchell, *The Kalela Dance: Aspects of Social Relationships among Urban Africans of Northern Rhodesia* (Manchester, England: Manchester University Press, 1956); A. L. Epstein, *Politics in an Urban African Community* (Manchester, England: Manchester University

Press, 1958); and J. S. Furnivall, *Netherlands India: A Study of Plural Economy* (New York: Macmillan, 1944).

40. For details of Kuper's criticism of primordialism, see Leo Kuper, "Plural Societies: Perspectives and Problems," in Leo Kuper and M. G. Smith, eds., *Pluralism in Africa* (Berkeley: University of California Press, 1969), pp. 7–26.

41. See Frederick Barth, *Ethnic Groups and Boundaries: The Social Organization of Cultural Difference* (London: Allen and Unwin, 1970); and Nathan Glazer and Daniel P. Moynihan, eds., *Ethnicity: Theory and Experience* (Cambridge, Mass.: Harvard University Press, 1975).

42. Saul Newman, "Does Modernization Breed Ethnic Political Conflict?" *World Politics,* 43, no. 3, April 1991, p. 454.

43. Smith, *Theories of Nationalism,* p. 46.

44. S. N. Eisenstadt, *Modernization: Protest and Change* (Englewood Cliffs, N.J.: Prentice-Hall, 1966).

45. Smith, *Theories of Nationalism,* p. 44.

46. Gellner, *Thought and Change* (Chicago, Ill.: University of Chicago Press, 1965 and 1978), p. 55.

47. Gellner, *Nations and Nationalism,* p. 39.

48. James Kellas, *The Politics of Nationalism and Ethnicity* (London: Macmillan, 1991), p. 43.

49. Walker Connor, "Nation-Building or Nation-Destroying?" *World Politics,* 24, no. 3, April 1972, p. 320.

50. Kellas, *The Politics of Nationalism and Ethnicity,* p. 44.

51. Ibid., p. 43.

52. Smith, *Theories of Nationalism,* pp. 57–58.

53. W. Kornhauser, *The Politics of Mass Society* (Glencoe, Ill.: Free Press, 1959).

54. Karl W. Deutsch, *Nationalism and Social Communication* (Cambridge, Mass.: MIT Press, 1953), pp. 86–130.

55. See, for example, Samuel P. Huntington, *Political Order in Changing Societies* (New Haven, Conn.: Yale University Press, 1968); and Daniel Lerner, "Communications and the Prospects of Innovative Development," in Daniel Lerner and Wilbur Schramm, eds., *Communication and Change in the Developing Countries* (Honolulu, Hawaii: East-West Center Press, 1967), pp. 305–317.

56. Newman, "Does Modernization Breed Ethnic Political Conflict?" pp. 454–455. For a detailed exposition of this view of strain theory prevalent in the 1960s, see Neil J. Smelser, "Mechanisms of Change and Adjustment to Change," in Bert F. Hoselitz and Wilbert E. Moore, eds., *Industrialization and Society* (The Hague: UNESCO and Mouton, 1963), p. 41. See also Charles C. Ragin, *The Comparative Method: Moving Beyond Qualitative and Quantitative Strategies* (Berkeley: University of California Press, 1987), p. 134.

57. Stein Rokkan, *Citizens, Elections, Parties* (New York: McKay, 1970), p. 121.

58. Alexis Heraclides, *The Self-Determination of Minorities in International Politics*, (London: Frank Cass, 1991), p. 8.

59. Walker Connor, "Nation-Building or Nation-Destroying?" pp. 328–331. See also Walker Connor, "The Politics of Ethnonationalism," *Journal of International Affairs*, 27, January 1973, pp. 1–21, and "Self-Determination: The New Phase," *World Politics*, 20, no. 1, October 1967, pp. 30–53.

60. For details, see Michael Hechter, *Internal Colonialism: The Celtic Fringe in British National Development, 1536–1966* (London: Routledge and Kegan Paul, 1975).

61. Michael Hechter and Margaret Levi, "The Comparative Analysis of Ethnoregional Movements," *Ethnic and Racial Studies*, 2, July 1979, p. 272.

62. The earliest indications of the plural society approach could be found in the writings of the Duke of Sully in the seventeenth century and John Stuart Mill in the nineteenth century. See Stephen Ryan, *Ethnic Conflict and International Relations* (Aldershot, England: Dartmouth, 1990), pp. 1–2.

63. J. S. Furnivall, *Netherlands India*, pp. 446–469.

64. M. G. Smith, "Some Developments in the Analytic Study of Pluralism," in Kuper and Smith, eds., *Pluralism in Africa*, p. 442.

65. Ryan, *Ethnic Conflict and International Relations*, p. 12.

66. Arend Lijphart, *Democracy in Plural Societies: A Comparative Exploration* (New Haven, Conn.: Yale University Press, 1977), and *Democracies: Patterns of Majoritarian and Consensus Government in Twenty-One Countries* (New Haven, Conn.: Yale University Press, 1984), pp. 23–30.

67. Eric A. Nordlinger, *Conflict Regulation in Divided Societies* (Cambridge, Mass.: Harvard Center for International Affairs, 1972).

68. Donald Rothchild, "Hegemonic Exchange: An Alternative Model for Managing Conflict in Middle Africa," in D. L. Thompson and D. Ronen, eds., *Ethnicity, Politics and Development* (Boulder, Colo.: Lynne Rienner, 1986), p. 72. Cited in Ryan, *Ethnic Conflict and International Relations*, p. 19.

69. Stephen Ryan, *Ethnic Conflict and International Relations*, (Aldershot, UK: Dartmouth, 1990), pp. 19–20.

70. Ibid., p. 20.

71. For details of the resource competition approach, see Michael Hannan, "The Dynamics of Ethnic Boundaries in Modern States," in Michael Hannan and John Meyer, eds., *National Development and the World System: Educational, Economic and Political Change, 1950–1970* (Chicago, Ill.: University of Chicago Press, 1979), pp. 253–277; Francois Nielsen, "The Flemish Movement in Belgium after World War II: A Dynamic Analysis," *American Sociological Review,* 45, 1980, pp. 76–94, and "Toward a Theory of Ethnic Solidarity in Modern Societies," *American Sociological Review,* 50, 1985, pp. 133–149; Charles C. Ragin, "Class, Status, and 'Reactive Ethnic Cleavages': The Social Bases of Political Regionalism," *American Sociological Review,* 42, 1977, pp. 438–450, and "Ethnic Political Mobilization: The Welsh Case," *American Sociological Review,* 44, 1979, pp. 619–635.

72. Heraclides, *The Self-determination of Minorities in International Politics,* p. 9.

73. Donald M. Snow, *Distant Thunder* (New York: St. Martin's Press, 1993), p. 60. For details of the theory of relative deprivation, see Ted Robert Gurr, *Why Men Rebel* (Princeton, N.J.: Princeton University Press, 1970).

74. See Brass, *Ethnicity and Nationalism.*

75. Heraclides, *The Self-determination of Minorities in International Politics,* p. 9.

76. See, for example, Robert D. Kaplan, *Balkan Ghosts: A Journey Through History* (New York: St. Martin's, 1993).

77. Frederick L. Shiels, eds., *Ethnic Separatism and World Politics* (Lanham, Md.: University Press of America, 1984), p. 11.

78. For details of the early 1990s turmoil in Afghanistan, see Salamat Ali, "Uneasy Truce," *Far Eastern Economic Review,* 17, September 1992, p. 30; "Pound of Flesh," *Far Eastern Economic Review,* 6, August 1992; Jayanta Bhattacharya, "Killing Fields," *Sunday,* September, 13–19, 1992, pp. 52–53; Edward A. Gargan, "Afghanistan, Always Riven, Is Breaking into Ethnic Parts," *New York Times,* January 17, 1993; "Leaders of Afghan Factions Seem Closer to Peace," *New York Times,* March 4, 1993.

79. See P. S. Suryanarayana, "Afghan Support to Pak. in the Event of War," *The Hindu,* International Edition, October 15, 1994, p. 3; and Chris Hedges, "Many Islamic Militants Trained in Afghan War," *New York Times,* March 28, 1993.

80. Steven Erlanger, "Tamarlane's Land Trembles: Bloodshed at Gates," *New York Times,* February 15, 1993.

81. Myron Weiner, "The Macedonian Syndrome: An Historical Model of International Relations and Political Development," *World Politics,* 23, no. 4, July 1971, pp. 673–674.

82. Ibid.

83. Stephen M. Saideman and R. William Ayres, *For Kin or Country: Xenophobia, Nationalism, and War* (New York: Columbia University Press, 2008).

84. Stephen M. Saideman, *The Ties That Divide: Ethnic Politics, Foreign Policy, and International Conflict,* (New York: Columbia University Press, 2001).

85. I. William Zartman, "Introduction: Posing the Problem of State Collapse," in Zartman, ed., *Collapsed States: The Disintegration and Restoration of Legitimate Authority* (Boulder, Colo.: Lynne Rienner, 1995), p. 1.

86. Barry R. Posen, "The Security Dilemma and Ethnic Conflict," *Survival*, 35, no. 1, Spring 1993, pp. 27–35.

87. Ibid., p. 32.

88. Stephen M. Saideman, "The Dual Dynamics of Disintegration: Ethnic Politics and Security Dilemmas in Eastern Europe," *Nationalism and Ethnic Politics*, 2, no. 1, Spring 1996, pp. 22–23.

89. Ibid., p. 25.

90. Ibid., pp. 25–26.

91. James D. Fearon, "Ethnic War as a Commitment Problem," paper presented at the 1994 Annual Meeting of the American Political Science Association, New York, August 30–September 2, pp. 1–24.

92. Roger D. Petersen, *Understanding Ethnic Violence: Fear, Hatred and Resentment in Twentieth-Century Eastern Europe*, (Cambridge, U.K.: Cambridge University Press, 2002), p. 1.

93. Ibid., pp. 17–18.

94. Ibid., p. 19.

95. David A. Lake and Donald Rothchild, "Spreading Fear: The Genesis of Transnational Ethnic Conflict," in David A. Lake and Donald Rothchild, eds., *The International Spread of Ethnic Conflict: Fear, Diffusion and Escalation*, (Princeton, N.J.: Princeton University Press, 1998), pp. 7–8. See also, David A. Lake and Donald Rothchild, "Containing Fear: The Origins and Management of Ethnic Conflict," *International Security*, 21, no. 2, Fall 1996, pp. 41–42.

96. Ted Robert Gurr, *Minorities at Risk: A Global View of Ethnopolitical Conflicts*, (Washington, D.C.: United States Institute of Peace Press, 1993), p. 59.

97. Frances Stewart, "Horizontal Inequalities: A Neglected Dimension of Development," World Institute for Development Economics Research (WIDER) Annual Lecture 5, Helsinki, December 14, 2001, pp. 1–37.

98. James D. Fearon and David D. Laitin, "Ethnicity, Insurgency, and Civil War," *American Political Science Review*, 97, no. 1, 2003, pp. 75–90. See also James D. Fearon, "Economic Development, Insurgency and Civil War," in Elhanon Helpman, ed., *Institutions and Economic Performance*, (Cambridge, Mass.: Harvard University Press, 2008).

99. Ole Magnus Theisen, "Blood and Soil? Resource Scarcity and Internal Armed Conflict Revisited," *Journal of Peace Research*, 45, no. 6, 2008, pp. 801–818.

100. H. I. Grossman, "Kleptocracy and Revolutions," *Oxford Economic Papers*, 51, 1999, pp. 267–283. See also H. I. Grossman, "A General Equilibrium Model of Insurrections," *American Economic Review*, 81, 1991, pp. 912–921.

101. Paul Collier and Anke Hoeffler, "Greed and Grievance in Civil War," *Oxford Economic Papers*, 56, 2004, pp. 563–595.

102. See Paul Collier, Anke Hoeffler, and Dominic Rohner, "Beyond Greed and Grievance: Feasibility and Civil War," *Oxford Economic Papers*, 61, no. 1, 2009, pp. 1–27.

103. See Ian Bannon and P. Collier, eds., *Natural Resources and Violent Conflict: Options and Actions* (Washington, D.C.: The World Bank, 2003).

104. See Michael T. Klare, *Resource Wars: The New Landscape of Global Conflict*, (New York: Henry Holt and Company, 2002).

105. See Thomas F. Homer-Dixon, *Environment, Scarcity and Violence* (Princeton, N.J.: Princeton University Press, 1999).

106. Henrik Urdal, "People vs. Malthus: Population Pressure, Environmental Degradation, and Armed Conflict Revisited," *Journal of Peace Research*, 42, no. 4, 2005, pp. 417–434.

107. Michael L. Ross, "What Do We Know About Natural Resources and Civil War?" *Journal of Peace Research*, 41, no. 3, 2004, pp. 337–356.

108. Päivi Lujala, Nils Petter Gleditsch, and Elisabeth Gilmore, "A Diamond Curse? Civil War and a Lootable Resource," *Journal of Conflict Resolution*, 49, no. 4, 2005, pp. 538–562.

109. Richard Snyder and Ravi Bhavnani, "Diamonds, Blood, and Taxes: A Revenue-Centered Framework for Explaining Political Order," *Journal of Conflict Resolution*, 49, no. 4, 2005, pp. 563–597.

110. Richard Snyder, "Does Lootable Wealth Breed Disorder?" *Comparative Political Studies*, 39, no. 8, 2006, pp. 943–968.

111. V. P. Gagnon, Jr., "Ethnic Nationalism and International Conflict: The Case of Serbia," *International Security,* 19, no. 3, Winter 1994/95, p. 131.

112. Ibid., p. 132.

113. Ibid.

114. Stuart J. Kaufman, "An 'International' Theory of Inter-ethnic War," *Review of International Studies,* 22, 1996, pp. 149–150.

115. Stuart J. Kaufman, "Spiraling to Ethnic War: Elites, Masses, and Moscow in Moldova's Civil War," *International Security,* 21, no. 2, Fall 1996, p. 109.

116. Alberto Alesina and Enrico Spolaore, "On the Number and Size of Nations" (Cambridge, Mass.: National Bureau of Economic Research, Working Paper No. 5050, March 1995). Cited in "A Wealth of Nations," *The Economist,* 29 April 1995, p. 90.

117. Gary S. Becker, "Why So Many Mice Are Roaring," *Business Week,* 7, November 1994, p. 20.

118. Ibid.

119. Ibid.

120. Gurr, *Minorities at Risk*, p. 10.

121. Ibid., pp. 6–7.

122. Ibid., p. 15.

123. The "militant sects" have been reconceptualised by Gurr in a more recent study (with Barbara Harff) as the less pejorative sounding politically active "religious minorities." See Ted Robert Gurr and Barbara Harff, *Ethnic Conflict in World Politics* (Boulder, Colo.: Westview Press, 1994)

124. Gurr, *Minorities at Risk*, p. 23.

125. Ibid., pp. 18–23.

126. Ibid., p. 76.

127. Ibid., p. 79.

128. Ibid.

129. Ibid.

130. David Brown, "Ethnic Revival: Perspectives on State and Society," *Third World Quarterly,* 11, no. 4, October 1989, p. 2.

131. Ryan, *Ethnic Conflict and International Relations*, p. xix.

132. See Weiner, "Peoples and States in a New Ethnic Order?" p. 317; and Heraclides, *The Self-determination of Minorities in International Politics,* p. xv.

# CHAPTER 2

# Ethnic Conflict and International Norms

## INTRODUCTION

Within the field of international relations, an important aspect of the study of ethnic conflict is the interrelationship between the **international normative regime** (universally recognized norms, rules, procedures, and principles of behavior within the international system that govern the interstate system and membership in that system) and ethno-political movements. It is worth noting in this context that while the international system is anchored by the principles of national self-determination and state sovereignty, the international normative regime has remained strongly biased against ethno-nationalists, who usually invoke these same principles to justify their movements. In this chapter, we analyze why the international normative regime is biased against ethno-nationalists, identify the main moral arguments that are advanced by ethnic groups to justify their right to secede from an existing state, and explore whether it is possible for the international community to devise a set of criteria that could be used to evaluate different ethnic groups' secessionist claims.

## INTERNATIONAL NORMS AFFECTING ETHNO-SECESSION

**Secession** "is an abrupt unilateral move to independence on the part of a region that is a metropolitan territory of a sovereign independent state"; it can involve a "formal act of declaration of independence" by the secessionist entity, or it can be an "incremental process" of political activity that gradually leads to separation and independence without a formal declaration.[1] Ethno-nationalists do not always advocate secession because several nonseparatist options are available to accommodate ethnic demands: consociational and corporatist arrangements, communalism, multiculturalism, ethnic cooptation, and affirmative action.[2] But in those cases when ethnic groups do make secessionist claims against an existing state (see Table 2.1),

## TABLE 2.1  Secessionist Movements in the 1990s and Beyond

| Secessionist Region | Existing State | Country or Group Giving Assistance |
|---|---|---|
| Abkhazia | Georgia | Russia |
| Assam | India | Bangladesh, Myanmar |
| Basque | Spain | |
| Cabinda | Angola | |
| Catalonia | Spain | |
| Chechnya | Russia | Islamists |
| Corsica | France | |
| Crimea | Ukraine | Russia |
| Irian Jaya (West Papua) | Indonesia | |
| Karen | Myanmar | |
| Kashmir | India | Pakistan, Afghanistan |
| Kosovo | Serbia | Albania |
| Kurdistan | Iran, Iraq, Turkey | United States, United Kingdom |
| Mindanao | Philippines | Saudi Arabia, Indonesia |
| Mohajir | Pakistan | India |
| Nagaland | India | China, Myanmar, Bangladesh |
| Nagorno-Karabakh | Azerbaijan | Armenia |
| Northern Kazakhstan | Kazakhstan | Russia |
| Ogaden | Ethiopia | Somalia |
| Ogun | Nigeria | |
| Oromo | Ethiopia | |
| Puerto Rico | United States | |
| Punjab | India | Pakistan |
| Quebec | Canada | |
| Scotland | Great Britain | |
| Serbs | Bosnia Herzegovina | Serbia |
| South Ossetia | Georgia | Russia |
| South Tyrol | Italy | Austria |
| Southern Sudan | Sudan | Uganda |
| Tamil Eelam | Sri Lanka | India |
| Tibet | China | India |
| Trans-Dniester | Moldova | Russia |
| Western Sahara | Morocco | Algeria |
| Xinjiang | China | Afghanistan, Kyrgyzstan |
| Zanzibar | Tanzania | |
| Zulu | South Africa | |

*Source:* Adapted from Karin von Hippel, "The Resurgence of Nationalism and Its International Implications," *The Washington Quarterly,* 17, no. 4, Autumn 1994, pp. 192–193. The table identifies the best known secessionist and irredentist conflicts; there are many others.

they are usually confronted by two fundamental international norms: (1) the **doctrine of state sovereignty** and (2) the **principle of national self-determination**. Whereas existing states invoke the first doctrine to justify their survival as a unified state, ethno-nationalists refer to the second principle to justify their demand for secession and independence through sovereign statehood.[3]

## The Doctrine of State Sovereignty

The current international system composed of sovereign states gradually came into existence after the **Peace of Westphalia** in 1648, an agreement that ended the Thirty Years' War in Europe and marked the breakup of medieval Christendom. At first, the Westphalian state system was confined to Europe, but then gradually it spread to all corners of the globe, helped by western colonialism. The main normative pillar on which the Westphalian system rests is sovereignty, "a legal, absolute, and unitary condition."[4] Sovereignty is legal in the sense that, under international law, a sovereign state is not subordinate to any other state. Sovereignty is also absolute because it "is either present or absent" and "there is no intermediate category."[5] Finally, sovereignty is unitary because a sovereign state exercises "supreme authority within its jurisdiction."[6] The Westphalian system therefore accommodates two contradictory ideas: by equating sovereignty with state power and authority (which varies from state to state across time and space), it accepts the notion of a vertical or hierarchical positioning of states in the international system;[7] simultaneously, because each state is legally sovereign, the Westphalian system promotes the principle of sovereign equality of states.[8]

Some scholars, such as Nicholas Onuf, have questioned the usefulness of treating state sovereignty as a normative pillar of the international system in the post–cold war era: "The cold war has come to an end; and so, perhaps, has the long period of sovereignty's conceptual stability." He contrasted how nineteenth-century nationalism fostered an identity between state and nation, with the state expected to be the fulfillment of the national idea. But in the new millennium "nationalism tends to promote a contrary sensibility. The well-formed nation-state is a rarity. When states and nations fail to coincide, popular opinion favors the nation with a measure of majesty no longer available to the state. Increasingly the nation as people, not land, delimits the span of rule."[9] This may be cold comfort to many secessionist ethnic movements in the twentieth and twenty-first centuries that have failed to attain sovereign statehood. In particular, three entailments of sovereignty continue to create massive trouble for ethnic groups in their quest for sovereign statehood. The first concerns international legal norms on the territorial sovereignty of states and the creation of new states. The second deals with the need for all units of the system to recognize each other as sovereign. The final entailment of sovereignty is the international legal requirement on states not to interfere in the internal affairs of other states.[10] Let us now consider each of these obstacles to ethnic secession in more detail.

**STATE FORMATION AND TERRITORY.**    A new state comes to be formed "when a community acquires, with a reasonable probability of permanence, the essential characteristics of a state, namely an organized government, a defined territory, and such a degree of independence of control by any other state as to be capable of conducting its own international relations."[11] This can be achieved through "the granting of independence, by the acknowledgment of already existing *de facto* independence, from the dissolution of an empire or federation, by the merger of two or more units (former colonies or parts of empires) or states, by partition (the formation of two or more states by mutual consent) and by the seizure of independence."[12]

For ethno-national movements that aspire to independence and sovereign statehood, the most direct way to create a separate state is either through the partition of an existing state (by mutual consent) or through the forcible seizure of independence. As long as the creation of a separate state is the result of a mutually agreeable partition, it is acceptable under international law. But with few exceptions, the international normative regime condemns the forcible seizure of independence. Although it seems that international law provides for a simple way for ethno-secessionists to acquire independence and separate statehood, in practice, this is not so easy. A major difficulty is distinguishing between forcible secession and mutually agreeable partition.

In Medieval society, with its vast empires, the main political objective was to have power over people. But with the emergence of the Westphalian international system comprised of sovereign states, territory or land became "the ultimate object of political life."[13] In the Westphalian system, the value that sovereign states can never sacrifice is their political independence. In practice, this means that states cannot surrender their territorial integrity except under special circumstances.[14] Therefore, hardly any existing sovereign state would acquiesce to loss of territory to ethno-secessionists because to do so would violate a basic condition of state sovereignty—the territorial integrity of states.

Along with this practical difficulty, international legal principles pertaining to the acquisition of territorial sovereignty—the exercise of authority over a piece of territory in a way that demonstrates the fullest right to that territory—is stacked against ethno-secessionists. International law identifies five principal ways of acquiring sovereignty over a territory: through occupation, prescription, cession, conquest, or accretion. Of these five, only physical occupation of territory as a means of acquiring territorial sovereignty is relevant to the case of ethno-secession.

**Occupation** generally means the acquisition of territory that is not already part of another state. Titles (legal right) to territory by occupation are now practically impossible because almost the entire global landmass has been carved up into states. But international legal principles pertaining to territorial acquisition by occupation continue to be important "because the occupations of the past often give rise to the boundary disputes of the present."[15] The law pertaining to title to territory through occupation was set by the Permanent Court of International Justice under the League of Nations system. In the *Legal Status of Eastern Greenland* case (involving Norway and Denmark), the permanent court ruled that a claim to territorial sovereignty must be based on two elements: the claimant must first demonstrate its intention and will to act as sovereign over the territory, and the claimant must then show evidence of some actual exercise or display of sovereign authority in the territory.[16]

The first part of the test is not a major hurdle for many ethnic groups because they usually demonstrate the intention and political will to act as sovereign over a territory they consider to be their homeland. The problematic aspect is the second part of the test. As the permanent court observed in the *Eastern Greenland* case, in the absence of any competing claim by another party, only a slight exercise of authority would be sufficient to grant title to territorial sovereignty.[17] However, barring exceptional circumstances, a territorial claim made by an ethnic movement is unlikely to go unchallenged by the state. In such circumstances, as the permanent court pointed out, the evidence of actual exercise of authority over the claimed territory has to be substantial. Most ethnic groups are unlikely to be able to meet this criterion because governments usually have more power to demonstrate sovereign authority over state territory. It would seem then that the only way ethnic groups could meet this criterion would be if they won a decisive military victory against the state's forces and actually controlled and exercised real authority in the claimed territory for a considerable length of time. Such instances are rare and, even with territorial seizures, there is no guarantee that statehood will result.

**THE PROBLEM OF RECOGNITION.**    **Recognition** of a state is the act by which another state acknowledges that the political entity in question possesses all the attributes of statehood. Recognition confers an international legal personality on a state and allows it to join the international states system with full rights, privileges, and duties. In their quest for separate statehood, ethno-secessionists must obtain international recognition; otherwise, they risk becoming a pariah or rogue state. However, international legal principles dealing with recognition of new states can prove to be a major obstacle for ethno-secessionists in their quest for independence and sovereign statehood.

Three political-legal principles are used internationally to determine which claimants are to be accorded recognition as sovereign states. The first is the **ideological theory of recognition**; it involves using ideological criteria to determine whether the government of a new state can pass a political eligibility test. In practice, recognition depends on whether a would-be state's government is likely to be friendly toward the recognizing party. For instance, for three decades after World War II, the United States of America refused to recognize the People's Republic of China because the U.S. government, for ideological reasons, refused to recognize a communist government that seized power through a revolution. It was only the U.S. Secretary of State Henry Kissinger's *realpolitik* in the 1970s that overcame the ideological blockage and extended U.S. recognition to communist leader Mao Zedong's government.

According to the **constitutive theory of recognition**, the act of recognition itself creates statehood and confers sovereign authority on a new state and its government. Hence, from this perspective, new states acquire a legal personality in international law only through the act of recognition. The act of recognition is not only constitutive but reciprocal; that is, it creates rights and obligations of statehood where none existed before. However, the constitutive approach leaves unclear the minimum number of recognitions from existing states that are needed before a new state could be said to have acquired legal personality and sovereign standing under international law. For example, Iceland was the first country to officially recognize the independence of the Baltic states in 1991, but this was pretty much meaningless until a host of other western states did likewise. A strict interpretation of constitutive theory would imply "that an unrecognized state has neither rights nor duties in international law."[18] But as the Baltic states demonstrated, this would be clearly unjust and absurd because states can have a shaky legal existence even before they have been widely recognized.

Given the shortcomings of the ideological and constitutive theories of recognition, some international legal experts accept the notion that the act of recognition is not a constitutive but a declaratory act. The **declaratory theory of recognition** posits that the formal recognition of statehood "does not bring into legal existence a state which did not exist before." Rather, a state may de facto exist prior to being recognized and if it does, then whether or not it has been formally recognized by other states, "it has the right to be treated by them *as* a state."[19] The main purpose of recognition from this approach "is to acknowledge as a fact something which has hitherto been uncertain, namely the independence of the body claiming to be a state, and to declare the recognizing state's readiness to accept the normal consequences of that fact, namely the usual courtesies of international intercourse."[20]

The declaratory theory of recognition centers on the ability of a state to govern and control its population and territory, but this legalist approach is also fraught with difficulties. For one thing, how is "control" to be measured? For another, although the declaratory approach regards recognition of states as a political act on the part of other states in the international system, in practice this question is often both "difficult and delicate, especially when part of an existing state is forcibly endeavoring to separate itself from the rest."[21] In the absence of fixed rules, recognition of independence of a region in revolt while conflict is ongoing, as in Chechnya between 1994 and 1996, would be premature and regarded by the international community as unjustified intervention in the internal affairs of the state experiencing the revolt. In contrast, the mere persistence of the old state in the struggle where ethno-nationalists are clearly winning is not sufficient cause for withholding recognition of the seceding new state: "even though recognition is an optional act, if an entity bears the usual marks of statehood, in particular if there is *de facto* control of a territory and its inhabitants by an organized government, other states put themselves at risk legally if they choose to ignore the basic obligations of state relations."[22] But under "normal circumstances, the existence of a rebellion within a state is a domestic matter with which other states have no concern."[23]

There are two exceptional situations, and they may be used by other states seeking to avoid charges of partisan interference in a secessionist ethnic conflict while recognizing political and military realities. Under international law, conferring the **status of insurgency** or the **status of belligerency** offers ethnic groups "halfway-house recognition" of their claims[24] because both situations reflect an "international acknowledgment of the existence of an internal war."[25] The acknowledgment by the international community of a state of internal war also means that the international legal principles pertaining to warfare apply.[26]

Conferring insurgent status on a group involved in an internal war with the state, whether done tacitly or expressly, is an indication that the recognizing state regards the insurgents as legal contestants and not as mere lawbreakers. At the same time, it does not automatically "entail the legal burdens of a neutral—possibly the recognizing state is still free to assist the legal government, and would be illegally intervening if it materially assisted the insurgents."[27] Therefore, although it shields insurgents from being treated as lawbreakers, the granting of insurgent status does *not* confer on the insurgents the status of a state.

In turn, to qualify for belligerent status, insurgent groups must meet a number of criteria—a so-called factual test. First, an armed conflict must exist within a state; second, the rebels must physically occupy and govern a substantial portion of national territory; third, the rebels must carry out hostilities in accordance with the laws of war and through an organized armed force operating under a clear chain of command; and fourth, outside states must recognize the rebels as belligerents.[28] But recognition of belligerency, too, does not automatically translate into recognition of the breakaway group as a sovereign state. The conferral of belligerent status is "purely provisional" because "it puts both belligerent parties in the position of states, but only for the purposes and for the duration of the war."[29] Ironically, the recognition of belligerency of the rebels by other states may be advantageous to the state facing the rebellion because this act automatically relieves the state "of responsibility for the acts of its own rebellious subjects towards other states."[30] Still, for the most part, the conferral of belligerency status to a rebel movement is resented by the state to which rebels belong because the belligerency label would provide the rebels with a degree of international legitimacy. Hardly any state faced with a secessionist insurgency would want even a small degree of international legitimacy to be conferred on the insurgents, regardless of whether it is for a limited purpose and applies only for the duration of the conflict.[31]

International recognition—whether of full statehood or of the more circumscribed status of insurgency or belligerency—has proved to be a nearly insurmountable hurdle for secessionist ethnic groups to overcome, as it has been with title to territory. The recognition requirement can frustrate ethno-secessionists who are able to demonstrate all the other attributes of statehood. They can even have forces strong enough to win modern-day equivalents of the battle of Gettysburg and still be denied recognition.

**NONINTERVENTION AND NONUSE OF FORCE.**   In an international states system based on the norm of sovereign equality of states, where only states can legally claim a monopoly of jurisdiction within their borders and where this right is recognized by all states in the system, it is logical that states be allowed to exercise this right within their territory free of outside interference. To do otherwise would make sovereignty meaningless. Thus, the **principle of nonintervention** in the internal affairs of states "is one of the cardinal principles of international law and can be seen as complimentary to the non-use of force prohibition."[32] Because intervention implies the use of or the threat to use force, it violates the principle of territorial supremacy of states and thus comes into conflict with international law.

The duty of states not to intervene in the affairs of another state received recognition in Articles 1 and 3 of the draft Declaration on the Rights and Duties of States adopted in 1949 by the United Nations International Law Commission. In Article 2, paragraphs 4 and 7, the United Nations Charter also prohibits intervention by calling on all member states to refrain from threatening or using force against the territorial integrity or political independence of any state. International law allows for departures from the **principle of non-use of force** in exceptional circumstances: (1) reasons of self-defense; (2) promotion and/or restoration of international peace and security, in which case there is collective intervention by an international governmental organization (IGO) or by its members following a specific resolution; (3) response to complex humanitarian emergencies, especially situations of mass murder and genocide; (4) in rare cases, flagrant instances of institutionalized racism and violence against a majority; (5) situations akin to classical colonialism; and (6) status of belligerency.[33] Recently, more reasons have been found to justify international intervention. They range from pure realist (power) considerations such as "might makes right" and the need to protect oneself by such intervention, to internationally accepted justifications (consent given by the subject government, collapse of governing authority in the subject country, consensus in the international community), to pure globalist explanations such as conforming with universal principles or decisions taken by supranational authorities.[34]

Although the international community continues "to 'chip away' at the sovereign autonomy of states,"[35] nevertheless "nonintervention" and "nonuse of force" remain fundamental principles of international law. Hence, under a traditional interpretation of international law, ethnic groups do not have the legal right to seek external support, not even from ethnic kin in neighboring states. A sovereign state, however, has the legal right to seek support from any third state. Under traditional international law, "in relations with third states a lawful government is in a privileged position compared with the insurgents, at least until there has been recognition of belligerency."[36] But the recognition of belligerency is extremely rare and provisional in nature, and at best it may create military parity between the ethno-secessionists and the state.[37]

The international norms of nonintervention and nonuse of force therefore puts ethno-nationalists and secessionists at a great disadvantage in their quest to procure external support, compared with sovereign state governments, because "governments have a mutual interest in their security of tenure," and therefore "the bias of the system against revolutionary challenge is a logical expression of the basic idea of sovereign states exercising exclusive control over territory."[38] As if these legal norms and *realpolitik* factors were not enough, the world of mutual treaty obligations and strategic considerations have also contributed to the creation of an international states system heavily biased against ethno-secessionists.

## The Principle of National Self-Determination

**THE ORIGINS OF THE PRINCIPLE.**  Political historians have long argued that as a political doctrine or ideology, nationalism originated in post-Medieval Europe and later spread around the world when western-educated native elites and intelligentsia imported the nationalist idea from Europe to their respective lands. But why did nationalism first originate in post-Medieval Europe? Kedourie offered two main reasons: a revolution in European philosophy and a breakdown in European society in the eighteenth century. The revolution in European philosophy coincided with the French Revolution of 1789, which advocated the idea that people possessed certain inalienable natural rights and hence society should be politically organized in order to protect and promote these rights; by this standard, Medieval European society was evil because it violated these rights. This revolutionary viewpoint, however, had an in-built contradiction: the idea that people possessed certain inalienable natural rights assumed "the existence of an orderly universe, capable of rational explanation, of natural laws holding sway over both men and things"; the problem was that "the fashionable philosophy of the enlightenment made such an assumption extremely difficult."[39] Enlightenment philosophy, therefore, had to resolve the following dilemma: if knowledge was not based on universal natural laws but on human sensations (as the Enlightenment preached), then how could it be reconciled with the assertion that liberty, equality, and fraternity are the inalienable natural rights of every individual?[40] In other words, liberty, equality, fraternity, and the rest may all exist and have reality, but the important issue was how to prove it.

The writings of Immanuel Kant offered a way out of this predicament. In epistemology, Kant suggested that knowledge is based on sensations because that knowledge emanates from things in the external world; therefore, one can never know things as they really are independent of one's observation. From this, it followed that if knowledge is based on human senses and if morality is not a mere illusion based on opinions, morality must then be separated from knowledge of the phenomenal world: "Morality is the outcome of obedience to a universal law which is to be found within ourselves, not in the world of appearances. For morality to be possible, it must be *independent* of the laws which govern appearances."[41] This independence for Kant was *freedom* in the strictest or transcendental sense.

Although Kant can hardly be described as the father of nationalist philosophy, his idea had far-reaching political ramifications. Because man is free only when "he obeys the laws of morality which he finds within himself, and not in the external world," Kant's doctrine made the individual "in a way never envisaged by the French revolutionaries or their intellectual precursors, the very center, the arbiter, the sovereign of the universe."[42] Politically, its implication was that individual *self-determination* constituted the supreme good. It also followed that the civil constitution of every state should be republican because a republican state "was one where, regardless of the forms of government, the laws were or could be the expressions of the autonomous will of the citizens. Only in such a situation could peace be guaranteed."[43] Later political philosophers such as Rousseau, Herder, Fichte, and Hegel drew on and transformed Kantian ideas into a nationalist political philosophy or doctrine whose core propositions were the following:

- Humanity is naturally divided into nations.
- Each nation has its peculiar character.
- The source of all political power is the nation.
- For freedom and self-realization, people must identify with a nation.
- Nations can be fulfilled only in their own states.
- Loyalty to the nation-state overrides other loyalties.
- The primary condition of global freedom and harmony is the strengthening of the nation-state.[44]

Smith has argued that the core propositions of the nationalist doctrine neither furnished a complete theory of social change and political action nor defined the unit of population that could claim and enjoy its own state and government. By leaving open "the form of self-determination as well as the content of the expression of national individuality," the nationalist doctrine "endowed nationalism with its tantalizing amorphousness, its doctrinal sketchiness and the multifarious nature of the movements' activities and goals."[45]

The revolution sweeping European philosophy in the eighteenth century was accompanied by a simultaneous upheaval and transformation in European social life. The dislocations of industrialization and urbanization revealed the weaknesses of the old system and the need for more innovative political institutions adaptable to the new socioeconomic conditions. The attractiveness of new political ideas espoused by Enlightenment philosophers was therefore that much greater under such chaotic conditions, and people "were driven to import philosophy into politics because society and state in eighteenth century Europe seemed cold and heartless."[46]

The coalescing of the right of self-determination with the idea of the nation gave rise to the notion of national self-determination, which conferred a right on nations to determine their own political fate by determining "the sovereign state to which they would belong and the form of government under which they would live."[47] The notion of national self-determination thus assumed that humanity is not only divided by race and gender but also by nationality; that this division is natural; that rule by foreigners constitutes a denial of fundamental human rights and leads to resentment; and that each nation, and no other entity, has the right to constitute a separate state.[48]

The formation of nation-states proceeded along two tracks in Europe. In a famous lecture given in 1882 entitled *Qu'est-ce qu'une nation?* ("What is a nation?"), the French historian Ernest Renan called the nation a "daily plebiscite," meaning that a nation comes into existence when the population of a given territory perceives itself to be a nation and equates citizenship with nationality (*Staatsnation*). In the late eighteenth and early nineteenth centuries, in France and England, and also in the United States, the nation-state came to be understood as "a community of politically aware citizens equal before the law irrespective of their social and economic status, ethnic origin and religious beliefs."[49] By contrast, continental Europe witnessed the development of the ethnic or cultural nation (*Kulturnation*), which envisioned the nation-state on the basis of the vernacular cultural community or "the folk" with a sense of shared descent (no matter how fictive), history, religion, customs, practices, and vernacular language.[50]

The exercise of the right of self-determination in the late eighteenth and early nineteenth centuries further altered the locus of state sovereignty. Under the Treaty of Westphalia of 1648, which had established the legal principle of sovereignty to govern interstate relations, the dynastic principle of political legitimacy had been left intact along with "the right of rulers to determine the sovereignty and form of government of 'their' territories."[51] But under the impact of self-determination, the **dynastic sovereignty** was replaced by **popular sovereignty**, which proclaimed that "government should be based on the will of the people, not on that of the monarch, and people not content with the government of the country to which they belong should be able to secede and organize themselves as they wish."[52] Following from this tradition, in the first half of the nineteenth century, popular national liberation movements struggled to take power in Latin America, while in the second half, within the British empire, Canada and Australia became sovereign dominions.

**NATIONAL SELF-DETERMINATION AT THE BEGINNING OF THE TWENTIETH CENTURY.** During World War I, the doctrine of national self-determination was reaffirmed when U.S. President Woodrow Wilson "led the United States into the war in order to make the world safe for democracy and national self-determination," while the leader of the newly formed Soviet Union, Vladimir Lenin, led his country "out of the war proclaiming the principle of nationalities as a new guiding principle for a socialist world order."[53] To both Wilson and Lenin, the doctrine of national self-determination conferred a right to nations to decide their own political fate, regardless of existing state boundaries and political structures. But whereas Lenin enunciated the doctrine of national self-determination in the *Declaration on the Rights of the Peoples of Russia* to justify the October Revolution, Wilson saw no "gap between national self-determination and democracy (for what other purpose would a people claim the right to self-determination if not to rule themselves?) and between both these concepts and the idea of a self-policing system of collective security to replace the discredited system of international power politics (for if all legitimate national and democratic aspirations had been met, would not all have a joint interest in deterring any disturbance of the peace?)."[54]

In the aftermath of World War I, both Wilson and Lenin believed, but for different reasons, that the right of national self-determination incorporated two essential elements: the right to secession and the right to independent statehood. But while the concept of national self-determination seemed fine in theory and formed a key element in Wilson's Fourteen Points, in practice, it was difficult to implement.

The main problem was this: if the right of self-determination had to be extended to different nations, then it had to be assumed that the existence of nations is either known beforehand or will be self-evident once we start looking for it. Both assumptions were highly questionable for the following reasons. First, no consensus existed among scholars and practitioners regarding the key attributes of nationhood. Second, the various attributes of nationhood were not equally present among or stressed by different ethnic groups. And, third, even within the same ethnic group, different attributes of nationhood were stressed at different times. Wilsonian liberals tried to overcome this problem through the use of the plebiscite: "an open test of public opinion designed to solicit the wishes of individuals with regard to their collective identity."[55] The idea of the plebiscite, however, suffered from two major weaknesses: first, it assumed the preexistence of a "collective identity" based on the decision on which "people" to poll; and second, it discounted the "agenda problem," which arose "because of the fact that whoever controls the questions on which a particular population is to be asked to vote, is in a very strong position also to control the outcome."[56]

The doctrine of national self-determination also exposed the problem of ethnic minorities. Over the course of European history, ethnic nations had become hopelessly scattered. Even if one assumed that all the different ethnic nations could be identified and given separate statehood, it would have still left significant numbers of people outside their respective ethnic nation-states. In other words, no matter how adroitly political maps were drawn and redrawn, ethnic minority populations were certain to remain in most states. This meant that any attempt to strictly implement the right of national self-determination was both futile and fraught with risks for minority populations. For instance, the strict implementation of the right of national self-determination would inevitably result in a massive population movement and exchange. The sheer physical hardship and dislocation that people would have to bear would be enormous, and many would probably perish in the process. It would also worsen the plight of "trapped" ethnic minorities once the new states were in place. These new states would naturally be suspicious of and therefore insist on absolute loyalty from their ethnic minorities for reasons of state integrity and security. This meant that these states would be inclined to increase assimilationist pressures on their ethnic minorities and deny them any group rights; in extreme cases, it could result in genocide, massacre, or ethnic cleansing of minority populations. The existence of trapped ethnic minorities and state persecution could also generate a plethora of powerful and destructive secessionist and irredentist movements, which would then bring the state and the minority population into direct military confrontation.

Finally, to confer the right of national self-determination to many subject ethnic nations, the victorious powers had to condone the breakup of established states, including some of their own, which they were hardly inclined to do. The British government, for instance, was unwilling to extend the right of national self-determination to the Irish, citing reasons of state security and sovereignty; it was only in 1922, six years after the Easter Uprising in Dublin, that Britain was prepared to recognize a quasi-sovereign and emasculated Irish Free State missing six Irish counties in the north. Because the victorious European powers desired to hold on to their colonies in Asia and Africa, granting the right of national self-determination to the native populations went against their self-interest. Hence, these colonial powers favored a narrower formulation of the doctrine of national self-determination so that it could be applicable only to Europe.[57]

After World War I, therefore, the victorious powers used the language of national self-determination but redrew "the map of Europe so that it roughly reflected the nationality principle but without any fixed procedure and subject to considerations of practicality and political interests."[58] Thereafter, the doctrine of national self-determination was not even included in the covenant of the League of Nations. Until the end of World War II, the right of national self-determination was also not extended to colonial possessions, which created a transparent paradox for Britain and France in the sense that both were possessors of far-flung colonial empires, but "were also the countries in which liberal constitutionalism was most securely anchored and where [civic] national unification had proceeded furthest."[59] Liberal imperialists in Britain and France tried to explain and justify the contradiction between the political values of liberal democracy and the idea of a nationally, and ultimately racially, defined imperial order by conceptually dividing the world between civilized powers and barbarians. But "since liberal values were ultimately grounded in the Enlightenment discovery of universal human rights, this distinction could no longer be regarded as part of the natural order" and therefore liberal imperialists had to come up with the **"white man's burden" argument**, which envisaged "a process whereby barbarian states could graduate into 'civilized' international society after a period of enlightened education and preparation for self-government."[60]

**NATIONAL SELF-DETERMINATION UNDER THE UNITED NATIONS.** When the United Nations system was being created toward the end of World War II, national self-determination was not included in the original draft of the charter as drawn up by the major powers at Dumbarton Oaks. At the San Francisco conference, however, under pressure from the Soviet delegation as well as from Latin America and the Arab world, "self-determination" was introduced into the charter in two places. First, under Article 1(2), one of the main purposes of the United Nations was stated as follows: "To develop friendly relations among nations based on respect for the principle of equal rights and self-determination of peoples, and to take other appropriate measures to strengthen universal peace." Second, under Article 55, the charter laid down general social, economic, and human rights based on the principles enunciated in Article 1(2).[61] Still, the issue remained contentious, and it was unclear whether self-determination was to be applied as a "political principle" or as a "legal right." The United Nations (UN) preferred to treat national self-determination more as a political principle and went on to identify its role in three areas: (1) to expound on the basic principles of the charter—carried out primarily through UN resolutions (such as the Friendly Relations Declaration of 1970) and the advisory opinions of the International Court of Justice (such as on Namibia and Western Sahara); (2) to elaborate a system of universal human rights—enacted in 1966 in the form of the international covenants on human rights; and (3) to address the problem of colonialism—the decisive resolution in this case was the Declaration on the Granting of Independence to Colonial Countries and Peoples made in 1960, which made it clear that, although "all peoples have the right to self-determination," any disruption in "the national unity and the territorial integrity of a country is incompatible with the purposes and principles of the Charter of the United Nations."

Although the UN used national self-determination to bring about an end to colonies, it preferred that people in the colonies "exercise this right once and for all and never again, without disrupting the territorial integrity of the colonial entity."[62] An unstated UN objective was clearly, therefore, to freeze the political and territorial map of the world (at the expense of the legitimate political aspirations of nonstate ethnic nations) once the process of decolonization was over.[63] The African and Asian post-colonial states went along with this UN plan for reasons of sovereignty, territorial integrity, and national security, even though many African and Asian nationalists and political elites had earlier argued for revising artificial boundaries created by the western colonials. The UN plan to use the right of self-determination only for decolonization purposes also received support from regional intergovernmental organizations, such as the Organization of African Unity (OAU), for the obvious reason that "they would be placing themselves in an almost untenable position if they were to interpret self-determination in such a way as to invite or justify attacks on the unity and integrity of their own member states."[64] The UN's policy on national self-determination thus opposed nonstate ethnic nations' efforts to secede from the newly created post-colonial independent states: "a colonial people wishing to cast off the domination of its governors has every moral and legal right to do so [but] a manifestly indistinguishable minority which happens to find itself, pursuant to a paragraph in some medieval territorial settlement or through a fiat of the cartographers, annexed to an independent state must forever remain without the scope of the principle of self-determination."[65] Other than colonies and non-self-governing territories, the UN extended the right of self-determination "only to territories under occupation [such as the Baltic states and East Timor] and to majorities subjected to institutionalized racism [blacks in South Africa under Apartheid] but not minorities that are victims of similar policies."[66] In short, the basis of national self-determination under the UN became political and territorial instead of ethnic.[67] The main reason for such a UN stance was, of course, fear of international anarchy: "Fears that [ethnic] secession would mean international anarchy led to attempts to dissociate endorsement of the right of [national] self-determination from recognition of a right [of ethnic nations] to secede."[68] In practice, this meant that the UN had to avoid linking minority ethnic nations' "rights" with minority ethnic nations' "political objectives."[69]

If UN practice and international norms worked in tandem to squash ethnic nations' political aspirations after 1945, two other developments also posed a stiff challenge for ethnic groups seeking their own independent sovereign state. First, constitutional law operated "in a way almost equally adverse to [ethno-national] secession as international law" because "only three post-war constitutions have recognized a right of [ethnic] secession: those of Burma between 1947 and 1974, Yugoslavia and the Soviet Union."[70] But as state practice showed, even these three states were not interested in *genuinely* upholding the right of ethno-national self-determination. Second, both Marxists and western liberals tended to view ethnic nationalism and religious fundamentalism "either as epiphenomena, that is, expressions of more fundamental group identities such as class, or as anachronisms which will soon disappear in an age of economic interdependence and secularization."[71] To be sure, Marxists had always regarded nationalism and religion to be "integral parts of the superstructure created by the dominant economic and political classes . . . to legitimize their rule."[72] Hence, they predicted that the victory of the proletariat, which for Marxists was the culmination of the process of modernization, would erode nationalism as well as other social manifestations of class domination. The liberals, in contrast, assumed that increasing advancement in communications and transportation, industrialization, and urbanization would create a "modern" political identity uniting all inhabitants of the state regardless of ethnicity and thereby eliminate the incentives for ethnic conflicts.

From the preceding discussion, it is clear that the international legal framework pertaining to state formation and recognition, the international norm of nonintervention, and the international interpretation of the principle of national self-determination all conspire against ethnic groups and their desire for independent existence. In addition to international law, constitutional law also creates hurdles for ethnic groups. Some exceptions to the international normative regime on ethnic secession can be identified, but they serve only to underscore the existing rules. Although most states support the contemporary interpretation of the right of national self-determination, some, such as Somalia, officially recognize secession to be part of this right. Some Islamic states have also done the same, especially in cases where Muslim groups are fighting for self-determination. Similarly, India's recognition of Bangladesh's secession in 1971, the recognition some African states gave to Biafra in 1968, and the relatively quick recognition western European countries gave to the Soviet and Yugoslav successor states are exceptions to the rule.

The rarity of recognized secession is clearly seen when we realize how few are the cases of successful secession. Between 1945 and 1990, many separatist movements existed, but only one—Bangladesh—succeeded. In the early 1990s, a number of successful secessions did take place, but they were mostly concentrated in communist states that were organized as federal systems and were in the throes of collapse. The line was drawn clearly to preclude legal recognition of other secessions even when they had won military victories, as in the case of Chechnya in Russia, Trans-Dniester (a Russian region) in Moldova, Abkhazia in Georgia, and Karabakh (an Armenian enclave) in Azerbaijan. So the spate of successful secessions in the 1990s signaled a modification of the international normative regime on secession only to the degree that it formally recognized the consequences of a political bloc losing the cold war.

This section of the chapter has argued that the international legal framework, norms, and actual state practice are opposed to ethnic secession. In the next section, we consider the main moral arguments that ethnic groups usually offer in justifying their desire to secede from an existing state. In the final section, we focus on the question of whether the international normative regime should exhibit sensitivity to particularly egregious cases of oppression of nationalities and minorities engendering secessionist sentiment, or whether it should follow established practice and give a blanket rejection to all secessionist claims, regardless of the circumstances involved.

## THE MORAL CASE FOR SECESSION

In normal circumstances, a secessionist policy pursued by ethno-nationalists is unlikely to find much support in the international community. Still, it is quite probable that the portrayal of minorities as being at risk will evoke considerable international sympathy for such groups. The moral case for secession would seemingly be stronger and more worthy of international support the more at risk a minority is; the more serious its grievances are; and the more realistic, flexible, and accommodating its demands have been over time.[73]

An important body of literature that addresses the topic of the morality of secession has emerged in recent times. Even moral philosophers have become alert to the beleaguered status of ethno-nationalist movements that are fighting the power of the existing state. This literature has framed the issue in terms of the morality of secession—a notion referring to the efforts by a national group to undo a political union as a prelude to pursuing its own sovereignty. To be sure, the grounds for leaving a union may not always be the same as those for claiming statehood. Claims of discrimination are more persuasive for the first case; claims of historical destiny are more persuasive for the second. Generally, however, groups seek to advance the most morally persuasive case to justify their actions and objectives.

Explicit demands for secession and statehood are partly a consequence of the notion that self-determination has become too ephemeral and arbitrary. Indeed, an indirect cause for the increase in ethno-secessionist movements is that self-determination, as evidenced in the legal framework described above, has become diluted and without practical implications. One writer traced the discrediting of the principle to Hitler's appropriation of it in the 1930s to justify Third Reich military aggression in defense of the purported national aspirations of Germans in Austria and Czechoslovakia. Thus "[F]rom its Wilsonian origins, the concept of self-determination has been more an instrument of international politics than a humanitarian principle associated with the law of nations."[74] In the twenty-first century, the moral grounds for secession resemble the moral case behind self-determination in the colonial era.

As noted above, the most compelling case for secession seems to concern a minority population that is at risk, but both what a minority is and when it is at genuine risk are ambiguous notions: "There is no generally acceptable normative definition of ethnic or national minorities. On this basis many a state does not recognize the existence of distinct minority groups with corresponding minority rights, and of the minorities in question as they choose to define themselves. Another problem is that few states are prepared to regard such rights as 'group rights'"[75] Taxonomies of at-risk groups have little practical significance then if states dispute the very existence of distinct minority groups on the territory they govern.

Legal and political scholars, too, disagree about the conditions under which a group would be entitled to exercise self-determination. In *The Power of Legitimacy Among Nations,* Thomas Franck advanced the broad principle of "entitlement to equality" as a basis for self-determination. In his view, "self-determination is a right applicable to any distinct region in which the inhabitants do not enjoy rights equal to those accorded all people in other parts of the same state."[76] Franck thus avoided the conceptual difficulties associated with defining minority groups and drew attention instead to the fundamental condition of inequality.

In his pioneering study *Secession: The Legitimacy of Self-Determination,* Buchheit examined whether self-determination constituted a natural right derived from natural law and represented a universal humanist principle. Studying such natural-rights theorists as Thomas Hobbes, Hugo Grotius, Emmerich von Vattel, and John Locke, the author concluded that "at no point in the evolution of natural rights thinking has the doctrine of a right to resistance on the part of individuals or groups of individuals been affirmed in an unqualified manner." He added: "Nor has this inherent right of resistance generally been viewed as including a group right of secession."[77]

Buchheit was persuaded, however, that a highly qualified right of secession had emerged under positive international law. The Congress of Vienna in 1815—in that part of its declaration promising national institutions for partitioned Poland—as well as the post–World War I treaties of Versailles (in 1919 between the allies and Germany), Trianon (in 1920, with Hungary), Sèvres (in 1920, with Turkey), and others with both defeated and emergent states—especially those parts specifying the obligations of states to their minorities—constituted empirical evidence of the right to self-determination. The 1960 UN Declaration on the Granting of Independence to Colonial Countries and Peoples and the Friendly Relations Declaration of 1970 reinstated the importance of self-determination as a desideratum, if not a legal right. Writing in 1978, Buchheit concluded that "the evolution of an international legal recognition of secessionist self-determination, although cautious and uniformly conservative, is nevertheless perceptible."[78]

Buchheit then sought to integrate this limited opportunity structure for secessionists with normative-based models that could justify secession in the contemporary world. One was **remedial secession**—"a scheme by which, corresponding to the various degrees of oppression inflicted upon a particular group by its governing State, international law recognizes a continuum of remedies ranging from protection of individual rights, to minority rights, and ending with secession as the ultimate remedy."[79] A second model was that of **parochialist secession**, which contends that "the only really inescapable requirement for a legitimate claim to self-determination is the existence of a genuine 'self' wanting to control its own political destiny."[80] The merits of the latter claim rested on two issues: (1) the extent to which a group is in fact a self capable of independent existence, and (2) the likelihood that a greater degree of harmony, or less social disruption, would follow if an existing union was dismantled to accommodate secession. Effects of a successful secession had to be measured both on the remaining state as well as on the general international order. Buchheit arrived at a persuasive calculus of the legitimacy of secession:

> Where the disruption factor is high, the claimant must make out an extraordinarily good case for its entitlement to self-determination. In other words, the higher the disruption factor, the more will be required by way of demonstrating selfness and future viability. Where little disruption is liable to ensue from the secession, or where the amount of current disruption outweighs the future risk, the community can afford to be less strict in its requirements for selfhood. . . . It may therefore accommodate to a greater extent the self-governing wishes of a particular people who cannot offer overwhelming proof of their racial, historical, or linguistic distinctness.[81]

Although it is a well-conceived formula, the fact that the international state system has generally exaggerated the degree of disruption that would result from even a small or inconsequential actor (e.g., Chechnya) being awarded statehood suggests that Buchheit's calculus has more scholastic than practical implications.

Recognizing the limitations on measuring the legitimacy or morality of separatism, Ruth Lapidoth's approach focused on bending the definition of *sovereignty*: "In a case of diffusion of power, both the central government and the regional or autonomous authorities could be the lawful bearer of a share of sovereignty, without necessarily leading to the disappearance or dismemberment of the state."[82] But here, too, merely broadening the meaning of *sovereignty* so that it might subsume disadvantaged groups seemed unlikely to satisfy the demands of ethno-secessionist movements.

An ambitious attempt to accommodate separatist demands by opening up new political space was made by Gidon Gottlieb. This legal scholar proposed the creation of "new space for nations," which entailed the need "to deconstruct the notion of sovereignty into two initial components: sovereignty as power over people and sovereignty as power over territory."[83] Alongside the established system of states, Gottlieb proposed setting up a system of nonterritorially-based nations and peoples. The extension of a legal personality to instrumentalities other than states would allow populations to enjoy a full range of political and civil rights without territorial definition. Thus, while being citizens of a sovereign state, people could simultaneously be inhabitants of a national home, including one that might stretch across existing state boundaries.

The idea of a **national home regime** was a solution to competing ethnic claims. It would be designed "to reconcile the integrity and sovereignty of states with the claims of national groups within them; to provide a context for common nationality links for nations that are divided by state boundaries; to address their yearning for national identity; and to do so without undermining the cohesion of multinational societies."[84] Such a functional approach to organizing peoples is utopian, as Gottlieb recognized. Mixing state entities with nonstate ones, while not ordering them in a hierarchy, seemed both good common sense and an unrealistic expectation. The case of failed UN blueprints for establishing a Jewish homeland within a Palestinian state after World War II indicates the overwhelming power of the traditional idea of sovereignty. However, imagining new structures for organizing peoples is not without merit in the face of intractable ethnic conflicts.

Mayall, an active contributor to the debate on self-determination, proposed the creation of a new transnational regime to cope with the proliferation of ethnosecessionist movements. Although designed for Europe, the **"Maastricht option"** (as Mayall termed it) could have a broader application: "A form of European unification in which some powers are progressively transferred to the center while others are devolved to the regions could possibly provide a way by which minorities could gain autonomy without opting out of either the state or the open economy."[85] Again, the criticism of such a proposal is the unrealistic expectation it has of existing states being willing to cede powers to both higher and lower authorities.

An unassailable conclusion about the difficulties of achieving new political structures was drawn by Myron Weiner: "We end the twentieth century with the same unresolved issue with which the century began: how can we reconcile the claims for self-determination with the sovereign claims of states that their borders remain sacrosanct?" The author underscored the need to "find an imaginative solution to this problem by devising autonomy arrangements for ethnic groups that are short of state sovereignty, but which assure communities of greater self-government within their own territories." He reviewed the traditional institutional arrangements employed for mitigating ethnic conflict:

> Federalism, the principle of dividing powers of a state between a central government and its territorial subdivisions; cultural autonomy for communities with established historical relations within a territory; guarantees for the rights of national minorities including representation in elected bodies; condominium, the principle of two states sharing sovereignty over a territory; and guarantees of religious freedom.[86]

Although he suggested that these arrangements continued to provide the most viable solution to situations of ethnic conflict within a state, Weiner added that "[P]art of the solution lies in legitimizing the idea that modern states need not be centralized, that centralism has outlived its usefulness."[87] Both the state and the potential ethnosecessionists had to learn that the modern centralized state is not a goal in itself. Apart from pressure from below—exerted by minorities and regions—the centralized state is today also eroded by functional imperatives from above—adapting to an increasingly interdependent global economy and to new international regimes.

The same goals that separation might achieve for disaffected groups could equally be realized in a system of more responsible and responsive government: "Since the ultimate purpose of self-determination is not self-determination per se but responsive government, mutual tolerance might be what many countries and ethnic groups need most and first."[88] As an example of this approach, "[T]he peoples of India desire and deserve a government that is responsive to them, but not necessarily a separatist one."[89] Indeed, Etzioni made the questionable claim that "self-determination movements gained support because they fought against oppression, not because they fought for separatism."[90] The fact is that many national liberation movements had no alternative but to strive for both objectives simultaneously.

Excessive self-determination may work against democratization, however. "What meaning does self-determination have when miniscule countries are at the economic and military mercy, even whim, of larger states—states in whose government they have no representation at all?"[91] Similar logic has been used by radical leaders such as Fidel Castro to cast doubts on the utility of liberal democracy and free enterprise; in Castro's opinion, when crucial decisions affecting smaller states are taken by international lending institutions and multinational corporations located in the advanced western states, neither self-determination nor democracy really exist.

For Etzioni, "Only when secessionist movements seek to break out of empires—and only when those empires refuse to democratize—does self-determination deserve our support. Otherwise, democratic government and community building, not fragmentation, should be accorded the highest standing."[92] Liberals may sympathize with the motives and moral claims that separatist movements embody, but they insist that other ways are available to satisfy their demands short of recognizing their right of secession.

The stark choice available to state actors confronting outbreaks of secession is "abandoning the weather-beaten (antisecessionist) normative ship and permitting unilateral independence at least for those who can achieve it on the ground," such as the case of Eritrea, or returning to the original normative regime to "shut the 'window of opportunity' for secessionist attempts."[93] Heraclides listed the dangers of following only the first alternative:

> [T]he fear of indefinite divisibility (internal as well as regional), otherwise known as the domino effect; the issue of stranded majorities or trapped minorities; the non-viability of the rump state; the danger of giving birth to unviable entities that would be a burden internationally; the damage done to the will of the majority and the resultant ability of a minority to constantly blackmail the majority with secession; and, above all, the opening up of a Pandora's box of self-determination *ad absurdum*.[94]

A leading contributor to the debate on the morality of secession has been political philosopher Allen Buchanan. Like political scientists, he recognizes that secession is a messy affair: "Secession can shatter old alliances, stimulate the forging of new ones, tip balances of power, create refugee populations, and disrupt international commerce. It can also result in great loss of human life."[95] It is identifying the contingent conditions that justify secession that Buchanan set out to discover.

Drawing on an obvious parallel, he noted that political union, like marriage, is a human creation designed to satisfy mutual needs, and it may be dismantled when such needs are not being served. As with divorce, one can conceive of no-fault secession, where no injustice has been committed or wronged party found. The velvet divorce that put an end to the Czechoslovak federation in 1991 is as good an example as we have of a no-fault breakup of a political union.

What does the moral right to secede entail? For Buchanan, "[t]o say that there is a moral right to secede is to say at least two things: (1) that it is morally permissible for those who have this right to secede, and (2) that others are morally obligated not to interfere with their seceding."[96] As an example, Lithuania's unilateral declarations of sovereignty and then independence in 1990–1991 were morally permissible, given how Lithuania was incorporated into the Soviet Union during World War II. It is worth considering the converse of these propositions. For even if some course of action, like secession, may be morally wrong, it does *not* follow that it is morally permissible to prohibit it by force. Thus, Gorbachev was morally obliged not to dispatch black berets (elite Soviet special forces team) to quash the secessionist movement in Vilnius. Another example illustrates this logic. Even if Chechnya had weak moral claims to justify its pursuit of independence from the Russian Federation after 1991, this did not provide Presidents Yeltsin and Putin with a moral carte blanche to use force—especially brutal and indiscriminate force against both civilians and soldiers— to prevent its breakaway, as they did from 1994 to 1996, and 1999 on.

Buchanan chided liberal theorists for having little to say about secession. In theory, liberalism countenances secession because it holds that legitimate political authority rests on the consent of the governed. Where that consent is withdrawn, as would be indicated by the formation of an ethno-secessionist movement, political authority becomes illegitimate. Buchanan attacked liberalism not only for being largely silent on secession but also for assigning low value to collective rights and the communal life of a group. Protecting a group's culture assures its individual members of a meaningful context for choice—an objective that liberalism would readily embrace. It follows that opposition to political authority is justified for reasons not usually envisaged by classical liberalism. Moral grounds for opposing rulers include not merely violations of individual rights but also situations where a group is a victim of systematic discrimination.

Following Buchanan, let us identify twelve prosecession arguments based on moral claims. A first reason can be the defense of liberty. Just as it is impermissible to interfere with a person's liberty as long as that person's choice does no harm to others, so it may be immoral to interfere with a group's exercise of liberty where no one is harmed. Of course, the secession of a group is likely to disrupt the national life of a state and may have an adverse impact on the state's resources, territory, and fiscal base. Justifying separation (or revolution, for that matter) in the name of liberty has occurred regularly in world history, but usually the harm principle is studiously ignored by moralists who seek to legitimate political independence.

A second moral case is the promotion of diversity. Here, a circuitous logic is at work to justify separation. The best guarantor of cultural diversity is the creation of independent political units that then freely interact with each other. Yet in the real world, relations are invariably soured by parties to a divorce (secession). France's relations with Algeria, Russia's with Lithuania, or Bangladesh's with Pakistan have been troubled ones after the separation decision. It is questionable whether promoting diversity under all circumstances is a good in itself. Fragmented states in Africa, for instance, might suffer more from diversity policies than from centralization ones.

Third, to safeguard liberalism, it is in the interest of a liberal state to permit illiberal groups to secede. Tolerance for various communal lifestyles may, on occasion, backfire on a liberal state, as when militant religious sects take up arms. For its own protection, the state should grant illiberal groups the right to secede. Indeed, there may even be an obligation for such groups to part ways with a state whose philosophic principles they do not share. Needless to say, this is an esoteric moral ground for secession: few ethno-secessionist movements would want to claim as their moral basis for secession the fact that they have no tolerance for a tolerant state.

A fourth case for secession evolves when the original goals for setting up a political union have become obsolete or irrelevant. Considerations that previously necessitated a common association of various groups no longer hold, and contracting parties are freed from the time-specific and delimited obligations imposed on them. Buchanan considered that states bound together by the articles of confederation to achieve independence from Britain were not necessarily bound to each other once this goal was achieved.

Related to this case, a fifth reason occurs when the right of secession is included in a constitution to attract new members and, at some later date, a member reconsiders its entry decision and decides to avail itself of the constitutional provision for exit. Thus, a country that joins the European Union but becomes disenchanted with its political evolution would have moral and legal justification for leaving it. These two grounds are very uncommon and, in political practice, also unrealistic.

In contrast, the sixth reason for secession is widely used by breakaway ethno-nationalist groups today who claim that they wish to escape discriminatory redistribution at the hands of the existing state. When a national government does not operate for genuine mutual advantage and discriminates against or exploits certain groups, then this "in effect voids the state's claim to the territory in which the victims reside."[97] Inequalities or differentials (to use Gurr's terminology) may exist among groups, but only when ruling elites skew benefits to favor some and block others in unjustified ways does this powerful moral argument in favor of secession become irrefutable. Whether inequalities constitute injustice depends on whether the redistributive pattern is morally arbitrary. Cases exist where "if a stark disadvantage does not exist in the first place it has to be invented."[98] However, as Gurr found, it is relatively uncommon for the victims of unjust, systematic discrimination to assert ethno-secessionist demands, even though they would be morally justified in doing so. Still, victims of perceived discrimination often couple this reason—intended more for mass consumption than as a bargaining resource with the ruling elite—with cultural preservation rhetoric, which is described below.

A seventh case marries efficiency considerations to morality. Applying the principle of Pareto optimality, as long as one party would be better off and everyone else no worse off if secession occurred, then such a course of action is justified. This logic is often embedded in peaceful breakups of political unions, for example, Norway from Sweden in 1905. Curiously, though, it is probably more often advanced to justify unification of separate units and centralization of decision making.

The normative principle of nationalism consisting in the notion that every group is entitled to have its own state is a further reason given to justify secession. The belief that political boundaries should coincide with cultural ones is widespread but, in reality, it is an unviable proposition in most cases. Buchanan took aim at this argument and found it among the least plausible grounds to justify political divorce because it implies that multicultural, pluralist states are an inferior arrangement to ones that embody the pure nationalist principle. Although it is more valid to invoke this normative principle when a group's culture or its economic opportunities are under severe threat, generally to argue this case is to become vulnerable to Ernest

Gellner's caustic critique: "It follows that a territorial political unit can only become ethnically homogeneous, in such cases, if it either kills, or expels, or assimilates all non-nationals."[99]

Instead of focusing on an often spurious national principle, the ninth possible case for secession directs attention to the preservation of a culture. Separatism can best enhance the flourishing of a culture and thereby contribute to the lives of the people who celebrate that culture. Important ethno-nationalist groups in the West— Basques, Flemish, Quebecers—often cite cultural factors as the main reason for wishing to have political sovereignty. Buchanan did not dispute such claims, but he did regard efforts made to prolong the life of a moribund culture or to prevent its members' assimilation into a more dynamic culture as unjustified. Thus, a culture may be pernicious to its own members and not worth saving, or it may both erode another culture *and* prevent assimilation of its members into the dominant one. Referring to Native North Americans, Buchanan wrote of the double jeopardy suffered when "those whose cultures have been most severely damaged also have been barred from genuine assimilation into the culture the whites brought."[100]

With regard to creating states to safeguard cultures then, the most compelling counterargument is the practical consideration that there is simply not enough space and resources for every group to have its own territorial state. Just as persuasive a pragmatic consideration is that the domino effect may lead to no end of self-determination struggles. As Etzioni noted, "new ethnic 'selves' can be generated quite readily, drawing on fracture lines now barely noticeable. Subtle differences in geography, religion, culture, and loyalty can be fanned into new separatist movements, each seeking their own symbols and powers of statehood."[101]

The intrinsic value of protecting a culture, especially where it is under threat, led Buchanan to stipulate conditions where invoking the cultural-preservation principle in order to seek separation would be justified. The five conditions include the following: (1) the culture really is in peril, (2) less disruptive ways of preserving the culture do not exist, (3) the imperiled culture meets minimal standards of justice itself (that is, it does not represent a Khmer Rouge–type culture bent on genocide), (4) secession should not lead to the building of an illiberal state, and (5) neither the extant state nor any third party has a historic claim to the seceding territory. Positing these as prerequisite conditions that justify separation on the grounds of cultural preservation severely limits the universe of morally sound ethno-secessionist claims.

Rather than self-preservation, self-defense can be given as a tenth reason to justify a separate state. Fear of extermination from either the existing state or a third party from whom the extant state cannot offer viable protection would be variants of the self-defense justification. Thus, in the first case, whatever legitimate claims the state has to the seceding territory becomes outweighed by the claims of victims of genocidal policy. In the second case, Buchanan speculated about the moral grounds Jewish groups had to create a separate Jewish state in central European countries occupied by Germans who were perpetrating the holocaust. More recently, Palestinian Arabs who feel that neither Israel nor Jordan safeguard their interests are driven to build their own state.

An eleventh reason, as persuasive as the case of discriminatory injustice, concerns rectification of past injustices. As Buchanan emphasized, "The argument's power stems from the assumption that secession is simply the re-appropriation, by the legitimate owners, of stolen property."[102] The argument for rectification justice subsumes the historical grievance claim: "The valid claim to territory that every sound justification for secession includes must be grounded in a historical grievance concerning the violation of a preexisting right to territory."[103] The best known instances of historical grievance claims originated in the secret protocol of the August 1939 Ribbentrop–Molotov pact that led to the incorporation of the Baltic states and northern Romania into the Soviet Union. Especially, as in this case, where groups can claim unjust loss of their territory, the right to secession is legitimate. We should be aware, however, of the sheer proliferation of historical grievances over the loss of territory (see Table 2.2), ranging from the random, colonially imposed borders of African and Asian states to Austria's claim on South Tyrol, to Guatemala's belief of jurisdiction over Belize. Rectifying demonstrated cases of past injustices, especially

### TABLE 2.2 Irredentist Movements in the 1990s and Beyond

| Territory on Which There Are Irredentist Claims | Countries Making Irredentist Claims | Current Sovereignty |
|---|---|---|
| Aegean Sea Islands | Greece, Turkey | Turkey, Greece |
| Arunachal Pradesh | China | India |
| Baluchistan | Iran, Afghanistan | Pakistan |
| Belize | Guatemala | Belize |
| Bosnia Herzegovina | Croatia, Serbia | Bosnia Herzegovina |
| Cyprus | Greece, Turkey | Cyprus |
| Diego Garcia | Mauritius | United Kingdom |
| Djibouti | Somalia | Djibouti |
| Falklands/Malvinas | Argentina | United Kingdom |
| Gibraltar | Spain | United Kingdom |
| Hatay | Syria | Turkey |
| Israel | Palestine, Syria | Israel |
| Kashmir | Pakistan | India |
| Kurile Islands | Japan | Russia |
| Kuwait | Iraq | Kuwait |
| Moldova | Romania, Russia | Moldova |
| Northern Ireland | Ireland | United Kingdom |
| North Ossetia | Ingushetia | Russia |
| North West Frontier Province | Afghanistan | Pakistan |
| Sabah | Philippines | Malaysia |
| South Tyrol | Austria | Italy |
| Taiwan | China | Taiwan |
| Transylvania | Hungary | Romania |
| Ukraine | Russia | Ukraine |
| Uzbekistan | Kazakhstan, Kyrgyzstan | Uzbekistan |

Source: Adapted from Karin von Hippel, "The Resurgence of Nationalism and Its International Implications," *The Washington Quarterly,* 17, no. 4, Autumn 1994, pp. 192–193. The table identifies the best known secessionist and irredentist conflicts; there are many others.

illegitimate incorporation into a larger state or empire, is as compelling a moral argument for separation as there can be.

Finally, adopting the liberal basis for legitimate authority and political obligation—consent—we can list a twelfth reason why secession can be justified: the disappearance of fair play in the liberal system. When fairness vanishes, consent can be withdrawn and political obligations can cease. This logic is often used as an ancillary reason in favor of secession by an ethno-nationalist movement claiming discrimination.

More parsimonious approaches to justifying secession than this twelve-point typology exist. Heraclides advanced a tautological one: "Potential separatist groups are all those that have the ability to generate a secessionist movement, that is, a legitimized secessionist organization that can engage the Center in a secessionist conflict, be it armed or peaceful."[104] This explanation is associated with the "heroic" argument: "That if a group is willing to suffer in order to gain its coveted goal of independence then it is such a movement."[105]

Heraclides spoke of "the two main pillars of the secessionist self-determination rationale—namely 'nationhood' and 'alien domination' (approximating Buchheit's distinction between parochial and remedial secessionist claims)." He was more persuaded by the rationale offered in the second case and went on to identify four prerequisites for accepting secession as a solution to intercommunal conflict: (1) the existence of a sizable, distinct, and compact community (not necessarily nation or national minority) that overwhelmingly supports statehood and demonstrates it by recruitment into the ranks of the separatists; (2) a pattern of systematic discrimination, exploitation, or domination against the community; (3) a policy of cultural domination (Buchanan's cultural threat argument) seeking erosion of the disadvantaged group's culture or assimilation of its members into the dominant culture; and (4) the state's rejection of dialogue with the aggrieved community. Two additional floating criteria lending support to the separatist cause are the realistic prospect of conflict resolution and peace as a result of secession, and liberal, tolerant policies to be pursued by the prospective state (corresponding roughly to Buchanan's second condition). Implicit in the foregoing set of conditions was Heraclides's recognition that an "oppressed non-nation" might have a stronger moral case for separatism than a partially disadvantaged nation.[106]

But the author recognized that there are cases where "it would be hair-splitting to tell whose case is more sound—that of the state, or of the secessionists."[107] He offered three examples of such moral deadlock: (1) when both parties to the conflict are opposed to fundamental principles of political liberalism (Tamils and Sinhalese in Sri Lanka, Serbs and Albanians in Kosovo, and Azerbaijanis and Armenians in Nagorno-Karabakh); (2) when the moral arguments of the state and the secessionists seem of equal weight (Nigeria in seeking to preserve a federal state and its eastern region in seeking to create an independent Biafra around an entrepreneurial community); and (3) when the state is committed to pluralism and tolerance, but the ethno-secessionist group demands nothing short of independence (radical Sikhs in India, ultranationalist Basques in Spain, and their Quebecer counterparts in Canada).[108]

## THE EMERGING GLOBAL REGIME ON ETHNIC MINORITIES

The much feared disintegration of the international system into a chaotic and conflicting system of warring ethnic statelets proved to be unfounded as the scope and intensity of intra- and interstate ethnic conflicts lessened significantly from the late 1990s onward, mainly due to "more effective international and domestic strategies for managing ethno-political conflict."[109] But did the "global shift from ethnic warfare to the politics of accommodation" signal the betterment of the international normative regime concerning ethno-political conflict?

The answer is a qualified yes. In *Peoples Versus States,* Ted Gurr argued persuasively that the implementation of international standards of individual and group rights was mainly responsible for reducing ethno-political conflicts from the late 1990s onward. It signaled, for Gurr, the gradual emergence of a **"regime of managed ethnic heterogeneity"** consisting of a range of conflict-mitigating doctrines and practices, a widely articulated and accepted set of principles about intergroup relations in multiethnic states, various strategies for institutionalizing these principles of intergroup relations in multiethnic states, and global agreement on domestic and international policies regarding the best way to respond to ethno-political crises and conflicts.[110]

The first and most basic principle of the emerging regime of managed ethnic heterogeneity is "the recognition and active protection of the rights of minority peoples: freedom from discrimination based on race, national origin, language, or religion, complimented by institutional means to protect and promote collective interests."[111] Second, as a corollary to the first principle, national peoples within multinational states have a right to enjoy and exercise a degree of autonomy in the governance of their own affairs, and if they constitute a regional majority in a heterogeneous democratic state, "then they should have the right to local or regional self-governance."[112] Finally, the new regime incorporates the principle that the best form of dispute resolution between ethnic groups and states is through negotiation and mutual accommodation. This principle is further endorsed and "backed up by the active engagement of major powers, the United Nations, and some regional organizations (especially in Europe and Africa), which use various mixes of diplomacy, mediation, inducements, and threats to encourage negotiated settlements of ethnic conflicts."[113]

Gurr further suggested that four recent general developments, both regional and global, have helped to strengthen the principles of accommodation in heterogeneous societies: (1) the vigorous promotion of democratic institutions, practices, and ideals by the Atlantic democracies, which has lessened interstate conflict (the democratic peace hypothesis that posits that democracies seldom fight one another) and encouraged political accommodation with minorities (because democracies seldom use repression against internal opponents); (2) proactive action by the UN, its various affiliated bodies, regional IGOs, and nongovernmental organizations (NGOs), to protect the rights of national minorities, to encourage and induce states to temper their aggressive policies toward minorities, and to move conflicts in the direction of negotiated peace agreements; (3) the development of a universal consensus among the global political elite about the need to reestablish and maintain global and regional order and stable economic relations by preventing, managing, and punishing empire building and warmongering tendencies and policies; and (4) regardless of political systems, the realization by both governing elites and leaders of ethno-political movements of the high cost of violent ethnic conflicts.[114]

However dominant this regime of managed ethnic heterogeneity has become, it is far from a panacea. Although it may be argued that almost all European democracies have implemented its principles, many states outside Europe and North America are either loath to pay them more than lip service or simply reject them outright. Very few of the intractable ethno-political conflicts in the Mediterranean (e.g., Cyprus, Israel, Turkey), Asia (e.g., India, Sri Lanka, Philippines), the Middle East and West Asia (e.g., Iraq, Afghanistan), and Africa (e.g., Uganda, Sudan, Congo, Nigeria, Ivory Coast, Liberia, Zimbabwe) hold out prospects for negotiated peace and the protection and promotion of minority rights. Furthermore, the creation of a global standard for judging the legitimacy of ethno-secessionist claims is still a dream, although a beginning of some sorts has been made. As Gurr has correctly pointed out, in the heterogeneous, interdependent, complex, and multilayered system that has emerged after the termination of the cold war and the settlement of several ethnic and regional conflicts, states continue to be the paramount actors but are increasingly finding themselves "constrained by a growing network of mutual obligations with respect to identity groups and supranational actors."[115] One would like to hope that this trend would continue to strengthen in the future.

## Conclusion

We have surveyed the wide range of moral arguments that can be advanced to justify ethno-secession and evaluated the emerging global regime of managed ethnic heterogeneity. Although some of the moral arguments for secession appear to be highly persuasive and deserving of international support, there is a crucial tension between such moral considerations and the need to maintain continuity, stability, and order in the state system. Any sustainable international regime will have to succeed in providing at least a minimal level of continuity, stability, and order; it remains to be seen to what extent this function can be reconciled with responsiveness to secessionist claims.

## Discussion Questions

1. What is meant by the concept of international normative regime? In what way is the international normative regime biased against ethno-nationalists?

2. It is often argued by scholars that implementing the idea of national self-determination is dangerous for the international system. Why?

3. Examine the relevance of the principles of nonintervention in the internal affairs of a state and of the nonuse of force to the study of secessionism. Which party to an ethnic conflict is favored by international adherence to these principles?

4. Why is international recognition so crucial for ethno-secessionists? What criteria should the international community use to decide which

secessionist claims to accept and which to reject?

5. While it is true that the international normative regime is biased against ethno-nationalists, it is also true that, under certain special circumstances, ethno-secessionist demands may be legitimate. How can they be accommodated by the international system?

6. Of the many moral arguments that are advanced to justify ethnic secession, which in your view carry the most weight? Explain your answer.

7. What is the new regime of managed ethnic heterogeneity and how does it differ from the previous set of international norms? Might this regime succeed at reconciling the imperative of systemic stability with moral considerations? Why or why not?

## Key Terms

constitutive theory of
   recognition
declaratory theory of
   recognition
doctrine of state
   sovereignty
dynastic sovereignty
ideological theory of
   recognition
international normative
   regime

"Maastricht option"
national home regime
occupation
parochialist secession
Peace of Westphalia
popular sovereignty
principle of national
   self-determination
principle of
   nonintervention

principle of nonuse of force
   recognition
"regime of managed ethnic
   heterogeneity"
remedial secession
secession
status of belligerency
status of insurgency
"white man's burden"
   argument

## Notes

1. Alexis Heraclides, *The Self-Determination of Minorities in International Politics*, (London: Frank Cass, 1991), p. 1.
2. William Safran, "Non-separatist Policies Regarding Ethnic Minorities: Positive Approaches and Ambiguous Consequences," *International Political Science Review*, 15, no. 1, January 1994, pp. 61–80.
3. Heraclides, *The Self-Determination of Minorities in International Politics*, p. 21.
4. Alan James, *Sovereign Statehood*, (London: Allen & Unwin, 1986), p. 25. Quoted in Robert H. Jackson, *Quasi-States: Sovereignty, International Relations, and the Third World*, (Cambridge, England: Cambridge University Press, 1990), p. 32.
5. Ibid.
6. Ibid.
7. Djura Nincic, *The Problem of Sovereignty in the Charter and in the Practice of the United Nations*, (The Hague, Netherlands: Martinus Nijhoff, 1970), p. 2.
8. James Mayall, *Nationalism and International Society*, (Cambridge,

England: Cambridge University Press, 1990), p. 18.
9. Nicholas Onuf, "Intervention for the Common Good," in Gene M. Lyons and Michael Mastanduno, eds., *Beyond Westphalia? State Sovereignty and International Intervention*, (Baltimore, Md.: Johns Hopkins University Press, 1995), p. 52.
10. Heraclides, *The Self-Determination of Minorities in International Politics*, p. 20.
11. J. L. Brierly, *The Laws of Nations: An Introduction to the International Law of Peace*, 6th ed., Humphrey Waldock, ed. (London: Oxford University Press, 1963), p. 137.
12. Heraclides, *The Self-Determination of Minorities in International Politics*, p. 24.
13. Mayall, *Nationalism and International Society*, p. 19.
14. Ibid., p. 20.
15. Brierly, *The Law of Nations*, p. 163.
16. Ibid.
17. Ibid., p. 164.
18. Ibid., p. 138.
19. Ibid., p. 139 (emphasis in original).
20. Ibid.
21. Ibid., p. 138.

22. Heraclides, *The Self-Determination of Minorities in International Politics*, p. 25. Emphasis in original.
23. Brierly, *The Law of Nations*, p. 141.
24. Heraclides, *The Self-Determination of Minorities in International Politics*, p. 25.
25. Rosalyn Higgins, "Internal War and International Law," in Cyril E. Black and Richard A. Falk, eds., *The Future of the International Legal Order.* Vol. III: *Conflict Management*, (Princeton, N.J.: Princeton University Press, 1971), p. 88.
26. James E. Bond, *The Rules of Riot: Internal Conflict and the Law of War*, (Princeton, N.J.: Princeton University Press, 1974), p. 49.
27. Higgins, "Internal War and International Law," p. 88.
28. Higgins, "Internal War and International Law," p. 88; and Bond, *The Rules of Riot*, p. 34.
29. Brierly, *The Law of Nations*, p. 142.
30. Ibid.
31. Ibid., p. 143.
32. Heraclides, *The Self-Determination of Minorities in International Politics*, p. 26.
33. Ibid.
34. Gene M. Lyons and Michael Mastanduno, "State Sovereignty and International Intervention: Reflections on the Present and Prospects for the Future," in Gene M. Lyons and Michael Mastanduno, eds., *Beyond Westphalia? State Sovereignty and International Intervention*, (Baltimore, Md.: Johns Hopkins University Press, 1995), p. 261.
35. Ibid., p. 264.
36. Higgins, "Internal War and International Law," pp. 93–94.
37. Richard A. Falk, ed., *The International Law of Civil War*, (Baltimore, Md.: Johns Hopkins University Press, 1971), p. 12.
38. Ibid., p. 13.
39. Elie Kedourie, *Nationalism*, 4th expanded edition, (Oxford, England: Blackwell Publishers, 1993), p. 12.
40. Ibid., p. 13.
41. Ibid., p. 14 (emphasis added).
42. Ibid., pp. 15–17.
43. Ibid., p. 20.
44. Anthony D. Smith, *Theories of Nationalism*, (New York: Holmes and Meier, 1983), p. 21.
45. Ibid., pp. 23–24.
46. Ibid., p. 33.
47. Carlton J. H. Hayes, *The Historical Evolution of Modern Nationalism*, (New York: R. R. Smith, 1931), pp. 10–11.
48. Mayall, *Nationalism and International Society*, pp. 40–41.
49. Peter Alter, *Nationalism*, translated by Stuart McKinnon-Evans (London: Edward Arnold, 1989), p. 15.
50. Ibid.
51. Benjamin Neuberger, *National Self-Determination in Postcolonial Africa*, (Boulder, Colo.: Lynne Rienner, 1986), p. 4.
52. A. Rigo Sureda, *The Evolution of the Right of Self-Determination: A Study of United Nations Practice*, (Leiden, Netherlands: A. W. Sijthoff, 1973), p. 17.
53. Ibid., p. 5.
54. Mayall, *Nationalism and International Society*, p. 44.
55. Ibid., p. 52.
56. Ibid.
57. Ibid., pp. 44–45.
58. Ibid., p. 54.
59. Ibid., p. 45.
60. Ibid., pp. 45–46.
61. Nincic, *The Problem of Sovereignty in the Charter and in the Practice of the United Nations*, p. 221.
62. Heraclides, *The Self-Determination of Minorities in International Politics*, pp. 21–22.
63. Mayall, *Nationalism and International Society*, p. 56.

64. Heraclides, *The Self-Determination of Minorities in International Politics,* p. 23.
65. Lee C. Buchheit, *Secession: The Legitimacy of Self-Determination,* (New Haven, Conn.: Yale University Press, 1978), p. 17.
66. Alexis Heraclides, "Secession, Self-Determination and Nonintervention: In Quest of a Normative Symbiosis," *Journal of International Affairs,* 45, no. 2, Winter 1992, pp. 404–405 (emphasis in original).
67. Heraclides, *The Self-Determination of Minorities in International Politics,* p. 22 (emphasis added).
68. Allen Buchanan, "Self-Determination and the Right to Secede," *Journal of International Affairs,* 45, no. 2, Winter 1992, p. 350.
69. The UN made an effort to update norms governing the status of minorities in the contemporary state system by enacting resolution 47/135 in December 1992. Titled Declaration on the Rights of Persons Belonging to National or Ethnic, Religious and Linguistic Minorities, it set minimum international standards for securing minority rights, for example, recommending measures for mother-tongue instruction for minorities and promoting knowledge about minority cultures. But as with most UN resolutions, piously expressed objectives may have little bearing on actual rights provided and protected by member states. Also, by ignoring the issue of minorities' possible desire to build their own state, the 1992 resolution reflected the persistence of the ethos of antisecessionism. For a summary and critique of the resolution, see Patrick Thornberry, "International and European Standards on Minority Rights," in Hugh Miall, ed., *Minority Rights in Europe: Prospects for a Transitional Regime* (New York: Council on Foreign Relations Press, 1995), pp. 14–21.
70. Heraclides, *The Self-Determination of Minorities in International Politics,* p. 23.
71. Myron Weiner, "Peoples and States in a New Ethnic Order?" *Third World Quarterly,* 13, no. 2, 1992, p. 317.
72. Saul Newman, "Does Modernization Breed Ethnic Political Conflict?" *World Politics,* 43, no. 3, April 1991, p. 453.
73. Ruth Lapidoth, "Sovereignty in Transition," *Journal of International Affairs,* 45, no. 2, Winter 1992, pp. 325–346.
74. Robert A. Friedlander, "Self-Determination: A Legal-Political Inquiry," in Yonah Alexander and Friedlander, eds., *Self-Determination: National, Regional, and Global Dimensions,* (Boulder, Colo.: Westview Press, 1980), p. 318.
75. Alexis Heraclides, "Secessionist Conflagration: What Is to Be Done?" *Security Dialogue,* 25, no. 3, 1994, p. 287.
76. Thomas M. Franck, *The Power of Legitimacy Among Nations* (Oxford, England: Clarendon Press, 1990), p. 168.
77. Buchheit, *Secession,* p. 55.
78. Ibid., p. 97.
79. Ibid., p. 222.
80. Ibid., p. 223.
81. Ibid., p. 241.
82. Lapidoth, "Sovereignty in transition," p. 345. For a further elaboration of Lapidoth's views on sovereignty and self-determination, see Ruth Lapidoth, "Redefining Authority: The Past, Present, and Future of Sovereignty," *Harvard International Review,* 17, no. 3, Summer 1995, pp. 8–11 and 70–71.

83. Gidon Gottlieb, *Nation Against State: A New Approach to Ethnic Conflicts and the Decline of Sovereignty* (New York: Council on Foreign Relations Press, 1993), pp. 36–37.
84. Ibid., pp. 42–43.
85. James Mayall, "Sovereignty and Self-Determination in the New Europe," in Hugh Miall, ed., *Minority Rights in Europe: Prospects for a Transitional Regime* (New York: Council on Foreign Relations Press, 1995), p. 12.
86. Weiner, "Peoples and States in a New Ethnic Order?" p. 332.
87. Ibid.
88. Amitai Etzioni, "The Evils of Self-Determination," *Foreign Policy*, 89, Winter 1992–1993, p. 33.
89. Ibid., p. 25.
90. Ibid., p. 35.
91. Ibid., p. 28.
92. Ibid., p. 35.
93. Heraclides, "Secessionist Conflagration," pp. 285–286.
94. Heraclides, "Secession, Self-Determination and Nonintervention," p. 408.
95. Allen Buchanan, *Secession: The Morality of Political Divorce from Fort Sumter to Lithuania and Quebec* (Boulder, Colo.: Westview Press, 1991), p. 2.
96. Ibid., p. 27.
97. Ibid., p. 44.
98. Heraclides, *The Self-Determination of Minorities in International Politics*, p. 17.
99. Ernest Gellner, *Nations and Nationalism* (Oxford: Blackwell, 1983), p. 2.
100. Buchanan, *Secession*, p. 54.
101. Etzioni, "The Evils of Self-Determination," p. 27.
102. Buchanan, "Self-Determination and the Right to Secede," p. 353.
103. Buchanan, *Secession*, p. 68.
104. Heraclides, *The Self-Determination of Minorities in International Politics*, pp. 14–15.
105. Ibid., p. 15.
106. Heraclides, "Secession, Self-Determination and Nonintervention," p. 409.
107. Heraclides, "Secessionist Conflagration," p. 290.
108. Ibid.
109. Ted Gurr, *Peoples Versus States: Minorities at Risk in the New Century* (Washington, D.C.: United States Institute of Peace Press, 2000), p. 275.
110. Ibid., pp. 277–278.
111. Ibid., p. 278.
112. Ibid.
113. Ibid., p. 279.
114. Ibid., pp. 280–281.
115. Ibid., 282.

# CHAPTER 3

# Ethnic Conflict and International Security

## INTRODUCTION

Ethnic conflicts usually (though not always) occur within states, but few of these conflicts remain confined within state boundaries for long. As ethnic conflict spills over and becomes internationalized, it poses threats to international security and world order. Hence, the international community cannot remain indifferent and inactive when confronted with the outbreak of ethnic conflict, although dealing effectively with these threats is neither easy nor straightforward.

But what kinds of threats to international security and world order are posed by ethnic conflict? In this chapter, we argue that the onset of violent ethnic conflict poses four different threats to international security and order. The first is the threat of a **complex humanitarian emergency** (CHE), with unimaginable levels of suffering for civilian populations caught in the crossfire of conflict. If not dealt with quickly and decisively, CHEs inevitably lead to massive population displacement, gross human rights violations, and mass civilian casualties. They also produce refugees, spread disease and deadly infections, and greatly magnify the challenges of development both in the refugee-generating and in the refugee-receiving states. The second threat from ethnic conflict is the creation of negative social, political, and economic side effects that may lead the state experiencing the conflict down the slippery slope toward state failure and even state collapse. Failed and collapsed states can quickly become international security risks not only because they exacerbate the complex humanitarian emergency that has already been created by the conflict, but also because they provide the perfect sanctuary for insurgents; warlords; terrorists; drug traffickers; weapons, contraband, and people smugglers; and other criminal gangs. Such states can then become the launch pad for terrorist and criminal activities on a global scale. A third threat to international security and order occurs when a state affected by civil war becomes subjected to partisan intervention and counter intervention by other states willing to take advantage of weak or nonexistent central government authority and a polarized population to further their own interests. The intervention–counter intervention spiral usually expands the scope and intensity of a conflict. The conflict may then spread beyond the borders of the originating state into the surrounding region and transform from a low-intensity intrastate conflict into a high intensity interstate war. Finally, once ethnic conflicts break out, they tend to last for a long time. The intractable nature of ethnic conflict stems mainly from ethnic groups' ability to operate internationally and procure international support and sympathy. This means that, once ethnic conflicts break out, they tend to quickly become international problems (even though most states facing ethnic conflict would deny that) requiring international intervention to manage or resolve them. This usually puts the international community in a bind for two reasons: (1) as we have seen in the previous chapter, international norms do not encourage international intervention in the affairs of sovereign states barring exceptional circumstances, and (2) as we shall see in the next chapter, even when the international community can act, the track record of international intervention aimed at ethnic conflict management has been far from good.

## COMPLEX HUMANITARIAN EMERGENCIES

When an ethnic rebellion or insurgency breaks out, especially if the insurgents make secessionist demands, the natural tendency of governments is to define the conflict purely in legalistic terms—that is, as a law-and-order problem—and to treat the insurgents as criminals.[1] The tendency on the part of governments to use overwhelming force against the insurgents increases if the insurgents are well connected abroad or seek outside military support.[2] In using overwhelming force against insurgent groups whose members usually hide among and draw support from the civilian populations, the state security forces often inflict enormous hardship and suffering on the people inhabiting the areas or regions of the country where the insurgency is taking place.[3]

If the ethnic insurgents are well organized and adequately supplied, they may respond to the government's counterinsurgency operations by demonstrating their own military prowess. They may carry out spectacular attacks on the security forces as well as launch physical attacks on the civilian population, especially against those that they consider to be their main enemies. Because adversaries in ethnic conflicts usually see the conflict as a zero-sum game, ethnic insurgents are more likely to regard civilians belonging to enemy groups as expendable—hence, insurgents frequently and deliberately employ destructive policies such as ethnic cleansing, forced expulsion, and genocide.

The complex humanitarian emergency thus generated by violent ethnic conflict usually requires a huge effort by the international community to provide relief, sanctuary, and protection to unarmed civilians; the task is by no means easy.[4] But CHEs also include three subsets of issues, which mostly the international relief and rehabilitation agencies have to deal with. First, the upheavals accompanying ethnic conflict usually force people to flee their homes; some resettle elsewhere within the country where conditions are safer, thus turning themselves into **internally displaced persons (IDPs)**, but many cross national boundaries to take refuge in other countries, thus turning themselves into **refugees**. The condition of most IDPs and refugees is usually poor; therefore, if they do not quickly receive adequate food, clothing, shelter, and medicines, most would risk dying. The intractable nature of ethnic conflict also means that the humanitarian relief agencies that care for IDPs and refugees must do so for an extended period, which can be problematic. Second, in complex humanitarian emergency situations, there is the potential for massive human rights violations of civilians by both government troops and armed insurgents, particularly through practices such as torture, abuse, and rape. Protecting innocent civilian populations from these violations becomes an important task of humanitarian relief operations. Third, in many ethnic conflicts, it is common to find a large number of **child soldiers** deployed as frontline combatants. Using children as soldiers severely affects their health (physical and emotional), education and well-being, and negatively affects the state's economic and social development. The practice is also in complete violation of the UN Convention on the Rights of the Child and is considered a war crime by the International Criminal Court.

## IDPs and Refugees

Large-scale internal displacement of the civilian population is a common side effect of ethnic conflict. The displacement of populations within a state inevitably threatens their livelihood and well-being. In response, the international community and humanitarian organizations launch large-scale relief operations. For instance, in recent years, this was the situation in Darfur, in western Sudan, where nomadic Arab militia known as the Junjaweed, in collusion with Sudanese security forces, repeatedly attacked black African pastoral and farming communities. This led the UN to mount a major relief operation in the region. To assist IDPs in a sovereign state, however, the international community may have to first receive permission from the state's government, which (as was the case in Sudan) can be difficult to obtain if it is the government's forces that are mainly responsible for the human rights violations. If the insurgents are responsible, they are likely to resist and hamper relief operations, especially in areas they control or operate. They may even target international aid workers—in Darfur, staff members of an international governmental organization (IGO) involved in caring for the IDPs were killed by the Junjaweed and government security forces.

Displaced population groups that cross an international boundary to escape from the war zone become refugees. A massive influx of refugees fleeing their own state for fear of persecution or as part of a state's and/or insurgent group's efforts to create ethnically homogeneous territorial enclaves may impose "a large economic and political burden upon the receiving country."[5] As was the case in 1971 between India and Pakistan, the issue of refugees can lead to war between refugee-generating and refugee-receiving countries. A profound problem for the international community is the humanitarian crises generated by refugee flows. Receiving states may seal their borders; however, more often they allow refugees in but put them in inhospitable camps as a way of discouraging others from fleeing their homeland.[6]

Dealing with IDPs is considered an internal issue of the generating state and falls under the restrictions of state sovereignty. In contrast, international law accords more protection to refugees, and international humanitarian efforts are usually coordinated and implemented by the UN High Commissioner for Refugees (UNHCR).[7] Over the past decade, however, there have been cases (such as with Hutu refugees in Eastern Congo, who fled the ethnic civil war in Rwanda) where armed militias formed within the refugee camps have diverted large amounts of international humanitarian relief aid to pay for weapons and ammunition. They then used the weapons and ammunition in reprisal attacks against the refugees' original state, turning international humanitarian relief aid for refugees into a way of prolonging the original ethnic conflict.[8]

## Torture, Abuse, and Mass Rape

Incidences of torture (by both security forces and insurgents) against civilians have become a common issue in violent ethnic conflicts. Whenever an insurgency is supported by the local population, there is a greater probability that the security forces involved in **counterinsurgency (COIN) operations** will torture and abuse local civilians who they might suspect of providing help to the insurgents. During armed insurgency warfare, insurgents typically mingle with the local population to hide and to launch unexpected attacks on security personnel. In response, the security forces routinely sweep through an area where insurgents are suspected to be and pick up civilians (usually males between the ages of 10 to 15 and 45 to 50) for questioning; these civilians are often beaten and tortured in police lockups or prisons in order to obtain information about militants. Examples include the incarceration and torture of many Saudi nationals by the Saudi security services in the wake of the 9/11 attacks in the United States, and the torture of Iraqi nationals in prison by American occupation forces. It is also not uncommon for detainees to be killed while in lockups. Government soldiers may even swing through an area occupied by noncombative civilians and loot private property, destroy infrastructure, and execute suspects or prisoners. Governments sometimes may even create renegade paramilitary "death squads" to eliminate insurgents and other enemies of the state, as happened in Colombia in the 1980s and 1990s.

Some state governments involved in fighting an internal war in which the adversaries are militarily powerful but not easily identifiable may feel that they have no other choice but to respond with repression, even though this course of action may cause human rights violations of innocent civilians. However, if a state is involved in consistent and serious human rights abuses, it may cause grave harm to its international reputation, prestige, and standing. This may lead the international community to impose political and economic sanctions on the state concerned. The state may use diplomacy to try and prevent the imposition of sanctions, escape from censure and condemnation, and improve its international image. It may approach an **international governmental organization (IGO)** on the assumption that an IGO, being an organization of states, would be supportive of its position. An IGO may be sympathetic to an ethnically troubled state if the claims of ethno-nationalists are seen as unfounded, if their modus operandi is considered brutal and in violation of accepted international norms of conduct, or if they are in league with actors of unsavory reputation. A state may also decide to take its ethnic problems to an IGO if it is losing the military fight with the secessionists and wants third party–mediated settlement to preserve its sovereign existence and territorial integrity.

Insurgents commit violence against civilians as well. In the Indian province of Kashmir, for instance, where armed insurgents have been fighting against the Indian security forces since the late 1980s, insurgents have killed and made death threats against local people whom they suspected of cooperating with the state. In Sierra Leone, the Revolutionary United Front carried out a brutal policy of limb amputation of people living in the villages that it attacked and overran. In the ethnic civil war in Bosnia, paramilitary forces belonging to all sides (Serbs, Croats, and Muslims) summarily executed captured enemy soldiers. In Iraq, suicide and car bomb attacks by insurgents against soft civilian targets have been a daily occurrence.

A growing problem in many ethnic wars is the wave of sexual violence directed against women. Rape has always been used as a weapon of war. During the civil war in East Pakistan in 1970–1971, Pakistani soldiers were alleged to have systematically raped more than 200,000 Bengali women. But the disturbing feature of the sexual assaults associated with the post–cold war era's ethnic civil wars is their genocidal nature. The problem of **genocidal mass rape** came to light during the ethnic civil wars in the former Yugoslavia. By 1993, the existence of rape camps in Bosnia was widely known. Although all groups involved in the conflict committed atrocities, a majority of the mass rapes in the rape camps were committed by Serb paramilitary forces against Bosnian Muslim and Catholic Croatian women. Some experts believe that the purpose of the mass rapes was **ethnic cleansing**[9] —to terrorize an ethnic group and induce its members to flee from a given area, thereby leaving the area in possession of the attackers—and **genocide**[10] —the deliberate extermination of an ethnic group or nation—of Muslims and Croatians in Bosnia Herzegovina.[11] Toward this end, Muslim and Croatian women were repeatedly raped by their Serb captors "to impregnate as many women as possible with 'Chetnik' babies."[12] Many Muslim women from the rape camps further "reported that . . . some women were held captive for a period of weeks to ensure that they did not abort the child they had conceived in rape."[13] In several other cases of ethnic conflict, mass rape of women was used by armed gangs, paramilitary forces, and regular soldiers as a means of dehumanizing their enemy and terrorizing the civilian population into submission. In the Democratic Republic of Congo, for instance, women from villages (especially in the lawless eastern provinces bordering Rwanda, Burundi, and Uganda) are routinely abducted by armed gangs and kept in captivity, where they are forced to work as cooks, porters, and sex slaves. Many of these women are infected with the HIV virus and some have even developed full-blown AIDS. Many more remain untested because they are either too scared to know the results of their tests or because there are not enough health centers in the remote areas. This puts Congo in danger of experiencing an HIV–AIDS pandemic.[14]

## Child Soldiers

Between 1994 and 1998, it is estimated that some 300,000 children under the age of 15 participated in thirty-five conflicts around the world. Most of the conflicts were in developing states, most notably in sub-Saharan Africa and parts of Asia. The problem of child soldiers reached such a crisis that the Convention on the Worst Forms of Child Labor (June 1999), organized by the International Labor Organization, moved to prohibit the forced or compulsory recruitment of children under the age of 18 for armed conflict.[15]

The armed forces and insurgent groups that recruit children below the age of 15 do so for a variety of reasons. They use children to work as cooks, cleaners, guards, messengers, and spies; many children also serve as frontline combatants; female children are usually sexually abused and are often taken as "wives" for the senior soldiers. Most of the child soldiers are brutally "initiated" into the world of armed combat. They are often severely beaten, injected with heroin and other types of drugs, and made to perform a brutal killing (usually of a family member or someone they know). Most of the child soldiers are abducted from their homes, schools, and localities and then forced into a life of armed combat. Some children, however, join voluntarily to escape poverty, hunger, child abuse, disease, death in the family, and general boredom. Some are even lured in by the prospect of earning a steady income.[16]

An important aspect of international humanitarian intervention and relief aid is to devise ways to prevent the further recruitment and use of child soldiers. Toward this end, the international community, represented by the UN, needs to take concrete steps to ensure implementation of the existing international laws and conventions regulating the use of child soldiers among the member states.[17] More robust methods of arresting and punishing politicians and military leaders who encourage and use child soldiers must also be pursued. Finally, there should be increased international effort toward developing states' capacity in the social and economic sectors to prevent the recruitment of child soldiers in the future.

## STATE FAILURE AND COLLAPSE

The onset of violent and protracted ethnic conflicts greatly increases the risks that the affected state may gradually but inevitably slide toward failure and even collapse. **Failed states** generally exhibit most or all of the following characteristics: the government's social contract with its citizens is severely weakened; the government relies mainly on force and coercion to enforce its existing authority; the government's political legitimacy is highly compromised; the government is in control of only a small fraction of the state's territory and borders; and the government's capacity to deliver public goods and services to all citizens is severely restricted, with warlords and nonstate entities having taken over most of this function.[18]

The onset of ethnic violence may result in the severe undermining of the political legitimacy of the government as some of the constituent ethnic groups within the state withdraw from their obligations under the social contract. The loss of political legitimacy of the government may go hand in hand with its loss of control over large chunks of the state's territory, as ethnic rebels seize these lands. The undermining of government control and legitimacy may also thwart democratic development as state institutions and the people become polarized and politically divided. This may provide fertile grounds for groups promoting ultranationalist ideology and rhetoric, which in turn may further erode liberal values of inclusion, tolerance, and protection of minority rights in society. As society becomes politically polarized and hypernationalistic, the government may try to break the onset of insurgency through the use of overwhelming military force. The prolonged use of the military to solve domestic political problems may, however, lead to the politicization of the armed forces. This in turn may increase the prospects of damaging splits within the armed forces and could lead to military coups d'état and the onset of undemocratic rule.[19]

As ethnic violence intensifies and the country disintegrates politically, the national economy will also suffer. For instance, economic growth declines rapidly when infrastructure is damaged and destroyed, free movement of goods and services becomes restricted, and industrial and agricultural production declines. The onset of ethnic conflict can also adversely affect export earnings, foreign direct investments, and the production and distribution of food. As unemployment, hunger, and poverty begin to rise, this would further inflame ethnic violence.[20] Under these difficult conditions, the government (civilian or military) would find it difficult to govern, and the country may slide further toward collapse, thereby exhibiting most or all of these features: nonexistent social contract; nonexistent rule of law and the onset of anarchy; the meltdown of all government institutions; the carving up of state territory among various substate paramilitary groups, ethnic warlords, and rebel armies; and the delivery of public goods and services completely performed by nonstate entities, relief organizations, and foreign governments.

## Ethno-terrorism

State failure and collapse inevitably leads to the creation of a **complex political emergency** and may promote further criminalization of society. The collapsed state may become a haven for terrorists, warlords, drug and human traffickers, gun runners, smugglers, and other types of criminal gangs. Ethnic insurgents may also launch sudden headline-grabbing acts such as bombings and sabotage, assassinations of political figures, kidnappings, extortions, and massacre of innocent civilians in order to stay in the limelight.[21] As reported in Chapter 1, ethnic insurgents may resort to terrorism because it is cheaper, easier to get away with, and allows them to reach a global audience due to the CNN effect.[22] In this context, Bertelsen has noted that "in order to avoid being dismissed as the domestic problem of an established nation-state and in order to prevent nation-states from imposing solutions upon them, [ethnic groups or non-state nations] may direct violence against nation-states other than the ones in which they reside."[23]

The international targets of **ethno-terrorism** are not exclusively foreign governments or leaders. Insurgents frequently direct their attacks toward their own state's government, property, and personnel at home or abroad. The insurgents can also claim victims among private businesspeople and citizens of its own state who live in other countries. Conducting terrorism against foreign nationals and foreign property, such as the Somali pirate attacks on foreign ships off the coast of Somalia, can internationalize an ethnic conflict by drawing reprisals from the foreign nationals' state(s). Dissatisfied ethnic groups also "have begun to pirate international passenger flights, assassinate diplomats in foreign lands, and even to extort ransom from multinational giants such as the Ford Motor Company. Kidnappings of businessmen and diplomats have become a familiar feature in international politics."[24]

Over the past four or five decades, technological advances in transportation and communication, the globalization of the mass media, and the development of an integrated global economy have turned the world into a "global village," leading to ever-increasing lines of interaction between the international system and an individual country's domestic economy, polity, and society, as well as between the international system and nonstate actors. Consequently, the ability of states to control their internal environment has been substantially reduced. One result is the proliferation of networks of transnational ties among ethnic groups across the globe that provide "greater opportunities for transnational interactions: the exchange of ideas, information, wealth, and political strategies."[25] This in turn provides the basis for powerful **"demonstration effects**."[26] The student protest movements in the 1960s, which spread across western countries and beyond, are a good example. Indeed, demonstrators from Chicago to Prague chanted, "The whole world is watching!" Similarly, the outbreak of ethnic conflict in one part of the world may produce demonstration effects on ethnic movements in other regions. Leaders can note mistakes committed by other ethnic groups and absorb or even emulate the lessons of successful ethnic movements. The linkages that such demonstration effects allow among ethnic movements in different geographical regions have consequently introduced a distinct international dimension to some of these movements. Ethnic groups engaging in international terrorism have taken advantage of the globalization of the mass media and advances in communication technology.[27] As Pierre has observed:

> Television gives the terrorist instant access to the world's living rooms, thereby enabling him to draw global attention to his cause. The mobility offered by the modern jet aircraft allows him to strike at will almost anywhere in the world and then move on to safe asylum. Hence, advances in technology have made it possible for a large society to be directly affected by a small band of terrorists.[28]

Technological advancements in worldwide communications and transportation may also stimulate and reinforce ethnic identities across state boundaries. "Highly politicized communication networks provide groups with the attributes of ethnicity, not through a common historical tradition that usually includes the immigration experience, but through a more synthetic process of rapid ideological and political conversion."[29] This may result in the establishment of ties among ethnic groups in different countries based not only on ethnicity but also on the strength of ideology, strategy, and political–economic objectives. The collaborative relationships forged at one time between the Japanese Red Army and the Palestine Liberation Organization (PLO), the Croatian Ustasa and the Internal Macedonian Revolutionary Organization (IRMO), the Sri Lankan Tamil Tigers and the Colombian drug lords, the Shia Hezbollah militia in Lebanon and the Iranian Revolutionary Guards, and the Hamas in the Israeli-occupied territories and the Muslim Brotherhood in neighboring Arab countries, all dramatize this point.[30] Furthermore, innovations in communications and transportation technologies bind states more closely together, thereby increasing the scope and intensity of intrasocietal penetration, as noted by Stack: "Intra-societal penetration contributes to the strengthening of ethnicity throughout the global environment. French-Canadian separatists are not unmindful of the battles waged by Basque, Welsh, or Irish nationalists."[31] Therefore, it has become common in international politics for ethnic groups to emulate each other's tactics, strategies, and goals. The gains recorded by ethnic insurgents in one country may even reinforce the legitimacy and feed the ambitions of ethnic groups in another.

## Guns-for-Drugs Syndrome

The covert arms trade across the globe, estimated to be between US$5 to US$10 billion annually,[32] and international drug trafficking have significantly boosted the military and financial capabilities of insurgent groups and have given them a degree of freedom that they never enjoyed before.[33] This is particularly true of insurgent groups in failed or collapsed states, where gun-smuggling and drug-trafficking networks are often well developed.

Jayawardhana has reported that the Liberation Tigers of Tamil Eelam (LTTE), a Sri Lankan Tamil insurgent group fighting for a separate Tamil state in Sri Lanka (see the detailed discussion in Chapter 7), has peddled drugs for Colombian drug cartels in order to finance their arms procurements and military campaigns.[34] Ethnic separatists and other internal dissident groups operating in Thailand, Laos, Myanmar, Turkey, and Afghanistan have also been reported to be closely involved in the covert trade in contraband and narcotics. For instance, more than 80 percent of the drug trafficking in Myanmar is controlled by the Shan, Karen, and Kachin ethnic rebels. In recent years, the narcotics trade that originates in Myanmar has reportedly been joined by several ethnic and tribal insurgent groups that operate in the Indian northeast (e.g., Nagas, Kukis, Mizos, Manipuris, and the Assamese) and in the Chittagong Hill Tracts region (e.g., Chakmas) of Bangladesh.[35] In Southwest Asia, the largest supplier of narcotics is Afghanistan, and it is believed that more than 70 percent of Afghan heroin arrives in the West through India.[36] Ethnic and tribal groups reportedly involved in the Afghan narcotics trade include the Ghilzai, Pashtun, Baluch, Shinwari, Tajik, Hazara, and the Turkmen; Afridi and Pathan mafia groups in Pakistan are also believed to be involved in the Afghan narcotics trade.[37]

Apart from the interplay of ethnic insurgents and drug traffickers in both the Golden Triangle (Myanmar, Thailand, and Cambodia) and the Golden Crescent (Iran, Afghanistan, and Pakistan), the long anarchy that prevailed in Lebanon in the 1980s brought the **guns-for-drugs cycle** directly into the heart of the Middle East. Lebanon's position as a producer and refiner of opium, hashish, heroin, and cocaine and as a major transit route for Asian opium and heroin enabled its ethno-religious-based militias to use the narcotics trade to finance their military operations.[38] With the rise in Palestinian militancy and the increased activities of the Shia fundamentalist Hezbollah, two more significant players entered this circle. With the narcotics trade providing an independent source of funding, the various militias continued to destabilize Lebanon, Israel, and Syria and came to adversely affect the Arab–Israeli peace process as a whole.[39]

## Partisan Intervention and Counterintervention in Ethnic Conflicts

Given the self-help nature of the international states system, the outbreak of ethnic conflict within a state opens up considerable opportunities for partisan external intervention and counterintervention, thereby opening up the possibility of conflict transformation through the expansion and intensification of violence. This scenario particularly suits failed and collapsed states because severely weakened or nonexistent central government authority, a politicized and factionalized military, and a polarized population may not be able to resist external intervention and counterintervention; also, the various ethnic groups fighting within the state may actually invite and welcome such external intervention and counterintervention. As noted earlier, external **partisan intervention** by one state usually leads to partisan counterintervention by another, most probably a rival of the first intervening state. The intervention–counterintervention spiral inevitably increases the intensity of the conflict and widens its theater of operations. This in turn may further increase the destruction and human suffering caused by the conflict. While the following analysis of intervention applies to ethnic conflict situations, we should bear in mind that much of the logic also holds for military interventions in other contexts, including the U.S. interventions in Afghanistan and Iraq.

**TYPOLOGY OF EXTERNAL PARTISAN INTERVENTION.** Theoretically, two types of partisan external intervention are possible in ethnic conflicts: diffusion and encouragement, and isolation and suppression. It is important to note that in following a policy of either diffusion and encouragement or isolation and suppression, the intervener becomes a partisan supporter of one side in the conflict.

When an external intervener pursues a **policy of diffusion and encouragement**, it chooses to help the ethnic insurgents against their state and government. The external intervener can provide two kinds of partisan support: tangible support and political–diplomatic support. It can provide **tangible support** in the form of military and material aid; access to transportation, media, communications, and intelligence networks; and special services either within or outside the secessionist region. When it offers tangible aid to the ethnic insurgents, the external intervener's role in the conflict may be regarded as direct: that is, the intervener is physically involved in the conflict as a direct participant in some capacity. Alternatively, the intervener may provide the ethnic insurgents with **political–diplomatic support**, which may include statements of concern, support in international organizations, publicity campaigns, and diplomatic recognition of a government-in-exile or statehood. In such cases, the intervention may be regarded as indirect: the external intervener does not physically participate in the conflict but reacts to the conflict in ways that influences it.

When an external intervener pursues a **policy of isolation and suppression**, it chooses to ally against the ethnic insurgents and help strengthen the state's forces. Such action may involve providing military and political–diplomatic aid to the state. The intervener can also mobilize the international community to undertake collective action on the state's behalf. In cases where the victory of the ethnic insurgents is a *fait accompli*, the intervener can take action to ostracize the new state by refusing recognition or blocking its admission to international organizations. The intervener can cut off all support to the ethnic insurgents (if such support was being provided earlier) and even undertake joint military action with the state's forces against the insurgents.

**REASONS FOR PARTISAN EXTERNAL INTERVENTION.**    Partisan external intervention in ethnic conflicts occurs for two main reasons. First, both ethno-nationalists and states confronted with such movements often seek external partisan support in order to tip the balance of power in the conflict in their favor. Second, external interveners may also have their own motives for becoming involved in such conflicts. Such motives could be either affective, instrumental, or a combination of both.[40] **Affective motives** include reasons of justice; humanitarian considerations; ethnic, religious, racial, or ideological affinity with one of the disputants; and even "personal friendships between top protagonists."[41] **Instrumental motives**, by contrast, are rooted in *realpolitik* and include "international political (including general strategic) considerations, short-term and longer-term economic motives, domestic motives (internal political reasons including the demonstration effect fears) and short-term military gains."[42]

An external party may become a partisan intervener in an ethnic conflict for reasons of justice only if it is convinced of one side's moral and legal position. During the ethnic war in Bosnia, for instance, few international actors believed in the moral and legal justness of the Bosnian Serbs' position and actions; consequently, the external interveners (such as the UN and the North Atlantic Treaty Organization [NATO]) came to the aid of the Muslim-dominated Bosnian government in order to isolate and suppress the Bosnian Serb forces. The opposite scenario occurred during the Bangladesh war of liberation in 1971; during that crisis, most international actors were persuaded by the Bengalis' legal and moral case for secession and therefore decided to back the Bengalis against the Pakistan government. Therefore, for both ethnic insurgents and states interested in seeking external partisan support, a convincing presentation in international circles of their legal and moral position vis-à-vis the conflict is crucial.

External parties most likely to intervene for reasons of justice are international organizations, major powers, and regional states.

Humanitarian motives—saving civilian lives; delivering food, medicine, and aid; preventing ethnic cleansing, genocide and other forms of human rights abuses—behind partisan external intervention have increased in importance in the post–cold war era. As the conflicts in Bosnia, Somalia, and Rwanda showed, the role and power of IGOs and international nongovernmental organizations (INGOs) vis-à-vis ethnic conflict had begun to change: these international actors were no longer willing to let well-established international norms of state sovereignty and nonintervention in the internal affairs of states prevent them from intervening in internal conflicts on humanitarian grounds. IGOs and INGOs are not the only external parties, however, to intervene in ethnic conflict for humanitarian reasons. States—both major and regional powers—may also intervene in a partisan manner on humanitarian grounds. Whose side they would choose mainly depends on which side in the dispute happens to be more culpable for perpetuating a humanitarian crisis.

Ethnic affinity of the external intervener with one of the disputants may lead to partisan support for that side.[43] Ethno-nationalists are more likely to receive aid from a neighboring state if that state is strongly influenced by their **ethnic kin** or conationals.[44] In such cases, the ethnic kin state may start to provide partisan support to the ethno-nationalists (e.g., India's help to the Bengalis in East Pakistan and to the Sri Lankan Tamils in Sri Lanka) or may even pursue an aggressive irredentist policy with the aim of redeeming its lost conationals (e.g., Somalia's policy toward the Ogaden region of Ethiopia and Pakistan's policy toward Kashmir).[45] In some instances, however, attempts by ethnic insurgents to attract partisan support from their ethnic kin in a neighboring state who are a small minority in that state and who are seen as a security risk by the government of that state may backfire on the insurgents as the ethnic kin state, fearing the possibility of a demonstration effect of the conflict on its own ethnic minority, may decide to isolate and suppress the insurgents by cooperating with the state forces. It may also start to repress its own ethnic minority.[46] For example, the outbreak of the Baluch insurgency in Pakistan in 1973 had the effect of producing greater cooperation between Pakistan and Iran because Iran was suspicious about the political ambitions of its own Baluch minority. Iranian armed forces not only massacred the Iranian Baluch population but also provided support to the Pakistani military in its operations against the Pakistani Baluch separatist organizations. Like Iran, Turkey has suppressed its own Kurdish minority and, at times, has taken military action against the Kurds of Iraq on the suspicion that they were providing support to the Turkish Kurds. Turkey remains wary of Kurd intentions in post-Saddam Iraq.

Religious-ideological ties may also lead an external party to become partisan supporters of the ethnic insurgents or the state forces. For instance, many insurgent groups in India and Israel who profess an Islamic fundamentalist ideology have received support from neighboring groups and states with a similar religious-ideological orientation. In the early 1990s, Islamic *mujahideen* ("soldiers of God"), who were once active in Afghanistan and still maintain close ties with that country, infiltrated Indian-held Kashmir to aid local ethnic insurgents. Islamic *mujahideen* and volunteers were also reported to have come to Kashmir from Bahrain, Saudi Arabia, Sudan, Indonesia, and Malaysia.[47] Israel has had to face a similar predicament: some factions of the Palestine Liberation Organization (PLO) had long enjoyed the sympathy of and direct support from a variety of guerilla and terrorist groups around the world—the

Japanese Red Army's massacre at Tel Aviv's Lod international airport in May 1972 is an early and dramatic illustration of this point. Militant factions within the PLO, militant Islamic groups such as the Hamas, and the Hezbollah militia in Lebanon have also received substantial support from similar religious-ideological groups in Lebanon, Iran, Iraq, Jordan, Egypt, Saudi Arabia, and Syria.

But there might be situations when an external party decides to pursue a policy of isolation and suppression of the secessionists because the ideology and aims of the secessionist movement are incompatible with or a threat to its own ideological position. Generally, partisan external interveners who decide to isolate and suppress the ethno-nationalists for affective reasons will do so mainly through nonmilitary means. Nonmilitary means may include providing economic aid and intelligence information to the victimized state, demonstrating diplomatic solidarity with and sympathy for the state forces against the ethnic insurgents, cooperating with the state forces and other international actors to undercut the appeal of the insurgents, and blocking all assistance to the insurgents. Compared with affective motives, which are driven by empathy, kinship, and at times the strength of moral and legal claims, instrumental motives for partisan external intervention are rooted in *realpolitik.* In other words, ethnic conflicts within states may tempt outside powers to intervene to promote their self-interest.[48] For such instrumentally driven intervention to occur, "gains should outweigh costs." Put another way, "gains should be as cheap as possible, that is, a large return for a small outlay."[49] Gains can be of different kinds and can be both short- and long-term. Where economic gains are concerned, states have a natural advantage over ethnic groups in being able to offer economic inducements in return for external partisan support. But there are cases when ethnic groups, depending on where they are located, can offer attractive economic incentives to external parties. For example, the Kurd homeland in Iraq includes vast deposits of oil. Kurdish nationalists may be able to offer future access to that oil as an inducement to an external party for its support for Kurdish independence. But generally, as Gurr and Harff contend, the more resources a state has, the more is the likelihood of its receiving support from external actors during instances of internal ethnic conflicts.[50]

Sometimes, external parties may decide to support the ethnic separatists precisely to prolong the conflict and thus drain its enemy's economic, technical, human, and military resources, thereby weakening it from within. For this reason, the longer an internal conflict lasts, the greater the possibility of partisan intervention by outside parties (especially the enemies of the state) on behalf of the insurgents. At times, an external intervener may use support for ethnic separatists as bargaining leverage in negotiations with the insurgents' state over other, more vital issues. In either case, support for ethnic insurgents may be a means to an end for the intervener.

Instrumental motives may also induce external parties to pursue a policy of isolation and suppression of the ethno-nationalists. For instance, an external state that at one time was a partisan supporter of ethnic insurgents may decide to alter its course and pursue a policy of isolation and suppression if it calculates that its earlier course of action has led or could lead to serious negative consequences for its internal security (demonstration or contagion effect); external security (raising the possibility of counter intervention); and national reputation, prestige, and economy (as a result of international sanctions). It may then distance itself from the ethnic insurgents and begin to cooperate with the state forces.

**CHARACTERISTICS OF PARTISAN EXTERNAL INTERVENTION.** Conventional wisdom suggests that instrumental motives for partisan external interventions in ethnic conflicts would take precedence over affective motives. Some writers have even gone so far as to argue that affective motives devoid of instrumental considerations would seldom lead to intervention; however, when affective and instrumental motives are combined, direct interventions in internal ethnic conflicts would become a strong possibility.[51] But Heraclides's comparative analysis of seven cases of attempted ethnic secession has shown that instrumental motives for partisan external intervention were less common than affective ones. Small states (the exception being Israel, which is an anomalous small state) usually intervened in internal ethnic conflicts for affective reasons, while medium-size states, regional powers, and superpowers intervened for instrumental reasons.[52]

Realists have hypothesized that high levels of military and political–diplomatic support are usually provided to ethno-nationalists by external interveners only if they expect strong instrumental gains.[53] Heraclides's analysis confirmed this realist hypothesis but only insofar as material support was concerned; conversely, high levels of political–diplomatic support were provided mainly for affective motives or a combination of affective and instrumental motives.[54] Realists have also suggested that in their quest for partisan external support, ethno-nationalists would find it easier to procure political–diplomatic support rather that material support (based on the premise that words are cheaper than material aids). However, Richard Little's study found that external political–diplomatic support for ethnic insurgents and secessionists were generally lower and harder to obtain than external material support, belying the expectation that words are cheaper than material aid.[55]

Another point made by realists pertains to the unreliability of partisan external intervention because ethnic groups are often "perceived as instrumentalities in the foreign policy armamentarium of one state to disrupt the internal affairs of another state."[56] Although Heraclides's study confirmed this, it also showed that external parties that intervened in ethno-national conflicts for instrumental reasons tended to be more reliable than those that intervened for affective reasons, and within the category of affective motives, those that intervened for reasons of justice or empathy tended to be more reliable than those intervening for ideological or religious solidarity.[57]

Heraclides's study also discovered a significant correlation between the type of external states that intervened in ethnic and secessionist conflicts and the type of support that was provided. Western states and less developed countries (LDCs) of a western orientation usually provided ethno-secessionists with material support. Nonaligned LDCs usually provided political–diplomatic support, especially of an open, verbal kind. Neighboring states adjacent to government-held territory (and not to that held by the secessionists) generally supported the government forces. Neighboring states that bordered both government- and rebel-held territory tended to support the ethno-secessionists. Neighboring states that were adjacent only to the secessionist-held territory tended to support the secessionists even more. But regional states rarely intervened militarily on behalf of ethno-secessionists; two exceptions were Indian military intervention in Bangladesh and Iranian border raids on behalf of the Iraqi Kurds. During the cold war, the two superpowers (the United States and the Soviet Union) were rarely interested in becoming involved in ethno-secessionist conflicts on opposing sides. Finally, the realist dictum of "the enemy's enemy is my friend" held true for ethnic conflicts; for instance, external states that were enemies of the state experiencing ethnic conflict were more likely to support the ethnic secessionists with material and political–diplomatic support.[58]

**CONSTRAINTS ON PARTISAN EXTERNAL INTERVENTION.**    As we have pointed out in earlier chapters, in spite of the constraints imposed by the international normative regime, partisan external intervention in intrastate ethnic conflicts is a rule of thumb in international relations. One reason for this is the self-help nature of the international states system in the absence of any supranational governing authority. In spite of this, however, direct intervention by a state in intrastate ethnic conflicts in another state has been less frequent than classic civil wars in the post-1945 period.[59] Even in those rare cases of direct external intervention in intrastate ethnic conflicts, "incumbent governments have tended to attract more support than insurgents have."[60]

Certain characteristics of internal conflicts may also act as constraints on external intervention. Deutsch has suggested that four specific characteristics of internal conflicts—their duration, extent or scope, degree of recruitment and attrition, and morale and intensity of motivation on each side—may have a bearing on external intervention. For external intervention to become a realistic possibility—especially high-level tangible involvement—an internal conflict must be prolonged. Conflicts that last for only a few days or weeks provide little opportunity for external intervention, but prolonged internal conflicts, by generating a military balance between the adversaries, open up considerable opportunities for external intervention. The adversaries may seek to tip the military balance in their favor and to acquire the resources and capacity needed to engage in a long war through external intervention. Duration of the conflict is itself heavily dependent on the extent or scope of the conflict—how large a population is involved and over how large a territory. If the extent or scope of the conflict is large, its prolongation increases the possibility of external intervention. Similarly, the ability of adversaries to recruit new troops and to continue the conflict until one side emerges victorious also determines the duration of hostilities.[61] Lack of capability, funds, and calculations of gains and losses by an external party may also act as constraints on intervention. External intervention is unlikely if the potential intervener lacks the resources to carry it out. The potential intervener's belief that its losses would outweigh its gains and that intervention may be untimely or imprudent may act as further constraints on intervention.[62]

Partisan external intervention on behalf of ethnic separatists can also come at a high cost for the intervener and thus act as a constraint. For example, if a state intervenes in an ethnic conflict for affective reasons, such as sympathy for fellow nationals, it may expose itself to the risk that if the level of support proves insufficient to ensure success of its separatist ethnic kin or if it fails to satisfy its fellow nationals, then the anger of its fellow nationals (and even some of its own population) may be directed toward itself for a poorly conceived adventure. The failure of Serbian president Slobodan Milosevic to come to the Krajina Serbs' rescue when they were attacked by Croatia stimulated Serb anger toward him. Some Krajina Serbs even swore vengeance on Milosevic, the man they once depended on but who now was considered a traitor.[63]

Finally, external parties may decline to intervene on behalf of the secessionists if they are opposed to the movement, are opposed to secession and armed conflict on principle, are supporters of the center, or are not convinced about the merits or justness of the secessionist claim. International political considerations (fear of reprisal from the incumbents, adverse reaction of the international community), domestic political and security imperatives, and apprehension about negative economic effects (the financial drain of providing support) may all act to prevent an external state from intervening on behalf of the secessionists. In addition, **bystander apathy**—that is, "the greater the number of onlookers in a situation in which a suffering or victimized person requires urgent assistance, the greater is the diffusion of responsibility"—may also act as a check on intervention.[64]

**CONSEQUENCES OF PARTISAN EXTERNAL INTERVENTION.**   As we have argued, partisan external intervention in ethnic conflict, by increasing its scope and intensity, may pose serious threats for international security and order. If the ethno-nationalists score substantial gains using the support provided by external parties, it may induce their state to seek a military solution to the conflict, causing enormous human suffering and damage in the process.[65] The Zapatista National Liberation Army in the southern Mexican state of Chiapas furnishes an example of this phenomenon: employing modern communications technology such as e-mail and faxes, this movement, representing the impoverished indigenous population of Mayan stock, quickly became an international cause célèbre in the mid-1990s. But the Zapatistas paid a price for such fame because Mexican president Ernesto Zedillo resorted to harsh counterinsurgency operations to take back rebel-held villages.

External support for ethno-nationalists is also seldom provided on the scale that would enable them to win a decisive military victory against the state. What ethnic insurgents need most for a decisive victory is direct military intervention by their external supporters. But very rarely are states willing to assume such a risk. Although there are notable exceptions to the rule (one is the Indian military intervention on behalf of Bengali secessionists in Pakistan in 1971), partisan external support usually augments ethno-nationalists' strength in the short run, thereby resulting in military stalemates and the onset of complex humanitarian emergencies.

When ethnic groups' ability to wage war is substantially dependent on external state support, they may become pawns in a wider political game played between states. For instance, the PLO's dependence on Egyptian, Jordanian, and Syrian support resulted in its giving up more control than it got back in terms of capability.[66] Similarly, in their fight against the Iraqi government, the Kurds depended heavily on support from Iran (and secretly from the United States until 2003, when the American invasion of Iraq led to overt U.S. support for the Kurdish leaders). Consequently, it was the Iranians and the Americans who came to acquire control over the conflict's intensity and duration. They could prolong the conflict and raise its level of intensity by providing more material support to the Kurds, or they could halt or lower the intensity by reducing the Kurds' fighting capability through aid cutoffs. In such cases, an ethnic group becomes "a tool by which a nation-state may (indirectly) perpetrate violence against another state at reduced cost to itself."[67]

Partisan support from external states may at times become a double-edged sword for ethnic secessionists in the sense that such intervention, by inducing counterintervention on behalf of the state, may actually lead to an intensification and prolongation of the conflict. The danger here was clearly addressed by Northedge and Donelan, who warned that "intervention always tends to lead to counter-intervention of some sort, if there is time and opportunity for it. When this happens . . . the dispute [becomes] protracted and raised to a higher level of violence."[68] Consequently, secessionists may no longer find themselves as a disputant in an internal conflict but as victims of a much wider and intense international war. This type of conflict transformation usually marginalizes the issues that had led to the conflict in the first place and introduces new issues, actors, and solutions. Conflicts such as those in Lebanon, Cyprus, Congo, and Angola all became protracted and more violent following external intervention and counterintervention.

## THE STAYING POWER OF ETHNIC INSURGENCY MOVEMENTS

Once they emerge, ethnic insurgency movements tend to become intractable, thereby engaging the state in a war of attrition. For example, in post-Saddam Iraq, various ethno-religious insurgencies (above all by the Sunni minority) emerged, dug in deep, and began to attack U.S. and coalition forces with a degree of ferocity that caught many U.S. policymakers and the newly created Iraqi government off guard.

For an insurgency to become intractable, it needs to be durable, visible, and audible. Ensuring physical durability refers to an insurgent group's capability and desire to exist as an organized political movement, even in the face of repression by the state, and to engage in prolonged insurgency warfare. To survive state repression and achieve success as a political movement, insurgents also need to be visible (to be seen) and to be audible (to be heard). In large measure, durability depends on a movement's ability to obtain material support (weapons, ammunition, finances, intelligence, personnel, base of operations, and training) from external sources. Visibility and audibility may accrue from a movement's ability to attract political and diplomatic support (such as recognition of a government-in-exile, and verbal encouragement and propaganda activities in international forums) as well as the attention and sympathy of the national and international media.[69]

Ethnic insurgents usually seek to enhance the durability, visibility, and audibility of their movements in different ways. For instance, they may engage in international diplomatic activity to gain sympathizers who could provide them with material and political–diplomatic support. In this search for partisan external support, a number of factors are crucial for success. First, ethnic insurgents have to be pragmatic in selecting and accepting aid from external parties. This may require the movement to adopt a more diffuse or flexible ideology than it otherwise would wish to embrace. Second, to be able to make a strong international impact, ethnic insurgents must be able to present their case persuasively before the international community. Finally, the ability to effectively use positive inducements (rewards for support) as well as negative sanctions (credible threats against external parties ignoring insurgents' demands) is also pivotal in securing outside partisan support.[70]

Ethnic insurgents usually undertake international diplomatic activities at different levels: individual, group, state, and systemic. At the individual level, the targets of lobbying usually are prominent personalities, such as influential foreign politicians, intellectuals, creative artists, and religious and media figures who may be able to publicize the insurgents' case in their own countries, carry out fund-raising activities, and act as spokespersons for the movement in their countries. International arms merchants, bankers and financiers, and even heads of criminal organizations may be opportune targets for insurgents because of their ability to provide weapons and money for insurgency warfare. At the group level, the most common targets of lobbying are ethnic or religious kin in neighboring states, who may be eager to provide military and financial aid, training, and sanctuary.[71] Ethnic diasporas are also a target of lobbying, especially if their economic and political clout is considerable. Ethnic and religious groups who are not conationals or coconfessionals but are engaged in similar insurgencies or profess a common ideology or religion may also be approached for assistance if they possess needed resources and are ideologically fellow-travelers; the alliance between al-Qaeda (religious fundamentalists) and Sunni insurgents and between Iran and Shia factions in Iraq are cases in point.

In general, however, the main targets of ethnic insurgents' international diplomatic activity are states, which are still the principal actors in international politics. Countries backing the central government under attack may be warned to cut off their support. States that are already staunch enemies of the central government and that may wish to exploit the situation for their own gain will be targets of insurgents' lobbying. Former colonial powers or current major powers represent another category of states that may be asked for assistance or, under certain circumstances, to act as a third-party manager of the conflict. Of course, neighboring states containing ethnic kin are also likely targets of lobbying. At the systemic level, IGOs, whether regional (such as the European Union, the Organization of African Unity, the Arab League) or global (such as the United Nations), are the most likely targets of insurgents. IGO sympathy and support may lend legitimacy to an insurgent movement, boost the morale of its members and leaders, provide a forum from which ethnic groups can reach a wider international audience and thus sway international public opinion in their favor, and put pressure on the central government to initiate political negotiations and seek a peaceful solution to the conflict.[72] **International nongovernmental organizations (INGOs)**, such as Amnesty International, Médecins Sans Frontières (Doctors Without Borders), and the Red Cross, as well as multinational corporations (MNCs), are also frequent targets of lobbying by insurgents to gain publicity and international sympathy.[73] INGOs are also often referred to as **Nongovernmental Organizations (NGOs).** Made up of non-state actors such as civil society, social movements, and private voluntary organizations, most NGOs today engage in transnational networking. Ethnic groups regularly lobby INGOs and NGOs without noting a difference between them.

Ethnic insurgents may also seek to maintain visibility and audibility by resorting to terrorism. This may happen more often when the insurgents lack the resources needed for conventional military and guerrilla warfare. More important, because the goal of insurgents is to reach a global audience to publicize their cause, terrorism can be an effective tool. Sensational terrorist attacks are likely to be given widespread coverage by the global electronic and print media.[74] The downside of this policy, of course, is that ethnic insurgent groups risk being labeled as terrorist groups. If that happens, ethnic insurgent groups may find little sympathy and support for their cause, no matter how sound their moral and legal arguments appear. They will also find it hard to procure weapons and raise funds internationally. The state against which ethnic insurgents are fighting may also suddenly find itself at the receiving end of greater international sympathy and support, which may induce it to seek a military solution (because hardly any state would agree to negotiate with terrorists). Also, no tears are likely to be shed for the ethnic insurgents in case of their massacre by their state. This has been the fate of the Liberation Tigers of Tamil Eelam (LTTE), or Tamil Tigers, the main insurgent group fighting for a separate state for Sri Lankan Tamils in Sri Lanka, in recent years. We discuss this case in more detail in Chapter 7.

## Conclusion

In this chapter, we have shown how the outbreak of violent ethnic conflicts usually produces a set of side effects or consequences that in turn pose a threat to international security and order. For the most part, intrastate ethnic conflicts exert a destructive influence on the world system, although an international normative regime unsympathetic to ethno-secessionist claims, however morally justified they may be, can try the patience of the most liberal-minded ethnic political movement. Hence, the international community cannot remain indifferent and inactive when confronted with these consequences of ethnic conflict. However, devising ways to deal effectively with these risks is neither easy nor straightforward. The next chapter focuses on how international third parties—both transnational organizations and state actors—can contribute to resolving ethnic conflicts.

## Discussion Questions

1. What is meant by a complex humanitarian emergency? How does ongoing ethnic conflict make it difficult to manage such an emergency? Who are the main victims of such humanitarian crises?

2. Why is partisan external support so crucial for most ethno-nationalists? Why is it so difficult to obtain?

3. Describe the links among state failure, the rise of ethno-terrorism, and transnational networks. What is the role of the mass media in this process?

4. There is growing evidence that many ethnic groups use drug trafficking to fund their political–military operations. Do you think that the guns-for-drugs nexus provides ethno-nationalists today with a greater operational advantage and flexibility? What are the costs of using the guns-for-drugs nexus for ethno-nationalists?

5. Discuss the proposition that partisan external intervention in an ethnic conflict usually brings about counter-intervention.

## Key Terms

affective motives
bystander apathy
child soldiers
complex humanitarian
    emergency
complex political
    emergency
counterinsurgency
    (COIN) operations
demonstration effects
ethnic cleansing
ethnic kin
ethno-terrorism

failed states
genocide
genocidal mass rape
guns-for-drugs cycle
instrumental motives
internally displaced
    persons (IDPs)
international governmental
    organizations (IGOs)
international
    nongovernmental
    organizations (INGOs)

nongovernmental
    organizations (NGOs)
partisan intervention
policy of diffusion and
    encouragement
policy of isolation and
    suppression
political–diplomatic
    support
refugees
tangible support

## Notes

1. See Lucian W. Pye, "The Roots of Insurgency and the Commencement of Rebellions," in Harry Eckstein, ed., *Internal War: Problems and Approaches* (New York: The Free Press of Glencoe, 1964), p. 170.

2. Judy S. Bertelsen, "An Introduction to the Study of Nonstate Nations in

International Politics," in Bertelsen, ed., *Nonstate Nations in International Politics: Comparative System Analysis* (New York: Praeger, 1977), p. 3.

3. Myron Weiner, "Peoples and States in a New Ethnic Order?" *Third World Quarterly*, 13, no. 2, 1992, p. 326.

4. Mark Duffield, *Global Governance and the New Wars: The Merging of Development and Security* (London and New York: Zed Books, 2001. See also Mary Kaldor, *New and Old Wars: Organized Violence in a Global Era*, 2nd ed. (Cambridge, U.K.: Polity Press, 2006), pp. 119–149.

5. Weiner, "Peoples and States in a New Ethnic Order? p. 321.

6. Ibid.

7. Myron Weiner, "Bad Neighbors, Bad Neighborhoods: An Inquiry into the Causes of Refugee Flows," *International Security*, 21, no. 1, Summer 1996, pp. 5–42.

8. Sarah Kenyon Lischer, "Collateral Damage: Humanitarian Assistance as a Cause of Conflict," *International Security*, 28, no. 1, Summer 2003, pp. 79–109.

9. For a detailed historical account of ethnic cleansing, see Michael Mann, *The Dark Side of Democracy: Explaining Ethnic Cleansing*, (New York: Cambridge University Press, 2005).

10. For a detailed historical account of genocide, see Adam Jones, *Genocide: A Comprehensive Introduction*, (London and New York: Routledge, 2006).

11. For an excellent account of mass rapes in Bosnia Herzegovina, see Alexandra Stiglmayer, ed., *Mass Rape: The War Against Women in Bosnia-Herzegovina* (Lincoln and London: University of Nebraska Press, 1994).

12. Caroline Kennedy-Pipe and Penny Stanley, "Rape in War: Lessons of the Balkan Conflicts in the 1990s," *International Journal of Human Rights*, 4, no. 3–4, 2000, p. 73. See also Todd A. Salzman, "Rape Camps as a Means of Ethnic Cleansing: Religious, Cultural and Ethical Responses to Rape Victims in the Former Yugoslavia," *Human Rights Quarterly*, 20, no. 2, 1998, pp. 348–378.

13. Kennedy-Pipe and Stanley, "Rape in War," p. 74.

14. See Rory Carroll's report on the wave of sexual violence sweeping through the Democratic Republic of Congo, *The Guardian,* January 31, 2005, G2 section, pp. 10–11.

15. For an excellent account of the problem of child soldiers, see P. W. Singer, *Children at War* (Berkeley and Los Angeles: University of California Press, 2006).

16. Astri Halsan Hoiskar, "Underage and Under Fire: An Enquiry into the Use of Child Soldiers, 1994–98," *Childhood*, 8, no. 3, 2001, pp. 340–360.

17. Some of the key conventions are the Convention on the Rights of the Child and its Optional Protocol, the Geneva Convention's Additional Protocols of 1977, the African Charter on the Rights and Welfare of the Child, the ILO Convention on the Worst Forms of Child Labor, and the International Criminal Court.

18. David Carment, "Assessing State Failure: Implications for Theory and Practice," *Third World Quarterly*, 24, no. 3, June 2003, pp. 407–427; I. William Zartman, "Introduction: Posing the Problem of State Collapse," in William Zartman, ed., *Collapsed States: The Disintegration and Restoration of Legitimate Authority* (Boulder,

Colo.: Lynne Rienner Publishers, 1995), pp. 1–11; Robert I. Rotberg, "The New Nature of Nation-State Failure," *Washington Quarterly*, 25, no. 3, Summer 2002, pp. 85–96.

19. See William Reno, "The Politics of Insurgency in Collapsing States," in Jennifer Milliken, ed., *State Failure, Collapse and Reconstruction* (Oxford, England: Blackwell Publishing, 2003), pp. 83–103. See also Paul Richards, *Fighting for the Rain Forest: War, Youth and Resources in Sierra Leone* (Oxford, U.K.: James Curry; Portsmouth, U.K.: Heinemann; in association with the International African Institute, 1996).

20. Paul Collier et al., *Breaking the Conflict Trap: Civil War and Development Policy* (Washington, D.C.: World Bank and Oxford University Press, 2003).

21. Bertelsen, "An Introduction to the Study of Nonstate Nations in International Politics," p. 4.

22. For an argument on the effectiveness of terrorism for ethnonationalists, see Andrew J. Pierre, "The Politics of International Terrorism," *Orben*, 19, no. 4, Winter 1976, p. 1252.

23. Judy S. Bertelsen, "The Nonstate Nation in International Politics: Some Observations," in Judy S. Bertelsen, ed., *Nonstate Nations in International Politics*, p. 251.

24. Abdul A. Said and Luiz R. Simmons, "The Ethnic Factor in World Politics," in Said and Simmons, eds., *Ethnicity in an International Context* (New Brunswick, N.J.: Transaction Books, 1976), p. 30.

25. John F. Stack, Jr., "Ethnic Groups as Emerging Transnational Actors," in John F. Stack, Jr., ed., *Ethnic Identities in a Transnational World* (Westport, Conn.: Greenwood Press, 1981), p. 21.

26. Walker Connor, "Nation-Building or Nation-Destroying?" *World Politics*, 24, no. 3, April 1972, p. 352.

27. Stack, "Ethnic Groups as Emerging Transnational Actors," p. 21.

28. Pierre, "The Politics of International Terrorism," p. 1253. Here quoted from Ibid.

29. Ibid.

30. For details of specific cases, see Walter Laqueur, *Terrorism* (Boston, Mass.: Little, Brown, 1977), p. 194; Walter Jayawardhana, "Guns For Drugs," *Sunday*, November 4–10, 1990, p. 84; Shireen T. Hunter, *Iran and the World* (Bloomington: Indiana University Press, 1990), pp. 123–127; Tabitha Petran, *The Struggle Over Lebanon* (New York: Monthly Review Books, 1987), pp. 374–375; Barry Rubin, *Revolution Until Victory: The Politics and History of the PLO* (Cambridge, Mass.: Harvard University Press, 1994), p. 203.

31. Stack, "Ethnic Groups as Emerging Transnational Actors," p. 25.

32. "The Covert Arms Trade," *The Economist*, February 12, 1994, p. 21.

33. Said and Simmons, "The Ethnic Factor in World Politics," p. 30.

34. Jayawardhana, "Guns for Drugs," p. 82.

35. For details, see Bertil Lintner, "The Indo-Burmese Frontier: A Legacy of Violence," *Jane's Intelligence Review*, 6, no. 1, January 1, 1994.

36. See David Pugliese, "Private Armies Threaten Established Borders," *Defense News*, April 4, 1994, p. 12; and Jayawardhana, "Guns for Drugs," p. 84.

37. Said and Simmons, "The Ethnic Factor in World Politics," p. 32.

38. Richard Clutterbuck, *Terrorism and Guerrilla Warfare: Forecasts and Remedies* (London: Routledge, 1990), p. 157.

39. Ibid., pp. 103–104; and Rachel Ehrenfeld, *Narco-Terrorism* (New York: Basic Books, 1990), pp. 52–73.
40. See Astri Suhrke and Lela Garner Noble, "Spread or Containment?" in Suhrke and Noble, eds., *Ethnic Conflict and International Relations* (New York: Praeger, 1977), pp. 226–230.
41. Alexis Heraclides, *The Self-Determination of Minorities in International Politics* (London: Frank Cass, 1991), p. 52.
42. Ibid.
43. See Stephen M. Saideman, "Explaining the International Relations of Secessionist Conflicts: Vulnerability Versus Ethnic Ties," *International Organization*, 51, no. 4, Autumn 1997, pp. 721–753.
44. Frederick L. Shiels, "Introduction," in Shiels, ed., *Ethnic Separatism and World Politics* (Lanham, Md.: University Press of America, 1984), p. 11.
45. Stephen Ryan, *Ethnic Conflict and International Relations* (Aldershot, England: Dartmouth, 1990), p. xvi.
46. See Bertelsen, "The Nonstate Nation in International Politics," p. 252.
47. See Sanjoy Hazarika, "Afghans Joining Rebels in Kashmir," *New York Times*, August 24, 1993; Ahmed Rashid, "No Longer Welcome" and "Pulls and Pressures: President's Peace Offer Marred by Ethnic Violence," *Far Eastern Economic Review*, April 2, 1992, p. 18; Shiraz Sidhva, "Days of Despair," *Sunday*, June 16–22, 1991, p. 22.
48. Ryan, *Ethnic Conflict and International Relations*, p. xvi.
49. Heraclides, *The Self-Determination of Minorities in International Politics*, p. 52.
50. Ted Robert Gurr and Barbara Harff, *Ethnic Conflict in World Politics* (Boulder, Colo.: Westview Press, 1994), pp. 85–86.
51. Ryan, *Ethnic Conflict and International Relations*, p. 36.
52. See Alexis Heraclides, "Secessionist Minorities and External Involvement," *International Organization*, 44, no. 3, Summer 1990, pp. 371–372.
53. See Astri Suhrke and Lela Garner Noble, "Introduction," in Suhrke and Noble, eds., *Ethnic Conflict and International Relations*, pp. 17–18.
54. Heraclides, "Secessionist Minorities and External Involvement," p. 372.
55. Richard Little, *Intervention: External Involvement in Civil Wars* (London: Martin Robertson, 1975), p. 9.
56. Said and Simmons, "The Ethnic Factor in World Politics," p. 29.
57. Heraclides, "Secessionist Minorities and External Involvement," p. 373.
58. For details, see Heraclides, "Secessionist Minorities and External Involvement," pp. 372–376.
59. Ibid., pp. 352–353.
60. Ibid., p. 353.
61. See Karl W. Deutsch, "External Involvement in Internal War," in Eckstein, ed., *Internal War*, pp. 104–106.
62. Heraclides, "Secessionist Minorities and External Involvement," p. 353.
63. See Jane Perlez, "Croatian Serbs Blame Belgrade for Their Rout," *New York Times*, August 11, 1995, pp. 1, 2, and "Demonstration in Belgrade," *New York Times*, August 10, 1995, p. 4.
64. Heraclides, "Secessionist Minorities and External Involvement," pp. 353–355.
65. See Pye, "The Roots of Insurgency and the Commencement of Rebellions," p. 170.
66. Bertelsen, "The Nonstate Nation in International Politics," p. 252.

67. Ibid.
68. F. S. Northedge and M. D. Donelan, *International Disputes: The Political Aspects* (London: Europa, 1971), p. 131.
69. George Modelski, "The International Relations of Internal War," in James N. Rosenau, ed., *International Aspects of Civil Strife* (Princeton, N.J.: Princeton University Press, 1964), pp. 14–15.
70. Heraclides, *The Self-Determination of Minorities in International Politics*, pp. 41–45.
71. Rajat Ganguly, *Kin State Intervention in Ethnic Conflicts: Lessons From South Asia* (New Delhi: Sage Publications, 1998); Frederick L. Shiels, "Introduction," in Frederick L. Shiels, ed., *Ethnic Separatism and World Politics*, p. 11.

72. E. Marlin and E. Azar, "The Costs of Protracted Social Conflict in the Middle East: The Case of Lebanon," in G. Ben-Dor and D. R. Dewith, eds., *Conflict Management in the Middle East* (Lexington, Ky.: Lexington Books, 1981).
73. Cynthia H. Enloe, "Multinational Corporations in the Making and Unmaking of Ethnic Groups," in Ronald M. Grand and E. Spenser Wellhofer, eds., *Ethno-Nationalism, Multinational Corporations, and the Modern State* (Denver, Colo.: Graduate School of International Studies Monograph Series on World Affairs, University of Denver, 1979), pp. 21–27.
74. Pierre, "The Politics of International Terrorism," p. 1252.

# CHAPTER 4

# Resolving Ethnic Conflicts Through International Intervention

## WHY RESOLVING ETHNIC CONFLICTS IS IMPORTANT

The explosion of violent ethnic conflicts at the end of the twentieth century confronted the international community with difficult normative and practical challenges, including two in particular: how to safeguard ethnic minorities' rights and interests within existing state structures, and how to devise a moral and legal framework that could be used to determine which secessionist ethnic claims are to be supported and recognized. The growing literature written on this subject, some of which we have mentioned and discussed in Chapter 2, proves that there is little international consensus on these issues. From a more practical perspective, the manifestation and persistence of ethnic conflicts around the world has brought the international community face to face with certain damaging consequences and risks associated with such conflicts—terrorism, drug trafficking, humanitarian crises, refugee flows, and the threat of wider systemic wars. In Chapter 3, we have alluded to some of these key consequences and risks of ethnic wars. For the sake of international peace and security, therefore, the international community must find ways to resolve ethnic conflicts peacefully or, if needed, through the use of force.

In this chapter, we focus on conflict resolution through the involvement of international third parties, with particular stress on two interrelated points. First, we identify and analyze the various roles that international third parties may play and the criteria needed for success in each of these different roles. Second, we discuss specific international actors that have either played or have the potential to play third-party roles in ethnic conflict resolution.

# ETHNIC CONFLICT RESOLUTION BY INTERNATIONAL THIRD PARTIES

Conflict is intrinsic to human nature and is often the agent of development, reform, and progress. But conflict can and often does degenerate into murderous violence and, at such moments, it becomes crucial to manage and ultimately resolve conflict peacefully and quickly.

Theoretically, conflicts may be resolved in one of three ways. First, disputants may resolve a conflict violently through war (as the Sri Lankan government and the Tamil Tigers have done; details of this conflict are discussed in Chapter 7), which may ultimately settle the dispute when one side secures a military victory (for instance, the Sri Lankan government). This method of dispute resolution is harsh and fraught with high risks (such as the massive violation of human rights and the creation of a severe humanitarian crisis, as has happened in Sri Lanka)—precisely what the international community seeks to avoid in ethnic conflict situations. Second, and diametrically opposite of the first, disputants may settle their differences through peaceful bargaining and negotiation on their own initiative (as the Czechs and Slovaks did after the fall of Communism in Czechoslovakia leading to the peaceful partition of the country). Although such peaceful methods are most favored by the international community, in the case of ethnic conflicts, which are usually perceived as zero-sum games by the adversaries, the disputing parties often fail to implement them (the instances of the failure of peace accords in ethnic conflicts are too numerous for us to document all; one good example would be the number of failed peace negotiations and agreements in the Sri Lankan conflict, which is discussed in detail in Chapter 7). The limitations of the first two approaches raise the importance of the third method—the involvement of a third party—especially in situations of protracted ethnic conflict, during which the disputants have exhausted their own attempts at compromise.[1]

Dispute resolution through third-party action can be defined as "the intervention into a dispute of a person or an agency whose purpose it is to act as an instrument for bringing about a peaceful settlement to that dispute, while creating structures whereby the foundations of a lasting settlement can be laid."[2] To that extent, an international third party can pursue any of the following three objectives: peace keeping, peace making, and peace building.

## Peace Keeping

When severe ethnic conflicts break out, the international community's first priority is to immediately stop the fighting. This is crucial in order to create a peaceful context (however unstable) for holding talks between the disputants and to provide humanitarian relief to civilian populations who are the victims of such violence. To create this peaceful context, an international third party may undertake **peace keeping** operations in the conflict. Peace keeping operations involve the physical interjection of outside military forces between the disputants' forces to keep them apart and halt the fighting.[3] The target of peace keeping operations are thus the foot soldiers of the disputing sides, and the aim of the operations is to curb the soldiers' bellicose behavior, at least temporarily, to create an environment conducive for political negotiations and relief operations.[4] The conventional wisdom, as developed through United Nations (UN) practice, is that, to be effective, international peace keeping operations must fulfill three requirements: first, all parties to the dispute must give prior consent to them; second, international peace keepers must be impartial when dealing with the adversaries;[5] and third, peace keepers must use limited force, meaning that peace keepers can use force only to defend themselves.[6]

The failure of UN peace keeping operations to halt spiraling ethnic violence in Bosnia Herzegovina, Somalia, and Rwanda in the early 1990s generated tremendous skepticism about the effectiveness of limited and impartial peace keeping operations conducted by international third parties. International relations specialist Richard Betts argued, for instance, that impartial and limited peace keeping operations had occasionally succeeded in the past not because they were undertaken to halt the violence between adversaries who were willing to fight on but because they were undertaken to monitor **ceasefires** worked out and accepted by the adversaries themselves before the peace keepers intervened. But in situations where no prior ceasefire agreements had been worked out, limited and impartial peace keeping operations by international third parties did not halt the hostilities. He concluded that UN peace keeping efforts in Bosnia, Somalia, and Rwanda had failed because the UN suffered from the "destructive misconception" that these types of limited and impartial peace keeping operations can keep peace where none exists. For Betts, the fundamental issue in any war is always determining who rules when the fighting stops. He argues that wars do not begin unless both parties in a dispute prefer to fight than concede and, as a corollary, wars do not end "until both sides agree who will control whatever is in dispute."[7] Therefore, in his opinion, it is a mistake to assume that peace keeping intervention, along with the offer of good offices, will alone influence the belligerents to recognize the advantages of peaceful negotiation.[8]

Instead, Betts suggested that it is far better to undertake international peace enforcement operations in ethnic conflicts in which the belligerents have yet to be convinced that they have little to gain by fighting on.[9] International **peace enforcement** can be undertaken in one of two ways. The peace enforcers may choose to operate with limited force, but must then do so partially by backing one of the adversaries. This may either tilt the military balance in favor of that side, which would help it to win the war and thus bring the conflict to a quick end, or else create a **hurting stalemate** by helping to balance military power between the disputants, which may then induce them to come to the negotiating table and jointly search for a peaceful resolution of their dispute. Contrary to the first option, if the international peace enforcement operation must remain impartial, then it must deploy overwhelming military might to quickly gain total control of the situation on the ground, which would then give it the power to impose and enforce a peace settlement on belligerents unwilling to stop fighting. Anything short of this, Betts argues, would block peace "by doing enough to keep either belligerent from defeating the other, but not enough to make them stop trying."[10]

## Peace Making

In contrast to peace keeping or peace enforcement, **peace making** by international third parties usually involves political–diplomatic activity, the objective of which is to bring the leaders of the disputing parties closer to a political settlement achieved through peaceful negotiations. International third parties thus may play the role of intermediary during the negotiation process between the adversaries. This role is particularly important during violent ethnic conflicts because once the fighting begins, the adversaries are likely to be "reluctant to continue consultations or come together in order to discuss their problem."[11]

An international third party can be the intermediary by employing methods such as arbitration, mediation, or facilitation. **Arbitration** refers to "binding, authoritative third-party intervention in which conflicting parties agree to hand the determination of a final settlement to outsiders."[12] Arbitration, therefore, is a legal or quasi-legal method of conflict resolution that works only if the disputants submit their respective claims for outside arbitration and agree to abide by the arbitrator's decision. It is most effective in those situations "where the conflict has a strictly legal character."[13] However, its effectiveness and utility in violent ethnic wars is likely to be limited.

Compared with arbitration, **mediation** by international third parties may offer greater hope for resolving violent and protracted ethnic conflicts. International mediators can offer their good offices to the adversaries to initiate meaningful political dialogue. In this way, lines of communication between the adversaries can be opened, and different ideas and information can be shared. International mediators can also assist in changing how the adversaries perceive each other by helping each side understand the other's position, concerns, and constraints. In this way, the mediator may succeed in extracting concessions from the adversaries by narrowing their differences. In addition, by suggesting face-saving compromises, stressing common interests between the adversaries outside the immediate conflict, offering alternative proposals for settlement, and "linking agreement on one set of issues to agreement on another set of issues" through the building of "coalitions of support for desired outcomes and against undesired outcomes," the mediator may be able to bring the adversaries closer to a settlement.[14] Finally, at the postagreement stage, the mediator

**TABLE 4.1** Resolving Ethnic Conflict Through International Third-Party Action: Techniques, Qualities, Targets, and Objectives

| Techniques | Qualities | Targets | Objectives |
|---|---|---|---|
| Peace making | Impartiality, substantial leverage mediation, prior consent of adversaries not essential | Leaders | Induce or coerce the adversaries to sign a peace accord |
| Peace keeping | Impartiality, limited use of force, prior consent of adversaries needed | Soldiers | Stop the violence and carry out relief operations |
| Peace enforcement | Take sides if needed, massive use of force, prior consent of adversaries not essential | Leaders/ soldiers | Induce/coerce unwilling adversaries to accept and implement a peace accord |
| Peace building | Can be pre- and postconflict, policy coordination among various agencies essential, socioeconomic development | Masses | Foster mutual understanding among adversaries, reconstruction of war-torn societies, socioeconomic development |

can offer guarantees that the terms of the agreement will be honored and implemented by all sides to the dispute.[15]

Mediation is a three-sided process, like a triangle, and to be effective as mediator, an international third party must possess leverage over the adversaries. Knowing that there is a possibility that the mediator may support the other side, adversaries may abandon their inflexible stance and become more supportive of the mediator's position.[16] Availability of resources (political, economic, financial, military, informational, conceptual, tactical, and supervisory) may increase the mediator's leverage and enhance its ability to induce concessions from the adversaries by using the carrot-and-stick (rewards for compliance, punishment for noncompliance, respectively) approach.[17] The mediator's own image, prestige, standing, and credibility in politics and international affairs may also determine the leverage it enjoys over the adversaries.[18]

Because mediation is a voluntary process, the mediator must have an impartial image in order to secure the adversaries' trust, confidence, and cooperation; otherwise, mediation will be ineffective.[19] Whether the mediator has an impartial image depends to a large extent on the prestige and credibility that the mediator enjoys internationally, the motives for its involvement, and its ability to treat all sides in the dispute fairly and equally. Credibility and prestige are crucial because an important source of a mediator's influence is "possession of resources (physical, financial, informational)" that can be used "as 'leverage' when dealing with tactical rigidities."[20] But if the adversaries question the mediator's credibility, then the mediator's use of resources to induce concessions will only cause the adversaries to harden their positions during negotiations. Similarly, a mediator that gets involved because of its own self-interests and calculations of gain will fail to secure the "positive attitudes" of the adversaries toward a peaceful settlement of the conflict. Furthermore, the failure of a mediator to be fair toward, and supportive of, all the disputants may rob it of its impartial image.[21]

As with peace keeping operations, not all critics agree that the mediator should be impartial. In fact, effective mediation, some critics argue, inevitably requires the mediator to threaten the adversaries with the ultimatum that their refusal to commit to the peace process will force the mediator to take sides in the conflict.[22] Touval argues that, in this context, adversaries will accept the peace roadmap advocated by the mediator only if they come to believe that the mediator can help them get a better deal than the one they can get themselves by fighting or if they believe that rejecting the mediator's offer will cause it to side with the enemy.[23] Some experts further argue that, because mediation represents a form of multilateral bargaining, all the parties, including the mediator, actually pursue their own interests; hence, mediators cannot, by definition, be impartial, although mediators may find that their own and the disputants' interests are best served by encouraging a fair and equitable settlement. Those who believe in this line of reasoning argue that the only qualification needed of an external mediator is its "acceptability" to the disputants.[24] Finally, it has been suggested that the best moment for mediation to succeed is when the conflict is "ripe"—when the conflict is at a stage of hurting stalemate, where adversaries are exhausted and come to believe that little can be gained by prolonging or escalating the conflict.[25] If the parties to a conflict have not reached this stage, then mediators may find it desirable to "induce ripeness [to a conflict] and contribute to the making of a 'hurting stalemate' [in order to] create a disposition among the disputants to settle the conflict."[26] But this would require the mediator to side with the weaker party, at least in the initial stages of the conflict, to create a military stalemate.

Another method of international third party peace making is **facilitation**, which differs from mediation in terms "of the assumptions on which it is based, its objectives, the participants, the identity of the third party, and the nature of the outcomes."[27] One such assumption is that conflicts are the result of the suppression and denial of basic and inherent human needs for survival and development, such as security, identity, and recognition. The facilitation approach thus focuses more on human than institutional behavior. Facilitation is cooperative, nonhierarchical, and noncoercive: "It does not include direct bargaining or negotiation, nor does the third party advocate or impose specific solutions."[28] Instead, the third party aims to "transform the situation from a 'conflict' that divides the parties into a 'problem' that they share and over which they need to cooperate if it is to be resolved."[29] In other words, by facilitating the interaction of the parties to the conflict and by provoking their creative thinking, the third party can play a constructive role in the process of finding a self-sustaining settlement. But that settlement can and must come only from the parties themselves because resolution of a conflict "means that a new set of relationships will eventually emerge which are self-sustaining and not dependent for their observance upon outside coercion or third parties. It is not a settlement imposed by a victor or a powerful third party, but rather a new set of relationships freely and knowledgeably arrived at by the parties themselves."[30]

Facilitation requires a third party to be knowledgeable about theories of human behavior (especially violent behavior); motivations and goals that influence human behavior; and the political value that human beings attach to their motivations, goals, status, and role. These are highly specialized qualifications; therefore, a third party must be professionally qualified and experienced "to ensure that there is available to the parties all possible relevant information."[31] At the same time, it is preferable that the third party does not possess any specialized knowledge about the conflict and about the parties involved because "the dispute or conflict is that of the parties. It is for them to define it, and to determine the issues, values and motivations that are relevant. An 'expert' is likely to know the answers before the parties have met!"[32]

## Peace Building

A third role that international third parties can play in attempting to resolve ethnic conflicts is that of peace builder. **Peace building** requires an international third party to undertake long-term socioeconomic activities aimed mostly at the ordinary members of the disputing parties in order to change members' perceptions and attitudes toward members of the other group. Thus, the main objective of peace building is to implement "peaceful social change through socioeconomic reconstruction and development."[33] An international third party can play this role either before ethnic conflict has erupted or in the postconflict years. If it plays the role of peace builder in the preconflict stage, the international third party, acting on early warning signals of impending conflict, may undertake certain measures in order to prevent the outbreak of violence and foster better understanding among suspicious and insecure ethnic communities. If it steps in during the postconflict stage, the third party's peace building activities may involve economic reconstruction of war-ravaged societies and the reconciliation of warring ethnic communities.[34] The important criteria for the success of peace building activities are the financial resources at the third party's disposal and its patience and perseverance in what is bound to be a slow and arduous process.

## ETHNIC CONFLICT RESOLUTION BY THE UNITED NATIONS

The United Nations (UN) is assumed to be ideally suited to play the role of a third party in ethnic conflict situations for at least three reasons. First, its impartial image as an international organization makes it readily acceptable to the adversaries. Second, UN intervention can deinternationalize a conflict—prevent partisan intervention and counterintervention—and therefore help prevent the conflict from escalating.[35] And third, the UN's specialized bodies and agencies make it better suited to perform a range of tasks important for the successful deescalation and resolution of ethnic conflicts. These tasks may include monitoring ceasefires and undertaking peace keeping operations; arbitrating, mediating, or facilitating a negotiated peace agreement between the adversaries; providing humanitarian relief to the suffering populations; and undertaking pre- as well as postconflict peace building measures.

In spite of these perceived advantages, in practice, the UN was neither very active nor effective in resolving ethnic conflicts during the cold war. It did not become involved in the war in Biafra (in Nigeria) or in the intercommunal clashes in Northern Ireland. It played only a token role in the India–Pakistan dispute over Kashmir and during the secession of Bangladesh. The UN also shied away from Sri Lanka's brutal ethnic war, failed to prevent ethnic clashes in Myanmar and Malaysia, did little to censure Indonesian atrocities in East Timor, and played no role in preventing the rise of ethnic passions in the former Soviet Union and eastern Europe.

What factors can explain this dismal UN record in resolving ethnic conflicts? First, the United Nations, contrary to its name, is an organization of independent states, and thus it is natural for the organization to take a pro-state stand in intrastate ethnic conflicts, which it has done repeatedly.[36] Second, because state sovereignty and nonintervention in the internal affairs of states are long-established international norms, the UN (under Article 2, Paragraph 7 of its charter) cannot legally intervene in intrastate ethnic conflicts unless the state concerned seeks UN intervention or unless a compelling case can be made to override the principles of state sovereignty and nonintervention.[37] But as we discussed in earlier chapters, states confronted with ethnic conflicts rarely seek international intervention because they fear that such intervention would legitimize ethnic demands and restrict their ability to use force against the insurgents. International law also does not clearly define the conditions under which the international community could override the norms of state sovereignty and nonintervention in states' domestic affairs. Finally, the UN's limited financial and military capabilities and the constraints of cold war politics contributed to its inability to play an active role in resolving ethnic conflicts.[38]

But to be fair to the UN, it must be pointed out that, in spite of these shortcomings, the UN was not always a bystander in internal conflicts during the cold war. As long as the maintenance of international peace and security remained as the major goal of the UN, as enunciated in Article 1 of its charter, the UN had to be involved in some internal conflicts that threatened international peace, security, and human rights. Also, although the principle of self-determination under the charter was not meant to confer a right of separate statehood to ethnic groups, it still imposed an obligation on the UN not to ignore this principle's implications for ethnic conflicts. Some states did seek UN intervention in their internal conflicts, especially when they could not resolve these conflicts on their own.[39] The next sections assess the UN's record in internal conflicts to judge how effective it has been as a peace keeper, peace maker, and peace builder.

# The United Nations as a Peace Keeper

**EVOLUTION AND CHARACTERISTICS OF UN PEACE KEEPING.**    Chapter VII of the UN Charter provides the Security Council with powers to take action under the principle of **collective security** when breaches of peace or acts of aggression take place. Under Article 41, the Security Council may recommend to UN members any measure short of the use of force to be carried out against any one or more of the parties to a dispute. If these measures fail, then under Article 42, the Security Council may "take such action by air, sea and land forces as may be necessary to restore international peace and security." Articles 41 and 42 of the charter, therefore, provide the UN with the power to intervene in a conflict and to resort to coercive action in order to maintain global peace and security.

For the UN to undertake any action under the principle of collective security, however, the full agreement of the Security Council's five permanent members (the United States, Britain, France, Russia, and China) is an essential prerequisite because each has the power to veto any proposed action. Achieving unanimity among the five permanent members was difficult during the cold war when the Security Council was ideologically split between the communist (the Soviet Union and China) and capitalist (the United States, Britain, and France) blocs. Consequently, the principle of collective security, as envisaged by the framers of the charter under Chapter VII, was never actually realized.

In this situation of political and operational paralysis, on Secretary General Dag Hammarskjöld's initiative, the UN devised the concept of peace keeping, which went beyond the provisions of Chapter VI (dealing with the peaceful settlement of disputes) but did not resemble the military enforcement provisions of Chapter VII. As defined by the UN, the main aim of peace keeping operations was to bring about a cessation of hostilities by interposing UN forces between the warring factions. Additionally, UN peace keepers could perform other tasks (such as relief operations) as defined in their specific mandates. Thus, peace keeping is not specifically mentioned in the charter but "evolved as a non-coercive instrument of conflict control at a time when Cold War constraints prevented the Security Council from taking the more forceful steps permitted by the Charter."[40]

To conduct peace keeping operations in a given conflict, seven requirements had to be met, as defined by the UN. First, UN peace keeping operations could be undertaken only if all parties to a dispute gave it their prior consent and promised cooperation. Second, UN peace keepers were required to remain impartial toward all sides in a conflict at all times. Third, UN peace keepers could use only the minimum amount of force required for self-defense and self-protection. Fourth, UN peace keeping operations required a mandate from the Security Council under Chapter VI and its continued support throughout the duration of operations. Fifth, any changes to the peace keeping mandate affected by the Security Council required the consent of all the disputants before it became applicable. Sixth, troops and personnel provided by member states for UN peace keeping duties were to be under the exclusive control of the secretary-general. And seventh, UN peace keeping operations were to be fully financed by the UN.

**UN PEACE-KEEPING OPERATIONS DURING THE COLD WAR.**    Between 1948 and 1988, the UN undertook several peace keeping operations. The record of these operations is mixed. Although in some cases, the interjection of peace keepers often provided brief periods of relief from war and suffering, the UN generally failed to turn these short-term gains into more lasting peace settlements. For example, in the Congo in 1960, crumbling state authority and the outbreak of conflict brought in UN peace keepers. For the next three years, however, fighting continued in the country in spite of their presence. In Cyprus, UN peace keeping operations ended up hindering rather than facilitating a settlement by "reducing any sense of urgency for a political solution to the stalemate."[41] Similarly, in Lebanon, apart from some minor successes, UN peace keepers failed to put an end to the festering conflict.

**UN PEACE KEEPING OPERATIONS AFTER THE COLD WAR.**    The end of the cold war led to a dramatic expansion in the UN's peace keeping duties. Since 1988, the UN has undertaken several new peace keeping operations under three broad categories. The first included peace keeping duties aimed at managing unresolved conflict between states. As part of these traditional military-type operations, UN military observers monitored the ceasefire between Iran and Iraq from 1988 to 1991. UN military personnel also continue to monitor the demilitarized border between Iraq and Kuwait. A second category included operations "to help implement negotiated settlements of long-standing conflicts, as in Namibia, Angola, Cambodia, El Salvador and Mozambique."[42] And the third category was comprised of peace keeping operations to bring intense ethnic conflicts, such as those in Bosnia, Somalia, Rwanda, Congo, and Sierra Leone, under control.

The UN's expanding peace keeping role in intrastate conflicts in the post–cold war period reflected the development of an international consensus regarding the conditions under which the norms of state sovereignty and nonintervention would no longer automatically prohibit the UN from intervening in domestic ethnic conflicts.[43] These conditions are threefold: (1) when domestic ethnic violence threatens to spill beyond international borders and threatens a wider conflict involving others not previously involved; (2) when ethnic violence results in massive civilian suffering and engenders refugee problems; and (3) when ethnic violence leads to crimes against humanity, including **genocide**, **ethnic cleansing**, repression, and **forced expulsion**.[44] Contrary to expectations, the UN has failed to stop ethnic violence and prevent human rights abuses, from Somalia to Sri Lanka. Consequently, its reputation has become tarnished because ultimately "it is the peace and security agenda that serves as the prism through which the UN is judged by the media and the public."[45]

**WHY HAS THE UN NOT LIVED UP TO EXPECTATIONS?**    In Michael Mandelbaum's opinion, UN peace keeping operations under the guise of humanitarian interventions often failed to restore and maintain peace because such interventions invariably led to political interventions.[46] In particular, the UN was called on to perform two political tasks for which it was clearly unprepared: the first was to protect the boundaries of states experiencing civil conflict, and the second was to rebuild the institutions of government where they had failed or they had completely collapsed.[47] For instance, in Iraq after the first Gulf War and in Bosnia in the immediate aftermath of the Yugoslavian state's collapse, where ethno-sectarian groups (Iraqi Shia, Muslim Bosniaks, Catholic Croatians, Orthodox Serbs) were trying to secede, the main goal of UN peace keeping operations was to provide humanitarian relief and aid to suffering civilian populations. Soon, however, the UN peace keepers became tangled in the web of local politics, which then raised fundamental questions about whether the UN should help ethnic groups to secede and whether it should condone and even contribute to the redrawing of borders.[48] UN peace keeping operations on humanitarian grounds in Somalia and Haiti, in contrast, required the peace keepers to engage in **state reconstruction**, a task for which they were again unprepared.[49] Mandelbaum suggested, therefore, that future international peace keeping operations should obtain the political backing of the international community through the UN but should be carried out on the ground by individual states—historically, the most successful agents of state building.[50] The exception to this rule was the United Nations Transitional Authority in Cambodia (UNTAC), which was successfully involved in policing the country, monitoring elections, and establishing a civilian administration. It is an open question whether the success of UNTAC could be replicated elsewhere.

Richard Falk put the blame for the UN's peace keeping ineffectiveness on an anachronistic Security Council.[51] The Security Council's permanent membership, in Falk's opinion, no longer reflects the present world power structure and the changes that have occurred in the relative power and wealth of states during the past six decades. Consequently, ascendant states have been reluctant to bestow the UN with substantial autonomy in matters relating to financing and enforcement—areas that are crucial to the UN's peace keeping and peace building effectiveness. Furthermore, an obsolete Security Council results in the UN being used almost as a foreign policy arm of its permanent members. In cases of domestic conflict perceived by the permanent members as affecting their national interests, they have preferred to pursue unilateral action based on the concept of spheres of influence. This was evident in France's policy in Rwanda, the United States's role in Haiti, Russia's interventions in its "near abroad," China's approach toward Sudan and the Darfur crisis, and more recently the Anglo-American military interventions in Afghanistan and Iraq.[52] In contrast, **orphan conflicts** (those conflicts in which no states are willing to mediate either because they have more pressing priorities or because they consider the conflict too risky and not directly affecting their interests) that carry no immediate threat to the permanent members have been dumped on the UN without simultaneously building up the organization's capacity to take effective action.[53]

Paul Schroeder offered a slightly different explanation for the failure of the UN to punish violators of international law in the so-called **new world order (NWO)**. He suggested that a key postbipolar trend in international politics (especially championed by those who believed in the formation of an NWO in light of the allied victory in the first Gulf War) was the growing confrontation between states that allegedly break international law and those that supposedly uphold it. But this trend is dangerous because, when carried to its logical extreme, "the concept of the NWO as the collective enforcement of international law against transgressors" provokes resistance and violence on the part of lawbreakers in several distinct ways. First, it makes international politics a zero-sum game and therefore violates a key assumption of the international system that "all essential actors should be preserved, because even an aggressive opponent, once curbed, has a necessary role to play."[54] Second, when the international community portrays the sanctions it imposes on states and regimes as law enforcement against violators, it impugns the honor of the accused parties, thus giving them strong incentives to resist the sanctions (after all, a government that cannot defend its honor can quickly lose power) and to mobilize domestic support against the international community; this is precisely what happened in Yugoslavia, Somalia, and Iraq.[55] Third, in strategic terms, the collective enforcement of international law against violators often causes the international community to pursue vague and indefinable goals.

This may raise the stakes for the international community in terms of prestige and credibility, while the means of enforcement remains limited. Thus, disunity, defections, and juridical challenges to the legitimacy of international actions may result within the international community.[56] And finally, the collective enforcement of international law against aggressors may create disputes among the coalition members over "sharing the costs and burdens of enforcement, and fears that enforcing the law will result in more suffering and damage than did the original alleged violation."[57] Schroeder therefore concluded that the NWO, "so long as it is conceived as a collective effort to enforce compliance with international law or the will of the international community," as the UN has done, is unworkable and counterproductive.[58]

**THE FUTURE OF UN PEACE KEEPING.** Given the various problems and difficulties mentioned above, how should the UN react if asked to initiate, restore, and maintain peace in situations of violent domestic conflict? Experts are mostly in agreement that limited and impartial military interventions undertaken with the prior consent of the adversaries (the traditional peace keeping approach) is unlikely to work. The UN must therefore reformulate its peace keeping role to meet the new peace enforcement demands that are increasingly thrust on it—as indeed it did in sending an implementation force to Bosnia in late 1995. A redefinition of the UN's peace keeping role in internal conflicts will not be easy, however, and the UN must be prepared to consider painful alternatives as a result of growing incongruity between available resources and increasing demand for intervention in internal wars with high civilian casualties, human rights violations, and other **war crimes**.[59]

But what exactly are the UN's painful alternatives? Some experts are of the opinion that the UN should stay out of situations that call for peace enforcement through military means.[60] Others argue that the UN has the moral duty to protect innocent civilians from slaughter and so must undertake military peace enforcement operations in situations of conflict where ethnic cleansing, genocide, forced displacement, and other human rights abuses are occurring. But such military peace enforcement operations should not be limited and impartial, nor should they be undertaken with the prior consent of the adversaries. In calling for UN peace enforcement operations, therefore, these critics envisage military operations that go beyond traditional peace keeping.[61]

## The United Nations as a Peace Maker

**CHARTER PROVISIONS ON PEACE MAKING.** Although the UN Charter does not explicitly mention the organization's peace making role in ethnic or other types of internal conflicts, under the provisions of Chapter VI, the Security Council is empowered in situations that threaten international peace to call on all parties to settle their dispute by peaceful means and to recommend appropriate procedures and actual terms of a settlement. But it is up to the parties themselves, acting voluntarily, to resolve their dispute peacefully in light of the UN's recommendation. The UN's traditional peace making role, as understood from the charter, is therefore closer to facilitation than mediation.

**UN PEACE MAKING DURING THE COLD WAR.** During the cold war, the UN realized that the permanent resolutions of conflicts could be achieved only through political negotiations and for that, leverage mediation was often required. It is in this context that Secretary General Dag Hammarskjöld introduced the concept of **preventive diplomacy**.[62] One common form that preventive diplomacy took was the establishment of commissions of inquiry or observation units to examine the facts of a dispute. Such fact-finding activities included interrogation, observation, area surveys, and inspection, as well as the analysis and interpretation of these facts.[63] Generally the office of the secretary general, often working under instructions from the General Assembly or the Security Council, supervised the commissions of inquiry, although these bodies could undertake their own investigative work. The UN could then make recommendations to the parties involved for a peaceful settlement. Another form of preventive diplomacy was the offer of the good offices of the UN by the secretary general to disputants in order to influence them to agree to political negotiations. In these negotiations, the UN often participated as a facilitator. In practicing preventive diplomacy, the UN used resources of the secretary general's office and the vast diplomatic network of the organization to establish behind-the-scenes meetings and contacts with various adversaries in order to win approval for peaceful settlements. Furthermore, the UN supervised elections, helped to draft constitutions, and provided early warnings of impending conflict.

While preventive diplomacy was a positive step forward, the UN's peace making efforts were miniscule when it came to resolving ethnic conflicts. Cold war restrictions aside, both the General Assembly and the Security Council were "inappropriate arenas for the settlement of ethnic conflict because they are composed of states and exclude ethnic groups that do not represent sovereign states."[64] There was also nothing in the charter that would allow the Security Council or the General Assembly to "relate to non-state agencies such as liberation movements, communal minorities, or political parties."[65] Ethnic groups, therefore, found it difficult to communicate their views to the UN unless they could find a state sponsor willing to raise their case, as Turkey did for the Turkish Cypriots in Cyprus and as the Arab states did for the Palestine Liberation Organization (PLO). But most ethnic groups did not have such state sponsors, and the result was usually UN inaction.[66] The UN's lack of enforcement capability further undermined its effectiveness as a peace maker, especially in cases where UN members passed resolutions in support of an ethno-nationalist movement. Finally, the General Assembly and Security Council's style of decision making (through the passing of resolutions) undermined the effectiveness of the UN's facilitating role in two distinct ways: (1) the tendency of UN members to outvote their opponents did little to encourage adversaries to negotiate on the issues that divided them,[67] and (2) the frequent adoption of closely worded resolutions, instead of providing the UN with a general framework for pursuing a peace settlement, actually restricted the organization's room to maneuver.[68]

**HAS THE UN BECOME A MORE EFFECTIVE PEACE MAKER AFTER THE COLD WAR?**
Between 1987 and 2000, the UN achieved success in settling several outstanding conflicts. In 1988, the UN secretary general brokered the end of the Iran–Iraq war. Through active mediation and promotion of human rights and reconciliation, the UN was successful in creating a peace agreement in El Salvador's civil war; for his role in this peace effort, Secretary General Javier Pérez de Cuéllar received the Nobel Peace Prize for 1988. Although the UN did not mediate the peace accords that brought an end to civil strife in Mozambique, it played a critical role in their implementation; it was due to the UN that the peace process remained on track, military demobilization took place as agreed, and free and fair national elections could

take place. The accords that helped get the Soviet Union out of Afghanistan in 1989 were also constructed under UN auspices. The UN shepherded Namibia and, more recently, East Timor to independence, although it did precious little to prevent the Indonesian military-sponsored carnage that took place after the **referendum** (an open test of public opinion) on independence. Finally, the UN was instrumental in securing the release of hostages in Lebanon and in working out a political settlement in Cambodia.

These UN successes in peace making were mainly attributable to the disassociation of the institution of the secretary general from use-of-force operations, unlike past UN practice.[69] This is because "the functions of the institution of the Secretary General and the Security Council are complementary and work best when separated at the key dividing line involving the use of force."[70] To do otherwise—to associate the institution of the secretary general with UN military actions under Chapter VII of the charter—would produce certain negative consequences, as the UN has come to experience. First, military action under the secretary general would be ineffective considering the limited tools at his or her disposal, and this would ultimately undermine the credibility of the UN and, through the UN, the credibility of the member states. Under the charter, the authority to use force is given to the Security Council. Even though the Security Council is dominated by strong states, they are rarely willing to provide the secretary general with the resources (financial, military, and intelligence) needed to launch large-scale military actions. Consequently, "the Secretary General has managed use-of-force operations with tools better suited to Chapter VI peace keeping ventures," and it is "this gap [that] has led to questionable results in Somalia and Bosnia."[71] Second, the involvement of the office of the secretary general in UN actions concerning the use of force "would undermine the Secretary General's impartial negotiating role, thus depriving the international community of a further instrument that it already possesses."[72] This impartial negotiating role of the secretary general is crucial if the UN is to play the role of the good cop during peace negotiations, as opposed to the bad cop image that the Security Council would acquire in conducting use-of-force peace keeping operations. Maintaining this distinction between good cop and bad cop is even more crucial if the secretary general is to hold high moral authority, which is usually a key factor in UN-brokered peace negotiations. This moral high ground would be lost if the secretary general ordered the use of lethal force, as operations under Chapter VII would entail.[73] Finally, compared with the Security Council, which represents the vested interests of its member states, the strength and effectiveness of the secretary general emanates from the office's high credibility and lack of vested interests. This standing could be damaged if the secretary general became closely identified with the use of force.[74]

Therefore, it is important that the tasks of the secretary general and that of the Security Council should be kept separate if the UN wants to become an effective peace maker in the future. The secretary general could more effectively play the role of a peace maker and negotiator by obtaining help from skilled colleagues and special representatives and by following a consistent approach. And the Security Council could play a more effective role in the UN's use-of-force operations: it has the means, the ability, and a favorable political climate to define the **red lines of international conduct**—those activities of states or nonstate groups that are impermissible because they threaten international peace and security. The Security Council can also play this role better by streamlining its decision making and making its operations more predictable and consistent. For peace keeping or peace enforcement purposes, it can even subcontract the use-of-force operations under Chapter VII "to a coalition of member states, as in the case of the war against Iraq [in 1991], to a military alliance or a combination of alliances and other states."[75]

To be sure, not everyone is convinced that the UN has turned the corner in peace making because most of the structural limitations that restricted the organization's peace making efforts during the cold war period have carried over into the post–cold war period. For instance, Touval has accounted for the UN's relative successes as peace maker by referring to "the exhaustion of local parties and the unwillingness of external powers to continue supporting clients whose usefulness had expired with the Cold War."[76] For instance, Iran and Iraq accepted the UN-brokered ceasefire only after they had exhausted themselves by fighting for eight years. In Afghanistan and Cambodia, the Soviet Union and China were no longer interested in providing partisan support, thereby robbing local factions of the ability to continue the conflict. Similarly, in El Salvador, the United States was interested in seeing an end to the conflict and therefore put pressure on the right-wing government to come to terms with the left-wing insurgency.

Touval therefore cautioned that the so-called UN successes after the cold war should not raise expectations about the UN's peace making capabilities. The UN continues to suffer from inherent structural limitations that make it less effective in mediating complex international disputes and orphan conflicts—[77] The UN also lacks one of the principal criteria for effective mediation—leverage. It has neither its own military nor vast economic resources—it cannot even "harness the assets of international financial or trading institutions."[78] The UN can mediate only to the extent that its members (especially the permanent members of the Security Council) allow it to. The resources (material and diplomatic) needed by the UN for successful mediation also must come from the states; while states have increasingly sought UN mediation in orphan conflicts, they have committed few resources to ensure its success. While the UN has a significant amount of legitimacy behind its actions, its credibility is "consistently eroded by its inability to formulate and pursue the kind of coherent policy essential to mediation."[79]

These problems, argued Touval, emanate from the UN's decision-making process that deprives the organization of dynamism and flexibility in pursuing mediation. Lack of credibility further decreases the leverage of the UN, hindering the bargaining process and diminishing the probability that the adversaries would accept the proposals put forward by the UN for settling the conflict. The erosion of credibility further hinders UN mediators from offering crucial "guarantees for implementing and observing an agreement."[80] For Touval, then, rather than becoming involved directly, the UN should encourage individual states to assume the responsibility for mediating conflicts in their region of influence.[81]

## The United Nations as a Peace Builder

**THE UN'S RECORD AS A PEACE BUILDER.**    Although experts' attention remains focused on the UN's peace keeping and peace making roles, it also performs the crucial long-term task of peace building. This requires changing the antagonistic attitudes held by people on each side of the conflict and initiating socioeconomic reconstruction to improve the well-being of people shattered by war. There are several ways to accomplish peace building: (1) by undertaking economic development projects; (2) by providing education to ordinary people on different sides of the conflict to increase their understanding of each other's culture, beliefs, religion, practices, fears, priorities, and interests; (3) by pursuing superordinate goals—urgent goals that can be achieved only through cooperation among the conflicting sides—that cut across parochial interests; and (4) by implementing **confidence-building measures** among the conflicting parties.[82]

The UN Charter underscores the importance of international cooperation in the economic and social spheres. Article 1, Paragraph 3 stipulates that a primary objective of the UN is to "achieve international cooperation in solving international problems of an economic, social, cultural, or humanitarian character." Further, Article 55 explicitly states that to create stability and well-being, which is necessary for peace, the UN shall promote:

> (a) higher standards of living, full employment, and conditions of economic and social progress and development; (b) solutions of international economic, social, health, and related problems; and international cultural and educational cooperation; and (c) universal respect for, and observance of, human rights and fundamental freedoms for all without distinctions as to race, sex, language, or religion.

Overall, the charter devotes two full chapters (IX and X) and a few other provisions toward these goals; though not explicitly stated, some clearly fall within the realm of peace building in ethnic disputes.[83]

At the time the UN was established, it was assumed that the UN's specialized agencies would play a central role in peace building activities. These agencies include the Economic and Social Council (ECOSOC); the United Nations Educational, Scientific, and Cultural Organization (UNESCO); the International Labor Organization (ILO); the Food and Agricultural Organization (FAO); the International Bank for Reconstruction and Development (IBRD); the International Monetary Fund (IMF); and the World Health Organization (WHO).[84] These agencies have not always succeeded in building peace for several reasons.

First, because it is not a supranational organization, the UN does not have the power to make decisions that are binding on member states and their citizens, especially with respect to economic and social matters that fall within a state's domestic jurisdictions.[85] In cases of ethnic conflict, which would require working with governments and ethnic groups that may be politically and militarily opposed to each other, this task has proven to be even more difficult.[86]

Second, although the charter explicitly spells out the general principles and aims of the organization in social and economic matters, it does not provide any specific guidelines about how these socioeconomic goals are to be achieved.[87] Consequently, the commitment of member states to pursue joint or separate action to achieve the aims of the charter in the socioeconomic sphere became a matter of good faith. In addition, the ECOSOC was composed of government representatives who often did not have the technical competence to tackle the large volume of complex questions that came before them. To obtain technical assistance, ECOSOC created several functional subsidiary organs and commissions. For these to work efficiently, they should be staffed by experts chosen on the basis of personal qualifications, as the Dumbarton Oaks Proposals recommended. At the San Francisco Conference, however, this proposal was dropped in favor of having appointed representatives of member states who may or may not be experts in their fields. This undermined the effectiveness of the ECOSOC and the UN in undertaking economic and social tasks.[88]

Third, lack of coordination between the UN and its specialized agencies has hampered the organization's limited peace building efforts. When the UN and its agencies were created, there were wide variations in the memberships of the UN and the agencies. Although these variations in memberships have been greatly reduced, the specialized agencies remain different from the UN in terms of their composition, power, and voting procedures. These specialized agencies have retained substantial autonomy. Coordinating the policies and operating practices of these various agencies has proved difficult for the UN, reducing its ability to engage in constructive and sustained socioeconomic development activities in conflict-torn areas.

And finally, the General Assembly's and ECOSOC's established procedures for passing resolutions and recommendations directed at member states and specialized agencies do not impose any legal obligation on them to take action. Members who disagree with a particular resolution are free to continue their dissent. Especially when the implementation of a resolution requires the support of crucial states—for example, asking states to contribute funds to the UN for undertaking economic development projects such as road and school construction in strife-torn areas—their participation is vital. Although the reports, studies, and surveys published by the UN and its specialized agencies provide information and draw attention to important questions, the contributions of these studies "to the actual achievement of useful results are likely to be overemphasized."[89]

In spite of these obstacles, the UN and its specialized agencies have done some useful peace building work in cases of ethnic and intercommunal conflicts. For example, in divided Cyprus, the Nicosia Master Plan (a project of the United Nations Development Program [UNDP]) has developed better understanding between, and found solutions to common socioeconomic problems of, the Greek Cypriot and Turkish Cypriot communities through collaborative efforts of technical specialists from both communities. UNESCO also initiated projects aimed at economic development and enhancement of mutual understanding between adversaries in Sri Lanka. The UN High Commissioner for Refugees (UNHCR) has done admirable work in Nicaragua, Cambodia, Somalia, Bosnia, and Rwanda.

**UN PEACE BUILDING UNDER POSTBIPOLARITY.**   With the resurgence of violent intrastate conflicts in a postbipolar world, increasing demands are being made on the UN to undertake peace building activities. Secretary General Boutros-Ghali stressed that political stability and security without sustained and durable economic and social development could not be achieved because the root causes of political strife and military conflict are often the deterioration in economic and social conditions. At the same time, sustainable economic and social development is impossible without peace and political stability. He recommended that the UN adopt the concept of postconflict peace building not only in cases of international conflicts but in cases of internal conflicts as well.[90]

Postconflict peace building was best illustrated in El Salvador, where a UN-sponsored peace agreement was signed in January 1992. After the signing, the UN disarmed the disputants and began "to play a central role in ensuring that far-reaching political, social, and institutional reforms agreed to in the negotiations were carried out to prevent the recurrence of violence."[91] But the UN peace building experience in El Salvador exposed the problem of coordination in implementing diverse policies involving multiple actors in complex situations. The peace accord called for the creation of a national civil police that would remain separate and distinct from the armed forces, and it also envisaged land grants to the former guerrillas in exchange for their arms. From the UN's perspective, implementing these two proposals was critical for returning normal civil life to the country. But the proposed reforms entailed high financial costs that were difficult for El Salvador to meet because of a drastic fall in the price of coffee (50 percent of El Salvador's export earnings come from coffee) after 1989. The lack of commitment on the part of foreign countries to help meet peace agreement requirements and, most important, the inability of the Cristiani government in El Salvador to increase the level of domestic financing to pay for these projects— the Cristiani government itself was constrained by the economic stabilization program put in place by the IMF—contributed to only partial realization of the peace plan.[92] UN and IMF peace building policies were at cross-purposes, therefore, and it seemed "as if a patient lay on the operating table with the left and right sides of his body separated by a curtain and unrelated surgery being performed on each side."[93]

According to de Soto and del Castillo, this type of botched surgery could be prevented in the future if the UN followed three of their recommendations. First, international organizations should allow greater transparency between actions of different institutions and agencies through periodic and systematic exchanges of information. This would provide the UN with "a unique source of early warning of potential clashes between different agencies" that in turn might "pave the way for action to enhance coordination."[94]

Second, international organizations must integrate their goals and activities to assist peace building efforts under the overall supervision of the UN. For this purpose, the long-dormant liaison committee—established in 1961 to include the UN secretary general, the president of the World Bank, and the heads of the UN technical assistance board and the UN special fund (both predecessors of the UNDP), and the aim of which was to review peace building by various international organizations and integrate them into a common set of goals—should be reactivated.

Finally, "flexibility in the application of rules of financial institutions or adjustment of such rules when UN preventive diplomacy, peacemaking, or post-conflict peace building so requires" is a must.[95] Establishing a closer link between the UN and the Bretton Woods institutions would introduce the concept of rewards into peace-building activities. Concessional financing, for example, could be linked to compliance with peace agreement provisions. In this way, conditionality would serve peace as well as achieve pure economic objectives. In addition, flexibility would also prove helpful in carrying out unconventional institutional reforms in the host country, such as the creation of the national civil police in El Salvador. International lending institutions are reluctant to fund such projects, but if a degree of flexibility were allowed to permeate their operations, they might be persuaded to reconsider their decisions on such projects.[96]

In making these proposals, de Soto and del Castillo recommend that the UN be able to draw on and utilize the expertise and resources of the various international institutions engaged in peace building activities. To make these bold changes, political will on the part of the major players is needed. The postbipolar environment might offer greater incentives for such exercise of will.

## States as Third Parties in Ethnic Conflict Resolution

Intervention by states in ethnic and other types of internal conflicts presents a dilemma for the international community. On the one hand, critics point to the long-established international norms of sovereignty and nonintervention and argue that intervention by a state in the affairs of another, even if for the ostensibly benign act of settling a conflict, violates these principles of international conduct and is akin to "an international version of assault or burglary."[97] Therefore, state intervention, even for conflict settlement, is impermissible. On the other hand, some argue that, in spite of the international norms of sovereignty and nonintervention, powerful states' involvement in the affairs of the weak has been a consistent feature of international politics. Because intervention cannot be wished away, it should be utilized in constructive ways to contain or settle conflicts. We consider this second view here.

## Major Powers and Ethnic Conflict Resolution

It is often argued that major powers have a special responsibility to help resolve ethnic conflicts because of these states' enhanced military and political capabilities and their global roles and interests. This, of course, does not mean that every ethnic conflict would attract major power intervention but that, in their respective spheres of interests, major powers could play the leading role in settling or containing ethnic and other types of conflict.

For an external third party to be an effective peace keeper or peace maker in ethnic conflicts, it must quickly and decisively react to threats to peace. Unfortunately, international organizations such as the UN often remain paralyzed for months in conflict situations while its member states debate various policy options. By contrast, major powers, because they have vital interests in their spheres of influence, are unlikely to remain passive for long in the face of threats in their regions.

Successful third-party peace making also depends on the resources, capabilities, and resolve of the third party. In these respects, major powers have an advantage over international organizations to make the intervention more effective. Whether acting unilaterally or in tandem with others, they are better suited to carry out military operations. For example, the UN does not have a standing army, nor does it have the resources to carry out the large-scale military operations often required to keep peace in some of today's brutal and intense ethnic conflicts. Major powers have both these things as well as the political will to use them to keep peace if the conflict affects their vital interests. In the post–cold war environment, European powers such as Britain, France, Russia, and increasingly Germany (forbidden by its constitution to engage in military action abroad) have demonstrated their resolve to intervene militarily in violent conflict situations.

Critics have pointed out that because states—in particular, major powers or superpowers—intervene in conflict situations primarily to exploit the conflict for their own gains, such intervention, instead of containing or settling the conflict, may actually lead to conflict escalation by inviting counterintervention. Critics also maintain that exploitative intervention, by lacking legitimacy and impartiality, will not be credible enough to produce conflict settlement through peaceful negotiations. Fearing the intentions of the third party, adversaries would be disinclined to cooperate with the intervener and each other.

Addressing the first criticism, it can be argued that, during the cold war, a major reason why the United States and the Soviet Union were able to contain ethnic and intrastate conflict within their respective spheres of influence was their tacit understanding that neither side would overtly intervene in the other's sphere of influence. Covert intervention was not ruled out but, if caught, the side trying to upset the status quo generally retreated without a showdown (the Soviet withdrawal during the Cuban missile crisis of 1962 is a good illustration). The mutual acceptance of these rules of the game meant that each superpower had almost unlimited powers to make unilateral decisions within its region. Both the United States and the Soviet Union regularly intervened in their backyards (Latin America for the United States and eastern Europe for the Soviet Union) to suppress conflict. The end of the cold war and the global disengagement of the major powers have not meant the abandoning of the idea of regional spheres of influence. The West has tacitly accepted a prominent Russian role in policing Russia's "near abroad." Western European states have taken the lead in managing European crises such as Bosnia. China and Japan are also increasingly seeking to manage domestic conflict in their regions. The United States has not lost sight of domestic conflict in its traditional sphere, Latin America, as evidenced by the U.S. effort to resolve disputes in Haiti, Colombia, and Mexico.

Regarding the second criticism, the lessons of the NATO-led peace enforcement operations in Bosnia make clear that impartial and limited military interventions, as attempted earlier by the UN through traditional peace keeping, may actually be more counterproductive than partisan but aggressive types of operations. In this context, Hopkins has argued that the real possibility of great power military intervention in ethnic civil wars may actually encourage ethno-nationalists to search for domestic solutions to their grievances and disputes because such interventions may prove more detrimental to their overall interests and objectives.

Still, there is no escaping the fact that during the cold war, the superpowers sowed the seeds of some of today's ethnic wars by enhancing the coercive capabilities of their respective allies and by ignoring these allies' repressive policies toward ethnic minorities within their borders. For instance, the United States supported the Pakistani and Indonesian governments in their repression of the Bengalis in East Pakistan and the Muslims in East Timor.[98] The United States also supported Turkey in its conflict with the Kurds. The Soviet Union, too, helped the government of Ethiopia in its fight with separatists in Eritrea and Tigre. The Soviet Union also provided support to Iraq in its conflict with the Kurds. These one-sided, pro-statist policies of the superpowers often forced injured ethnic groups to wait for the opportune moment to assert their demand for separate political existence. Unless they could find a negotiated solution to their internal problems, however, states (especially weaker ones) that depended on superpower support for resolving their internal problems risked becoming engulfed in civil turmoil if that support were to be withdrawn suddenly.[99]

Peace building is a costly and complex process requiring the simultaneous performance of different tasks at different levels of operation. Considering the limitations of the UN and its specialized agencies, and the disinclination of major powers to make money available for peace-related projects in remote conflicts, it may be more realistic to ask major powers to undertake peace building exclusively in their own regions. For this purpose, as Muscat has argued, major powers may be in an advantageous position to use development aid to build and nurture peace in their backyards.[100] Such a division of labor would also provide much needed relief to an already overburdened UN.

## Ethnic Conflict Resolution by Third-World Regional Powers

In a more multilateral world, some scholars have argued that third-world regional powers should take the lead in settling ethnic and other types of internal conflicts in their regions. As Chester Crocker points out, "If nobody else gets involved in conflict resolution in regions around the world, you can be pretty sure that regional hegemons will."[101] Crocker is also skeptical that in a period of postbipolarity, increasingly cooperative relationships between the great powers can diminish the importance of third-world regional powers as third-party reconcilers of regional ethnic conflicts because, in his opinion, solutions and settlements of regional conflicts are ultimately reached by regional powers.[102]

What factors explain the growing assertiveness of certain third-world states in their respective regions? Using Modelski and Riggs's classification of states in the contemporary world, third-world states such as India, Brazil, Egypt, Nigeria, Turkey, Argentina, Thailand, Indonesia, and Malaysia can be classified as advanced transitional states.[103] While not as developed and powerful as states of the developed world, they nonetheless possess greater power capabilities compared to their regional neighbors. Because a state's foreign policy behavior is a function of its power capability, an advanced transitional state may have an expanded foreign policy capability.[104] Therefore, at least in regional affairs, these states may be attracted to the role of playing regional cop, especially when the major powers show little interest.

Self-interest could also motivate regional powers to play the role of third-party reconciler of regional ethnic conflicts. Advanced transitional states are particularly keen to use foreign policy to foster national development, for which regional peace and stability is an important prerequisite.[105] Thus, the outbreak of ethnic conflict in a neighboring country may be perceived by a regional power as destabilizing and harmful to its interests. Such states, therefore, cannot remain indifferent toward the conflict, nor can they assume that the adversaries will be able to settle their differences without outside help.

Protection of ethnic kin in neighboring states may also motivate a regional power to intervene in ethnic conflicts. States may have both affective and instrumental reasons for supporting their ethnic kin neighbors, especially when they are a persecuted minority. Regional powers may be tempted to provide partisan support to their conationals, but a policy of diffusion and encouragement may at times be deemed too risky, especially if the possibility of conflict transformation through counterintervention is high. At such times, a regional power may decide to follow a policy of reconciliation toward the conflict as a compromise option.

Other instrumental factors, such as security and geopolitical considerations, as well as pressures of domestic and international politics, may also influence a regional power to intervene in a neighboring ethnic conflict with the aim of reconciling the adversaries. For instance, the desire to prevent a regional rival from exploiting a conflict close to its borders (thereby posing a security threat) may motivate a regional power to intervene to find a solution quickly. A regional power may favor a negotiated settlement of a neighboring state's ethnic conflict to stem the flow of refugees, which almost always puts an enormous socioeconomic burden on the receiving state. Sometimes, the fear of a contagion effect may motivate a regional power to seek a quick end to ethnic violence in a neighboring state. Pressure exerted by the international community may also induce a regional power to play the role of a third-party reconciler. Such pressure may be brought by the UN to avert a humanitarian disaster, or it may be brought by a major power if it is engaged elsewhere.

Although it is clear that regional powers have strong incentives to become involved in regional ethnic conflicts as third-party reconcilers, it is not clear whether these states possess the qualities needed to be effective in such a role. If we accept Ryan's view, then we have to conclude that this intervention ends up transforming the conflicts into ones that are more complex and protracted and that are less amenable to resolution.[106]

There are several reasons for expecting such a complex outcome. If a regional power intervenes in a neighboring ethnic conflict for purely instrumental reasons, it may come to see the conflict "as something to be exploited rather than resolved."[107] In that case, the primary concern of the regional power would be to promote its own interests rather than to help the adversaries overcome their mutual antagonism and suspicion and find a mutually acceptable political solution. The regional power may begin to demonstrate lack of sensitivity toward the issues in dispute, to start taking sides, and even to introduce new issues and priorities, thereby complicating the conflict. The failure of the Indian peace keeping mission in Sri Lanka is a good example of this type of outcome.

If a regional power intervenes primarily for affective reasons, however, such intervention may be seen as biased, leading to the intervener's loss of legitimacy and credibility. The regional power will fail to secure the compliance and cooperation of all the disputants for a negotiated political settlement. This, in turn, may lengthen the conflict. The only way biased intervention may succeed in bringing an end to conflict is if the force introduced by the third party is great enough to ensure the outright victory of one side.[108] A good example is the Indian military intervention on behalf of Bengali secessionists in East Pakistan in 1971; such events are rare, however.

Finally, the capabilities of regional powers in the third world are inadequate for any major peace building operations, a task best left for international organizations operating in close association with major powers. The role of regional powers is to help with the implementation of various peace building projects.

## REGIONAL ORGANIZATIONS AS THIRD PARTIES IN ETHNIC CONFLICT RESOLUTION

The involvement of regional organizations as third-party reconcilers of ethnic conflict is not a new phenomenon. During the cold war period, two kinds of regional organizations played active roles in diffusing tension in crisis situations: regional organizations representing specific geographic areas often took an active part in maintaining peace in case of conflicts within that region, and regional organizations making up political blocs or alliances took an active part in diffusing subsystemic or intrabloc crises.[109] In the first category of interventions were those undertaken by the Organization of American States (OAS) in several Latin American conflicts; the peacekeeping operations undertaken by the Arab League in Lebanon in the mid-1970s, ostensibly to encourage Syrian disengagement from the conflict; and intervention by the Organization of African Unity (OAU) in several internal conflicts such as in Congo, Chad, and Western Sahara, as well as in interstate conflicts such as those between Morocco and Algeria and between Ethiopia and Somalia. In the second category were NATO efforts to deal with the Cyprus crisis in an effort to defuse the tense relations between two bloc members, Greece and Turkey. The political committee of the Warsaw Treaty Organization also sought to prevent friction between bloc members, such as between Hungary and Romania over Transylvania.

Regional organizations possess certain characteristics that allow them to play the role of a third-party conflict manager effectively. Although some are little more than forums for their members and lack the independence needed to become an effective third party, actions undertaken under the auspices of regional organizations are often more highly valued than state action. Regional organizations tend to acquire an image of impartiality that makes them more acceptable to the adversaries. In this context, Young has noted that the "parties responsible for shaping the actions in question [that is, conflict management or resolution] are likely to be the same whether the regional organization acts or not but the promulgation of actions through a regional structure sometimes makes a real difference in terms of a factor such as subjective impartiality."[110]

During the cold war, regional organizations "tended to exhibit a strong 'external orientation' and to concern themselves with the security of their area vis-à-vis outside threats rather than with the processes of interaction among their members."[111] As a result, they were not usually considered to be salient third-party reconcilers of intraregional disputes. To a large extent, this was a function of bipolar politics, although notable exceptions existed: the OAS and the OAU played important third-party roles in intraregional conflicts. In the postbipolar environment, however, with the growth in the popularity of multilateral approaches toward peace and security, regional organizations have demonstrated more willingness to become active in intraregional conflicts.

For instance, the European Union (EU) and the Organization on Security and Cooperation in Europe (OSCE) have been active in regional crisis management and resolution, and the Council of Europe has sought to enforce state compliance with minority and linguistic rights to avert future conflicts. The EU and NATO were at the forefront of international action in Bosnia. The OSCE sent fact-finding and *rapporteur* missions to the Balkans to support the sanctions and humanitarian measures taken by the UN, EU, and NATO. OSCE missions designed to provide early warning of the spillover of the hostilities in Bosnia into the nearby regions of Serbia, Montenegro, Kosovo, and Macedonia were undertaken in 1992 and continued until mid-1993. The OSCE also sent missions to Hungary, Bulgaria, Romania, Ukraine, and Albania to monitor compliance with sanctions. Under OSCE auspices, international efforts were made to solve the conflict in Nagorno-Karabakh—an Armenian enclave in Azerbaijan. The OSCE was active in the former Soviet Union, undertaking limited peace building missions in Moldova, Estonia, and Georgia to promote better understanding among communities in these states. It established a mission in Latvia to monitor issues related to the Russian minority. The OSCE also sent peace keepers to other areas of the former Soviet Union where local wars had broken out. In Africa, the African Union (AU) was engaged in Angola, Chad, Mozambique, Somalia, Congo, Rwanda, Liberia, and Sierra Leone. In Southeast Asia, the Association of Southeast Asian Nations (ASEAN) emerged as a powerful actor in fostering cooperation between regional states.

Given the growing importance and influence of regional organizations and the difficulties faced by the UN in maintaining peace and security around the globe, some experts have suggested that it would be better for the UN to lighten its load and delegate future peace keeping, peace making, and peace building operations to regional organizations, provided they accept the UN secretary general's overall command of these operations. For instance, as Bosnia, Kosovo, and now Afghanistan have demonstrated, peace keeping and peace enforcement operations may be better performed by NATO rather than by UN forces. This idea envisages NATO as a military arm of the UN and especially appealed to those who believed that the end of the cold war and the loss of a common enemy had eroded much of NATO's earlier purpose as a defensive military alliance against the Soviet Union. The idea also appealed to those who advocated the creation of a permanent UN military force but were aware of the practical difficulties involved; for this group, NATO forces acting as the military arm of an active UN were the next best alternative.

Another alternative to NATO in Europe is the Western European Union (WEU), formed by the Brussels Treaty of 1948 after the dissolution of the wartime Western Union. During the cold war years, the WEU was made part of the NATO defense system, but with the ascendancy of NATO as the dominant security structure of the western alliance, it gradually lost most of its original relevance, power, and influence. The revival of the WEU started in the mid-1980s. In 1987, many European powers, concerned that the United States and the Soviet Union were conducting bilateral nuclear disarmament talks and then imposing the outcomes on Europe, demonstrated a desire to strengthen the WEU to bring about greater European integration in social, economic, and security matters. As the WEU grew in importance after 1989, its position relative to NATO became blurred and it was thought to have acquired certain advantages over NATO. Unlike NATO, the WEU is a European organization that previously represented European security concerns and interests within NATO, so it may be more effective as a peace keeper and peace enforcer in European conflicts. The WEU may also have greater freedom of maneuver than NATO in defense matters outside the European theater, as was evident during the Gulf War, when the WEU—not NATO—deployed European forces from all three services in the Gulf.

Other regional organizations may be more suited to play the roles of peace maker and peace builder than peace keeper or peace enforcer. As the failure of the OAU peace keeping operations in Chad demonstrated, regional political organizations, when asked to keep peace, often face the same kinds of problems that the UN faces. Ryan maintained that the OAU peace keeping mission in Chad failed mainly because of the disinclination of regional states to contribute troops, the lack of adequate financial resources, the disinclination of the adversaries to seek a negotiated political settlement (the force went in without a ceasefire agreement being signed by the adversaries beforehand), and the continued support that was provided by some members of the OAU to one or other of the parties to the dispute.[112] Similar problems have at one time or another undermined the effectiveness of peace keeping operations undertaken by the UN. Regional political organizations, therefore, may be more effective as peace makers because this involves less financial cost and because these organizations usually have high stakes in and better knowledge about intraregional conflicts. Local mediators may also have personal contacts with key leaders of the disputing parties that may prove useful at the negotiating table. Similarly, regional economic organizations may be able to play effective peace building roles both in the pre- and postconflict phases.

## INTERNATIONAL NONGOVERNMENTAL ORGANIZATIONS AS THIRD PARTIES IN ETHNIC CONFLICT RESOLUTION

International nongovernmental organizations (INGOs) have made significant contributions as third parties in conflict situations. A case in point is the International Committee of the Red Cross, which has provided invaluable service in several conflicts dating back to the early years of the cold war. For instance, during the Algerian war of the 1950s and the Hungarian crisis of 1956, the Red Cross was able to provide medical services and humanitarian relief to combatants and civilians.[113] More recently, the Red Cross has been involved in several conflicts—Cambodia, Afghanistan, Somalia, Bosnia, Congo, Rwanda, and Iraq, to name a few. Similarly, Amnesty International has played an important role in highlighting abuses of human rights in various regions of the world. Humanitarian services have also been rendered by Médecins Sans Frontières (Doctors Without Borders).

How effective are INGOs in containing or resolving conflict? They cannot be very effective as peace keepers or peace enforcers because they lack too many of the important physical resources needed for such operations. Their real strength lies in their impartial image, freedom of operations, and unique ability to rise above the political struggles; hence, INGOs have the potential to be effective as peace makers. Still, INGOs have certain deficiencies that can inhibit them from effectively playing this role. INGOs may not possess substantial powers of leverage over the adversaries. Mediators need to earn the respect of the adversaries by offering innovative suggestions, ideas, and frameworks for a political solution. INGOs may not always have full information, first-class diplomatic skills, and an authoritative image. As Young points out, the "lack of such qualities as salience and respect, coupled with typically low scores in such areas as relevant information and diplomatic skill, severely limits the interventionary roles which non-governmental organizations might undertake successfully."[114] These deficiencies may further limit INGOs from performing various service roles "such as inspection and supervision, which are useful in maintaining rules during a crisis or in implementing agreed-upon termination arrangements."[115]

Humanitarian assistance, as well as preventive and postconflict peace building functions, are areas in which INGOs can and do play positive roles. Because of the resurgence of violent conflicts in the postbipolar world and the increasing demand being made on the international community to avert or cope with humanitarian disasters, the international community's perception of the usefulness of INGOs in such operations is changing. A clear sign of this change came in 1988, when the UN General Assembly passed a resolution upholding the principle of intervention within a sovereign state by INGOs on humanitarian grounds, such as in the case of systematic violations of human rights, persecution and genocide of ethno-religious minorities by state machineries, and the need to deliver humanitarian aid urgently. In adopting this principle, the UN recognized that force may be used if necessary to help and support the work of INGOs in these circumstances.

A special task for the international community in the future will be preventive and postconflict peace building. The lead role rightfully belongs to the UN, but the UN will need a great deal of assistance. In this respect, a historic opportunity exists to create an interactive mechanism among the UN, regional associations and agencies, and INGOs with global reach and operations. Specifically, INGOs could play a constructive role in implementing, monitoring, and overseeing a range of UN peace building operations. Because they are active in the field, INGOs could also serve as early warning mechanisms for the UN and the international community by providing information on potential or actual violations of peace agreements, problems of project implementation or coordination, the failure of disputants to respect human rights, and so on. This not only would help the international community to better coordinate peace building activities, it would also pinpoint regions where preventive diplomacy, peace keeping, and peace enforcement activities must be directed or redirected.

## Conclusion

In this chapter, we conceptually addressed the role of international third parties in ethnic conflict resolution. We also surveyed the various international actors that may be drawn into domestic ethno-nationalist disputes, and we suggested types of actors and the roles seemingly best suited to them as they try to resolve such conflicts. We recognize that these actors, the roles they play, and the modes of operation they pursue may be redefined in the course of the conflict. Almost by definition, each ethnic conflict is idiosyncratic and different in important ways from others. A dynamic perspective that describes the evolution of a conflict has many advantages over a static, snapshot approach. The case studies in Part II provide such a dynamic perspective.

## Discussion Questions

1. Why is it important to resolve ethnic conflicts? What roles can the international community play in this regard?
2. What are the essential differences between peace keeping and peace enforcement? Do you feel that traditional international peace keeping in ethnic conflicts should be abandoned in favor of international peace enforcement?
3. In your assessment, has the United Nations succeeded or failed as an international third party in resolving ethnic conflicts? Are other international actors better able to play this role in the future?
4. What is preventive diplomacy? Can it be an effective strategy for preventing future ethnic conflicts?
5. Most scholars argue that the most difficult aspect of ethnic conflict resolution by international third parties is both pre- and postconflict peace building. Why is this so?

## Key Terms

arbitration
ceasefire
collective security
confidence-building
   measures
ethnic cleansing
facilitation
forced expulsion

genocide
hurting stalemate
mediation
new world order (NWO)
orphan conflicts
peace enforcement
peace building
peace keeping

peace making
preventive diplomacy
red lines of international
   conduct
referendum
state reconstruction
war crimes

## Notes

1. Jacob Bercovitch, "Third Parties in Conflict Management: The Structure and Conditions of Effective Mediation in International Relations," *International Journal*, 40, no. 4, Autumn 1985, p. 736–738.
2. Michael Harbottle, "The Strategy of Third Party Intervention in Conflict Resolution," *International Journal*, 35, no. 1, Winter 1979–80, p. 120.
3. Ibid., pp. 120–121.

4. Peace-keeping operations are generally conducted under the guise of international humanitarian intervention. For an excellent discussion of the ethical, legal, and political dilemmas associated with conducting humanitarian interventions, see J. L. Holzgrefe and Robert O. Keohane, eds., *Humanitarian Intervention: Ethical, Legal and Political Dilemmas* (Cambridge,

England: Cambridge University Press, 2003).

5. *Impartiality*—not taking sides—is not the same as *neutrality*—having no effect on the outcome—because the very presence of a third party changes the nature and structure of the dispute. See Bercovitch, "Third Parties in Conflict Management," p. 739, fn. 5.

6. For a detailed discussion of the historical development of peace keeping, see Alex J. Bellamy, Paul Williams, and Stuart Griffin, *Understanding Peace Keeping* (Cambridge, England: Polity Press, 2004).

7. Richard K. Betts, "The Delusion of Impartial Intervention," *Foreign Affairs,* 73, no. 6, November/December 1994, p. 21.

8. Ibid., pp. 21–22.

9. Ibid., p. 20.

10. Ibid., p. 21.

11. John W. Burton, "The Procedures of Conflict Resolution," in Edward E. Azar and John W. Burton, eds., *International Conflict Resolution* (Boulder, Colo.: Lynne Rienner, 1986), p. 100.

12. Mark Hoffman, "Third-Party Mediation and Conflict Resolution in the Post–Cold War World," in John Baylis and N. J. Rengger, eds., *Dilemmas of World Politics: International Issues in a Changing World* (Oxford, England: Clarendon Press, 1992), p. 264.

13. Ibid.

14. Ibid., pp. 268–269.

15. Saadia Touval, "Why the U.N. Fails." *Foreign Affairs,* 73, no. 5, September/October 1994, p. 51.

16. Ibid.

17. On this point, see Oran Young, *The Intermediaries: Third Parties in International Crises* (Princeton, N.J.: Princeton University Press, 1976).

18. Bercovitch, "Third Parties in Conflict Management," p. 749.

19. Ibid., p. 749. See also, Jacob Bercovitch and Allison Houston, "The Study of International Mediation: Theoretical Issues and Empirical Evidence," in Bercovitch, ed., *Resolving International Conflicts: The Theory and Practice of Mediation* (Boulder, Colo.: London: Lynne Rienner Publishers, 1996), pp. 11–35.

20. Ibid.

21. Burton, "The Procedures of Conflict Resolution," p. 105.

22. See D. G. Pruitt, *Negotiation Behavior* (New York: Academic Press, 1981); S. Touval, ed., *The Peace Brokers: Mediators in the Arab-Israeli Conflict 1948–1979* (Princeton, N.J.: Princeton University Press, 1982); S. Touval and I. W. Zartman, "Introduction: Mediation in Theory," in Touval and Zartman, eds., *International Mediation in Theory and Practice* (Washington, D.C.: Westview Press for the SAIS, 1985).

23. Touval, "Why the U.N. Fails," p. 47.

24. Hoffman, "Third-Party Mediation and Conflict-Resolution in the Post–Cold War World," p. 268.

25. See D. G. Pruitt and J. Z. Rubin, *Social Conflict: Escalation, Stalemate and Settlement* (New York: Random House, 1986); and Touval, "Why the U.N. Fails," p. 51.

26. Touval, "Why the U.N. Fails," p. 51.

27. Hoffman, "Third-Party Mediation and Conflict Resolution in the Post–Cold War World," p. 270.

28. Ibid., p. 271.

29. Ibid., p. 272.

30. A. J. R. Groom, "Problem Solving and International Relations," in E. Azar and J. W. Burton, eds., *International Conflict Resolution* (Brighton, England: Wheatsheaf, 1986), p. 86.

31. Burton, "The Procedures of Conflict Resolution," p. 105.

32. Ibid.

33. Harbottle, "The Strategy of Third Party Interventions in Conflict Resolution," p. 121.

34. For a detailed discussion of what postconflict peace building and development may entail, see Roland Paris, *At War's End: Building Peace after Civil Conflict* (Cambridge, England: Cambridge University Press, 2004); Gerd Junne and Willemijn Verkoren, eds., *Postconflict Development: Meeting New Challenges* (Boulder, Colo.: Lynne Rienner, 2005); Anthony Oberschall, *Conflict and Peace Building in Divided Societies* (London and New York: Routledge, 2007); Ho-won Jeong, *Peacebuilding in Postconflict Societies: Strategy and Process* (Boulder, Colo.: Lynne Rienner, 2005).

35. Stephen Ryan, *Ethnic Conflict and International Relations* (Aldershot, England: Dartmouth, 1990), pp. 42, 176.

36. Frederick L. Shiels, "Introduction," in Shiels, ed., *Ethnic Separatism and World Politics* (Lanham, Md.: University Press of America, 1984), p. 10.

37. Milton J. Esman and Shibley Telhami, "Introduction," in Esman and Telhami, eds., *International Organizations and Ethnic Conflict* (Ithaca, N.Y.: Cornell University Press, 1995), pp. 9–10. For an excellent analysis of the norm of "collective non-intervention" under the UN Charter, see Ann Van Wynen Thomas and A. J. Thomas, Jr., *Non-Intervention: The Law and Its Import in the Americas* (Dallas, Tex.: Southern Methodist University Press, 1956), Chapter 7.

38. Raymond E. Hopkins, "Anomie, System Reform, and Challenges to the UN System," in Esman and Telhami, eds., *International Organizations and Ethnic Conflict,* p. 89.

39. Ryan, *Ethnic Conflict and International Relations,* pp. 120–121.

40. See Boutros Boutros-Ghali, "Empowering the United Nations," *Foreign Affairs,* 72, no. 5, Winter 1992/1993, p. 89; and Jack Donnelly, "The Past, the Present, and the Future Prospects," in Esman and Telhami, eds., *International Organizations and Ethnic Conflict,* p. 59.

41. W. Andy Knight and Mari Yamashita, "The United Nations' Contribution to International Peace and Security," in David Dewitt, David Haglund, and John Kirton, eds., *Building a New Global Order: Emerging Trends in International Security* (Toronto: Oxford University Press, 1993), p. 300.

42. Boutros-Ghali, "Empowering the United Nations," p. 89.

43. Two developments promoted this consensus. First, the end of the bipolar ideological rivalry eliminated the main reason for the norm of nonintervention—that is, the prevention of conflict between the superpowers, each of whom tried to impose its own model of legitimacy on other states—and created a broad agreement as to what the appropriate domestic system within states should be. The First Gulf War demonstrated this when the UN General Assembly adopted a resolution demanding that Saddam Hussein's regime stop the repression of Iraq's own citizens. Second, the widespread endorsement of human rights as an international norm encouraged humanitarian intervention by the international community to alleviate the suffering of those whose rights were violated by their own governments, by rival groups or nations, or by other states. See Michael Mandelbaum,

"The Reluctance to Intervene in Foreign Country Problems," *Foreign Policy,* 95, June, 1994, pp. 13–14.

44. See Esman and Telhami, "Introduction," p. 12.

45. Richard Falk, "Appraising the U.N. at 50: The Looming Challenge," *Journal of International Affairs,* 48, no. 2, Winter 1995, p. 625.

46. Mandelbaum, "The Reluctance to Intervene in Foreign Country Problems," p. 4.

47. Ibid., p. 5.

48. Ibid., pp. 4–5.

49. Ibid., p. 11.

50. Ibid., p. 10.

51. For a detailed discussion of the UN Security Council's role in international politics, see Bruce Cronin and Ian Hurd, eds., *The UN Security Council and the Politics of International Authority* (London and New York: Routledge, 2008).

52. Falk, "Appraising the U.N. at 50," pp. 630–631, fn. 10.

53. Ibid., pp. 637–638, 642–643.

54. Paul W. Schroeder, "The New World Order: A Historical Perspective," *Washington Quarterly,* 17, no. 2, Spring 1994, p. 29.

55. Ibid.

56. Ibid.

57. Ibid.

58. Ibid.

59. Thomas G. Weiss, "Intervention: Whither the United Nations?" *Washington Quarterly,* 17, no. 1, Winter 1994, pp. 123–124.

60. See Mandelbaum, "The Reluctance to Intervene in Foreign Country Problems"; Falk, "Appraising the U.N. at 50"; Weiss, "Intervention."

61. See Betts, "The Delusion of Impartial Intervention"; Boutros-Ghali, "Empowering the U.N."

62. See Inis Claude, *Swords into Plowshares: The Problem and*

*Progress of International Organization,* 4th ed. (New York: Random House, 1984), p. 312.

63. Knight and Yamashita, "The United Nations' Contribution to International Peace and Security," p. 301.

64. Ryan, *Ethnic Conflict and International Relations,* p. 143.

65. Sydney D. Bailey, "The U.N. and the Termination of Armed Conflict—1946–64," *International Affairs,* 58, no. 3, 1982, p. 469.

66. Ibid.

67. See Claude, *Swords into Plowshares,* p. 179.

68. Sydney D. Bailey, *How Wars End: The United Nations and the Termination of Armed Conflict, 1946—1964* (Oxford, England: Clarendon Press, 1982), vol. 1, p. 168.

69. The only instance in this period where force was used by the United Nations was in the Gulf War. In that conflict, however, the UN Security Council empowered the U.S.-led military coalition to take action against Iraq, and the secretary general's office was kept outside these actions in a de facto fashion.

70. Giandomenico Picco, "The U.N. and the Use of Force: Leave the Secretary General Out of It," *Foreign Affairs,* 73, no. 5, September/October 1994, p. 15.

71. Ibid.

72. Ibid.

73. Ibid., p. 18.

74. Ibid., p. 16.

75. Ibid.

76. Touval, "Why the U.N. Fails," p. 44.

77. Ibid., pp. 45–46.

78. Ibid., p. 52.

79. Ibid.

80. Ibid., p. 54.

81. Ibid., pp. 45–46.

82. Ryan, *Ethnic Conflict and International Relations,* pp. 61–76.

83. For a case-by-case approach to the UN's role in peace building,

see James Dobbins, Seth G. Jones, Keith Crane, Andrew Rathmell, Brett Steele, Richard Teltschik, and Anga R. Timilsina, *The UN's Role in Nation-Building: From the Congo to Iraq* (Santa Monica, Calif.: RAND Corporation, 2005).

84. Under the charter, the central organ responsible for discharging the duties of the UN in the social and economic sphere is the General Assembly. This was a concession to the smaller states in return for their reluctant acceptance of the prominence given to the Security Council and the major powers in matters of peace and security. However, being a large and cumbersome body, it was anticipated that the General Assembly would have difficulty in discharging these functions. So the framers of the UN Charter created the Economic and Social Council (ECOSOC—a subsidiary organ of the General Assembly) to undertake more specialized tasks to realize this goal of the UN. The ECOSOC consists of eighteen members elected by the General Assembly and its powers are enunciated under Chapter X of the charter.

85. Leland M. Goodrich, *The United Nations* (New York: Thomas Y. Crowell, 1959), p. 268.

86. Ryan, *Ethnic Conflict and International Relations*, p. 147.

87. Goodrich, *The United Nations*, p. 267.

88. Ibid., p. 272.

89. Ibid., p. 281.

90. Boutros-Ghali, "Empowering the United Nations," pp. 101–102.

91. Alvaro de Soto and Graciana del Castillo, "Obstacles to Peace Building: United Nations," *Foreign Policy*, 94, Spring 1994, p. 70.

92. Ibid., p. 71.

93. Ibid., p. 74.

94. Ibid., p. 79.

95. Ibid.

96. Ibid., pp. 80–81.

97. Mandelbaum, "The Reluctance to Intervene in Foreign Country Problems," p. 13.

98. For a good description of U.S. policy toward East Pakistan and East Timor, see Seymour M. Hersh, *The Price of Power: Kissinger in the Nixon White House* (New York: Summit Books, 1983), pp. 444–464; and N. Chomsky, *Radical Priorities*, in C. P. Otero, ed. (Montreal: Black Rose, 1984).

99. Hopkins, "Anomie, System Reform, and Challenges to the U.N. System," p. 86.

100. Robert J. Muscat, *Investing in Peace: How Development Aid Can Prevent or Promote Conflict* (New York: M. E. Sharp, 2002).

101. "Resolving Conflict in the Post-Cold War Third World: The Role of Superpowers," *In Brief* (Washington, D.C.: United States Institute of Peace), May 29, 1991, no page number.

102. Ibid.

103. For details of Riggs's and Modelski's study, see F. W. Riggs, "International Relations as a Prismatic System," and George Modelski, "Agraria and Industria: Two Models of the International System," in Klaus Knorr and Sydney Verba, ed., *The International System: Theoretical Essays* (Princeton, N.J.: Princeton University Press, 1961).

104. See Jayantanuja Bandyopadhyaya, *The Making of India's Foreign Policy* (New Delhi: Allied Publishers, 1979), p. 16.

105. Ibid.

106. Ryan, *Ethnic Conflict and International Relations*, p. 37.

107. Ibid.

108. Ibid.

109. Young, *The Intermediaries*, p. 105.

110. Ibid., p. 106.

111. Ibid.

112. Ryan, *Ethnic Conflict and International Relations*, pp. 130–131.

113. Young, *The Intermediaries*, p. 108.

114. Ibid., pp. 109–110.

115. Ibid., p. 110.

# CHAPTER 5

# Nationalism and the Collapse of Empire: The Russian–Chechen Conflict

In Part I, we explored the meanings of nationalism and ethnic conflict, and we considered the international dimensions of the two phenomena. In Part II, we apply the analysis of the domestic and international aspects of ethnic conflicts to specific cases. We organize the analysis of each case (each chapter) into four sections: why ethnic conflict occurred, how the international system reacted, why the conflict was or was not internationalized, and the extent to which external parties sought to intervene.

In addition, each of the chapters in Part II considers a distinct theme related to ethnic conflict. In this chapter, we examine how the collapse of an **empire** can provide an opportunity structure for the emergence of new kinds of nationalism. In Chapter 6, we focus on the theme of constitutional secessionism as a form of ethnic quarrel, which is left to be resolved by the parties involved. By contrast, Chapter 7 is concerned with a prolonged and bloody civil war and the changing forms that third-party intervention has taken. Chapter 8 looks at the political outcomes that result from ethnic conflict occurring in weak states. Finally, Chapter 9 examines western military intervention in already divided countries since the 1990s and its impact on ethno-religious cleavages.

## THE DISINTEGRATION OF EMPIRES

Empire has been defined as the existence of a multinational state in which a core dominant nation exercises disproportionate authority over peripheral nations which are made subordinate to it. Because of fundamental unequal relations between nations, empire can be understood as, ultimately, a failed multinational state. Does the collapse of an empire, understood this way, fan ethnic conflicts because of the power vacuum created by the decline in the authority of the core nation? Is there a ripple effect by which one hitherto powerful nation's nationalism is mimicked by smaller nations—all former parts of the same empire? Can a lost empire be reconfigured after an imperial nation has recovered its power and will? The case we study to answer these questions is the dismantling of the Soviet empire and its replacement by a Russian state bent on a restoration of great power status.

An unusual alliance between Russian nationalism and the nationalisms of other peoples of the Soviet Union—Balts, Ukrainians, nations of the Caucasus—put an end to the Soviet imperium in 1991. It led to a phenomenon dubbed **matrioshka nationalism**: like the brightly painted Russian wooden dolls that contain ever-smaller dolls within them, the emergence of anti–Soviet Russian nationalism in the late 1980s spawned "lower-order" nationalisms and, with them, ethnic conflicts. The most dramatic example is Chechnya's fierce struggle for independence from Russia.

It is surprising to discover that the literature on the rise and fall of empires rarely identifies nationalism as a pivotal factor; historians and political scientists theorizing about the fate of empires have looked to other explanations. One understanding of empire is that it is primarily shaped by the economic needs of a great power. British political historian John Strachey developed a simple chronology of empire in history: "(i) the original, servile empires based upon slave labor; (ii) the mercantile empires based upon the plundering sort of commerce which we have described ... in the case of the East India Company's eighteenth century empire in India; and (iii) the fully developed capitalist empires."[1] The latter developed "a distribution of income and other characteristics that leave their directing classes little choice but to attempt the conquest, colonization and exploitation of as much of the world as they can get hold of."[2] Strachey recognized that shortly after World War II, even the latter type of empire had become unprofitable and anachronistic.

Influential twentieth-century theories describing how empires were formed and the **imperialism** they engendered include those of John Hobson in his *Imperialism* (1902) and Vladimir Lenin in his *Imperialism: The Highest Stage of Capitalism* (1917). Political scientist Michael Doyle regarded both Hobson and Lenin as adherents of the **metrocentric theory of empire building**, in which it was essential "to look within the dominant metropoles and examine the internal drive to external expansion."[3] This "domestic structures" approach stood in contrast to the **systemic theory of empire building**, which "combines an account of motives with a portrait of opportunities and arrives at a determinate result."[4] Realists in international relations such as Hans Morgenthau could be included in this category. Doyle also described the **pericentric theory of empire building** whose primary focus is on a secondary actor beyond the metropole, for instance, smaller or peripheral nations.

This framework can be used to explain how the collapse of empires can be metrocentric, systemic, or pericentric. In his magisterial *Decline and Fall of the Roman Empire,* eighteenth-century scholar Edward Gibbon offered a nuanced social explanation for the decay of Rome during its 1,300-year history. He favored a primarily metrocentric explanation, though he acknowledged that systemic features, such as disparity of power and states' struggles for survival, were also influential. The avarice and materialism of both Romans and peoples ruled by Rome weakened the human fiber of society. But Gibbon identified as "the most potent and forcible cause of destruction, the domestic hostilities of the Romans themselves."[5]

Although describing not empires but great powers, Paul Kennedy singled out imperial overstretch as a cause of decline. He employed the notion not in some vague way as a state gobbling up more than it could digest, but in quantifiable terms as a state's rate of terrirtorial expansion that outpaces its rate of economic growth. Its level of industrial capacity generating material resources was particularly critical to whether a state succumbed to imperial overstretch:

> . . . The fact remains that all of the major shifts in the world's *military-power* balances have followed alterations in the *productive* balances; and further, that the rising and falling of the various empires and states in the international system has [sic] been confirmed by the outcomes of the major Great Power wars, where victory has always gone to the side with the greatest material resources.[6]

A country's industrial base was crucial, therefore, in helping it attain great-power status. Pursuing a metrocentric explanation, Kennedy also contended that disequilibrium between productive capacity and expanding great-power commitments would lead to a country's military weakening and hasten its decline:

> The history of the rise and later fall of the leading countries in the Great Power system since the advance of western Europe in the sixteenth century—that is, of nations such as Spain, the Netherlands, France, the British Empire, and currently the United States—shows a very significant correlation *over the longer term* between productive and revenue-raising capacities on the one hand and military strength on the other.[7]

In focusing on twentieth-century empires, Doyle adopted a multicausal explanation of their rise and fall: "The course of modern empire has been determined by changes in the character of the international environment, in the domestic society of the metropole, and in the development of social change and the balance of collaboration in the peripheries."[8]

Instead of examining great powers, some scholars have focused on world orders, that is, cycles in which interactions among states are stable. For Torbjorn Knutsen, five world orders are distinguishable: (1) a sixteenth-century Iberian one, (2) a seventeenth-century Dutch one, (3) an eighteenth-century British one, (4) a nineteenth-century British one, and (5) a contemporary U.S. one. As can be seen, each world order was headed by a system-managing great power. In a first phase, this great power enjoyed hegemony based on its economic, military, and especially normative strength, that is, the international consensus around the great power's value system. A second phase involved a challenge to the great power, and a third led to its decline, producing greater equality among states.[9]

The crumbling of a world order owes most, claims Knutsen, to sudden international conflicts that the hegemon was not prepared for—for example, Spain's war with England in 1739 and Russia's with England in 1854. An initial international loss of prestige led to dissent at home, a secondary factor that came to erode the power of the hegemon. For the author, in the latter part of the twentieth century, U.S. hegemony faced interstate (the Soviet nuclear threat, Vietnam, third-world revolutions) and world economic challenges (inflation in the 1970s), together with normative dissent domestically (the antiwar movement). But the United States recovered, largely due to the strength of its democratic values and its economy, and may be constructing a second world order. Knutsen's analysis of hegemons and world orders pays little regard to nations and nationalism as a catalyst for change. In contending that U.S. "citizens do not constitute an *ethnos* but a *demos,*"[10] he implies that at no time soon will ethnicity, race, or other forms of collective identity shake U.S. hegemony.

Yet the case of the collapse of the **Union of Soviet Socialist Republics (USSR)** underscores the importance of ethnicity and the nationalism based on it as factors producing change in a world order. Studying anticolonial and ethno-secessionist movements can help us understand why an empire is toppled and, with it, a world order.

## WHY DID ETHNIC CONFLICT OCCUR?

### Soviet Imperialism and Great Russian Nationalism

The disintegration of the Soviet Union raised a number of historical controversies concerning the nature of the communist system that Lenin had constructed. Three controversies are particularly relevant to the relationship between Soviet power and Russian nationalism. First, there has been considerable debate about whether the Soviet Union represented a mere variation of long-standing Russian imperialism or, to accept Soviet leaders at their word, it marked a departure from the imperial idea and a shift toward socialist internationalism. A second historical controversy is whether the Soviet period represented a sustained effort at the **russification** of non-Russian peoples (captured by the notion of *sliyanie,* or merger of cultural groups), or whether Soviet federalism provided significant cultural space for over 100 national groups. A third controversy is whether, despite the existence of an elaborate system of repression, non-Russians strongly opposed the Soviet state or whether they were so persecuted that a nationalist explosion could occur only once the Soviet center had lost its ability to govern.

We can shed light on all three issues by examining the character of the Soviet political system. There are important similarities and differences between the former Soviet empire and other empires.[11] The imperial thrust, evidenced in the conquest and acquisition of new territories, is a defining characteristic of all empires. Expansion of Soviet power into the Caucasus (then called Transcaucasia) in the early 1920s and into Central Asia in the late 1920s—even though indigenous socialist forces had already gained considerable power—testified to Soviet leaders' concern for ensuring Russian rather than mere communist control in peripheral lands. Hugh Seton-Watson caustically pointed out how "[t]he arguments of Soviet historians that the conquest of Central Asia by the Tsars was objectively progressive are essentially a Marxist–Leninist version of the arguments of Kipling."[12] As in the case of most imperial conquests, Seton-Watson was correct to emphasize how "the journey to 'socialism' of the Soviet type is a one-way trip: there is no return ticket."[13]

There were notable differences between the Soviet model of empire and other ones. Seton-Watson noted two points:

> The first is that the non-Russian peoples of the Russian Empire were very much more advanced in their general level of civilization than the peoples of the British colonies in Africa, and even than those of India.

The second is that the proportion of the metropolitan to the colonial peoples was quite different. The proportion of Russians to all non-Russians was about 1:1, and of Russians to Central Asian Moslems about 5:1, whereas the proportion of British to Asian and African colonial subjects was about 1:10.[14]

The Soviet empire was unique in ways other than the use of the ideology of socialist internationalism to justify Russian conquest and domination.

We come to the important question: Did Soviet interests coincide or conflict with the agenda of Russian nationalism? Some historians contend that Lenin became the founder of a new Russian dynasty disguised as national bolshevism. In this role, he was effectively a promoter of Russian national interests. But those skeptical about his Russian nationalist credentials questioned his—and other Bolshevik leaders'—*sang pur*. Lenin's "impure" origins included a maternal grandfather who had been Jewish, while early bolshevik leaders like Trotsky, Sverdlov, Kamenev, and Zinovyev were indisputably Jewish. The assumption by "authentic" Russian nationalists was that Jewish bolsheviks leaders could not be serving the country's national interests.

Neo-Stalinists claim that it was the native of Georgia—Stalin—who, paradoxically, accelerated Russian empire building.[15] The proof of Stalin's nationalist credentials was supposed to be his policy resulting in many non-Russian groups (Baltic peoples) being forcibly annexed, exiled (Tatars, **Chechens**), starved (Ukrainians), targeted for purges (Jews), or simply denied any semblance of political autonomy (the various federal republics). In the Stalin era and especially during World War II, expansionist-oriented tsars such as Ivan the Terrible, Peter the Great, and Catherine the Great were romanticized as builders of a greater Russia. To some, all of this constitutes compelling evidence that Stalin was the first communist representative of Russian nationalism.

If Soviet leaders were simply disguised Russian empire builders, they failed to russify conquered peoples. This is a characteristic the Soviet empire shares with the Ottoman or Habsburg empires, which also did not force the imperial language on subject peoples. The results of russification were poor, whether looked at in 1920, 1950, or 1990. In a book published in 1952 in the period of high **Stalinism**, one historian of Eastern Europe polemicized:

> A convincing proof of the invincible national oppositions against Soviet Moscow and of their strength lies in the fact that the Russian Communist Party faced in 1950 practically the same problems as in the late 20's. In Europe the "orientation to the West" of the non-Russian nationalities; in Asia Pan-Islamism, Pan-Turkism and Pan-Afghanism, offer encouragement to the national independence movements of the non-Russian peoples.[16]

Studies of language acquisition among non-Russians showed that non-Slavic peoples learned very little Russian, while Russians who lived outside their own republic (Russia was one of fifteen republics within the Soviet federative system) also infrequently picked up the language of their host region because they already enjoyed a privileged status across the Soviet Union. The absence of *parity bilingualism,* whereby Russians living outside Russia learned the local language, accentuated the grievances of other Soviet nations.[17] More consequential distortions were reflected in the overrepresentation of Russians in positions of political, economic, and military leadership.

But if the USSR was a Russian empire in disguise, there were features about it that were unsatisfactory to more ardent Russian nationalists. During the Gorbachev years (1985–1991), moderate Russian nationalists were more concerned about dismantling the ossified Soviet structure than they were about stripping non-Russians of their rights. By contrast, Russian ultranationalists lamented the failure of Soviet policy to have russified minority peoples. The most reactionary nationalist elements sought to exclude non-Russians from the Russian polity altogether, either through expulsions, as during Stalin's day, or through political and economic marginalization.

The new wave of Russian nationalism was at odds with earlier official Soviet nationality policy. It had championed the idea of a *sovietskii narod*—a Soviet nation—that would allow all nationalities to retain their formal cultural identities while injecting a socialist content and value system into them. Over time, this proved to be mere rhetoric rather than actual policy, and the Soviet Union failed to integrate not only the **titular peoples** (those nations after whom Soviet republics were named), such as Lithuanians, Georgians, and Uzbeks, but also second-order titulars (minorities within the Russian republic itself): Tatars, Chuvash, Bashkirs, and Mari in the Middle Volga region; Chechens, Balkars, and Karachai (all deported peoples) in the north Caucuses; and Yakuts, Buryats, and Tuvans in Siberia.

Some writers have argued that the failure to assimilate minorities was due to the nature of Soviet federalism rather than to communist malevolence. Gregory Gleason suggested that:

> Soviet national federalism has not produced a mobilizational conduit for political loyalties, shifting them first from ethnic group to republic, then from republic to the union, then from union to the larger international-ist community of man. On the contrary, Soviet national federalism has resulted in divided loyalties. In precisely this way, Soviet federalism has become an instrument by which ethnic identities are reinforced, aspirations for collective ethnic advancement are encouraged, and the visions of minority national futures are legitimized.[18]

A policy of russification would deny any measure of autonomy to national minorities and, indeed, "[a]ny American town has a larger measure of independence and self-government than a Soviet republic."[19] Russian nationalists had little reason to complain about too much decentralization of power in the former USSR. Whether the acculturation of minorities was aggressively pursued by Soviet authorities was, however, a different issue.

It does seem clear that when the Soviet center did try to linguistically assimilate nontitular nations—Jews, Crimean Tatars, Lithuanian Poles, Volga Germans—it largely succeeded. In addition, in a number of special cases, Soviet leaders used proxies to push for assimilation of smaller peoples. For example, Siberia's largest non-Russian minority, the Yakuts, were charged with assimilating the smaller minority peoples in the region. Therefore, russification was one of a number of forms of dominance employed by Soviet rulers to keep nationality groups in check. Soviet central authorities based in the Kremlin were usually successful whenever they bullied the weak, and it was this legacy that engendered ethnic conflict between Russians and others when the Soviet Union fell apart.

## Democratization as a Source of Ethnic Conflict

The Russian nationalism that emerged under Mikhail Gorbachev's leadership seemed on the surface to be inclusionary. It encouraged other nations to assert themselves, too, against highly centralized rule. In his first years in power, the agenda of reform—*perestroika* (restructuring) and *glasnost* (candidness)—overshadowed all other issues including, incredibly, the priorities of the 45 percent of the Soviet population that was not Russian. The major institutional changes envisaged by the reform-minded Gorbachev were unprecedented in the seventy-year history of the Soviet Union. Preoccupied with restructuring the system, he was dismissive about the threat posed by nationalist challenges to the Soviet system—even by its dominant nation, the Russians. The probability that a powerful Russian nationalist movement would emerge, that it would be led by a high-ranking Soviet apparatchik (Boris Yeltsin), and that it would then create a parallel set of political institutions (foreign ministry, interior ministry) in Moscow, in the shadows of the Kremlin walls where Soviet institutions were housed, remained a far-fetched scenario at the beginning of the 1990s. The unintended consequence of Gorbachev's liberalization policies was therefore unforeseen. As historian John Dunlop starkly put it: "Presumably the last thing that Mikhail Gorbachev wanted to accomplish when he took power in 1985 was to prepare the emergence of an independent Russian state."[20]

During the next five years, the issue of nationalism came to dominate politics in the USSR. In 1989 the Communist party leadership sought to remake Soviet federalism by investing republics with real political and economic responsibilities. But it ended up being stillborn, and the devolution of power that occurred was the result not of top-down policies but of **centrifugal tendencies** originating with titular and nontitular nations.

In April 1991, a new union treaty was drafted and submitted to the Soviet population for approval. While it was approved in those areas where the referendum was held, six Soviet republics refused to conduct it, rendering the overall result moot. Two months later, Yeltsin was elected president of the Russian republic in a general election. Unofficially he became leader of all nations struggling to free themselves from Soviet rule. In August, a coup attempt was staged in Moscow by hard-line communists to wrest power back from the ineffectual Gorbachev. When it was defeated, largely due to Yeltsin mobilizing the Russian republic's resources against it, it became clear that the USSR's days were numbered.

The three Baltic republics were now joined by the remaining twelve republics of the USSR in issuing declarations of sovereignty—by this stage, tantamount to full independence. To cobble together some unifying structure to replace the Soviet Union, eleven of these republics (the Baltic states and Georgia refused to take part in the negotiations) signed an agreement in December 1991 creating a **Commonwealth of Independent States (CIS)**. It recognized Russia as the legal successor to the USSR, giving it the place formerly occupied by the USSR on the UN Security Council and other international organizations, as well as sole inheritance of Soviet nuclear forces. When the Soviet military formally pledged allegiance to

Yeltsin as commander-in-chief and Gorbachev was forced to hand over nuclear codes to him later that month, all that remained was for the tricolored Russian flag of the tsars to be raised in place of the hammer-and-sickle flag over the Kremlin on Christmas.

## The Conflict of Identities

Scholars east and west have disagreed over the causes of the nationalities explosion that brought down the USSR. One explanation was to attribute the systemic crisis to mistakes committed early in the Soviet period. A one-time Gorbachev adviser asked observers to "look at the intense national feelings and hatreds that are erupting around the country. All these problems were created by the authoritarian past."[21] A political dissident noted: "We ourselves created this danger by trampling these republics, disregarding their national interests, culture, and language. Our central authorities planted the roots of the emotional explosion of national sentiment we are now witnessing."[22]

These views largely ignore the deep-rooted identities and attachments that were awakened among many nations as the Soviet Union veered toward collapse. But a focus solely on the overbearing Soviet center as the source of subsequent ethnic conflict was also reflected in much western literature. One comprehensive study of the nationalities question, *Soviet Disunion,* argued that Russian domination implemented through the Soviet state was responsible for nationalist unrest.[23] Russian specialist Timothy Colton, too, discounted the importance of grassroots nationalism in overthrowing the communist empire. In *After the Soviet Union,* he wrote:

> In sum, the Soviet Union's end was crafted, not by representatives of the state in concert with a political opposition and private groups, but by public officials alone, working for the most part behind closed doors. The compact reached was one *among governments,* meaning by this time the cooperating republic governments. Nongovernmental players were not welcome at the table and were informed of what had been decided only after the fact.[24]

Not all scholars were prepared to blame Soviet authoritarianism exclusively for nationalist awakening. In her seminal study of Latvia's road to independence, Rasma Karklins provided a nuanced analysis of the self-reinforcing processes leading to the establishment of new states. She distinguished among three types of ethno-political identities: the ethnic community proper, the territorial state, and the political regime.

> Although many theorists ask what economic, social, or other factors promote or assuage ethnic assertiveness, few examine the links between types of political regimes and types of ethnic politics. The Soviet experience suggests that regime type is crucial to whether nations want to identify with an established multinational state or seek to form new states.[25]

The author emphasized the multicausal character of the attack on the Soviet system. The struggle was over regime change and it, in turn, affected ethno-politics. Karklins asked, "Does it matter whether a multinational state—be it the former USSR or another state—is ruled autocratically or democratically, and if so how? Moreover, once a transition to democracy starts, does multiethnicity play a constructive or destructive role, and under what conditions?"[26] For her, a democracy could not be reconciled with an ethnic control system. As a corollary, empowerment of ethnic communities went hand in hand with empowerment of democratic forces.

The linkage between democratic and nationalist projects is clear from this analysis. Claus Offe conceptualized it somewhat differently as the "ethnification of the politics of transition."[27] Yeltsin's first term as president had exemplified how fusing democratic and nationalist objectives was good politics in the transition phase, but it became perilous politics subsequently when, each in their turn, more committed democrats and more determined nationalists each accused Yeltsin of betraying their cause.

Regime identity was an especially significant factor in the rise of separatist movements throughout the Soviet Union. The rejection of an identity based on the USSR brought democrats from many republics together in a common cause. They assisted each other's efforts to find new political and ethnic identities. Karklins concluded that, above all, "[t]he changing self-definition of Russians was crucial for the collapse of the USSR. During the late 1980s more and more Russians rejected a Soviet identity and opted for the self-rule of people and peoples."[28] This was because, "[f]or most Russian democrats and some traditionalists, any territorial state larger than the RSFSR became discredited due to links to Communist Soviet identity."[29] Mark Beissinger echoed this point: "The construction of a modern Russian identity could occur only on the basis of the deconstruction of the symbiosis between Russian and Soviet imperial identities."[30]

The unresolved nature of Russian national identity and its effect on Soviet nationalities policy (see Box 5.1) was taken up by historian Roman Szporluk. Russia's crisis of identity, he contended, was an important issue at the time of Lenin's seizure of power in 1917:

> Precisely because Russia itself had not yet resolved the key issues of its modern identity when the Bolsheviks won—the relations between state and society, between nation and empire—the same issues reemerged as Soviet power was disintegrating. In a real sense, among the post-Soviet nations facing the problem of nation and state building, the Russians are in a particularly difficult situation. They were used to being "the leading nation" in the USSR, but they were also an object of manipulation and a victim of political manipulation—their identity made and remade by the party.[31]

A key assumption made in the late 1980s by Russia's nascent democratic movement was that a nation oppressing others could not itself be free. Russian democrats came to believe that the separatist claims of non-Russian nations had to be treated as part of a broad movement toward participatory democracy. But by the mid-1990s, much of the idealism of the democratic movement had dissipated. When separatist movements in Russia proper arose, even democrats supported their suppression. The north Caucasus became a crucial testing ground for the collision between the national aspirations of non-Russians and a newfound democratic Russian nationalism that still could not fully let go of the country's imperial past. When in 1999, under former KGB head and recently appointed prime minister Vladimir Putin, the Russian military launched a brutal invasion and occupation of Chechnya, few Russian voices could be heard opposing it.

**BOX 5.1**

**Theorizing the Linkage Between the Soviet Internationalism Versus Russian Nationalism Conflict and Its International Dimension**

*Complementary Perspectives from Comparative Politics and International Relations*

**Soviet Versus Russian Conflict**

**1. Domestic factors**

Weakness of internationalist (Soviet) identity formation versus power of fusing democratic and nationalist aspirations

Russian imperial identity

Reactive ethnicity: Russian backlash at Soviet affirmative action program for minorities

Failure of coup attempt to preserve the Soviet Union

**2. International factors**

Ease of obtaining international recognition for state independence for anti-Soviet movements

International norm of recognizing constitutional and peaceful secessionist outcomes

**3. Conflict resolution**

Triumph of the principle of national self-determination in post-Soviet space

Failure to replace the USSR with a new supranational federation (Commonwealth of Independent States)

## Nationalist Mobilization in Post–Soviet Russia

Historian Walter Laqueur summed up the momentous impact on the Russian psyche that the collapse of the USSR was to have: "Three centuries of Russian history were undone in a few days in August 1991 as the result of the weakness of the center."[32] There could be no question, in his view, that the calamity of losing many Russian-ruled territories when the Soviet Union went out of existence would eventually produce a backlash in Russian society: "The breakup of the Soviet Union is the central event bound to shape the course of Russian nationalism and of Russian politics, as far ahead as one can see. It could be compared with the impact of the Treaty of Versailles (1919) on postwar Germany and with the loss of North Africa for French politics in the 1950s and 1960s."[33] The collapse of the USSR also produced a reaction in Russia's political elite. In 2005, President Vladimir Putin labeled the event as the greatest geopolitical catastrophe of the twentieth century.

The theory of reactive ethnicity can help explain why Russian nationalist mobilization occurred. It highlights the infiltration of a peripheral, subnational area by members of the dominant cultural group. A "cultural division of labor" results, thereby fomenting ethnic backlash. Russians were clearly the dominant nation in the USSR, and other peoples bridled at this fact.

But many Russians believed that it was *their* country that had been infiltrated by other nations—the Soviet Muslim republics, the peoples of the Caucasus, the indigenous groups of the Far East. These Russians came to the view that there were now too many non-Russians living in a purportedly Russian-dominated state. As a result, reactive ethnicity was palpable in Moscow, St. Petersburg, and above all in Russian provincial towns, not just in non-Russian regions.

Furthermore, lands considered historically Russian, such as the Crimea—indeed, most of Ukraine—as well as much of the Caucasus, were also viewed by Russian nationalists as having been infiltrated and stolen by other nations. On the streets of Almaty (Kazakhstan), Kiev (Ukraine), Chisinau (Moldova), Simferopol (Crimea), and Kazan (Tatarstan), a Russian backlash against the titular nationality coalesced. In 1991, most of the 25 million members of the Russian diaspora stranded outside the Russian Federation felt that they had become second-class citizens in traditional Russian lands. Reactive ethnicity, then, could apply to the status of a dominant nation that felt it was losing its dominance.

Russian ethnic mobilization can also be explained by the ethnic competition perspective. Under conditions of competition, "[e]thnic political mobilization is sparked when ethnic groups (dominant and subordinate) are forced to compete with each other for the same rewards and resources."[34] Of former constituent republics of the USSR, only Ukraine was demographically robust enough to pose a challenge to Russian dominance. But competition for centrally allocated resources can be viewed in relational as well as absolute terms. Russian nationalists raised the question of inequity: why were small and/or backward states apparently receiving more than their fair share of resources from the central government? These nationalists invoked the predatory behavior of many non-Russians. "Why do Estonians and Latvians, Armenians and Georgians enjoy higher standards of living than we do?" was a question asked more frequently.

This became the new *kto kovo* **question**—who is exploiting whom? Many Russians came to believe that they were being forced to compete for dwindling resources with smaller, undeserving nations. One writer traced Soviet economic stagnation to "the system of patronage inherent in the affirmative action programs which, in turn, led to the rise of regionally and/or ethnically based criminal networks that operated at the expense of the official economy."[35] Perceptions of unequal competition, therefore, helped fuel the nationalist tide within Russia. In turn, it led to ethnic countermobilization by many non-Russian peoples.

International relations expert James Rosenau has argued that most societies increasingly use performance criteria to evaluate their governments. He believed that the more this happened, the more patriotism and nationalism would decline, and "unabashed assertions of sovereign rights [would] diminish in frequency and intensity as adequate proof and appropriate performance [became] increasingly salient as criteria of national conduct."[36] Unfortunately, in the first decade of the new century, there was not much evidence—whether from western democracies like Italy or the United States, or personalist authoritarian systems like Russia or her politically shaky neighbors—that citizens *were* more concerned with performance rather than patriotism. In fact, adopting performance criteria when the performance is poor may exacerbate parochial or nationalist sentiments. Security specialist Jack Snyder has asserted that

> [t]he failure of some post-Soviet states to provide economic security may also galvanize nationalist reactions. This would be especially dangerous in Russia, where economic nationalists are politically allied with nationalists calling for the forceful protection of co-ethnics whose security is seen to be at risk in neighboring states. An economic depression sweeping

nationalists into office might, therefore, change not only Russian economic policy, but also foreign and military policy.[37]

In short, political leaders' nationalist assertion may be the performance criterion that much of the public values above all else. On this measure Putin scored very high.

## The Core Ideas of Russian Nationalism

Russian nationalists launched their drive for independence when they concluded that Sovietization had served to weaken rather than strengthen the Russian nation. But it would be wrong to deduce from the swiftness with which independence was achieved that Russian nationalists comprised a united group.

Historian John Dunlop identified the different groups that articulated versions of Russian nationalism, beginning with the early *perestroika* period.[38] These groups included liberal nationalists who renounced Russia's authoritarian past but took pride in its cultural achievements. Centrist nationalists were modern-day counterparts of nineteenth-century **Slavophiles**, proud of Russia's communitarian traditions, cautious about westernization, but avoiding xenophobia (a fear of foreigners). By the early 1990s, nationalists with more authoritarian platforms emerged to compete with democratic ones. A decade later, Putin, elected president in March 2000, put forward a nationalist program that blended Russian traditions of authoritarianism and imperialism.

Putin did not belong to the nationalist right, sometimes called the National Bolsheviks, who manipulated Leninism to achieve nationalist aims, nor was he as authoritarian and anticommunist a nationalist as Vladimir Zhirinovsky (discussed in the next section). A Russian nationalist who did not fit into any of these categories was former dissident Alexander Solzhenitsyn, a Nobel Prize laureate in literature. A longtime critic of the evil that the USSR had perpetrated on Russia, Solzhenitsyn not only attacked the nihilism of communist ideology but also praised the fundamental goodness of traditional Russian life: its spirituality, its innocence, its villages. He simultaneously criticized western civilization—its materialism, veniality, and misguided notion of political democracy that produced feebleness and naiveté.[39]

For Solzhenitsyn, Russia was not defined by an imperial mission; indeed, the West had been mistaken to equate Russia with the Soviet Union. "The word 'Russia' has become soiled and tattered through careless use; it is invoked freely in all sorts of inappropriate contexts. Thus, when the monsterlike USSR was lunging for chunks of Asia and Africa, the reaction the world over was: 'Russia', the Russians."[40] Stressing the importance of regaining inner spirituality, Solzhenitsyn made clear what paths post–Soviet Russia had before it: "The time has come for an uncompromising *choice* between an empire of which we ourselves are the primary victims and the spiritual and physical salvation of our own people."[41]

Russian nationalist empire builders were disappointed by Solzhenitsyn's views, but as an indication of how quickly politics changed in the early 1990s, his reservations about statehood for Kazaks, Ukrainians, and Belarusians came in for harsh criticism by nationalists in these countries when they attained independence in 1992. Solzhenitsyn held out hope that a voluntary union of Slav peoples could be formed among Russia, Ukraine, and Belarus. It would encompass the notion of *rossiiskii* (an older term was *rossiianin*) that subsumed ethnic Russians and related ethnic groups. The English language lacks an adequate term for this notion, but the word

*Russland* that exists in some other languages captures well its territorial dimension. The narrower idea of **russkii,** exclusively subsuming ethnic Great Russians, is embodied by the term *Russia*. A more appropriate spelling, for a multinational Russia, therefore, as Valery Tishkov contended, is *Rossia*.[42]

Solzhenitsyn's view on the new minorities in independent Russia—Chechens, Tatars, Siberian peoples—was that they needed to remain within Russia more than Russia needed to have them in the federation. Consequently he did not consider a multicultural Russia as necessarily good: "Even after all the separations, our state will inevitably remain a multicultural one, despite the fact that this is not a goal we wish to pursue."[43]

Solzhenitsyn's writings had little influence on nationalist circles in the chaotic conditions prevailing in post–Soviet Russia. But his views did reflect the contradiction many nationalists confronted:

> It is paradoxical that so many of the Russians who wish to see her borders expand should be unwilling to face the consequences of living in a multinational state. Instead, they have been dismayed to see recreated—even in the "truncated" Russian Federation—what from their point of view were the worst features of the USSR.[44]

## Russian Nationalists Resurgent

Solzhenitsyn represents a benign side of Russian nationalism. There are darker forces on the nationalist right that exert influence in Russian politics. Laqueur surveyed a variety of such forces. One was the monarchist movement, seeking a return to the Romanov tsarist dynasty. The most extreme right-wing monarchists were organized into *Zemshchina,* an antidemocratic group opposed to rights for minorities and religions other than Russian Orthodoxy. Supporting the nineteenth-century Romanov slogan of "Autocracy, Orthodoxy, Nationality," this group believed the role of ordinary citizens was to show subservience to the rulers. But the weakness of the monarchist movement lay in the fact that those Russians who held antidemocratic, autocratic sentiments were far more likely to support political dictatorship.

Another right-wing movement consists of the **Cossacks**. Romanticized in Russian literature as horseguards of the steppe who protect Russia's borders and conquer new lands, they were originally a mobile people of different ethnic backgrounds: Tatar, Turkic, Ukrainian. In the nineteenth century, Cossacks sometimes attacked minorities (such as the Poles) and carried out pogroms of the Jews. Not surprisingly, because of their close association with the brutality of tsarist rule, they were persecuted in the Soviet period. A Cossack revival began in the early 1990s. They lobbied the defense ministry to permit them to become border guards again, and Cossack units were subsequently legalized once again. In the Caucasus, especially Chechnya and Abkhazia (a breakaway region of Georgia), they played a pivotal role in supporting pro-Russian forces.

One of the first Russian right-wing organizations to emerge in the Soviet period was *Pamyat* (often translated as "Memorial"). Its initial innocuous goal was the restoration of Russian historic monuments and sites. With this platform *Pamyat* was able to curry the favor of well-known Russian poets, novelists, and filmmakers; even Yeltsin attended one of its gatherings. It undertook efforts to recruit the more nationalist elements of the Communist party, but in the Gorbachev years *Pamyat* became outflanked on the right by noisier, more outrageous groups like that headed by Zhirinovsky. As Laqueur wrote, "Seen in historical perspective the role of Pamyat was that of a precursor; it was the first in a field that later on became crowded."[45]

Russian nationalism is also found within the Orthodox church, revived at the end of the Soviet period. Laqueur highlighted its psychological dimension: "Most clergymen feel more at home with the nationalists than with the liberals. The nationalists will not constantly remind them of their past collaboration with the Communist regime and demand purges in their leadership."[46] Right-wing nationalists were initially attracted to the church as a distinctly Russian national institution, but many became disillusioned, having no interest in an alleged "Jewish" Old Testament; in mystic "theologians" such as Berdyayev, Bulgakov, or Florensky; or in spiritual redemption in the afterlife.

The canonization in 2000 of Nicholas II and his wife Alexandra as saints gave Orthodoxy added appeal. But a more significant event was Putin, after his inauguration as president in 2000, making the short walk through the Kremlin grounds to the Cathedral of the Annunciation for a thanksgiving service presided over by Patriarch Aleksii II. The Russian Orthodox leader prayed that Putin would "help us to disclose the soul of the nation."[47] Under Putin's leadership, the Russian Orthodox church has attained the status of de facto state religion. The ascendancy of the Orthodox church was captured by the bold statement made by Metropolitan Kirill, who was elected patriarch of the church in 2009: *Rossia-pravoslavnaia, a ne mnogokonfessionalnaia strana* ("Russia is Orthodox, not a multiconfessional country").[48]

In the West, Russian nationalism is most closely identified with one person, Zhirinovsky. As head of the misnamed Liberal Democratic Party, he obtained nearly 6 million votes in the 1991 presidential elections—"as many as all the people in Switzerland" in his words. Liberal Democrats were one of the three strongest parties in the state Duma following the legislative elections of 1993 and 1995. Zhirinovsky's populism, drinking, fistfights, outrageous statements (insults to women, to Islamic peoples, to Jews—though himself of Jewish background), and associations with heavy metal rock bands gave the ultranationalist right the outrageous publicity it craved.

Zhirinovsky has been described as a character out of Dostoyevsky and as a "holy fool" who regularly reappears in Russia's history. "Holy fools embrace self-humiliation and self-abasement, then get up from the dirt and present themselves to the world in their revealed spiritual beauty and power."[49] Zhirinovsky scandalized people with his obscenities while charming them with stories of his youth as an underpriviled child—"the smallest and the weakest, underfed, ugly, badly dressed, and often without shoes.... This ugly duckling grows up to be an equally ugly gander.... In videos, Zhirinovsky, displaying a hairy beer belly, drinks vodka and gesticulates exaggeratedly."[50]

Predictably, much of the respectable nationalist right disowned Zhirinovsky because his pronouncements—expose the Baltic peoples to radiation, drop nuclear bombs in the Atlantic to flood Britain ("the most barbaric country on the planet"), deport the Chinese population from Russia's Far East, regain Alaska, impregnate women to boost Russia's population—invited ridicule. His imperial agenda was encapsulated in the dream he described of one day seeing Russian soldiers washing their boots in the warm waters of the Indian Ocean and switching to year-round summer uniforms. In the Caucasus, he suggested using nuclear weapons against

Chechnya while he became personally engaged in supporting Abkhaz rebel leaders who broke from Georgia. One observer pointed to the suspicion with which much of the right views Zhirinovsky: "a dubious cheat, a traitor, the agent of a global conspiracy against the rebirth of Russia."[51]

Zhirinovsky's popularity peaked with the 1993 Duma elections, when his party captured 23 percent of the popular vote. He finished far behind the leading vote-getters in the 1996, 2000, and 2008 presidential elections (he did not even run in 2004). Still, he picked up 7 million votes (nearly 10 percent) in 2008 and became one of the deputy chairpersons of the state Duma.

In his study of the extreme right in Russia's twentieth-century politics, Laqueur identified the Russian tendency toward extremism. He acknowledged that "nationalism can still be a powerful force for the mobilization of dissatisfied and disadvantaged elements," but he added:

> There is the time-honored Russian tendency toward radicalism and extremism, toward pursuing an idea or ideal relentlessly, well beyond the confines of good sense. The Russians did take socialism, a political doctrine that elsewhere led to social democracy and the welfare state, and turned it into a nightmare. There is the danger that nationalism, an explosive force at the best of times, might fare similarly, fueled by hatred and selfishness and pursued at the expense of all other values, and become yet another monster.[52]

Our account of contemporary Russian nationalism's sources would be incomplete without reference to right-wing street violence in Russian cities. Fascist groups, often made up of skinheads, have organized and frequently targeted citizens from former Soviet republics, especially the Caucasus and Central Asia. In 2006, in a small town in the Karelian Republic, several Chechens were killed by a Russian mob in an outbreak of "interethnic violence." Some referred to the killings as Caucasian pogroms. The Russian government estimated there were about 60,000 members of skinhead groups in 2008, and the Moscow Human Rights Bureau claimed there had been well over 100 racially motivated murders in the country that year.[53] In December 2008, a gang of seven skinheads accused of murdering eighteen non-Slavic migrants in Moscow and posting videos of the crimes on the Internet received jail sentences. That day, racist groups rallied on the streets in their support. Such activity may appear more anarchic or criminal than political but, like the brownshirts in Nazi Germany, racist gangs can pose a political threat, especially if more savvy ultranationalist organizations decide to make use of them.

## Russia's New Minorities

At the time of Soviet collapse, many of Russia's minority peoples undertook concerted efforts to liberate themselves from rule by Moscow. Disturbances in Yakutia and the north Caucasus were among the first to demonstrate minorities' dissatisfaction at still being ruled by the Kremlin, whether it was inhabited by a communist or a democratic ruler. The 7 million Tatars, scattered throughout Russia and now its largest minority group, also became restless. The center of the Russian Federation seemed as remote from Tatars and Yakuts as before. During 1990–1991, most of the republics within Russia declared state sovereignty. These "sovereignty games" were intended to consolidate local rulers' positions as well as enhance the status of their republic within Russia. In rare cases, sovereignty declarations were intended for an international audience. Thus, addressing the Islamic world, Tatarstan asserted that it was the northernmost Muslim state in existence.[54] The rhetoric of sovereignty was largely instrumental, therefore. As we see below, Chechnya alone took the sovereignty game literally.

After 1991, the new minorities in Russia hoped for a fresh start in interethnic relations.[55] Some of them had distinct identities (Chuvash, Mari); others were sizeble (Bashkirs, Mordovians), counted on outside support for their cause (Chechens, Ossetians), or still possessed significant natural resources (Yakuts). The success of what might be termed the first round of self-determination movements in the former USSR had a demonstration effect on the new minorities, a number of which considered themselves equally worthy of full statehood. As Dunlop observed:

> Just as Yeltsin's idealistic vision of a future confederation [the Commonwealth of Independent States] had been rudely rebuffed by the other union republics, so did his model of a harmonious Russian federation encounter suspicion and outright rejection on the part of certain minority peoples of the Russian Republic, as well as by some ethnic Russians who began to push for full independence of their regions from Moscow. If Estonia could be fully independent, then why not, they argued, Tatarstan, Chechnya, or the Russian Far East?[56]

It was Chechen president Dzhokhar Dudayev's bid for independence that led to the most tragic case of ethnic conflict in the Russian Federation. It was punctuated by two Russian military invasions, in November 1994 and September 1999. In each case, Russian forces used air power and artillery indiscriminately, causing many civilian casualties and eliciting condemnation for human rights abuses by various international organizations. Both Yeltsin and Putin (Putin was elected to the presidency in large part because of the popularity of the campaign against Chechnya) backed Chechen puppets, which only exacerbated the conflict. The wars had all the appearance of a classic confrontation between the subnationalism of an upstart nation and the imperial nationalism of a humiliated great nation.

Russian nationalism alone, however, did not explain the decisions to carry out military intervention in Chechnya. Strategic considerations and national interest were important factors as well. Alternatives to attacking Chechnya existed; for example, Russia could have showed its contempt for the Chechen "gangster state" by expelling it from the Russian Federation. Let us review the Chechen nationalist challenge, the Russian response, and the international reaction.

## Russia and Chechnya

As the USSR crumbled in 1991, Chechen leader Dzhokar Dudayev joined with Soviet republics such as Ukraine and neighboring Georgia in proclaiming his nation's independence. Even though Gorbachev was still Soviet president, it was Yeltsin who, as president of Russia, had to tackle the problem of secession in his own country. Initially Yeltsin made a feeble attempt to impose martial law, but when that did not work, he opted for a policy of benign neglect of the region, until 1994. This three-year interlude provided Chechen forces with the time to stockpile a massive quantity of weapons, most purchased in shady deals with the Russian military itself. Clandestine Russian efforts in this period included planting a car bomb that narrowly missed killing Dudayev in 1994. The following year, Russians organized a puppet "Chechen" movement opposed to Chechnya's independence; it launched an unsuccessful military campaign on Dudayev's forces.

# Chechnya

Yeltsin's decision finally to invade Chechnya was explained in ways unrelated to a simple ethnic conflict: the need to keep the Russian Federation together; to demonstrate Russia's resolve; to show that the Russian military remained a cohesive fighting body; to create conditions for a declaration of a state of emergency that would allow Yeltsin to postpone the 1996 presidential elections; to distract attention from hyperinflation, unemployment, poverty, and general economic decline; to combat organized crime in the region; to maintain Russian control over the trans-Chechnya oil pipeline running from Baku on the Caspian Sea to Novorossiisk on the Black Sea; to sabotage an $8 billion oil contract between nearby Azerbaijan and a consortium of multinational oil companies that Russia questioned in terms of who had jurisdiction over the Caspian Sea shelf; to prevent the unification of Moslem peoples of the north Caucasus into a confederation of mountain peoples (as had happened in the early 1920s) that would be dominated by Chechen leaders in Grozny; to send a signal that a hard-line "war party" in the Russian government, made up of military, security, and industrial leaders, was now in charge of Russia's national security policy. Best-selling Canadian author Naomi Klein even suggested that the Russian invasion was intended to cause a national shock that would allow the Russian government to apply a neoliberal program favored by multinational corporations.[57]

Nearly all these reasons could also explain the decision to invade Chechnya again in September 1999, a decision attributed to both president Yeltsin *and* to his recently appointed prime minister and former Federal Security Services (the old KGB) chief Putin. For Yeltsin in 1994, most of these calculations backfired. His popularity had eroded, the military fell into disarray, and decision making proved chaotic. Chechen society became more nationalistic and militarized. Other minorities (as in neighboring Ingushetia) found even less appeal in remaining within a federation threatened with renewed authoritarianism and whose relations with the West were set back. And NATO's expansion into central Europe followed in 1999.

In 1999–2000, it was Putin who assumed responsibility for prosecuting the war against Chechnya, paying no attention to Russian casualty figures or human rights abuses. He was able to project the war as the start of Russia's return to great-power status, and most Russians, desperate for a political savior by 2000, gave him the benefit of the doubt. As much as we may criticize the brutality of the Russian forces in prosecuting this war, the resurgence of Russian power over the next decade can be traced back to Putin's anti-Chechen crusade.

The 1994 attack on Chechnya reversed a policy of settling disputes over autonomy between the central government and the regions through peaceful means. Tatarstan and Chechnya were the only republics that refused to sign the Russian Federation treaty. However, after hardheaded negotiations, Yeltsin and Tatarstan leader Mintimir Shaimiev signed an accord in 1994 granting that nation considerable autonomy. It secured sovereignty over its oil and other natural resources and obtained recognition for its self-proclaimed constitution and presidency, republican citizenship laws, and special rights for military service in the territory of Tatarstan. During the rest of 1994, Russia concluded similar treaties with the republics of Bashkortostan and Kabardino–Balkaria (the latter is next door to Chechnya).

The 1994 invasion of Chechnya was a caesura in Russia's relations with other nationalities. It demonstrated that Yeltsin had abandoned his policy of encouraging minorities to demand as much political autonomy from the center as they could manage. Until then, he was aware of the destructive dynamics of interactive ethno-nationalism. A notion used by Shantha Hennayake to study Sri Lanka (see Chapter 7), it refers to how majority nationalism is the principal cause behind minority ethnic nationalism.[58] According to this proposition, exclusionary policies toward minorities are invariably counterproductive and inclusionary ones are efficacious.

Pressured by Russian empire restorers, Yeltsin stopped pursuing the inclusive, accommodative policies toward minority nations exemplified in the 1994 agreements. He had turned to scorched-earth policies: on Grozny in 1995 and on Pervomaiskoye (a Russian village where Chechen rebels and their Russian hostages were shelled) in 1996. His inconsistency on nationalities issues was reflected in the succession of advisers appointed to counsel him on the subject. That he reluctantly accepted the conditions for an end to the war negotiated by his national security chief, then promptly fired him, further illustrated how much agonizing Yeltsin, other leaders, and indeed all Russian society had experienced in dealing with Chechen ethno-secessionism.

Putin, too, was part of a broad consensus in 2000 holding that Russian power had to be restored. On New Year's Day 2000, when he took office from Yeltsin, he flew to Russian-occupied Chechnya to award medals to Russian commanders. There he reiterated Russia's goal: "It is about putting an end to the breakup of the Russian Federation." The suppression of Chechnya was of a piece: tough-talking Putin also began to rein in the powers of other ethnic republics and of Russia's regions. If there was one message the new president was sending out across the Russian Federation, it was that the games of sovereignty and the agenda of secession were over.

## Chechen Ethno-secessionism

Russian nationalism cannot, by itself, be held accountable for the fierce wars fought in Chechnya since 1994. The basis for the conflict was Chechnya's ethno-secessionism. Its armed struggle against Russia in the nineteenth century, its unilateral declaration of independence in 1991, and its highly charged form of nationalism in the wake of Soviet collapse explain the confrontation with Moscow. Dudayev, a former Soviet Air Force general, was elected to the presidency by a council of clan elders with a mission to create an independent state of **Ichkeria** (the preferred Chechen name for the country).

While personal animosity between Dudayev and Yeltsin may have hardened this ethnic conflict, the Chechen leader was far from the gangster depicted in the Russian media. In Dudayev's view, the war in Chechnya "demonstrated to the world what the Russian leadership is capable of, and what direction it is headed in"—a statement that reverberates nearly two decades later. He imputed the cause of war to "the rapid nationalist shift in Russia's leadership" and called for UN intervention because the war was neither an internal Russian nor regional Caucasus problem, but a human rights tragedy. He appealed for international recognition of Chechnya.

Instead of a short victorious war, Russian forces suffered heavy casualties, even after their initial capture of Grozny and after the technologically sophisticated assassination of Dudayev in early 1996 (reports say that he was making a pre-arranged call to an international mediator in a remote part of Chechnya when a Russian military jet appeared overhead and launched a laser-guided missile at him). Chechen fighters took the fight to southern Russia, where they struck in the towns of Budennovsk and Kizlyar, taking hostages. Even so, no one seriously believed that the Russian army would be defeated militarily.

There were other reasons for Yeltsin to negotiate an early end to the conflict. Much of Russian society, exposed to graphic television coverage of the carnage in Chechnya, became opposed to the war effort and wanted to cut losses, even if it meant admitting defeat. Russia may have lost as many as 10,000 military personnel in combat. Some Russian leaders asked publicly whether it was worth fighting to keep Chechnya in the federation. They did not believe that Chechnya's independence would necessarily produce a domino effect felt throughout the country: "The centrifugal forces unleashed by the collapse of the Soviet Union have dissipated. The republics and states on Russia's fringes are seeking the security of closer ties with the center, not the freedom of more distant ones."[59]

In a surprise attack in August 1996, Chechen forces retook Grozny from the Russians. The pro-Russian puppet government and some Russian politicians claimed that the city had been deliberately surrendered to the rebels. The military debacle in Grozny, coupled with deep cuts in defense spending, demoralized the Russian army. Finding an honorable way to leave Chechnya seemed the only alternative. On August 31, at **Khasavyurt**, General Alexander Lebed, Yeltsin's security adviser, dramatically declared: "The war is over. That's it. Finished. We're sick of fighting." Acting largely on his own, Lebed signed an armistice agreement with one of the Chechen leaders, Aslan Maskhadov. By the end of January 1997, all of the more than 30,000 troops had left. The agreement also foresaw a referendum in Chechnya on independence in five years' time.

For the next few years, Russia's rulers sent mixed signals to Chechnya. For example, the Kremlin proposed turning all of Chechnya into a free economic zone on the model of Hong Kong. But the moderate post-Dudayev Chechen leadership was unable to assert full authority over its territory, thus allowing criminal gangs, kidnapping, and clan feuds to carry on. Islamic militants organized into conservative Wahabbi groups and began to infiltrate a neighboring republic of Russia, Dagestan. One radical warlord, Movadi Udugov, boasted that Chechens would help create an Islamic state from the Caspian to the Black Sea. Shamil Basayev, the most infamous of Chechen warlords, announced the creation of a government of an independent Islamic Dagestan and promised to expel all infidels from the north Caucasus. In August 1999, the Russians formally accused Chechnya of attacking its neighbor.

Over the next weeks, a series of bombs exploded in Moscow's largest mall, in apartment buildings in the capital, and in two other Russian cities. Some 300 people were killed. Putin blamed these attacks, too, on Chechen terrorists, although rumors persisted that Russian security forces had carried out the bombings in order to galvanize public opinion in favor of another war. On September 30, the full-scale invasion of Chechnya was launched.

The Russian army offensive that captured Grozny in February 2000 cost several thousand casualties (the Russian leadership proved more skillful this time in censoring and providing disinformation to the media). The total Russian casualty figure in the Chechen wars, including guerrilla attacks, may have reached 10,000 by 2009. The overall Chechen death toll, including the years of "pacification" after 2000, was closer to 100,000. Nearly one half of the 1.3 million Chechen population became refugees in neighboring republics. The Russian leadership advanced a ready-made excuse for the human suffering that accompanied the war: NATO had done just the same in Kosovo less than a year earlier.

In June 2000, President Putin appointed Akhmad Kadyrov, a disaffected Chechen spiritual leader opposed to independence, as head of the pro-Kremlin civilian administration. He presided over a dubious constitutional referendum in 2003 that affirmed Chechnya's status as a Russian republic and had himself elected president that year. In 2004, however, he was killed by a bomb blast in Grozny—part of a terror campaign by Chechen insurgents that had been preceded by hostage taking in a Moscow theater that had resulted in the deaths of hundreds of people. In late summer 2004, two Russian passenger planes were blown up simultaneously by Chechen women suicide bombers, closely followed by another hostage taking in a school in the Russian town of Beslan, which led to hundreds more deaths. Rebel Chechen leaders even took credit for the sinking of Russia's nuclear-powered submarine, the *Kursk*, and the fire that caused serious destruction to Moscow's Ostankino television tower, in 2000.[60]

In 2005, two Chechen resistance leaders, former president Maskhadov (elected in 1997 when Chechnya was not occupied by Russian forces in what international observers called a generally fair election) and warlord Basayev (who claimed to have organized the Beslan assault) threatened further attacks on Russia. Within a year, both had been killed by Russian security forces. The conflict in Chechnya had tilted in favor of Putin and the Russians.

Some human rights officials claim that, since 2000, tens of thousands of Chechens have disappeared and many others tortured. There are regular reports of anti-Russian terrorist attacks, not just in Chechnya but in the neighboring republics of Dagestan and Ingushetia. Pro-Russian strongman Ramzan Kadyrov (son of the assassinated president) began to employ his presidential security service forces as an instrument of counterterrorism. But historical grievances, continued repression, extreme poverty, a warlord culture, and different Islamic strategies suggest that Chechnya's struggle against Russian domination is not over.

## INTERNATIONAL REACTION

We have observed how, in a remarkably short time after 1991, the internal affairs of the USSR were transformed into international relations among fifteen new states. According to Barry Posen, the breakdown of an empire and the accompanying disappearance of a hegemonic power have traditionally produced anarchy in the international system:

> In areas such as the former Soviet Union and Yugoslavia, "sovereigns" have disappeared. They leave in their wake a host of groups—ethnic, religious, cultural—of greater or lesser cohesion. These groups must pay attention to the first thing that states have historically addressed—the problem of security—even though many of these groups still lack many of the attributes of statehood.[61]

The security interests of Russia, the fallen hegemon, were of greatest concern to the international community. As the long-standing anchor of order and stability in Eurasia and as a nuclear superpower, the task of ensuring Russia's sense of security and helping it make the transition to a more democratic capitalist state was of particular importance to the West. What was the role of the United States, the Soviet Union's long-standing adversary, in the process of Soviet disintegration and the emergence of Russia as an independent state?

In late 1991, then U.S. secretary of state James Baker toured many of the Soviet republics and announced five principles that the United States supported and that should govern relations in the region: (1) a peaceful process leading to self-determination of Soviet peoples, (2) respect for existing internal and external borders, (3) support for democracy and the rule of law, (4) protection for human rights, and (5) adherence to international law and treaty obligations. Thus, while the nationalist movements that had mobilized across the USSR had diverse origins, statehood for the republics was to be decided upon by established international rules and norms, with the United States playing an important role as adjudicator.

These norms were stacked against international recognition of breakaway states. Once the USRR had disintegrated into fifteen pieces, the West was cautious about lending support to independence struggles within these new states. Whether it was Chechnya and Tatarstan within Russia, Abkhazia and South Ossetia within Georgia, the Armenians of Nagorno-Karabakh in Azerbaijan, Trans–Dniester and Gaugazia in Moldova, or Crimea in Ukraine, almost all states in the international system abided by the principle that this "second round of ethno-secessionist demands" was purely the internal affair of the new states.

In the case of Chechnya, there was mild rebuke by western states of Russia's violation of human rights in its conduct of the war. But no reference was made to Russia's violation of the *group rights* of the Chechen people. The international response to Chechen ethno-secessionism was therefore one of feigned concern. The practical consequence of such a response was that the battlefield would determine the winner of the struggle, and the West would stay out. Thus, at the height of the 1999 Russian invasion of Chechnya, the United States made clear that it continued to support the Blue Stream project, by which Russia piped natural gas through the Caucasus (Azerbaijan and Georgia) to Turkey. War in the Caucasus was not seen as grounds for disrupting trade between Russia and the West.

The regional reaction to the Chechen conflict is also important to consider. Meeting in the Ingushetia capital of Nazran in 1996, the leaders of eight republics and the regions of the north Caucasus endorsed the Khasavyurt Accords, though they expressed concern about the domino effect on the region if Chechnya did secede from Russia. In particular, if Chechnya became an independent state, the issue of how to draw new international borders would be contentious. Chechnya's borders had been repeatedly redrawn in the Soviet period. First, Stalin merged Chechens and Ingush into a single territory in 1934. Then in 1944, he deported the Chechens and created different administrative units in the Caucasus. Finally in the mid-1950s, after Stalin's death, Chechens returned to their homeland and to new borders.

Three of Chechnya's borders are contentious. First, Chechnya's rebel leaders claim a larger territory, one extending beyond the present western border with Ingushetia. Second, Chechnya makes irredentist claims on parts of Dagestan to the east. The Khasavyurt district just on the border is inhabited primarily by Chechens; in addition, the Aukhovsky district was Chechen-settled until the 1944 expulsions. Third, the northern border with the Stavropol district in Russia itself is in dispute. Russian settlement spills over from Stavropol into northern Chechnya, especially into the historically pro-Russian Nadterechny district. If Chechnya had become independent, current regional territorial disputes would become future international border conflicts, with a high potential for third-party intervention.

## NONINTERNATIONALIZATION OF THE CHECHEN CONFLICT

In 1970, Soviet dissident Andrei Amalrik published a seminal book called *Will the Soviet Union Survive Until 1984?* It presented a scathing critique of the Soviet system, but it also contained an oblique attack, recognized by few readers at that time, on Russian empire builders. Amalrik wrote: "I have no doubt that this great Eastern Slav empire ... has entered the last decades of its existence. Just as the adoption of Christianity postponed the fall of the Roman Empire but did not prevent its inevitable end, so Marxist doctrine has delayed the break-up of the Russian Empire— the third Rome—but it does not possess the power to prevent it."[62] Thus, Amalrik anticipated not only the breakup of the USSR as a result of nationalist movements such as those in Russia, Ukraine, and the Baltic states, but also the rise of separatist forces, such as the Chechens, within Russia itself.

Spillover of ethnic conflict inside Russia into the international arena can occur as a result of increasing instability in a region, tempting outside parties to intervene. The disintegration of the USSR provided new opportunities for regional states to expand their influence. Indeed, Turkey, Iran, and Afghanistan were lured into the politics of Central Asia.; none, however, has become involved in the Caucasus. Indeed, a Kremlin source disclosed that only four foreigners had been captured in Chechnya during the fighting in 1999–2000.[63] The level of tangible international (in particular, Islamic) support for the Chechens was therefore exaggerated.

Reasons that states become involved in an ethnic conflict in another country are numerous. They may have affective links to one of the parties, ranging from ethnic solidarity with another state's minority to irredentist claims on the other state. In the case of Chechnya, however, there is no other ethnic (as opposed to religious) group that has *affective* ties to the Chechens, so third-party intervention on these grounds has been ruled out. Beyond that, "[r]arely ... will affective concerns prompt action without fears relating to security and loss of geopolitical advantage."[64] Accordingly, intervention based on *instrumental* concerns entails a state's pursuit of its own national interests, which include the interrelated issues of national security, balance of power, and geopolitics. Russia had the strongest instrumental reasons to intervene in its breakaway republic.

A third party that *has* played an important role in the Caucasus is Islam, a resurgent transnational religious force that also frequently dictates political agendas. It is indisputable that the Islamic world has both affective and instrumental ties to Chechnya. There are 4 million Muslims in the north Caucasus and another 15 million in the Russian Federation. Although most mosques and *medrese* ("seminaries") were shut down in the Soviet period, Muslims of the north Caucasus, especially those living in mountainous areas, continued to adhere to Sufi brotherhoods. The collapse of Soviet power provided an opportunity for the "re-Islamization" of the region as people searched for a new identity. While one possible identity was ethnically crosscutting, stressing the common bonds found in the **Umma** (Muslim community), another type of reidentification was based on ethno-religious fusion, where to be Chechen was to be Muslim. Applying this latter type of identification, the Russian–Chechen wars cannot be reduced to the clash of Christianity and Islam, but instead they reflect respective Russian and Chechen variants of them.

In the wars with Russia, Islam became the ideology of the Chechen resistance. Rebels declared a *jihad* ("holy war") and attacked Russian positions shouting *Allahu akbar!* ("God is great"). Yet when Dudayev declared an Islamic state in 1991, it had little appeal to the Chechen population, partly because of some Soviet-era success in fashioning a secular, agnostic way of life there and partly because Islam came late to Chechnya—in the nineteenth century, compared with southern Dagestan, where it was introduced by the Arabs in the seventh century. Dudayev himself did not set out to politicize the Muslim faith and repeated how "Russia forced us into Islam."

When Russia started the war in 1994, Islam quickly gained many new supporters in Chechnya. Islam became their distinguishing marker. It had already served as the ideological adversary of Russian Marxism and now of Russian Orthodoxy, and it was embraced by Chechens because of the logic of resistance. **Shariat** courts based on the teachings of the Qur'an operated in rebel-controlled territory throughout the 1990s, and a new legal code that followed the Shariat replaced the Russian criminal code.

Broader Islamic solidarity led to isolated support by militant Islamic groups for the Chechen cause. Fighters were recruited from Saudi Arabia and other Persian Gulf states. The number was low compared with the thousands of fighters—many of them professional and well equipped—from the Islamic world who took part on the Bosnian Muslims' side in the war with Serbia. Only one state recognized Chechnya's independence—Afghanistan in 2000, itself a rogue state under the fundamentalist Taliban. Chechen commander Basayev refuted claims that Osama bin Laden, blamed by the United States for financing terrorist attacks around the globe, had given aid to the Chechens. But Russian officials insisted that Islamic militants from abroad, including groups connected to al-Qaeda, had infiltrated the republic.

No countries in the Caucasus stood to gain from siding with the Chechen separatists. Although independent Georgia had a mountainous border with Chechnya, transportation and communication links were limited. The Georgian government was bogged down with Russian-supported secessionist movements on its own territory. Instability in Chechnya presented an opportunity to weaken Russia, but when Georgia, under a pro-Western leader tried in 2006, Putin quickly took countermeasures to bring it into line.

Ethnic conflict can be internationalized in conditions when a group is spread over more than one state but forms a majority in none. Any ethnic strife arising in one state may therefore spill over to another. Borders in the north Caucasus do not coincide with ethnic divisions, so spillover of conflict from one republic to another is probable, as we see with Ingushetia. But Russia's brutal invasions of Chechnya had a demonstration effect on other republics, and its swift retaliation for Chechen involvement in Dagestan in 1999 was a singular lesson for all the peoples of the Caucasus.

Internationalization of ethnic conflict occurs when a dominant group in one state is separated from conationals that form a minority in another. Chechens had few conationals anywhere: some ethnic kin did live in neighboring republics and others resided in Moscow, but after the 1999 apartment bombings, many were expelled from the city. Clearly in the Chechnya case, this scenario was tangential.

One other way that ethnic disputes may be internationalized is through terrorism. In 1996, Dudayev threatened to spread political terrorism to western Europe if it continued to ignore Russia's military intervention in the republic. Another threat was to set off a nuclear device in Moscow; as supposed evidence of their ability to do so, at one point, a Chechen group left radioactive material in a Moscow park. Although terrorist acts, especially hostage taking, have taken place, ethno-political violence has generally been limited to the clash of armies and militias.

We should note that, for Chechen rebels, as for most secessionists, the conflict with Russia was fundamentally an international one. Referring to a different case, Karklins made the point that "[s]ome ethnic conflicts are internationalized; in Latvia an international conflict has been 'ethnicized.'"[65] Some Chechen leaders would argue that the same applied to their country. By contrast, the Kremlin sometimes depicts the conflict in ethnic terms, as a majority group fighting a rebellious minority one; more often, it refers to the conflict as merely a campaign against terrorists and bandits.

In summary, the international system has conveniently ignored neoimperialist tendencies emerging in Russia. International actors such as the **Organization on Security and Cooperation in Europe (OSCE)**, the International Monetary Fund (IMF), and the **Council of Europe** have regularly chided Russia for human rights violations, believing that the best way to civilize the country is through its incorporation in western structures. Because of the balance of power in Europe, no country has wanted to become militarily involved in Russia's ethnic conflicts (though Poland allowed Chechens to establish an information bureau in the country). Ethnic conflicts in Russia have not become internationalized, but the reasons for this may provide more grounds for pessimism than optimism (see Box 5.2).

On the other hand, the wars in Chechnya were the object of considerable efforts at third-party mediation. As a general rule, third-party conflict management initiated by a regional actor can escalate rather than reduce conflict, rendering it more complex and intractable.[66] Yet managing conflict early is of utmost importance: it will determine "whether a conflict relationship is expressed through acts of violence and hostility, or whether it produces a more fruitful form of interaction...." Conflict management efforts need to devise "a range of mechanisms to limit the destructive effects of a conflict and increase its potential benefits."[67]

---

**BOX 5.2**

**Theorizing the Linkage Between the Russian Nationalism Versus Chechen Ethno-Secessionism Conflict and Its International Dimension**

*Complementary Perspectives from Comparative Politics and International Relations*

### Russia Versus Chechnya Conflict

**1. Domestic factors**

Distinct (primordial) character of identities among nations of the Caucasus

Construction of a Russian imperial identity versus instrumentalist use of Chechens' Islamic identity

Chechen historical grievances

**2. International factors**

Transnational Islamic religious ideas (but not the existence of ethnic kin)

International norm of nonintervention in a state's internal affairs

**3. Conflict resolution**

Use of scorched-earth and counterterrorism strategies

International acquiescence to the use of force as a means of resolving a domestic conflict

Impotence of diplomacy

Two international organizations in Europe that are well placed to assume a conflict management role are the OSCE, a pan-European body consisting of more than fifty states, and its Office of the High Commissioner on National Minorities. Shortly after the USSR's collapse, when wars over sovereignty and borders seemed imminent, the OSCE established peace-keeping operations in three former Soviet republics: Georgia (3,000 peace keepers in Abkhazia), Moldova (5,000 peace keepers in the Trans–Dniester Republic), and Tajikistan (where most of the 20,000 non-Tajik troops were Russian). The objectives of these OSCE missions were to negotiate peaceful settlement to conflicts, to promote respect for human rights, and to build democratic institutions and a legal order. Notably absent from OSCE operations was Russia, which preferred peace keeping in the region to be entrusted to the CIS (the organization set up by Russia after the Soviet collapse that was envisaged to be a post-Soviet confederation of independent states).

As early as 1994, the UN Security Council supported CIS deployment of peace-keeping troops in Georgia's breakaway region of Abkhazia. Under Chapter VIII of the UN Charter, member states are enjoined to make every effort to settle local disputes peacefully through regional arrangements. For the first time, the UN sanctioned a CIS-organized peace-keeping force. The caveat was that the troops sent to Abkhazia were Russian. The danger arose that the Kremlin would use its peace-keeping forces to regain control over Georgia and other new states, using the CIS as cover. Indeed, by 1995 Russia's combined "peace-keeping" strength in Abkhazia, Tajikistan, Moldova, and Azerbaijan (alongside a bilateral agreement with Belarus) had reached about 100,000 troops.

Russian diplomats countered that in Abkhazia and elsewhere, Russia was acting at the request and with the consent of the parties to the conflict. Perhaps because of the OSCE umbrella under which it was operating, Russian peace keepers at first discouraged Abkhazian separatists from declaring independence from Georgia. But as relations with the Georgian government deteriorated, Putin began to encourage Abkhazian separatist ambitions.

Following the Russian invasion of Chechnya in 1994, the OSCE established a permanent mission in Grozny. Its delegation, calling itself the Assistance Group, set itself up as a facilitator between the warring sides, but Russian leaders did not trust the OSCE because of the contacts its representatives had with the Dudayev group. Monitoring of human rights was often obstructed by Russian officials. In turn, the Chechens were upset that the OSCE called separatist forces "rebels" and did not recognize Chechen independence.

When the Russian army launched its next invasion in 1999, the OSCE chairperson, Kurt Vollebaek, made repeated efforts to visit the war-torn region, but Putin was able to delay his arrival. The OSCE at times acted timidly and even indirectly encouraged Russian actions: in late 1999, at the height of the Russian onslaught on Grozny, the OSCE summit held in Istanbul declared that its members "fully acknowledge the territorial integrity of the Russian Federation."

Other international governmental organization (IGO) heads condemned Russia's excessive brutality. These included Kofi Annan, United Nations secretary general; Mary Robinson, United Nations high commissioner for human rights; Michel Camdessus, director of the IMF; and Chris Patten, European Union (EU) commissioner for external affairs. A chorus of western leaders including U.S. president Clinton, French president Chirac, British prime minister Blair, and German chancellor Schroeder, added their criticism of Russian heavy-handedness. The U.N.

Commission on Human Rights adopted a resolution in 2001 condemning egregious human rights violations by Russia's forces. That same year, the United States acknowledged that it had opened diplomatic contacts with the rebel Chechen foreign minister, prompting a sharp rebuke from Moscow. In 2005, an American television network carried an interview with rebel leader Basayev, again incurring Kremlin wrath. The following year Alexander Dugin, a leading member of the Eurasian circle, which holds that Russia's identity is defined as much by its Asian expanses as by its European territories, contended that the Caucasus is at the heart of U.S. strategy to cripple Russia while simultaneously creating a pro-American "Greater Middle East." In place of international mediation of the Chechen conflict, Russia and the United States seemed headed for a more direct confrontation in the Caucasus. This finally took place in August 2008 in Georgia.

## THE INTERNATIONALIZATION OF ETHNIC CONFLICT IN GEORGIA

Nobel Peace Prize winner and Soviet dissident Andrei Sakharov once described Georgia as "a little empire." Though supportive of national independence movements after Soviet disintegration, he was critical of the ultranationalist policies pursued by Zviad Gamsakhurdia, first president of post-independence Georgia in 1991–1992. His slogans of "Georgia for the Georgians" and "one state one nation" were directly aimed at disenfranchising sizable, territorially concentrated minority groups in this south Caucasus republic—Abkhazian, Adjars, Ossetians—as well as smaller minorities who had ethnic kin in their own independent states—Armenians, Azeris, Greeks, and Russians. At a time when, across former Soviet territories, the principles of devolution of power, cultural autonomy, self-rule, and minority rights were being glorified, Gamsakhurdia viewed the administrative autonomy enjoyed by Abkhazia and South Ossetia as relics of the Soviet system and moved to eliminate them (see Box 5.3).

## Georgia

*Source*: Courtesy of the University of Texas Libraries, The University of Texas at Austin.

---

**BOX 5.3**

**Theorizing the Linkage Between the Georgian-Versus-Minorities Conflict and Its International Dimension**

---

*Complementary Perspectives from Comparative Politics and International Relations*

**Georgian State Versus South Ossetia/Abkhazia Breakaway Republics**

**1. Domestic factors**

Construction of a Georgian imperial identity by Georgian leadership supported by Georgian autocephalous Orthodox identity

Construction of distinct Abkhaz and Ossetian ethnic identities

Ethnicization of interstate conflict between Russia and Georgia

**2. International factors**

U.S. political and military backing for Georgia

Russian political and military support for South Ossetia and Abkhazia

International norm of the territorial integrity of a state and the refusal to recognize breakaway states' sovereignty

**3. Conflict resolution**

Battlefield outcome

---

Ethnic conflicts in post-independence Georgia were fanned by the chauvinism of its first president—a counterpart to Serbia's ultranationalist Slobodan Milosevic. The nationalist majority in the Georgian parliament was eager to support him:

First, it passed a law making Georgian the sole official language, a measure blatantly discriminatory toward the republic's non-Georgian minorities. Later in 1989, it banned parties that operated only "regionally" from participating in general elections in the Georgian republic, a transparent ploy to disenfranchise Abkhazian and South Ossetian voters. In 1990, as the Ossetians moved toward secession from the soon-to-be-independent republic of Georgia, a newly elected Georgian parliament, led by Gamsakhurdia, simply revoked their autonomous status altogether. In March 1991, Gamsakhurdia banned Georgians from voting in Gorbachev's USSR-wide referendum on preserving the Soviet Union. The Abkhazians defied this ban and organized their own balloting for the referendum, while Gamsakhurdia held a separate vote on Georgia's secession from the USSR. Some 90 percent of Georgians voted for independence, and the Abkhazians voted even more overwhelmingly to preserve the union—which they saw as the only guarantor of their autonomous rights—and, notably, were joined by large majorities of all the region's other non-Georgian peoples as well.[68]

Political differences overlapped with ethnic and linguistic ones, therefore. Sectarian ones also were salient: Georgians had their own autocephalous Orthodox church. Abkhazians (a minority of whom was Sunni Muslim), Ossetians, and

Russians, of course, were Orthodox, too, but they were organizationally separate. The patriarch of the Georgian Orthodox church felt at liberty, then, to insult ethnic minorities, even though the majority was Orthodox Christian.

Paradoxically, the major non-Orthodox minority in Georgia, the Adjaris, about half of whom are Muslim and whom Gamsakhurdia had disparaged as "Tatardom," ended up avoiding armed conflict. It helped that their spoken language and written alphabet were similar to Georgian. More important in keeping the peace in Adjara was the impact of the so-called **Rose Revolution** in 2003—a populist movement that organized demonstrations in the capital, Tbilisi, and succeeded in bringing a young American-educated, anti-Russian leader to power. Shortly after becoming president, Mikheil Saakashvili hailed Gamsakhurdia (who died at the end of 1993) as a great Georgian patriot and nationalist, in this way legitimating renewed efforts to impose central authority in Adjara. He successfully deposed the region's corrupt and autocratic leader, then passed a law reducing its political autonomy. Emboldened by these successes, Saakashvili then demanded the removal of a large Russian military base in Batumi. Having no contiguous friendly territory through which to resupply the base (other than by way of the Black Sea), the Russians pulled out in 2007 and handed the base over to Georgian forces. This seamless process gave the Georgian president every reason to believe he could repeat the success and force Russian troops out of Abkhazia and South Ossetia.

But these two breakaway regions *were* different. The Russian military had intervened on their side in the early 1990s when all of Georgia was caught up in a civil war pitting militia leaders against each other. In Abkhazia, about 200,000 ethnic Georgian residents had been driven out and were permanently displaced. With Putin's support it, and South Ossetia, had become de facto separatist enclaves for fifteen years—before Saakashvili was to turn his attention—and artillery—on them in 2008.

Georgia's ethnic makeup was an invitation to third-party intervention from the outset. The Rose Revolution was the first in a series of public, supposedly spontaneous mobilizations in various countries that aimed at overthrowing traditional authoritarian regimes with populist prowestern—and invariably pro-American—ones. Ukraine's Orange Revolution followed in 2004, Kyrgyzstan's Tulip Revolution occurred the next year, as did Lebanon's Cedar Revolution. The Bush administration, which had launched its invasion of Iraq just months before the first of these revolutions, claimed that these spontaneous events had confirmed that its policy of democracy promotion was bearing fruit. A more sinister view, particularly resonant in the Kremlin, was that the Bush administration's own imperialist agenda was taking shape. Encirclement of Russia was one of its pivotal cornerstones.

President Saakashvili was an ardent advocate of Georgia's admission into NATO and had invoked the resurgence of Russian nationalism, manifested in its intervention in the north and south Caucasus, as the main reason to accelerate membership talks. But at a NATO meeting in April 2008, his hopes had been dashed when four of the EU's largest countries—France, Germany, Italy, and Spain—came out against a fast-track process, thereby revealing their disagreement with the United States. Saakashvili needed a crisis with Russia to regain the initiative, and retaking Georgia's pro-Russian breakaway regions—especially when the world's attention was focused on the Beijing Olympics—seemed a high percentage strategy for rallying the West around his cause.

Evidence suggests that the shooting war began when Georgian artillery bombarded the South Ossetian capital of Tskhinvali in early August 2008. Given that there was an enormous mismatch in Georgian and Russian firepower, and that South Ossetians would clearly side with Russia against Georgia, the question arises why Saakashvili gambled on a surprise attack. Full-scale military combat lasted five days before a ceasefire was signed. During that short time, Saakashvili spoke several times with U.S. vice president Dick Cheney, even as the Russian army poured through the breakaway states and occupied Georgia itself. Russia's ambassador to the United Nations observed: "It is hard to imagine that Saakashvili embarked on this risky venture without some sort of approval from the side of the United States."[69]

President Putin, in turn, charged the Georgian leader with genocide and demanded a war crimes tribunal, modeled on the Yugoslav one, be set up to try him. He suggested that Saakashvili deserved the same fate as Saddam Hussein. The Russian and Georgian presidents were known to despise each other: former U.S. ambassador to the U.N. Richard Holbrooke put it colorfully: "It's about a tiny man from the big country and a big man from the tiny country."[70] Putin is five feet six, almost a full foot shorter than Saakashvili.

Putin prevailed. By the end of the month, as Russian forces began to withdraw from Georgia proper, he had recognized the independence of Abkhazia and South Ossetia, lost forever to Georgia, a fact that he emphasized. A Russian military analyst put Russia's ambitions candidly: "It's impossible to imagine a weak Russia in the Caucasus."[71] One despondent Georgian opposition leader attacked Saakashvili for creating a state of siege in the country from the first day of his rule. "I don't want to live in the new Caucasian Israel," he inveighed.[72]

Third-party mediation that ended the conflict quickly was provided by French president Nicolas Sarkozy, who at the time was also rotating EU president (see Box 5.4). With OSCE backing, he concluded a ceasefire agreement that required all parties to the conflict to return to their prewar positions. But bilateral agreements between Russia, on the one hand, and "independent" Abkhazia and

---

**BOX 5.4**

**Theorizing the Linkage Between the Georgia-Versus-Russia Nationalist Conflict and Its International Dimension**

*Complementary Perspectives from Comparative Politics and International Relations*

## Georgia Versus Russia Conflict

### 1. Domestic factors

Personal animosity between political leaders

Clash of imperial identities of the two states

### 2. International factors

Role of Russia's "international peace-keeping Force" in the region

EU disagreement over recognizing Georgia's effort to restore territorial integrity versus applying norm of nonuse of force

### 3. Conflict resolution

Third-party diplomatic mediation (by then EU as well as French President Sarkozy)

Refusal of key third parties (NATO, the United States) to intervene

South Ossetia, on the other, provided the legal cover for Russian troops to bolster their presence in these regions. The Russian government also refused to extend beyond the end of 2008 the OSCE mission in Georgia, which had first been set up in 1992.

To deepen Saakshvili's losses—and those of the Bush administration, which had supported him so strongly (it is thought that during the war, Russia made off with five years' worth of American military equipment sufficient to have made Georgia into a NATO-compliant force)—a NATO summit in December 2008 opted for intensified NATO–Georgia dialogue rather than designing a membership action plan (MAP) for the country's admission into NATO. Western powers seemed more interested in establishing a *modus vivendi* with a resurgent Russia than in backing Georgia's insistence on respect for its national sovereignty and territorial integrity.

## Conclusion

Nationalism was both cause and effect of the collapse of the Soviet empire. The reawakening of a nation's historic identity—in particular, of Russia's—can contribute to the breakup of an empire (see Box 5.1). Equally important is the demonstration effect on the other nations who are not designated as the legal successors to the empire. These smaller nations may feel that dominant–subordinate relations are being reproduced in a new form. They soon discover, as the Chechens have, that the international community is not prepared to support so-called second-round nationalists in their struggle against central authority, however just their cause may be or however much suffering they have endured at the hands of the imperial center.

While elite discourse in Georgia after independence also emphasized a return to imperial identity, its problem was that control over the ethnicities it sought to rule over in the Caucasus was contested—by Russia. Even enlisting the support of a superpower that was led at the time by George W. Bush could not help Georgia, as a "little empire," match up evenly with a resurgent Russia.

The international normative regime discourages tampering with the state system, even one whose membership numbers were expanded in the early 1990s following the breakup of the Soviet empire. Post 9/11 *realpolitik* has further stacked the deck against recognizing an Islamic insurgency like that in Chechnya. But it also discriminates against authentically pro-Russian ethnic mobilization, as was the case in Abkhazia and South Ossetia. The major benefit Russia obtains from the international normative regime, as currently reconfigured, is noninterference by outside actors in its declared sphere of influence. This is an advantage that Russia, under Medvedev and Putin, can parlay further to its advantage.

## Discussion Questions

**1.** What are the main causes given by historians for the collapse of empires? Has nationalist assertion on the part of subjected peoples represented an important factor?

**2.** Was the Soviet Union a Russian empire in disguise? Did it successfully russify non-Russian peoples? Were the interests of Russia promoted by the Soviet system of government?

3. Describe the different forms that Russian nationalism has taken from the 1990s onward. Which forms are threats to Russia's fledgling democratic system? To Russia's minorities? Which types are compatible with western liberalism?

4. What were the reasons for Russian military intervention in Chechnya in 1994 and 1999? What type of identity did Chechen rebel leaders embrace? What identity did Russians ascribe to Chechens?

5. Describe international reaction to the 1999–2000 war in Chechnya. Did the Chechens receive outside help? Which major international organizations were prepared to offer mediation?

6. Make the case for treating the 2008 war between Georgia and Russia as a case of the ethnicization of an international conflict. Were Georgian leaders' nationalist policies responsible for driving Abkhaz and Ossetians into the Russian camp? What type of policy on minorities could have led to a restoration of Georgia's territorial integrity?

## Key Terms

centrifugal tendencies
Chechens
Commonwealth of
   Independent States
   (CIS)
Cossacks
Council of Europe
empire
Ichkeria
imperialism
Khasavyurt

*kto kovo* question
matrioshka nationalism
metrocentric theory of
   empire building
Organization for Security
   and Cooperation in
   Europe (OSCE)
pericentric theory of
   empire building
Rose Revolution
*rossiiskii*

*ruskii*
russification
Shariat
Slavophiles
Stalinism
systemic theory of empire
   building
titular peoples
*Umma*
Union of Soviet Socialist
   Republics (USSR)

## Notes

1. John Strachey, *The End of Empire* (New York: Frederick Praeger, 1966), p. 325.
2. Ibid., p. 340.
3. Michael W. Doyle, *Empires* (Ithaca, N.Y.: Cornell University Press, 1986), p. 123.
4. Ibid., p. 125.
5. Edward Gibbon, *The History of the Decline and Fall of the Roman Empire,* Vol III, David Womersley, ed. (New York: Allen Lane, 1994), Chapter LXXI, p. 1073.
6. Paul Kennedy, *The Rise and Fall of the Great Powers: Economic Change*

   and Military Conflict from 1500 to 2000 (New York: Random House, 1987), p. 439.
7. Ibid., p. xvi.
8. Doyle, *Empires,* p. 353.
9. Torbjorn L. Knutsen, *The Rise and Fall of World Orders* (Manchester, England: Manchester University Press, 1999), pp. 1–8.
10. Knutsen, *The Rise and Fall of World Orders,* p. 298.
11. For one comparison, see Richard L. Rudolph and David F. Good, eds., *Nationalism and Empire: The Habsburg Monarchy and the Soviet*

*Union* (New York: St. Martin's Press, 1992).

12. Hugh Seton-Watson, *The New Imperialism* (Totowa, N.J.: Rowman and Littlefield, 1971), p. 135.

13. Ibid., p. 133.

14. Ibid., p. 131.

15. Walter Laqueur, *Black Hundred: The Rise of the Extreme Right in Russia* (New York: Harper Perennial, 1994), pp. 156–157.

16. Roman Smal-Stocki, *The Nationality Problem of the Soviet Union and Russian Communist Imperialism* (Milwaukee, Wis.: Bruce Publishing Company, 1952), p. 260.

17. Rasma Karklins, *Ethnopolitics and Transition to Democracy: The Collapse of the USSR and Latvia* (Washington, D.C.: Woodrow Wilson Center Press, 1994), p. 152.

18. Gregory Gleason, *Federalism and Nationalism: The Struggle for Republican Rights in the USSR* (Boulder, Colo.: Westview Press, 1990), p. 135.

19. Stephan Kux, "Soviet Federalism," *Problems of Communism,* March–April 1990, p. 1.

20. John Dunlop, *The Rise of Russia and the Fall of the Soviet Empire* (Princeton, N.J.: Princeton University Press, 1993), p. 3.

21. Fyodor Burlatsky, in Stephen F. Cohen and Katrina vanden Heuvel, eds., *Voices of Glasnost* (New York: W.W. Norton, 1989), p. 195.

22. Lev Karpinsky, in Stephen F. Cohen and Katrina vanden Heuvel, eds., *Voices of Glasnost* (New York: W.W. Norton, 1989), p. 303.

23. Bohdan Nahaylo and Victor Swoboda, *Soviet Disunion* (New York: Free Press, 1990), p. xii.

24. Timothy J. Colton, "Politics," in Timothy J. Colton and Robert Legvold, *After the Soviet Union: From Empire to Nations* (New York: W.W. Norton, 1992), p. 21.

25. Karklins, *Ethnopolitics and Transition to Democracy,* p. 9.

26. Ibid.

27. Claus Offe, "Ethnic Politics in East European Transitions," paper for conference on European Nationalisms, Tulane University, New Orleans, April 1994, p. 2.

28. Karklins, *Ethnopolitics and Transition to Democracy,* p. xviii.

29. Ibid., p. 48.

30. Mark B. Beissinger, "Elites and Ethnic Identities in Soviet and Post-Soviet Politics," in Alexander J. Motyl, ed., *The Post-Soviet Nations: Perspectives on the Demise of the USSR* (New York: Columbia University Press, 1992), p. 150.

31. Roman Szporluk, "Introduction: Statehood and Nation Building in Post-Soviet Space," in Szporluk, ed., *National Identity and Ethnicity in Russia and the New States of Eurasia* (Armonk, N.Y.: M.E. Sharpe, 1994), p. 6.

32. Laqueur, *Black Hundred,* p. x.

33. Ibid., p. 276.

34. Charles Ragin, *The Comparative Method* (Berkeley: University of California Press, 1987), p. 136. Examples of the ethnic competition approach include Michael Hannan, "The Dynamics of Ethnic Boundaries in Modern States," in Hannan and John Meyer, eds., *National Development and the World System* (Chicago, Ill.: University of Chicago Press, 1979), pp. 253–277; François Nielsen, "Toward a Theory of Ethnic Solidarity in Modern Societies," *American Sociological Review,* 50, 1985, pp. 133–149. The resource mobilization view is described in Charles Tilly's magisterial *From Mobilization to Revolution* (Reading, Mass.: Addison-Wesley, 1978).

35. Kurt Nesby Hansen, "Continuity Within Soviet Nationality Policy:

Prospects for Change in the Post-Soviet Era," in Miron Rezun, ed., *Nationalism and the Breakup of an Empire: Russia and its Periphery* (Westport, Conn.: Praeger, 1992), p. 15.

36. James N. Rosenau, *Turbulence in World Politics* (Princeton, N.J.: Princeton University Press, 1990), pp. 435–436.

37. Jack Snyder, "Nationalism and the Crisis of the Post-Soviet State," in Michael E. Brown, ed., *Ethnic Conflict and International Security* (Princeton, N.J.: Princeton University Press, 1993), pp. 95–96.

38. John Dunlop, "The Contemporary Russian Nationalist Spectrum." *Radio Liberty Research Bulletin,* December 19, 1988, pp. 1–10.

39. Aleksandr Solzhenitsyn, *Warning to the West* (New York: Farrar, Straus and Giroux, 1979).

40. Aleksandr Solzhenitsyn, *Rebuilding Russia: Reflections and Tentative Proposals* (New York: Farrar, Straus and Giroux, 1991), pp. 5–6.

41. Ibid., p. 11.

42. Valery Tishkov, *Ethnicity, Nationalism and Conflict in and After the Soviet Union* (London: Sage, 1997). The distinction approximates that in the case of the United Kingdom between *English* and *British*.

43. Solzhenitsyn, *Rebuilding Russia,* p. 19.

44. Dixon, "The Russians," p. 61.

45. Laqueur, *Black Hundred,* p. 221.

46. Ibid., p. 243.

47. John Anderson, "Putin and the Russian Orthodox Church: Asymmetric Symphonia," *Journal of International Affairs* (September 2007).

48. Metropol Kiril, "Rossia—pravoslavnaia, a ne mnogokonfessionalnaia strana," *Radonej,* 8 (2002).

49. Mark Yoffe, "Vladimir Zhirinovsky, the Unholy Fool," *Current History,* October 1994, p. 326.

50. Ibid.

51. Graham Frazer and George Lancelle, *Absolute Zhirinovsky: A Transparent View of the Distinguished Russian Statesman* (New York: Penguin Books, 1994), p. xxxii.

52. Laqueur, *Black Hundred,* p. xi.

53. "Russian Gang Faces Murder Charge," BBC News (June 30, 2008), at http://news.bbc.co.uk/2/hi/europe/7482125.stm.

54. See John W. Slocum, "Sovereignty Games in the Russian Federation," paper prepared for the ISA–West Annual Meeting, October 20, 1995, University of Colorado, Boulder.

55. Regions of Russia also demanded more devolution of powers from Moscow. Some demanded the same powers as the ethnically determined republics, and in a few, separatist tendencies even emerged. Because they are not ethnically driven, we do not consider such movements here.

56. Dunlop, *The Rise of Russia and the Fall of the Soviet Empire,* p. 63.

57. Naomi Klein, *The Shock Doctrine: The Rise of Disaster Capitalism* (New York: Metropolitan Books, 2007).

58. Shanta K. Hennayake, "Interactive Ethnonationalism: An Alternative Explanation of Minority Ethnonationalism," *Political Geography,* 11, no. 6, November 1992, pp. 526–549.

59. "Yeltsin's Vietnam?" *The Economist,* February 10–16, 1996, p. 52.

60. The Chechen website, which has extended Russian-language and more limited English-language reports, is www.kavkaz.org.

61. Barry R. Posen, "The Security Dilemma and Ethnic Conflict," in

Michael E. Brown, ed., *Ethnic Conflict and International Security* (Princeton, N.J.: Princeton University Press, 1993), p. 104.

62. Andrei Amalrik, *Will the Soviet Union Survive Until 1984?* (New York: Harper and Row, 1970), p. 65.

63. "Are Foreigners Fighting There?" *The Economist*, July 8–14, 2000, pp. 51–52.

64. Stephen Ryan, *Ethnic Conflict and International Relations* (Aldershot, England: Dartmouth, 1990), p. 36.

65. Karklins, *Ethnopolitics and Transition to Democracy*, p. 133.

66. For evidence, see David Carment and Patrick James, eds., *The International Politics of Ethnic Conflict: Theory and Evidence* (Pittsburgh, Pa.: University of Pittsburgh Press, 1997).

67. Jacob Bercovitch, "Third Parties in Conflict Management: The Structure and Conditions of Effective Mediation in International Relations," *International Journal*, 40, no. 4, Autumn 1985, pp. 736–737.

68. Robert English, "Georgia: The Ignored History," *New York Review of Books*, 55, no. 17, November 6, 2008.

69. Vitaly Churkin, quoted at http://afp.google.com/article/ALeqM5iqi9FuxxzlQbV9-dL-kcNtRqylSQ.

70. Wendell Steavenson, "Marching Through Georgia," *New Yorker*, December 15, 2008, p. 65.

71. Sergey Markedonov, quoted in Steavenson, "Marching Through Georgia," p. 70.

72. Erosi Kitsmarishvili, quoted in Steavenson, "Marching Through Georgia," p. 66.

# CHAPTER 6

# Separatist Movements in Constitutional Democracies: Canada and Quebec Nationalism

## INTRODUCTION

Why is it that some separatist movements produce violent confrontations between dominant and minority groups and others do not? What are the factors that can lead to the successful secession of a nation disenchanted with an existing political system? What are the conditions—domestic and international—that can impede successful secession? Specifically, do constitutional democracies make it easier or more difficult for a group to break away from the parent state? These are issues we explore in this chapter.

There is probably no greater contrast in recent times between constitutional and coercive efforts to attain sovereignty than the respective cases of Canada and Yugoslavia.[1] Indeed, some scholars would challenge the essential "comparability" of the two cases. Cultural differences between North America and the Balkans, divergent historical paths leading from the Westminster model of democracy and that of socialism, the relative newness of the Canadian confederation contrasted with the supposed "ancient curses" that have set Balkan peoples against each other for a long time, and differing stages of social and economic development can explain the respective peaceful and violent approaches taken to challenging federations. While the wars of Yugoslav secession received much attention from world leaders, the constitutional impasse in Canada has become, for many informed observers, a one-night drama—when the results of the Quebec referendum on sovereignty, held in October 1995, showed how close Canada had come to fracturing.

In theory the constitutional road to independence may pose a more serious danger to the integrity of states than simmering ethnic wars. Especially in established western liberal democracies such as Canada, Britain, Belgium, and Spain, nationalist movements that can demonstrate at the ballot box that they have the support of a substantial majority of "their" people may build strong cases for proceeding with separation.

The problem for such movements is that it is not easy winning the votes of nationalists in competitive elections from other political parties that may boast of a prestigious past, mobilize an enormous bureaucracy, or dispose of political patronage. Frustrated by the "traps" that democracy can spring, some nationalist movements break with the electoral process and turn to the use of force to achieve their objectives. While it has not come to that in Scotland or Catalonia, Basque separatists in Spain encompass separate political and military organizations. The military wing of the ETA (*Euzkadi Ta Askatasuna,* or Basque Fatherland and Liberty), the most militant separatist group, has carried out political assassinations and bombings. By contrast, the political wing of the ETA (*Herri Batasuna*) has become more engaged in the Spanish electoral system and stressed political means of separation. An even more moderate group, the Basque Nationalist Party (PNV), which exercises power in the Basque lands, is committed to nonviolence. Spanish democracy has tried to blunt Basque separatist ambitions, channel them into parliamentary means, and divide the nationalist movement. Democracy can provide a real **political opportunity structure** for separatists to create a broad political movement. But it can also effectively accommodate and weaken ethno-separatist groups.

To examine the dilemmas of separatism's challenge to democracy and democracy's challenge to separatist movements, this chapter considers the evolution of nationalism in Quebec and its near-success in 1995 in obtaining majority support for separation from English Canada. In Quebec—as in Yugoslavia, Czechoslovakia, the Soviet Union, and Ethiopia—a separatist movement emerged from the failure to construct enduring, crosscutting identities based on a federal system. Only in Canada and Czechoslovakia were ethno-secessionist challenges largely devoid of violence. In Czechoslovakia, it was elite consensus that in 1993 produced the split of the federation into two separate states. In the case of Canada, breakup would occur only as a result of an electoral verdict because all parties are committed to respecting a fair referendum outcome.

We need to understand, therefore, what type of response a democratic federal state should make to a centrifugal challenge. The appeal of cultural explanations for why nationalism becomes or does not become violent—the most famous is the survival of ancient ethnic hatreds—needs to be complemented by reasoned explanations focusing on the institutionalized interaction between parent state and would-be breakaway movement. It is, after all, the acceptance of rules of the game that distinguish a democracy. When outcomes stemming from these rules are contested and an aggrieved party resorts to violence, then the focus on rules has to be replaced with one on political culture.

# WHY IS THERE CONFLICT? SOURCES OF QUEBEC NATIONALISM

Quebec nationalism, and the sovereignty movement engendered by it that first took power in the province in 1976, is based primarily on historical grievances, territorial rights, and cultural defense claims. Indeed, the majority of those opposed to Quebec secession do not question that the French constitute—together with the First Nations of Indians and Inuits, as well as the British—a founding nation. But Canadian federalists—those opposed to the breakup of the country and therefore to

Quebec's separation—do challenge the argument that French speakers have historically not been treated as equals in Canada.

Recorded European involvement in Canada began in 1534 when Jacques Cartier landed in the Gaspé Peninsula and claimed the land for the king of France. The first settlement was established by Samuel de Champlain in 1608, but little French colonization followed. In 1666, the non-native population was barely 3,500. France was weakened by wars with England, and her possessions in the New World were vulnerable. By the Treaty of Utrecht in 1713, New France (as Canada was called at the time) had to surrender Acadia (parts of today's New Brunswick and Nova Scotia), Newfoundland, and lands around Hudson Bay to Britain.

## British Colonization

English domination of North America was the result of massive English-speaking colonization of the New World, overwhelming the few French settlers. At about the time of the battle on the **Plains of Abraham** in 1759, 65,000 French settlers faced 1 million English colonists. Britain's greater interest in the colonies was also reflected in its decision to send the Royal Navy to North America. By contrast, the government in Paris seemed indifferent to the fate of its possessions. It was entirely predictable, then, that British forces led by General Wolfe would defeat the French army commanded by General Montcalm on the plains overlooking Quebec City. As with other nations' historic defeats—the loss of the Alamo to Santa Ana's army in 1836, the defeat of the Serbs by Turkish armies on Kosovo Field in 1389, or the heroic battle waged by Zulu warriors against the British in Ulundi in 1879—"the Conquest" became etched in the minds of generations of French Canadians, or *Canadiens.*

British colonization policy was neither consistent nor ruthless. The 1774 Quebec Act reinstated the borders of New France, and British governors strengthened the power of the large French landholders, or *seigneurs,* and of the Catholic church hierarchy, seeing them as allies against the type of popular democratic revolution that was breaking out in the thirteen colonies. The Constitutional Act of 1791 divided the British colony in North America into two provinces, Upper (Ontario) and Lower (Quebec) Canada, each with a governor and legislative assembly.

These postconquest institutional arrangements were meaningful enough to have English and French communities join forces—together with Native American tribes both within and outside Canada—in beating back the American invasion of 1812. The War of 1812 was the first manifestation of an emerging pan-Canadian national identity, and it was based, as it has been ever since, on a common unwillingness among those living above the forty-ninth parallel—a long stretch of the Canadian–U.S. border—to become American. James Madison's boast that the conquest of Canada was "a mere matter of marching" thus helped deepen loyalty to Canada.

Over time, rivalry between the dominant English merchant class of Lower Canada, living almost exclusively in Montreal, and the French population scattered throughout the rest of Quebec, grew. In 1837, a French nationalist movement, the *Patriotes,* staged a revolt in Montreal. The rebellion was crushed by British forces, and political oppression of the *Canadiens* followed.

Of special symbolic importance to the historical grievance claim made by contemporary Quebec nationalists is the "Report on the Affairs of British North

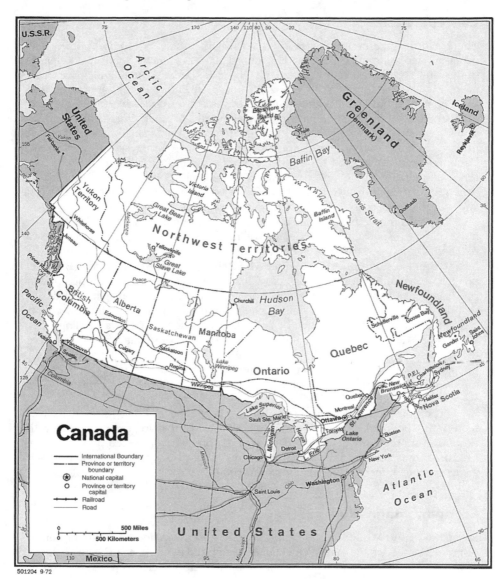

501204 9-72

America," written by British Governor General Lord **Durham** and published in 1839. Seeking to avoid a repeat of the 1837 rebellion, he advanced the idea of responsible government for all of Canada, together with the recommendation that French speakers should be forced to assimilate into English culture. To achieve these twin goals, he proposed a legislative union of Upper and Lower Canada that would have erased the political autonomy and cultural identity of French Canada. Lord Durham resigned after five months as governor general and his report was never implemented. But his anti-French report remained implanted in the minds of French Canadians thereafter.

## Confederation

The political uncertainty caused by the Durham report, combined with a deep economic recession in Lower Canada, induced 500,000 French Canadians to emigrate to the United States, mostly to New England states, between 1840 and 1900. Others moved to the Canadian west and established small French-speaking communities, as in Manitoba, but French settlement in the western territories was discouraged by English Canadian leaders. The threat to the survival of French Canadian culture was never as great as in the mid-nineteenth century. Although a small nationalist movement demanded full independence for Lower Canada, progressive liberal French Canadian leaders decided to join talks about creating a new federal union. The renewed threat from the United States, seemingly intent on punishing British North America for England's sympathy toward the South during the United States Civil War, made negotiations to form a Canadian union urgent.

A conference was convened in Charlottetown, Prince Edward Island, and after much debate, especially over federal–provincial power sharing, a compromise was reached. On July 1, 1867, a confederation of Canada was created—a sovereign state having the status of a British dominion. The **British North America Act (BNA Act)** of that year enumerated the powers of the federal government and those of the provinces. Even though Canada was nominally a confederation, which indicated that the provinces were to enjoy far-reaching autonomy, in practice the new country was a federation, with its central, or federal, government in Ottawa holding extensive powers. For more than a century since, most provinces (but especially Quebec, the successor to Lower Canada) have fought for decentralization of power. Another question about the confederation pact, often posed by those seeking Quebec sovereignty, is, How was Canada cobbled together without popular approval being sought, as through a plebiscite?

The constitutional procedures that led to the act of confederation have affected the political process ever since. Demands for greater powers for the provinces are regularly made at meetings of the premiers of the ten provinces.[2] Just as Canada was constructed through constitutional means, Quebec nationalists seek to deconstruct it through constitutional procedures.

## Economic Stagnation

From 1867 up to World War I, Ontario experienced a sustained industrial boom, as did much of the United States. Quebec, however, did not.[3] French Canadian society remained largely agrarian, and the all-powerful Catholic clergy wished to keep it this way. The strategy of *survivance* (survival) of French Canadian culture was shaped by the church, but it had its own institutional interests: it wished to retain its monopoly over education, welfare, and other social services rather than share it with government institutions. French Canadians were encouraged to have large families as part of the strategy of *survivance* and historians wrote of *la revanche des berceaux*—the revenge of the cradles. But if demographic growth helped keep a culture alive, it did nothing to empower it.

The assimilation of more and more immigrants from Europe into anglophile society produced a worsening ratio between French and English speakers. The growth of Montreal as an economic center simultaneously represented the growth of a powerful English community isolated from francophone Quebec. Up to the late

1960s, socio-occupational mobility in Quebec was only possible through integration into the English-speaking business community.

If French Canadians seemed resigned to being second-class citizens, it had much to do with "the old nationalism" of French Canadians in the first part of the twentieth century. In the view of McGill University political philosopher Charles Taylor,

> The old nationalism was defensive; it was oriented around the defense of a way of life that was held already to exist but was in danger of being, if not submerged, at least undermined by the more robust North American culture alongside which it lived. It was meant to defend a civilization based on a set of values, mainly the religious values of a certain interpretation of Roman Catholicism and the linguistic values of the ancestral language. It was feared that these values would ultimately lose out to the North American values of material progress, of wider communication, of the cult of achievement.[4]

## Conscription Crises

The sense of backwardness, of persecution, and of forming a society under siege was exacerbated by the call to arms issued by the Canadian government on two occasions early in the twentieth century. From 1899 to 1902, Britain was at war with the Afrikaner Dutch Calvinist settlers in South Africa, who had proclaimed two free states. Urged on by British empire builder Cecil Rhodes, the Canadian government agreed to send troops to help the British defeat this minority. For many French Canadians, however, the Boer War did not involve Canadian interests, and it set an ominous precedent: launching an attack on a minority that sought political autonomy. They were aware that Quebec, even with its limited provincial autonomy, could become the next target.

For somewhat different reasons, French Canadians balked at fighting in World War I. British participation in the war constitutionally forced its dominions (sovereign states that did not have powers in foreign policy matters) to go to war. Contending that they could not identify with king and country when these were British, French Canadian leaders organized an anticonscription movement.

In 1932, the Statute of Westminster finally gave the Canadian government control over its foreign policy. Nevertheless, when Britain declared war on Germany in 1939, Canada again was at war too, not as one of the Allies, as the United States or the Soviet Union were to become, but directly on behalf of the British government. Another anticonscription movement, bolstered by pacifist sentiments in Quebec society, welled up in the province.

## Disputed Borders

A territorial dispute also brought into question whether the treatment of Quebec within Canada was fair. In 1927, the Judicial Committee of the British Privy Council awarded Labrador, a vast territory situated on the Canadian mainland, to Newfoundland—then a British colony (it became a Canadian province in 1949). New France had first obtained the territory by statute in 1774. In 1809, it was annexed by

Newfoundland, but in 1825, it was returned to Lower Canada. The Judicial Committee's ruling was based on a 1763 commission giving Newfoundland jurisdiction over "the coasts of Labrador." The British lords considered that the word *coast* did not mean a one-mile-wide strip of land along the seashore but instead a more remote watershed line that in places extended 200 miles inland from the shoreline.

Quebec was not even permitted representation in this legal dispute between Canada and Newfoundland, but it was the main victim. The manner in which the territorial award was made worried many Quebecers. Neither they nor Newfoundlanders lived in great numbers in Labrador; consequently the catalyst of so many ethno-secessionist conflicts—claims of rival ethnic groups to the same territory—was nonexistent. When in 1999, Newfoundland's official name was changed to Newfoundland and Labrador, there was barely a protest from Quebec. Irredentism plays no part in Quebec nationalism. But the threat of another partition of Quebec, should it choose independence, is taken seriously by nationalists.

## Society in Transformation

Major social and economic changes took place in Quebec during the interwar period. The proportion of Quebec's production accounted for by the agricultural sector fell from 37 percent in 1920 to 10 percent in 1941. By contrast, manufacturing increased in this period, from 38 percent to 64 percent. Even though the Quebec economy expanded, the balance of power between federal and provincial governments, set out by the 1867 BNA Act, shifted further to the central government.

The interwar period produced the intellectual father of the Quebec sovereignty idea, Lionel-Adolphe Groulx. This Catholic priest was drawn to the notion of an autonomous French Canadian, or "Laurentian," state. It seemed to him the best form of defense of francophone culture and language and, of course, the Catholic religion in an increasingly Anglo-Saxon Protestant-dominated world of business.[5]

After World War II, power in Quebec was concentrated in the hands of a conservative, proclerical, and generally corrupt government. At the same time, the ethnic makeup of Quebec was radically transformed by massive immigration at the end of World War II. On arriving in Montreal, most immigrants spoke neither English nor French. Most were unaware of how Quebec constituted a distinct society within Canada. Most assumed that it was as natural to opt for English in Quebec as elsewhere in North America. In making this choice, immigrants were encouraged by the disinterest that francophone authorities displayed.[6] A second wave of European immigrants in the late 1950s, numerically spearheaded by Italians, also chose integration into English society. This was to lay the groundwork for a nationalist backlash that shifted the relations of ethnic power in Quebec.

## The Quiet Revolution

A **Quiet Revolution** began in Quebec in 1960 when the Quebec Liberal Party (QLP), led by Jean Lesage, was elected to power. Spawned in part by a francophobe Canadian prime minister, John Diefenbaker, from rural Saskatchewan; by the spread of French-language television; and even by the 1959 Cuban revolution that brought a nationalist, Fidel Castro, to power, the Quiet Revolution accelerated institutional and societal changes. It also made Quebec sovereignty a plausible alternative. In 1960, the Movement for National Independence (*Rassemblement pour l'Independance*

*Nationale* [RIN]) was formed, and it produced a number of future sovereigntist leaders (and even a handful of terrorists).

The BNA Act had made education a provincial government responsibility, but in Quebec, educational policy had long been formulated by the *Comité Catholique,* a nongovernmental institution linked to the church. As one of his first reform measures, Premier Lesage created a department of education and, shortly after that, a department of cultural affairs. Simultaneously, his government expanded the provision of social services. An economic development council was established to map out economic strategy, and the government also nationalized the profitable hydroelectricity industry. Through negotiations, it obtained new taxation powers from Ottawa and also reached an agreement allowing Quebec to opt out of certain federally administered social programs.[7]

Well before the sovereignty movement captured power, Lesage had established Quebec diplomatic missions abroad, the first being the *Maison du Québec,* which opened in Paris in 1961. The employment opportunities created for francophones by this institutional expansion produced greater self-confidence and ambition in the young generation. The coming of age of a French Canadian middle class, conscious of itself as a distinct nation, started in the 1960s. The most successful and enduring of the nationalist political organizations formed in this decade was the ***Parti Québécois*** (PQ, or ***Péquistes***), created in 1968.

Explaining the societal transformation, one writer contended that rising expectations, not economic adversity, had contributed to nationalism: "The surge of nationalism and collective self-confidence in the 1960s, including the rapid growth of the *Parti Québécois* and the enthusiasm it prompted among francophone youth, appeared to be the product of optimistic expectations in an environment of economic expansion and global decolonization, rather than a response to specific threats or grievances."[8]

Equally important developments affecting Quebec nationalism were taking place at the federal level. The 1965 report of the Royal Commission on Bilingualism and Biculturalism (known as B & B) recognized the threat that French Canadians felt to their culture and language. In 1968, new Canadian prime minister Pierre Elliot Trudeau, a highly educated, cosmopolitan Montrealer, undertook reform of the federal government in the spirit of the B & B report. The 1969 Official Languages Act declared French and English to be coequal official languages, requiring that all federal services be available in each, at the client's choosing. The number of ministerial posts and civil service positions staffed by native French speakers increased dramatically during Trudeau's long tenure (1968–1979, 1980–1984).

Trudeau's vision of a united country functioning smoothly in two languages was put to the test in 1970 when a terrorist cell, calling itself *Front de Libération du Québec* (FLQ), kidnapped a British diplomat and murdered a profederal Quebec government minister. The Canadian prime minister overreacted: he swiftly invoked the War Measures Act—in practice, martial law—and the Canadian army was sent onto the streets of Montreal to project federal power. Leading French intellectual and cultural figures with nationalist leanings were rounded up and interned. While the handful of terrorists eventually released their British hostage in return for safe passage to Cuba (two decades later, they made a triumphant return home), the impact of Trudeau's harsh response to the October crisis was to alienate many Quebecers from the government in Ottawa and the federal Liberal Party. The 1970 events have been the one case of nationalist violence in recent Quebec history.

Quebecers expressed their nationalist sentiments through the ballot box in 1976 when they elected the PQ to power for the first time. Under its charismatic leader, René L'évesque, economic expansion was promoted and Quebec was transformed into a dynamic, secular, technologically advanced society, leaving behind its agrarian, clerical past. L'évesque also secured the position of French language and culture through the enactment of the Charter of the French Language, or **Bill 101**. It enshrined French as the language of work, business, and education in the province, not merely a language spoken only at home or in the tavern. For the PQ, Quebec had little choice but to become a unilingual state: only by making French the sole language to be used in schools, corporations, the professions, and public signs could it hope to survive the remorseless pressures of creeping anglicization. L'évesque referred to the greater sense of cultural security resulting from the enactment of the French Language Charter as the reason why Quebecers, by a margin of 60 to 40 percent (52 to 48 percent among francophone Quebecers) turned down a first referendum on independence held in 1980.

Quebec's new nationalism was not defensive, argued Taylor. Rather,

[i]ts aim was not to defend the traditional way of life but to build a modern French society on this continent. In its pure form, practically the only value it had in common with the old was the French language itself. The rest of what has been defined as the French-Canadian tradition was seen in a very negative light. The modern nationalists were often anticlerical, if not unbelievers, and in any case the traditional conception of Catholicism in this society was anathema to them.[9]

Taylor suggested that "[i]ndependence could be the symbol even if not always the actual goal of the new nationalism because, in the era of decolonization, it represented the awakening of underdeveloped societies that were determined to take control of their own history and in doing so to wrest it from both foreign domination and the dead hand of millennial tradition."[10] In this new society, the priest and the historian would be displaced by the businessperson and the technocrat. By 1995, however, it became clear that sovereignty was, in fact, the goal of many Quebecers, and the movement did not just possess symbolic importance.

## Quebec's Exclusion from the Canadian Constitution

In 1982, Prime Minister Trudeau, encouraged by the referendum result, pressed on with his vision of centralized federalism by **patriating the Canadian constitution**. Hitherto, all laws passed by the Canadian parliament had to receive royal assent—a formality, to be sure, but it was a reminder of Canada's past status as a British dominion.

At the provincial premiers' meeting held in late 1981 in Ottawa, which hammered out a patriation formula, Quebec leader L'évesque was kept out of the all-night negotiations in which the other nine provincial premiers participated. According to Trudeau, "Levesque left himself out," but as far as the Quebec leader was concerned, he had been "tricked by Trudeau" on that "day of anger and shame."[11]

Not only did the new constitution eliminate the need for royal assent for Canadian legislation, it also weakened provincial powers, something both major parties in Quebec—the nationalist PQ and the profederalist QLP—opposed. Quebec had not given its consent to the constitutional accord and has never, since then, ratified it. As a result, Quebec governments do not feel bound by the constitution, even though they honor its provisions. The unintended consequence of Trudeau's constitution was to trigger a simmering three-decades-long constitutional crisis that remains unresolved.

The constitutional impasse can be explained in terms of disagreement over the desirability of asymmetry. The Federal Task Force on Canadian Unity set up by Trudeau had recommended in 1979 that all provinces should enjoy augmented, equal powers, but that only Quebec should be permitted to exercise all of them. Such a political solution to a legal matter acknowledged the need to build in asymmetrical arrangements that could accommodate Quebec within the new constitution. But the Canadian prime minister rejected such a solution. "Trudeau's image was of French-speaking Canadians as individuals without the collective dimensions of identification with *la nation canadienne-française*."[12] In their turn, Quebec leaders from across the political spectrum concurred that the new Canadian constitution, especially if it limited the power of the Quebec National Assembly to legislate on language issues, would reinforce the province's minority status within confederation.

It would be simplistic to attribute the resurgence of Quebec nationalism solely to the constitutional crisis or to Trudeau's centralizing policies. In economic terms, while Quebec had recorded impressive absolute gains throughout the 1970s, it suffered relative losses compared with Ontario, Alberta, and British Columbia. Toronto became corporate headquarters for many Canadian and foreign-owned businesses, easily overshadowing Montreal, which for a long time had been Canada's largest metropolis. By the early 1990s, Montreal became the city with the highest unemployment rate nationwide. Militant *syndicats* (trade unions) were a discouragement for outside investment, while "the Canadian business establishment sealed the fate of Pierre Trudeau's brand of federalism by refusing to integrate French-speaking persons in the upper reaches of management and in head-office operations."[13] Yet the causal argument that Quebec would wither economically if it grew "nationalistically" appeared to be refuted by developments in the 1990s.

## The Failure to Bring Quebec Back In

The deadlock on the constitutional crisis seemed to be broken when a new Canadian prime minister was elected in 1984. The Progressive Conservative Party, led by another Quebec native, Brian Mulroney, won the federal elections with the largest majority in Canadian history and put an end to the long rule of Trudeau's Liberals. Traditionally, the Conservatives were more open to decentralization of power. Mulroney himself was more sympathetic to Quebec's desire for greater political autonomy within a decentralized federal system. He declared that he wanted to integrate Quebec into the constitution "with honor and enthusiasm."

Another election result seemed to further improve the chances of a deal to bring Quebec into the constitutional fold. In 1985, after nearly a decade in power, the PQ was defeated in Quebec elections by the provincial Liberals headed by a pragmatic economist, Robert Bourassa. As Quebec premier between 1970 and 1976, Bourassa had introduced legislation giving priority to the French language but, as a Harvard-trained economist, he had also mapped out a strategy of economic growth for the province and was less concerned with cultural issues.

For a period of eight years, after both Mulroney and Bourassa were reelected, an opportunity for reaching an agreement on a renewed Canadian federalism beckoned. But the most that the decentralizing Canadian prime minister and the profederalist Quebec premier could produce in the period their terms overlapped was the so-called **Meech Lake Accord**.

Agreed upon in 1987 by Mulroney, Bourassa, and the nine other provincial premiers, it provided for Quebec's accession to the Canadian constitution in return for concessions on five principal Quebec demands: constitutional recognition of Quebec as a **distinct society**, a constitutional veto for the province, three of nine judges on the Supreme Court, the right to opt out of future federal programs, and shared immigration powers. Bourassa spoke of these demands as the minimum any Quebec premier would ever be able to put forward.

The flaw in the agreement was procedure. In accordance with his ideal of centralized government, the amending formula for the Canadian constitution enacted by Trudeau required unanimity among all ten provinces. In 1990, the two provincial governments of Manitoba and Newfoundland, for idiosyncratic reasons of their own, refused to approve the Meech Lake Accord. The effort to incorporate Quebec into the constitutional order had failed.

Predictably, its failure led to a resurgence in nationalism in Quebec. An opinion poll conducted in late 1990 found that 62 percent of all respondents and 75 percent of francophone ones expressed support for Quebec sovereignty—a high-water mark for the sovereignty cause.[14] Quebec was growing in self-confidence:

> Quebec's emergence as a confident nation has been the result of various factors, including a more politically sophisticated population, a militant trade union movement, a more enterprising business class, better educated state elites, examples of successful nationalist movements elsewhere, perceived slights or injustices committed by officials in the rest of Canada and best exemplified by the failure of the Meech Lake Accord, ambitious politicians with their own political motives, and a sense that francophone and non-francophone goals are incompatible."[15]

After the defeat of the Meech Lake Accord, Bourassa blustered that "the Quebec government will not return to the constitutional negotiating table," and that Quebec was "free and capable of taking responsibility for its destiny and development."[16] His own party was moving toward a sovereignty position. But at this point, Bourassa was satisfied to limit post–Meech Lake protest to a temporary boycott of federal–provincial meetings rather than hold a referendum on sovereignty, which he feared would pass.

In 1992, the Quebec leader rejoined talks with other premiers. A new proposal, incorporating the substance of the Meech Lake Accord, was floated under the name Charlottetown Accord. But the "constitutional moment" had passed, and in English Canada, too, a mood not to compromise with Quebec had taken hold. In a referendum held across Canada that fall, the Charlottetown formula was defeated in six provinces. While English provinces generally turned down the constitutional compromise because it gave in to Quebec "blackmail," the 56 percent of Quebecers who opposed the accord did so primarily because it did not grant Quebec sufficient new powers. Faring poorly at the polls, in 1993, both Bourassa and Mulroney resigned as leaders of their parties.

## The Growth of the Sovereignty Movement

Quebec nationalism was running so strong that sovereigntists decided to form a party that would contest federal seats in the province on the platform of Quebec independence. In 1990, a Mulroney associate, Lucien Bouchard, broke from the Conservative cabinet and established the ***Bloc Québécois*** (BQ), a sister party of the PQ. It did not have to wait long to record its first success. In the 1993 national elections, the Liberals, led by former Trudeau deputy Jean Chrétien (also a native of Quebec) returned to power in place of the scandal-plagued Conservatives. But the strongest showing in Quebec was recorded by the BQ, which captured fifty-four of the seventy-five federal ridings in the province. The BQ, seeking the breakup of Canada, ironically became the official opposition party in the Canadian House of Commons.

Within a year of the BQ's success, the PQ won a comfortable majority of seats in Quebec provincial elections. Even though it had edged out the PLQ in the popular vote by the slimmest of margins (44.7 percent to 44.3 percent), the PQ under its new leader (and premier) Jacques Parizeau was committed to fulfilling its campaign promise of holding a referendum on sovereignty as soon as possible. Its Executive Council explained the rationale for sovereignty: "The Canadian federal system is a major obstacle to the pursuit of the goals of both societies. Quebec and English Canada are caught in a constitutional trap that prevents both of them from enjoying the benefits of their sovereignty and adopting strategies to meet the most important challenges of our time. Canada is at an impasse, and it is clearly in the interest of both partners to get out of this impasse as quickly as possible."[17]

The wording of the referendum question would be crucial to determining the result. Reference to independence would limit supporters to the 25 percent of hardline unconditional *indépendantistes* in the province. Coupling Quebec sovereignty with continued economic association with Canada would expand the support base. A disagreement arose between sovereignty party leaders. Whereas Parizeau, representing the *pur et dur* ("purist and hard-line") wing of the PQ, wanted a "hard" question addressing independence, BQ chief Bouchard preferred a "softer" question stressing continued association with Canada.

Another problem for *indépendantistes* was that, for a sovereignty referendum to succeed, at least 61 percent of francophones would have to vote yes because English speakers and immigrant communities would vote heavily against the proposal. For Quebec's bargaining position on independence vis-à-vis Ottawa to be strong, at least 60 percent of all voters would have to support sovereignty, thereby requiring 77 percent support among French speakers.

On October 30, 1995, Quebecers went to the polls to give a yes or no to the following question: "Do you agree that Quebec should become sovereign, after having made a formal offer to Canada for a new economic and political partnership, within the scope of the bill respecting the future of Quebec and of the agreement signed on June 12, 1995?" The bill in question, introduced in the Quebec legislature in September 1995, provided for drafting a new Quebec constitution and clarified the territories, citizenship, and currency that a sovereign Quebec would have; the June agreement cited in the referendum question was one concluded by the three major prosovereignty movements: the PQ, BQ, and the *Action Démocratique du Québec* (the ADQ, a third party—in addition to the Quebec Liberals—represented in the Quebec National Assembly).

The referendum result was closer than the complacent federal forces had imagined: 50.6 percent of voters opposed the question and 49.4 percent supported it. Slightly more than 60 percent of francophones opted for the sovereignty option, while the overwhelming majority of English speakers and members of Quebec's ethnic groups rejected it. Public opinion polling just before the vote, done on behalf of the yes campaign, showed that the yes side was poised to win, and premier Parizeau even prerecorded a victory speech in which he referred to Quebec joining the international family of nations.

The final result was a shock to both sides. The federalists had been slow to react to the surge of support for sovereignty, had no one to counter Bouchard's charisma, and were badly divided on tactics. The sovereigntists had seen victory slip away as large "unity rallies" in Montreal were staged. Well-intentioned pledges by sovereigntists to provide employment in the Quebec public service to Quebecers who presently worked for federal agencies backfired. Civil servants of the Quebec government felt they would lose out, and in predominantly francophone Quebec City, a surprising number of voters opposed sovereignty. In such a close election, this swing was decisive.

But for Parizeau, conceding defeat in the referendum, the loss was attributable to two sources: ethnic groups and big money (the large corporations operating in Quebec). Even though there was evidence to support his claim, his remarks were viewed as incendiary and he resigned the day after the referendum. A few months later, Bouchard changed jobs from BQ head in Ottawa to PQ leader in Quebec.

A lesson learned from Parizeau's fall was that, in contemporary democracies, nationalistic rhetoric must not undermine liberal principles such as tolerance and diversity. Subsequent debates within the PQ over the definition of a Quebecer (Is it someone born in Quebec? Someone speaking French or of French ancestry? Anyone living in Quebec?) have revealed a concern—even if only on pragmatic grounds—that an ethnocratic approach to Quebec identity is likely to backfire. Nationalists in democracies who adopt a purely ethnic understanding of citizenship are vulnerable to criticism that they breach the international liberal norm of multiculturalism.

In the first six months after the referendum, the rhetoric between sovereigntists and federalists was heated. Each side accused the other of voting irregularities. Hard-line nationalists talked of a unilateral declaration of independence, while uncompromising federalists threatened to partition Quebec if the province left Canada.

By the end of 1996, however, support for sovereignty waned and premier Bouchard was forced to turn his attention to Quebec's economic problems. To win reelection, he had to focus on good governance rather than sovereignty. Because dropping the sovereignty option from his party's program altogether was not viable, Bouchard began to speak of holding another referendum only when "winning conditions" had been achieved. There would never again be a losing referendum on Quebec sovereignty, he pledged.

The PQ was reelected in 1998, but opinion polls showed support for Quebec independence had shrunk to under 40 percent. Canadian prime minister Chrétien won reelection, too, and his government enacted a bill giving parliamentary (though not constitutional) recognition to Quebec as a distinct society. The threat to Canadian unity was fading as Canada and Quebec became victims to "constitutional burnout." In 2003, the PQ, seemingly without a cause to champion, lost power in Quebec to the profederalist PLQ leader Jean Charest. The PQ showed signs of recovery in the December 2008 election, but they were not enough to prevent a Charest majority government from forming.

In 2003, Quebec nationalists had received a political windfall with the outbreak of the "sponsorshop scandal." It was alleged that the Liberal government in Ottawa had allocated US$100 million to Chrétien-friendly agencies in Quebec to promote a Canadian unity message. In an anti-Liberal backlash, Conservative Party leader Stephen Harper was elected to head a minority government in 2006. His "open brand of federalism" initially appealed to Quebecers, who returned ten Conservative Members of Parliament (MPs) in the province (compared to none in 2004). In a bid to form a majority government, which was predicated on winning even more seats in Quebec, Harper called early elections in 2008. This time, however, the Calgary native was accused of "Quebec bashing" because of purported disparaging remarks about and federal funding cuts for Quebec artists. In the electoral campaign, the Bloc accused him of assaulting Quebec's cultural sovereignty. The result in Quebec was almost the same as two years earlier with Conservatives winning ten seats and the BQ winning forty-nine.

Deprived of a majority government by Quebec nationalists, Harper's postelection rhetoric included an attack on the alleged antidemocratic character of the BQ: it held the balance of power in the Canadian Parliament yet wanted to break up the country. Almost the entire Quebec political establishment denounced Harper, while opposition leaders in Ottawa accused him of wanting to provoke a national unity crisis. The selection of a new Liberal Party leader, Michael Ignatieff, a former Harvard scholar of nationalism whose views on Quebec nationalism were generally conciliatory, appeared to increase the vulnerability of Harper's minority government.

## The Canadian Supreme Court on Secession

The close referendum result in 1995 prompted interested parties, including the government of Canada, to seek juridical clarification from high courts concerning the legality of separation. One scholar conceptualized the issue in the following way: "Separatism is not primarily about how government or its assignees exercise their authority. It is about who is to be accepted as the definitive group for selecting a government to decide our fundamental obligations and which groups should assign roles. Separatists subordinate the division of roles and responsibilities to recognition of a people as a primary source of authentic authority."[18]

For Quebec to obtain sovereignty, the province would have to seek an amendment to the Canadian constitution recognizing its secession. But the amending formula requires the approval of the House of Commons and Senate, and the consent of a minimum of seven provinces containing at least 50 percent of the Canadian population. Holding a referendum on the question, as the Parizeau government did, was to assume a mandate not conferred upon it by the constitution.[19] In a legal sense, then, those antiseparatist forces claiming that Parizeau was guilty of planning a constitutional coup d'état were not far off the mark.

The Péquiste government refused to contest the legal case for sovereignty brought to the Canadian Supreme Court in 1996, and so an *amicus curiae* was appointed to represent Quebec. Three questions were referred to the Supreme Court for adjudication:

> Question 1: Under the Constitution of Canada, can the National Assembly, legislature or government of Quebec effect the secession of Quebec from Canada unilaterally?

Question 2: Does international law give the National Assembly, legislature or government of Quebec the right to effect the secession of Quebec from Canada unilaterally? In this regard, is there a right to self-determination under international law that would give the National Assembly, legislature or government of Quebec the right to effect the secession of Quebec from Canada unilaterally?

Question 3: In the event of a conflict between domestic and international law on the right of the National Assembly, legislature or government of Quebec to effect the secession of Quebec from Canada unilaterally, which would take precedence in Canada?[20]

The court's ruling was published in 1998. The answer to the first question gave some satisfaction to each of the parties in the case. A referendum victory for the sovereignty side could be the basis for separation: "A clear majority vote in Quebec on a clear question in favor of secession would confer democratic legitimacy on the secession initiative which all of the other participants in Confederation would have to recognize." On the other hand, Quebec separation could not be unilateral: "Quebec could not, despite a clear referendum result, purport to invoke a right of self-determination to dictate the terms of a proposed secession to the other parties to the federation."[21]

The court ruling showed particular ingenuity in balancing the exigencies of democracy and constitutionalism: "The democratic vote, by however strong a majority, would have no legal effect on its own and could not push aside the principles of federalism and the rule of law, the rights of individuals and minorities, or the operation of democracy in the other provinces or in Canada as a whole."[22] Specifically, "[t]he relationship between democracy and federalism means, for example, that in Canada there may be different and equally legitimate majorities in different provinces and territories and at the federal level. No one majority is more or less 'legitimate' than the others as an expression of democratic opinion."[23] Furthermore, "Canadians have never accepted that ours is a system of simple majority rule"[24] because democracy and popular sovereignty include respect for constitutionalism and the rule of law as well as for voting majorities.

The court's interpretation subsequently formed the basis of the Clarity Act of 2000, pushed through parliament by the Chrétien government. It stated that a referendum question not referring specifically to secession would be considered "unclear." The act also left it to the Canadian parliament to determine whether a "clear majority" had expressed itself in a referendum. In short, "Democratic rights under the Constitution cannot be divorced from constitutional obligations." However, "[t]he other provinces and the federal government would have no basis to deny the right of the government of Quebec to pursue secession should a clear majority of the people of Quebec choose that goal, so long as in doing so, Quebec respects the rights of others."[25]

In a carefully researched answer to the second question concerning international law, the Supreme Court focused on the principle of the right of a people to self-determination. It recognized that "the precise meaning of the term 'people' remains somewhat uncertain," even though "[i]t is clear that 'a people' may include only a portion of the population of an existing state."[26] The court did not consider whether Quebecers constituted a people but examined the hypothetical circumstances that would justify a people's right to unilateral secession.

It found that international law "leaves the creation of a new state to be determined by the domestic law of the existing state of which the seceding entity presently forms a part."[27] It "expects that the right to self-determination will be exercised by peoples within the framework of existing sovereign states and consistently with the maintenance of the territorial integrity of those states."[28] Put differently, "the right to self-determination of a people is normally fulfilled through **internal self-determination**—a people's pursuit of its political, economic, social and cultural development within the framework of an existing state."[29] The right to external self-determination, in practice, statehood, is accorded only to peoples of "former colonies; where a people is oppressed, as for example under foreign military occupation; or where a definable group is denied meaningful access to government to pursue their political, economic, social and cultural development."[30]

Quebec's people were not colonized or oppressed. "For close to 40 of the last 50 years, the Prime Minister of Canada has been a Quebecer.... During the 8 years prior to June 1997, the Prime Minister and the Leader of the Official Opposition in the House of Commons were both Quebecers. At present, the Prime Minister of Canada, the Right Honorable Chief Justice and two other members of the Court, the Chief of Staff of the Canadian Armed Forces and the Canadian ambassador to the United States, not to mention the Deputy Secretary-General of the United Nations, are Quebecers."[31]

In sum, Quebec did not qualify under any of the circumstances envisaged under international law for a people to exercise external self-determination. Because the answer to the second question submitted to the Supreme Court was consistent with the answer to the first question and that therefore neither under international nor domestic law did Quebec have the right to unilateral secession, question 3 inquiring which body of law has precedence became moot.

The Supreme Court's arguments about the right of secession in the country reveal how difficult it is for a would-be breakaway group to secede in a western democracy. The penultimate paragraph of the ruling was categorical: "*A state whose government represents the whole of the people* or peoples resident within its territory, on a basis of equality and without discrimination, and respects the principles of self-determination in its internal arrangements, is entitled to maintain its territorial integrity under international law and to have that territorial integrity recognized by other states."[32] It follows from this that a democracy *qua* democracy cannot be rent asunder. Two concessions only are offered to a democratic separatist movement within a democratic state. First, "one of the legal norms which may be recognized by states in granting or withholding recognition of emergent states is the legitimacy of the process by which the *de facto* secession is, or was, being pursued." Compliance with the legitimate obligations arising out of its earlier status and with procedural rules can "weigh in favor of international recognition."[33]

Second, the **effectivity principle**, that is, recognition of a factual political reality, can give hope to democratic secessionists. It "proclaims that an illegal act may eventually acquire legal status if, as a matter of empirical fact, it is recognized on the international plane." Squatters do sometimes acquire property rights, for example, and a change in factual circumstances may produce a change in legal status. But these two exceptions only highlight how democracies believe themselves to be nearly invulnerable in legal and moral terms to the claims of secessionists.

# WHY PEACEFUL SECESSION IS RARE

In a major study of the potential consequences of a successful Quebec separation from the **Rest of Canada (ROC)**, a Canadian political scientist explored the theory of peaceful secessions. Outcomes of secessions are path dependent; that is, they reflect the process through which they occur. The secession outcome is contingent on historical events, the procedure of separation, the antecedent institutional structures, and the nature of the transition moment.[34] In this chapter, we have described the path dependence of the Quebec sovereignty movement.

Economic studies of Quebec secession usually distinguish between the immediate impact of the transition to sovereignty and Quebec's long-term prospects as an independent state. In both cases, the province's resource endowment and industrial base are constant, but the short-term impact would be negative for both Canada and Quebec due to transaction costs (such as institutional restructuring), fiscal costs (increased tax burdens), and uncertainty (affecting currency markets, investment, and migration). Estimates of Quebec's budget deficit in the first year of independence have ranged from US$10 billion to US$22 billion.[35] Either of two contrasting economic scenarios could result from secession:

> In the optimistic view, a cohesive, flexible Quebec, with a loyal business class and state policies tailored to its needs, outward looking and with access to markets assured through international trade regimes, would fare better than it currently does. In the pessimistic view, either Quebec would fail to gain adequate access to international markets, or its sociocultural endowment would fail to produce economic growth, or the effects of the transition to sovereignty would hobble its long-run prospects.[36]

To contextualize Quebec's bid for separation, the same author examined the comparative politics of peaceful secession. He noted that few cases existed, limited in the twentieth century to Norway's secession from Sweden in 1905 and Singapore's from Malaysia in 1965. In these cases, secession events happened abruptly, negotiations involved few political participants and centered on a few significant provisions, agreements were accomplished constitutionally, and foreign powers played an important role. Cases of separatism from the former Soviet Union (1991) and Czechoslovakia (1993) were different because they followed the complete disintegration of a "predecessor state" into separate parts rather than one unit (prospective "secessor state") seeking to break away.[37]

Czechoslovakia's **velvet divorce** was the product of increasing political polarization within the federation. "This is a process of growing mutual hostility between two communities, accompanied by a sense among members of each that their interests are distinct and can only be met through separation."[38] Thus, whereas in mid-1990 only 5 percent of Czechs and 8 percent of Slovaks favored dividing the country into two separate states, by fall 1992, 56 percent of Czechs in Bohemia and 43 percent in Moravia, and 37 percent of Slovaks thought separation was necessary. The more general inference, applicable to the Canada–Quebec case, is that "how polarization took place in Czechoslovakia is a reminder that political competition is not restricted by the rules of the game: politicians will try to shift public opinion and even to reshape society for their own advantage."[39]

Successful Quebec secession would also be the result of contingent circumstances. Milton Esman referred to a political opportunity structure within which ethnic movements operate. It "furnishes incentives, limitations, permissible boundaries, potentials, and risks that inform the behavior of ethnic entrepreneurs and activists and influence the expectations of their constituents. It enables and facilitates certain actions, constrains and proscribes others."[40] Esman identified two principal dimensions to the political opportunity structure:

(a) the rules and practices that enable or limit the ability of the ethnic movement and its component organizations to mobilize, to propagandize, and to assert claims for access, participation, redress, or benefits; and (b) the propensity of the political establishment to consider such claims as legitimate and subject to possible accommodation.[41]

Esman contrasted three cases of ethnic mobilization with different process features. In Northern Ireland, Catholic groups had the opportunity to mobilize but could not obtain recognition from political leaders for the legitimacy of their grievances. In South Africa, the absence of established rules and practices and of an accommodation-oriented regime did not permit mobilization so, according to Esman, violent or revolutionary strategies were adopted by ethnic groups. By contrast, in Canada, both dimensions were positive, thereby encouraging Quebec nationalists to rely on constitutionally oriented methods. Their legal strategy is an outcome of a political opportunity structure that is both open and accommodative.

We should emphasize that nationalism often has a momentum and direction of its own. The authors of a political science text on Quebec observed how Quebec nationalism's "evolution began with the Church, moved to the State, and now is expressed by individual francophones in the market economy. Nationalism is a permanent fixture of Quebec political culture."[42] There has been a parallel change in this nationalism's ideological content, too: "Gradually, nationalism evolved from this insular, collectivist perspective—rooted in a deep-seated conservatism—to a confident, functional, statist orientation, to, finally, an entrepreneurial, materialistic individualism rooted in economic liberalism."[43]

The most important fault line in Canada remains language and ethnolinguistic identity. Taylor argued how, "for English Canadians, who are acutely aware of the diversity of the country, of the tenuous and indefinable nature of what holds it together, the question of unity is paramount. For any part of Canadian society to demonstrate that it prizes its part over the whole smacks of treason."[44] He suggested that "if French Canadians must learn to understand the English anxiety about unity, English Canadians must learn that the identification with *la nation canadienne-française* is not at all the antechamber to separatism."[45]

In 2007, Taylor, a supporter of Canadian federalism, along with sovereigntist sociologist Gérard Bouchard, were appointed to head a Quebec government Royal Commission on Reasonable Accommodation. The combination of French Quebecers' cultural insecurity and immigrant groups' demands for special rights triggered the investigation into what measures might be reasonable for Quebec to take to help integrate and provide autonomy for its so-called cultural communities. What Quebec identity ultimately entailed was debated at the hearings held throughout the province.

The commission's main recommendation was for the promotion of **interculturalism**—a model in which French–Canadian society is at the center of a wheel with spokes connecting it with its minority groups. Taylor explained: "The reason why people use the prefix 'inter-' as against 'multi-' is that they want to accentuate the exchanges between different cultural groups [using] the French language." Bouchard added: "A minority culture like Quebec is naturally more concerned with integration and more fearful of fragmentation. So in interculturalism you have this focus on interaction and integration."[46]

The commission also advocated the building of a secular society in Quebec. Neither mainly Catholic French Quebecers nor members of cultural communities for whom religion was often central to their identity were enthusiastic about this idea.[47] The rejection of the Bouchard–Taylor secularization proposal was best symbolized by the Quebec legislature's reaction to the recommendation that the crucifix overlooking the Speaker's chair in the National Assembly be removed. The Assembly, made up of members of different ethnic, racial, and religious backgrounds, convened soon afterward and passed a motion—unanimously—to retain the crucifix where it was. In justifying this decision, the approved motion affirmed Quebec's attachment to its "religious and historic heritage."[48]

## INTERNATIONAL REACTION

Outside Canada, two contrasting reactions greeted the results of the 1995 referendum. The first, the reaction of sovereign states in the international community, was of relief that Canadian democracy had survived a stiff challenge and produced an electoral majority, however tenuous, favoring national unity. In particular, liberal democracies such as the United States and Great Britain, both of which wished to appear neutral in the dispute, were pleased that the referendum maintained the status quo.

Most other states in the international system also endorsed the result. Canada's image in the world had been nearly without blemish (other than for its seal hunting), and the World Development Report issued by a United Nations agency was to rank it as having the highest quality of life of any country in the world for seven consecutive years through 2000. Many states had significant diaspora populations in Canada: Italy, Portugal, Poland, India, Sri Lanka, China, and the Philippines. Like the immigrants settling in Canada, leaders of these states could not fathom the historical and cultural nuances underlying Quebec's dispute with English Canada. Because Canada claimed to be a multicultural state, most immigrants from these countries understandably concluded that there was no difference in status between being a Chinese Canadian or a French Canadian: each ultimately had to master English. If Canada's other ethnic groups in Canada did not demand autonomy, the logic went, why should the French? The question that English Canadians first posed shortly after the Quiet Revolution—What do Quebecers want?—now had international resonance.

By contrast, the reaction of nationalities that themselves sought greater political independence from centralized states was that of being heartened by the closeness of the Quebec referendum result. Nationalist leaders in Scotland, Catalonia, northern Italy, and elsewhere were given reason to follow democratic procedures, given how close Quebec nationalists had come to success. Especially since ethno-secessionism had been stigmatized by the wars taking place in Bosnia, Chechnya, Kashmir, and Sri Lanka, the Quebec referendum had demonstrated the compatibility between national assertion and liberal democracy.

Probably the most influential reaction emerging from the international system and having a direct bearing on Quebec's future is that of foreign investors. We alluded to Canadian and international corporations that pulled their operations out of Quebec, wholly or in part, in the 1970s and 1980s. Corporations largely sided with the no campaign in the 1995 referendum, and they urged Bouchard after that to get rid of political uncertainty by announcing a moratorium on referendums. Yet, as we see below, the calculations of Quebec sovereigntist leaders has been just the opposite: an independent Quebec would provide better investment opportunities than a province shackled by Ottawa-imposed red tape. Quebec forms an integral part of the North American economy, they assert, and its functioning is regulated not only by the Canadian government but also by various international trade regimes.

## CAN A CONSTITUTIONAL DISPUTE BE INTERNATIONALIZED?

If there is any circumstance in which the international principle of noninterference in the internal affairs of a sovereign state should be strictly upheld, it must be when there is domestic disagreement over a country's constitution. An international system that respects the noninterference principle will allow Canada and its parts to decide the country's future for themselves. However, the stakes may be high for neighboring states, in particular, which might fear the chaos that could follow the country's breakup. In the case of Canada, the interested neighbor happens to be a superpower. Not surprisingly, then, economic relations with the United States are pivotal for Canadian federalists and Quebec's sovereigntist leaders alike.

It may be surprising to learn that American leaders historically have assumed an agnostic position on Quebec independence. One scholar has observed:

> the United States has long maintained that an independent Quebec would be a viable country and a good neighbor. It acknowledges that Quebec would likely support all of Canada's existing defense and economic commitments and remain a staunch supporter of American policies in a broad sense. The most pertinent reason for U.S. opposition to Quebec's sovereignty, then, has less to do with Quebec per se and more to do with the fractionalization of Canada that could result.[49]

According to a Quebec journalist, beginning in the 1970s, the U.S. State Department regularly studied the options it would have if Quebec seceded, but it did not engage in any diplomacy that could be interpreted as interfering in Canada's internal affairs.[50] The international dimension of the Canada–Quebec dispute was most in evidence in economic rather than political relations with the United States. In 1978, about 73 percent of Quebec's material (or tangible) exports went south; by 1995, with the implementation of most of the articles in the **North American Free Trade Agreement (NAFTA)**, the proportion rose to 84 percent. Forty-five percent of Quebec's imports originated in the United States and, astonishingly, this one Canadian province represented the seventh largest export market in the world for the United States. Quebec's trade balance per capita with the United States was more positive than even Japan's.[51] All political parties in Quebec, then, whether federalist or sovereigntist, have supported the NAFTA agreement.

If we focus on the U.S. perspective, we can find a number of examples of a two-track policy on Quebec. In 1991, President George H. W. Bush stated that his country had no desire to interfere in domestic Canadian politics. But, he added, "[w]e are very, very happy with a united Canada."[52] Similarly, during President Bill Clinton's visit to Canada in 1995, protocol required a meeting with the official opposition leader, who was the Bloc's Bouchard. Some parliamentarians criticized Clinton for going ahead with the meeting, which was cordial. But true to form, Clinton then made a speech in the House of Commons that included the exhortation: "*Vive le Canada.*" In this way, he antagonized Quebec nationalists seeking to leave confederation. The latter were especially incensed with perceived U.S. involvement late in the 1995 referendum campaign. U.S. secretary of state Warren Christopher praised the excellent relationship between his country and Canada and then warned that there would be no guarantee of a similar framework with Quebec if Canada were reorganized. This statement came in response to a request from the Chrétien government to make a statement as fear of a referendum defeat became palpable.[53]

The U.S. two-track policy is contingent on a number of factors. "If the threat of sovereignty were somehow to have devastating economic implications or strategic costs for the United States, then American officials would undoubtedly rethink their position."[54] An independent or unstable Quebec could pose a security threat to the United States in an age of global terror, especially if border controls were weakened. Nevertheless, in recent times, Quebec has vigorously sought to ingratiate itself with its southern neighbor—perhaps more than has English Canada—a phenomenon that has not passed unnoticed in Washington.

The role of France in encouraging Quebec separatism is easily exaggerated. Other than President Charles de Gaulle's famous cry from Montreal City Hall in 1967, "*Vive le Québec libre,*" successive French leaders have avoided giving the appearance of helping break up Canada. To be sure, the author of a study on French–Quebec relations did conclude: "Did France have a Quebec policy? The answer is clearly yes." Even if France has generally reacted to, rather than engineered, events in Quebec, nevertheless, "thanks to direct cooperation, France has strived to reinforce Quebec autonomy and has de facto converted Quebec's constitutional grievances into international relations."[55]

A second study, this one by an English Canadian, depicts France's role in Canada in more insidious terms. It identified a "Quebec mafia" in France that has thrived under the hothouse conditions created by the Gaullist movement—de Gaulle and his successors. While officially committed to the French variant of a dual-track policy—noninterference in but nonindifference about Quebec—most French leaders have cultivated diplomatic contacts with Quebec sovereigntists. As a result, "the history of Franco–Quebec relations these past thirty years teaches us what these meeting are for: to conspire once again for the separation of Quebec from Canada."[56] Some circumstantial evidence does partly support this otherwise overblown conclusion. In 1997, former PQ Leader Parizeau reported that Giscard d'Estaing, French president in the 1970s, had encouraged him in 1995 to issue a unilateral declaration of independence if he had won the referendum. It is significant that it was a past French president, not the incumbent, who may have recommended such unconstitutional action.

Jacques Chirac, who became French president in 1996 soon after the Quebec separatists' near-success in the referendum, had gone on record as saying that France would recognize Quebec independence if it was produced by a democratic verdict. Ironically his successor, Nicolas Sarkozy, elected in 2007, chastised his socialist party opponent, Ségolène Royal, for reaffirming this commitment to Quebec during the election campaign. Sarkozy further antagonized Quebec sovereigntists during a visit to Canada in 2008. In expressing a wish to bring Quebec closer to Canada, he remarked: "Quebecers are our brothers, but Canadians are our friends."[57]

In 2009 the French president took on the Quebec issue again. He defined "the message of the *Francophonie*"—a loose global association of francophone states under the direction of Paris—as "the universal values we hold in Quebec as in France—the rejection of bigotry, the rejection of division, the rejection of self-confinement, the refusal to define one's identity through fierce opposition to another." When pressed if he was abandoning the longstanding French policy of noninterference, nonindifference with regard to Quebec, Sarkozy replied "it's not my thing." The riposte of Bloc Québécois leader Gilles Duceppe was equally dismissive: if Sarkozy was referring to sovereigntists as bigots and dividers, "he's making an eloquent demonstration of his crass ignorance of Quebec's political situation."[58] French Quebecers have long objected to what they perceive is a condescending attitude by France to their former colony. It is significant that no recent Quebec nationalist leader has made closer ties to the French-speaking world a priority.

If Quebec did establish a separate state, doubts have been cast about the ROC's ability to survive. The resulting uncertainty would become a serious concern to U.S. policymakers. The United States might then be tempted to incorporate parts or all of English Canada. Admittedly, there are few "annexationists" in U.S. politics, the only notable exception being Patrick Buchanan. Policy specialists in Washington are aware that the Canadian region most likely to wish to join the United States would be the "poorhouse" Maritime provinces. Economically endowed provinces such as Ontario and Alberta would be least enthusiastic, while British Columbia's robust union movement and left-of-center provincial governments would make the province radical by U.S. standards.[59]

Canada is well equipped to survive Quebec's secession. While in the early 1990s, Quebec accounted for 25 percent of Canada's population and 23 percent of its gross national product (GNP), it had only a 17 percent share in Canadian exports. All these figures have declined since then. About 80 percent of interprovincial trade in Canada takes place between Quebec and Ontario, with Quebec's economy more dependent on trade with Ontario—more than 40 percent of its cross-Canada trade was with its western neighbor—than the reverse.[60] The economic costs of Quebec leaving Canada would be borne proportionally more by Quebec. English Canadian nationalist and newspaper magnate Conrad Black (convicted and imprisoned in 2007 by a U.S. court for mail fraud) once boasted that "a Canada no longer subject to Quebec's endless threats of secession. . . . would be a steadily more important G7 country. It would fully occupy the political role available to one of the world's ten or twelve most important countries."[61]

The international dimension to the Quebec sovereignty issue is circumscribed, therefore. There is little sense of threat felt by the United States or any other countries brought on by the constitutional stalemate involving Canada and Quebec.

## IS EXTERNAL MEDIATION NECESSARY IN CANADA?

Because the issue of Quebec sovereignty has been managed consistent with Canada's established democratic procedures, international organizations have been superfluous to the process of mediation. Should the sovereignty question ever lead

---

**BOX 6.1**

**Theorizing the Linkage Between Ethno-Secessionism in Quebec and Its International Dimension**

*Complementary Perspectives from Comparative Politics and International Relations*

**1. Domestic factors**

Parliamentary (but not constitutional) recognition of a French-Canadian nation

Political tradition of constitutional management of conflicts within the confederation

Canadian policies of civic nationalism and multiculturalism

Quebec's historical grievances

Quebec claim of cultural and linguistic sovereignty

**2. International factors**

International community's adherence to principle of noninterference in a sovereign state's internal affairs

"Words are cheap": U.S. and France's verbal "nonindifference" to fate of Quebec and Canada

**3. Conflict resolution**

Constitutional impasse

---

to a major crisis, Canada's membership in institutions such as the UN, NATO, and the G8 (group of eight highly industrialized nations) may make them the first to attempt mediation.

The only conceivable third-party mediation outside an international governmental organization (IGO) would be by the United States (see Box 6.1). We have highlighted the guarded U.S. approach to the Canada–Quebec dispute. Two additional factors would make the United States circumspect about becoming involved. Its experience in mediating conflicts in Bosnia, Kosovo, and Northern Ireland has taught U.S. leaders that good faith peace-making efforts are fraught with dangers. American pressure may have helped bring about the 1985 Anglo–Irish agreement on the future of Northern Ireland.[62] But over twenty years later, the agreement has still not been fully implemented. As for Bosnia and Kosovo, U.S.-brokered independence for the states has created fragile ethnic peace rather than lasting stability.

The other factor inhibiting profound U.S. involvement in the Canada–Quebec dispute is the proximity of the country in crisis. The United States is likely to be especially hesitant to become involved in mediating internal disputes in neighboring states because it can set off latent anti-American sentiment. Good faith mediation that produces an unsatisfactory outcome for one of the parties could lead directly to a backlash against the United States.

Canada has a long history of sending troops to carry out peace-keeping missions in various parts of the world and, more recently, combat operations in Afghanistan. For many specialists on Canada, it is unimaginable that the federal government will not be able eventually to reach a solution to a problem at home: how to accommodate Quebecers' desire for asymmetrical status.

A step in that direction was taken in 2006 when the Canadian parliament passed a resolution sponsored by Prime Minister Harper to recognize *the French-speaking people of Quebec as a nation within a united Canada*. The main opposition parties—the Liberals, the Bloc, and New Democrats—all supported the resolution, which had symbolic rather than constitutional value but which went a step further than parliamentary recognition of Quebec as a distinct society (as enacted under the Chrétien government).

Despite overwhelming parliamentary approval, concerns were raised about recognizing French-speaking Quebecers' nationhood. Harper's intergovernmental affairs minister, Michael Chong, resigned, complaining that he would not accept the ethnic nationalism implied in the resolution as a substitute for Canada's traditional civic nationalism. Other political observers feared that recognition of French-speaking Quebecers' nationhood could reignite the Quebec sovereignty movement—but it did not.

When a state uses constitutional procedures to manage an ethnic conflict, chances are that external involvement will be unnecessary. Respect for the principle of nonintereference in a country's domestic affairs by interested third parties— France and the United States are the major stakeholders in the Quebec–Canada disagreement—is likely to be cemented when the domestic actors at the heart of the dispute are committed to reaching a legal resolution. Norway's peaceful secession from Sweden over a century ago is evidence of this and may be relevant to the Canadian case. To be sure, peaceful breakups are rare, and conflicting nationalisms may easily spin out of control. It is difficult to see this happening in Canada's culture of civility.

## Discussion Questions

1. What are the historical grievances advanced by Quebec nationalists to justify separation from English Canada? Are these more important than arguments emphasizing Quebec's cultural and linguistic development?

2. In what way has Canada's political culture, stressing constitutional procedures for resolving disputes, affected the nature and methods of the Quebec sovereignty movement? How has the Canadian Supreme Court been involved in setting the ground rules for secession?

3. Which external parties have a stake in Canada's possible breakup? What role, if any, have they played in the dispute between Quebec and Ottawa?

Would that role change if a majority of Quebecers voted for sovereignty?

4. What are the major characteristics of peaceful secession? Why is it so rare? Would Quebec's peaceful secession from Canada have a demonstration effect on national minorities living in other western liberal democracies?

5. Using Quebec as an example, how does global economic interdependence affect secessionism? Does it offer an opportunity structure for smaller nations to conduct their own economic affairs, or does economic interdependence leave the future of smaller nations in the hands of large international actors?

## Key Terms

Bill 101
*Bloc Québécois*
British North America Act
    (BNA Act)

distinct society
Durham
effectivity principle
interculturalism

internal self-determination
Meech Lake Accord
North American Free Trade
    Agreement (NAFTA)

| *Parti Québécois* | Plains of Abraham | Quiet Revolution |
| patriating | political opportunity | Rest of Canada (ROC) |
| *Pequiste* | structure | velvet divorce |

## Notes

1. For an argument about the commonalities, see Mihailo Crnobrnja, "Could It Happen Here?" *The Gazette* (Montreal), October 29, 1996, p. B3.
2. See Richard Simeon, *Federal–Provincial Diplomacy: The Making of Recent Policy in Canada* (Toronto: University of Toronto Press, 1977).
3. For an excellent introduction, see Paul-André Linteau, René Durocher, Jean-Claude Robert, *Quebec: A History 1867–1929* (Toronto: Lorimer, 1983).
4. Charles Taylor, *Reconciling the Solitudes: Essays on Canadian Federalism and Nationalism* (Montreal: McGill–Queen's University Press, 1993), p. 5.
5. See Paul-André Linteau, René Durocher, Jean-Claude Robert, *Quebec Since 1930* (Toronto: Lorimer, 1991).
6. On language of education for immigrants, see Donat Taddeo and Raymond Taras, *Le débat linguistique au Québec* (Montreal: Les Presses de l'Université de Montréal, 1986).
7. See Claude Morin, *Quebec Versus Ottawa: The Struggle for Self-Government 1960–72* (Toronto: University of Toronto Press, 1976).
8. Milton J. Esman, *Ethnic Politics* (Ithaca, N.Y.: Cornell University Press, 1994), p. 164.
9. Taylor, *Reconciling the Solitudes*, pp. 5–6.
10. Ibid., p. 6.
11. Pierre Elliot Trudeau, *Memoirs* (Toronto: McClelland and Stewart, 1994), pp. 325–326.
12. Taylor, *Reconciling the Solitudes*, p. 34.
13. Dominique Clift, *Quebec Nationalism in Crisis* (Montreal: McGill–Queen's University Press, 1982), p. 142.
14. On the evolution of sovereigntist support in Quebec in the period 1962–1994, see Jonathan Lemco, *Turmoil in the Peaceable Kingdom: The Quebec Sovereignty Movement and Its Implications for Canada and the United States* (Toronto: University of Toronto Press, 1994), p. 75. See also Jean-François Lisée, *The Trickster: Robert Bourassa and Quebecers 1990–1992* (Toronto: Lorimer, 1994), p. 360.
15. Lemco, *Turmoil in the Peaceable Kingdom*, p. xiii.
16. Lisée, *The Trickster*, pp. 16–17.
17. National Executive Council of the Parti Québécois, *Quebec in a New World: The PQ's Plan for Sovereignty* (Toronto: Lorimer, 1994), p. 6.
18. Howard Adelman, "Quebec: The Morality of Secession," in Joseph H. Carens, ed., *Is Quebec Nationalism Just? Perspectives Anglophone Canada* (Montreal: McGill–Queen's University Press, 1995), p. 177.
19. See Supreme Court of Canada, "Quebec Constitutional Amendment Reference," no. 2, December 1982, 45 N.R. 317, 331.
20. "Reference re Secession of Quebec," *Supreme Court Reports*, File No. 25506, August 20, 1998.
21. "Reference re Secession of Quebec," "Reference by Governor in Council," Section (2).

22. "Reference re Secession of Quebec," "Reference by Governor in Council," Section (2).
23. "Reference re Secession of Quebec," para. 66.
24. "Reference re Secession of Quebec," para. 76.
25. "Reference re Secession of Quebec," "Reference by Governor in Council," Section (2).
26. "Reference re Secession of Quebec," paras. 123–124.
27. "Reference re Secession of Quebec," para. 112.
28. "Reference re Secession of Quebec," para. 122.
29. "Reference re Secession of Quebec," para. 126.
30. "Reference re Secession of Quebec," para. 138.
31. "Reference re Secession of Quebec," data cited in para. 135.
32. "Reference re Secession of Quebec," para. 154. Emphasis added.
33. "Reference re Secession of Quebec," para. 143.
34. Robert A. Young, *The Secession of Quebec and the Future of Canada* (Montreal: McGill–Queen's University Press, 1995).
35. Lemco, *Turmoil in the Peaceable Kingdom*, p. 135.
36. Young, *The Secession of Quebec and the Future of Canada*, pp. 94–95.
37. Robert A. Young, "How Do Peaceful Secessions Happen?" *Canadian Journal of Political Science*, 27, no. 4, December 1994, pp. 773–792.
38. Ibid., pp. 147–148.
39. Ibid., p. 292.
40. Esman, *Ethnic Politics*, p. 31.
41. Ibid., pp. 31–32.
42. Guy Lachapelle, Gerald Bernier, Daniel Salee, and Luc Bernier, *The Quebec Democracy: Structures, Processes and Policies* (Toronto: McGraw–Hill Ryerson, 1993), p. 70.
43. Lachapelle et al, *The Quebec Democracy*, p. 70.
44. Ibid., p. 31.
45. Ibid., p. 32.
46. "Quebec's Diversity Is Different, Taylor Says", *Montreal Gazette* (May 23, 2008). See also the debate "Unreasonable Accommodation?" in *Inroads*, no. 22 (Winter/Spring 2008).
47. "Minority Report Makes 37 Recommendations on Culture, Religion," CBC News (May 22, 2008), at http://www.cbc.ca/canada/montreal/story/2008/05/22/qc-boutayrecommendations.html.
48. "We'll Keep Crucifix Up, Charest Says," *Montreal Gazette*, May 23, 2008.
49. Lemco, *Turmoil in the Peaceable Kingdom*, pp. 149–150.
50. Jean-Francois Lisée, *In the Eye of the Eagle* (Toronto: HarperCollins, 1990).
51. See Alfred O. Hero, Jr., and Louis Balthazar, *Contemporary Quebec and the United States, 1960–1985* (Lanham, Md.: University Press of America, 1988). See also Alfred O. Hero and Marcel Daneau, eds., *Problems and Opportunities in U.S.–Quebec Relations* (Boulder, Colo.: Westview Press, 1984).
52. Quoted in Keith G. Banting, "If Quebec Separates: Restructuring North America," in R. Kent Weaver, ed., *The Collapse of Canada?* (Washington, D.C.: Brookings Institution, 1992), p. 176.
53. See the special issue on "The 1995 Quebec Referendum: An American View," in *American Review of Canadian Studies*, 25, no. 4, Winter 1995. See also the memoirs of then U.S. ambassador to Canada: James J. Blanchard, *Behind the Embassy Door: Canada, Clinton and Quebec* (Toronto: McClelland and Stewart, 1998).
54. Lemco, *Turmoil in the Peaceable Kingdom*, p. 147.
55. Frederic Bastien, *Relations Particulières: La France face au*

*Quebec après de Gaulle* (Montreal: Les Editions du Boreal, 1999), pp. 353–354.

56. J. F. Bosher, *The Gaullist Attack on Canada, 1967–1997* (Montreal: McGill–Queen's University Press, 1999), p. 126.

57. "Sarkozy's Quebec Comments Stir Anger," *Toronto Star*, May 9, 2008.

58. "The Sarkozy Code on Quebec Sovereignty," *CBC News* (February 4, 2009)

59. See Lansing Lamont, *Breakup: The Coming End of Canada and the Stakes for America* (Toronto: Key Porter Books, 1995).

60. Lemco, *Turmoil in the Peaceable Kingdom,* pp. 92–95.

61. Conrad Black, "Canada's Continuing Identity Crisis," *Foreign Affairs,* 74, no. 2, March/April 1995, pp. 114–115.

62. Adrian Guelke, "The United States, Irish Americans, and the Northern Ireland Peace Process," *International Affairs,* 72, no. 3, July 1996, p. 535.

# CHAPTER 7

# Intractable Ethnic War?: The Tamil-Sinhalese Conflict In Sri Lanka

## INTRODUCTION

In this chapter, we shift our focus to South Asia and to "dirty wars" by studying the prolonged Tamil–Sinhalese ethnic conflict in Sri Lanka. Typically **dirty wars** are deep-rooted and highly internationalized ethnic conflicts, that are ruthlessly fought by the adversaries, produce great human suffering and human rights abuses, and are difficult to resolve through international third-party involvement. As recent developments in Sri Lanka vividly demonstrate, such conflicts often end with the complete military defeat and destruction of one side. But, while a "fight to the finish" may lead to the end of the conflict, it usually leaves behind a war ravaged country and a complex humanitarian emergency. At the conclusion of dirty wars, therefore, peace building, reconstruction and reconciliation emerge as the main challenges. Sustained international commitment and support is usually needed to meet these challenges.

## WHY DID ETHNIC CONFLICT OCCUR IN SRI LANKA?

Sri Lanka (formerly Ceylon), a small island off the southern coast of India, has a total population of around 20 million, of which roughly 74 percent are **Sinhalese**; 18 percent are Tamils; 7 percent are **Moors**; and the rest are **Burghers**, **Malays**, and **Veddhas**.[1] In terms of the population's religious orientation, approximately 70 percent are Sinhalese-Buddhists, about 15 percent are Hindus, around 7 percent are Muslims, and Roman Catholics and other Christian groups account for 8 percent.[2] The Sinhalese mostly inhabit the wetter southern, western, and central parts of Sri Lanka. The roots of their civilization are largely Indian, although over the years, they have been influenced by other cultures, including the Portuguese; the English; and to a lesser extent, the Dutch, the Burmese, and the Thais. The bulk of the Tamil population is concentrated in the drier northern and eastern parts of Sri Lanka and is split into two distinct groups: the **Sri Lankan Tamils**, who are mainly descendants of tribes that first arrived on the island well over 1,500 years ago, and the **Indian Tamils**, who originate from indentured plantation workers brought to the island by British tea planters during the nineteenth and early twentieth centuries.[3]

Historically, Tamil–Sinhalese ethnic relations have been marked by both traditional rivalry and peaceful coexistence. During British colonial rule, however, contentious issues that could inflame interethnic relations remained firmly in check. But after independence in 1948, successive Sinhalese-dominated governments openly pandered to Sinhalese-Buddhist nationalist sentiments, and they tried to resolve these contentious issues in ways that favored the Sinhalese community at the expense of the minorities, especially the Tamils. The result was a steep deterioration in interethnic relations in the immediate postindependence era, which turned into a brutal insurgency–counterinsurgency war starting in the early 1980s.

One of the most serious issues between the Sinhalese and Tamil communities concerns the Sri Lankan Tamils' demand for political autonomy or independence, based on their notion of a national territorial homeland comprising the northern and eastern provinces of Sri Lanka. The Sri Lankan Tamils' insistence on their "right" to a national homeland derives from their belief that they had been the first people to settle on the island and that they had a long history of separate political existence

## Sri Lanka

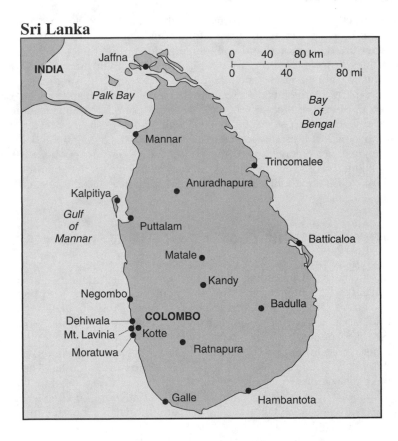

from the Sinhalese prior to British rule. The Sinhalese community and the Sri Lankan government, however, completely refute the Sri Lankan Tamils' territorial claims over any parts of Sri Lanka. Myths and legends composed by **bhikkhus** (Buddhist monks) maintain that the Sinhalese were the first civilized people to settle on the island, long before the Tamils came. These stories also allege that the Sinhalese arrival in Sri Lanka was at the request of Lord Buddha himself, and hence it is the "religious–ethnic destiny" of the Sinhalese community to control the entire island so that the Buddhist religion can be protected and promoted there. Based on this schema, the Hindu Tamils, whose presence in Sri Lanka are claimed by the Sinhalese to be the result of invasion, conquest, and British labor and emigration policy, are denied any territorial rights to a separate national homeland.

Cultural and religious differences and insecurities have also contributed to destroying ethnic harmony in Sri Lanka. The Tamils are mostly Hindus, although their identity has no specific religious or Hindu dimension. This probably explains why the Sri Lankan Tamils have historically not expressed fears about the Sinhalese community's desire to protect and promote Buddhism, which many Hindus consider to be an offshoot of Hinduism that expounds similar themes on life and religion.[4] In contrast, the Sinhalese, who are overwhelmingly Buddhist, despite some conversions to Christianity in the colonial period, have an aversion to the Tamils. The *bhikkhus* have been apprehensive that the preeminent position of the Buddhist religion in Sri Lanka faces a grave threat from Hindu Tamils, not only from within Sri Lanka but also from the strong Tamil diaspora in India, numbering about 80 million. The *bhikkhus'* apprehension was formed over centuries due to repeated invasions of Sri Lanka by South India's powerful Tamil kingdoms, which eventually led to the overthrow of the ancient Sinhalese-Buddhist kingdom in the north and the forced migration of Sinhalese people from the north to the south in the thirteenth century. Spurred also by the fear that their privileged position within the Sinhalese-Buddhist community would be at grave risk if Sri Lanka ever came under the political domination of Hindu Dravidian rulers,[5] the *bhikkhus* tried to influence Sinhalese national consciousness in the postindependence period "by deliberately exaggerating historical events dealing with Sinhalese–Tamil conflict."[6] For instance, the *bhikkhus* evoked legends and myths to advocate the view that Sinhalese-Buddhist society faced the constant danger of being destroyed or polluted by the Dravidian Hindu civilization and that past Sinhalese rulers had made heroic efforts to curb Tamil invasions. Such legends and myths made a deep impression on Sinhalese national consciousness, leading to the creation of a minority complex—that is, the majority Sinhalese community came to see itself as a small minority living under the shadow of a grave threat posed to its religious, cultural, and national identity by 100 million Hindu Tamils in Sri Lanka and India. To a large extent, this explained "the negative way [the] Sinhalese.... reacted to Tamil demands for regional autonomy for the northern and eastern areas of the country, which the Tamils [considered] to be their traditional homeland."[7]

Another issue that contributed to the conflict was language rights and the choice of a national language after independence. The Tamil and Sinhalese communities are both essentially linguistic groups, and within each community, language acts as a source of emotional identification.[8] But this issue also had important implications for the economic and financial well-being of both communities. When Sri Lanka was under Portuguese and Dutch colonial rule, administrative functions were generally carried out in the island's languages, and the languages of the colonial power were used only for record keeping and some central government tasks. Under the British, however, Sri Lanka was governed in the English language. After the British established a centralized form of government in 1833, the local demand for English education rose swiftly because people realized that knowledge of English was essential for employment. But the colonial administration faced such enormous difficulties in providing English education that, by 1885, the government changed its education policy to emphasize vernacular education for the masses. This left Christian missionaries as the only ones still teaching English in schools they established.[9] As a consequence of this new education policy, the division between the English-educated (who were mainly Tamils because they wholeheartedly embraced English education offered by Christian missionaries) and the vernacular-educated local people (who were mainly Sinhalese because they were suspicious about Christian missionaries and English education) grew rapidly and formed a formidable class hierarchy.[10] The people who obtained an English education (mostly the Tamils) found it easier to procure well-paid government jobs and thus came to enjoy greater wealth, prestige, and power compared with the vernacular-educated masses (mostly Sinhalese) who worked mainly as cultivators, laborers, village traders, and service workers. Friction gradually grew between the Sinhalese and the Tamils when it became apparent to the Sinhalese that the Tamils had secured a huge advantage in the competition for government jobs by virtue of their proficiency in the English language.[11]

Another aspect of the economic problem concerned the status of a substantial number of Indian Tamils who were brought by the British from southern India in the 1830s to work in the coffee, tea, and rubber plantations located mainly in the Kandyan Hills.[12] The Sinhalese considered the Indian Tamils to be foreigners with no abiding interest in the country except for their low-wage jobs on the plantations. The Sinhalese also feared that the Indian Tamils and the Moors, together with the Sri Lankan Tamils, would dominate the island's economy and pose a challenge to the survival of the Sinhalese race, religion, and civilization. Right after the island obtained independence from the British, Sinhalese politicians and the *bhikkhus* fanned these fears within the Sinhalese community for their own political advantage.

The conflict over language rights and the choice of a national language after independence took the form of the **Swabhasha movement** ("the people's own language movement"), which pushed for the Sinhalese language to be the sole official language of government instead of English.[13] Supported by the *bhikkhus* and Sinhalese political parties, the *Swabhasha* movement symbolized for the Sinhalese "their aspirations to retrieve their ancestral heritage and reassert their position and prerogatives as the majority, which they felt were denied them under colonial rule."[14] To the Tamils, however, the *Swabhasha* movement symbolized the Sinhalese majority's dreaded domination, which could threaten Tamil existence as a separate group.[15]

The fallout from these differences, fears, and insecurities occurred on the political front. Under British colonial rule, communal representation in the legislative council was the vehicle through which the various communities participated in the political process. Starting in the 1920s, however, Sinhalese politicians began to demand that communal representation be replaced by some form of territorial representation that would reflect the majority community's size relative to that of the minority communities.[16] Anxious for self-government, the Sri Lankan Tamils at this stage were willing to accept a Sinhalese majority in the legislative council provided that the Ceylon National Congress (CNC) "actively supported the proposal for the reservation of a special seat for the Tamils residing in the Western Province."[17] When no such support came from the CNC, the Tamils began to suspect that Sinhalese politicians were willing to sacrifice Tamil interests, a suspicion that was reinforced when the CNC came under the sway of the Buddhist Revivalist Movement. Subsequently, the Sri Lankan Tamils sought to convince the Donoughmore Commission, which was given the task of recommending constitutional reforms, to retain communal representation. In this effort, the Tamil community failed. The Donoughmore Constitution, which was adopted in 1931, abolished communal elec-torates, granted the franchise to all adults over 21 years of age, and created a state council whose members were to be elected through a territorial electoral system based on area and population. In the state council, Sri Lankan internal administration was to be carried out under the direction of elected ministers, and the powers re-served for the governor were to be handled by the British officers of state.

The implications of the Donoughmore Constitution for interethnic relations were obvious: with the Sinhalese constituting two-thirds of the island's population, the introduction of universal suffrage was bound to create an overwhelming num-ber of territorial constituencies that had a Sinhalese majority, in turn allowing the Sinhalese community to assert its strength politically. The Sri Lankan Tamils, there-fore, demanded that any constitutional arrangement for an independent Sri Lanka must incorporate safeguards for minority interests. Toward this end, it recom-mended to the **Soulbury Commission**, which was asked to draft a new constitu-tion for an independent Sri Lanka, to incorporate a **50:50 formula** in the new constitution—that is, 50 percent of the seats in the parliament of independent Sri Lanka to be reserved for the Sinhalese and the remaining 50 percent for the Sri Lankan Tamils and other minorities, such as the Muslims and the Burghers. The Soulbury Commission rejected this proposal. Instead, the Soulbury Constitution pro-hibited the parliament of independent Sri Lanka from enacting laws prejudicial to minority interests. Except for this limitation, which could be overcome by constitu-tional amendment, the Soulbury Constitution did not provide any other safeguards for the minorities.[18] This made the country ripe for the emergence of postindepen-dence ethnic conflict.

The first sign of trouble came when, contrary to assurances made by Prime Minister D. S. Senanayake, the first prime minister of independent Sri Lanka, that no harm would come to the minorities, the United National Party (UNP) government passed the Ceylon Citizenship Act of 1948 and the Indian and Pakistani Residents (Citizenship) Act of 1949. These two pieces of legislation, along with the Parliamentary Elections (Amendment) Act of 1949, laid down strict requirements and documentation for eligibility for Sri Lankan citizenship, which very few Indian Tamils could meet. Consequently, a vast majority of Indian Tamils became stateless, and the minorities' overall parliamentary capacity to defend their legitimate civil rights as citizens was reduced.[19] Thereafter, successive Sinhalese-dominated govern-ments utilized their parliamentary strengths to implement discriminatory measures such as the Official Language Act of 1956,[20] the policy of "standardization,"[21] and state-aided programs of colonization of Tamil areas by Sinhalese peasants,[22] which reduced the minorities, particularly the Sri Lankan Tamils, to an inferior status. Even at the societal level, persecution of minorities continued, often with tacit govern-mental approval. The resurgence of extremist Sinhalese-Buddhist nationalism after independence greatly influenced the governments of Sri Lanka in these efforts.[23]

Faced with grim prospects after independence, the Sri Lankan Tamils resorted to agitation, strikes, demonstrations, and civil disobedience movements to "protect their community from domination and possible assimilation by the large Sinhalese majority."[24] Throughout the 1950s and 1960s, Sri Lankan Tamil demands were mainly autonomist in nature: to protect the Sri Lankan Tamils' cultural, linguistic, economic, educational, and political rights through decentralization and devolution of political power that could lead to substantial autonomy for the Sri Lankan Tamil homeland. Sri Lankan Tamil leaders believed that, without regional autonomy, it would be impossible to protect and promote their civil rights and liberties and improve the economic condition in their traditional homeland. But they never demanded a separate Tamil state. It was only in the mid-1970s that "serious calls for a separate Tamil state were made by leading political figures and organizations."[25] A primary reason for the rise of secessionist sentiments among the Sri Lankan Tamils was the failure of negotiations between the Sinhalese and Tamil political leaders and the impatience of Tamil youths with conventional methods of agitation.[26] The Tamil youths were further encouraged by the successful secession of East Pakistan in 1971 and the creation of the new state of Bangladesh.[27]

The Tamil youths' drift toward militancy received an impetus in 1978 when the ruling UNP government of J. R. Jayewardene introduced a new constitution that created a presidential form of government (with Jayewardene as the first executive president) and provided certain concessions to the minorities: it gave Tamil the status of a "national language," although Sinhalese remained the only "official" one; it introduced a new system of voting whereby minorities' votes would count in national politics;[28] and it created new district councils that gave the Sri Lankan Tamils considerable autonomy in Tamil-majority areas. But all these concessions came to nothing because the ruling party was not serious in implementing them. For instance, the increased official use of Tamil did not come about as the minorities had expected; district councils were not given enough powers of autonomy; and parliamentary elections, in which the Sri Lankan Tamils could have played an important part, were declared unnecessary by the ruling party.[29] To the frustrated Tamil youths, therefore, militancy seemed to be the only option left. By the early 1980s, several Tamil insurgent organizations had cropped up. The largest and the most powerful of these groups was the **Liberation Tigers of Tamil Eelam (LTTE)**, led by Velupillai Prabhakaran. Founded in 1972 as the Tamil New Tigers, the group changed its name to Liberation Tigers of Tamil Eelam in 1976, which coincided with the demand for a separate state to be called **Tamil Eelam**. In 1981, a faction of the LTTE broke away to form the People's Liberation Organization of Tamil Eelam (PLOTE). A host of other groups also emerged in the early 1980s: chief among these were the Tamil Eelam Liberation Organization (TELO); the Eelam People's Revolutionary Liberation Front (EPRLF); the Tamil Eelam Liberation Army (TELA); and the Eelam Revolutionary Organization of Students (EROS).

The Tamil insurgency became more potent in the aftermath of the anti-Tamil riots of 1983. During the riots, senior government personnel used state machinery and resources in a blatant and concerted effort directed against the lives and properties of the Tamils.[30] In retaliation, the LTTE and the other guerrilla organizations changed their style of operation "from isolated attacks on policemen and Tamil politicians who cooperated with the government to organized attacks on [Sinhalese] military units."[31] These attacks brought about harsh reprisals from the Sri Lankan security forces against the Tamil civilian population of Jaffna, which further increased support for the Tamil insurgents in the north and east. The growing popularity of the Tamil insurgents also drove the final nail in the coffin of moderate Tamil politics practiced by political parties such as the Tamil United Liberation Front (TULF).[32] Full-blown secessionist war thus can be traced to the events in 1983.

## INTERNATIONALIZATION OF THE ETHNIC CIVIL WAR

International reaction to the onset of full-blown ethnic civil war in Sri Lanka after the July 1983 anti-Tamil riots was immediate. One of the states directly affected was neighboring India, which had more than 80 million Tamils in the southern province of Tamil Nadu who were naturally sympathetic toward their ethnic kin and urged the Indian government to protect the Tamil community in Sri Lanka. New Delhi therefore formed the view that the protection and promotion of India's national interest required an immediate deescalation of violence and the start of a peace process aiming at a peaceful settlement of the Tamil–Sinhalese conflict. From the Indian perspective, a peaceful settlement required the preservation of Sri Lanka's territorial integrity and sovereignty, and the simultaneous accommodation of the Sri Lankan Tamils' demand for regional autonomy.[33]

Other states generally followed India's line toward Sri Lanka's ethnic conflict. Through Indian diplomatic channels, the Sri Lankan Tamil political parties and insurgent organizations were able to reach a wide global audience with accounts of systematic Sinhalese discrimination against their community, which helped to earn them international goodwill and political support. For instance, Britain offered prominent Sri Lankan Tamil politicians asylum and allowed the LTTE to open a public relations office in London. Canada also took a sympathetic stand and allowed many Sri Lankan Tamil refugees to settle in the country. The United States and the Soviet Union also accepted as legitimate India's concerns for the Sri Lankan Tamils and professed full faith in New Delhi's ability to effect a peaceful settlement of the conflict. Consequently, when President Jayewardene visited the United States in 1984 to seek U.S. support for the Sri Lankan government's position on the ethnic issue and to obtain military assistance, Washington declined to provide such help.[34]

Sri Lanka, however, received military help from some other states. Within South Asia, it received some arms and military training from Pakistan.[35] China, South Africa, Singapore, and Malaysia also supplied some weapons to Sri Lanka.[36] The Sri Lankan government even hired some British, Rhodesian, and South African mercenaries to train its armed forces in counterinsurgency warfare.[37] The Sri Lankan government also sought assistance from Israel, a country with which it had severed diplomatic relations in 1970. Responding to Sri Lanka's call, Israel set up an interests section in the U.S. embassy in Colombo; the Mossad, Israel's external intelligence agency, and Shin Beth, which dealt with counterinsurgency, started providing training in **counterinsurgency operations** to Sri Lankan security forces.[38]

While New Delhi was officially using diplomacy to push for a peaceful settlement of the ethnic conflict in Sri Lanka, by 1984, the existence of guerrilla training camps in India for Sri Lankan Tamil insurgents was an open secret. These training camps were located mostly in southern Tamil Nadu and were under the aegis of the **Research and Analysis Wing (RAW)**, India's foreign intelligence agency. RAW's interest in Sri Lanka's ethnic conflict had started in the late 1970s for a number of reasons: the election of the pro-West and anti-India Jayewardene as the prime minister of Sri Lanka in 1977, increased American interest in the strategic Trincomalee Harbor in eastern Sri Lanka as a potential forward base for its rapid deployment force, and the formation of Tamil insurgent groups on the island. The first Sri Lankan Tamil group to be trained by RAW was the TELO. RAW also provided military training to the LTTE, the PLOTE, and the EROS. Training consisted of field craft; tactics; map reading; jungle and guerrilla warfare methods; and the operation of weapons such as light and medium machine guns, automatic rifles, pistols, and rocket-propelled grenades. Apart from RAW instructors, regular Indian army personnel were also reported to have taught the insurgents how to use bombs, set mines, and establish telecommunications.[39] Political parties in Tamil Nadu also provided the Sri Lankan Tamil insurgent groups with substantial material and financial support, as well as lots of free publicity and media exposure. The Indian government was well aware of the help that Tamil politicians in India were providing to Sri Lankan Tamil insurgent groups but chose to turn a blind eye to such developments.

As we have discussed in Chapter 3, one way that intrastate ethnic conflicts become internationalized is through the flow of refugees. This issue assumes a greater importance as the duration and intensity of the conflict increases. The anti-Tamil riots of 1983 drastically intensified Sri Lanka's ethnic conflict and resulted in substantial numbers of Tamil refugees fleeing the war zones in northern and eastern provinces and crossing over into Tamil Nadu in India. These refugees brought with them stories of Sinhalese atrocities against the Sri Lankan Tamils that fueled local anger in Tamil Nadu against the Sinhalese. Tamil political parties in turn applied intense political pressure on the Indian government to intervene on behalf of the Sri Lankan Tamils. For internal security and political reasons, the Indian government could not ignore these pleas for action. Prime Minister Indira Gandhi therefore warned that India could not remain indifferent toward the ethnic conflict in Sri Lanka because it affected people of Indian origin.[40]

## India's Attempt at Conflict Resolution

India's decision to intervene in Sri Lanka's ethnic conflict as a third party interested in conflict resolution stemmed from New Delhi's realization that undertaking such a role was the perfect "compromise option" between the two extreme policies of supporting Eelam and doing nothing. To prepare for this role, in the immediate aftermath of the 1983 ethnic riots in Sri Lanka, New Delhi enunciated the **Indian Doctrine of Regional Security**.[41] This clarified India's position that, if any south Asian state required external assistance to deal with serious internal conflict, it should seek it from within the region, including from India, and that the "exclusion of India in such circumstances will be considered an anti-Indian move."[42]

In August 1983, Prime Minister Indira Gandhi announced that President Jayewardene of Sri Lanka had accepted India's offer of good offices and agreed to have a broad-based conference with the Sri Lankan Tamil leaders to work out a peaceful settlement to the ethnic conflict. This set the stage for intense diplomatic efforts to induce the various Sri Lankan Tamil and Sinhalese parties to come to the negotiating table. Indira Gandhi's personal envoy, G. Parthasarathy. was given the task of mediating between the Tamil groups and the Sri Lankan government. What emerged from Parthasarathy's efforts came to be known as the **Parthasarathy Formula**. Its key provision was Annexure C, which envisaged the formation of elected regional councils in the northern and eastern provinces of Sri Lanka, with the power to levy taxes and with jurisdiction over law and order, social and economic development, and administration of justice and land policy.[43] An **all-party conference** was called to discuss these proposals. Most recognized political parties, including the TULF and several Sinhalese-Buddhist religious and nonpolitical organizations, participated in a series of meetings throughout 1984, but the discussions failed to provide a breakthrough.

There were no more Indian initiatives to resolve Sri Lanka's ethnic conflict until the middle of 1985. In the interval, India faced a major domestic tragedy when Prime Minister Indira Gandhi was assassinated by her Sikh bodyguards; she was succeeded as prime minister by her eldest son, Rajiv Gandhi. Meanwhile, in Sri Lanka, ethnic violence reached unprecedented levels after the Sri Lankan government announced plans to settle 3,000 Sinhalese families in the north and provide them with military training and weapons. Colombo also initiated a major program of weapons procurement from all possible sources. The Tamil insurgents reacted by forming a government in exile in Tamil Nadu and by stepping up violent attacks against the Sri Lankan security forces. Sensing that the situation was getting out of hand, New Delhi organized another round of talks between the Sri Lankan government and the Sri Lankan Tamil insurgents in Thimpu, the capital of Bhutan. At the negotiating table, the Sri Lankan Tamil delegation insisted that the Sri Lankan government's acceptance of the following principles were crucial for a settlement:

- The Sri Lankan government must recognize the Sri Lankan Tamils as a distinct nationality.
- The Sri Lankan government must recognize that the northern and eastern provinces together constitute the Sri Lankan Tamils' traditional homeland.
- The Sri Lankan government must recognize the Sri Lankan Tamils' right of self-determination.
- The Sri Lankan government must grant Sri Lankan citizenship to all Tamils on the island.[44]

The Sri Lankan government countered that recognizing the above principles was tantamount to conceding Eelam. The talks fell through as a result.

Following the failure of the Thimpu talks, the Tamil insurgents and the Sri Lankan security forces sought a military solution to the conflict and engaged in heavy fighting in the northern and eastern provinces. Simultaneously, severe infighting broke out among the Tamil insurgent organizations. The Sri Lankan government tried to take advantage of this situation by dealing directly with the LTTE, which had emerged as the most powerful of the Tamil insurgent groups. Recognizing that it was losing the initiative to resolve the conflict, India made another effort in 1986 to work out a negotiated settlement between the Sri Lankan Tamil insurgents and the Sri Lankan government. Under Indian pressure, President Jayewardene met Prime Minister Rajiv Gandhi, Tamil Nadu chief minister Ramachandran, and LTTE supremo Prabhakaran in Bangalore, India. In this meeting, President Jayewardene "proposed the break-up of the present Eastern Province into three separate units representing Tamils, Sinhalese and Muslims."[45] This proposal refuted the Tamils' traditional-homeland theory that was based on the merger of the northern and eastern provinces in two ways: the Sri Lankan government signaled that it did not consider the eastern province to be a predominantly Tamil area and furthermore that any merger of the northern and eastern provinces would be detrimental to the interests of the Sinhalese and Muslim populations of the eastern province.[46] The LTTE rejected this proposal outright, setting the stage once again for renewed fighting.

As fighting once again intensified in Sri Lanka, President Jayewardene, acting under pressure from Sinhalese nationalists and *bhikkhus*, imposed a food and fuel embargo on the Jaffna Peninsula and ordered the aerial bombardment of the area with the aim of destroying or at least severely weakening the LTTE. The humanitarian crisis that rapidly unfolded in Jaffna created a tremendous backlash in Tamil Nadu. Shaken by the severe criticism emanating from Tamil Nadu, New Delhi announced its intention to send relief supplies to the civilian population of the beleaguered and embattled Jaffna Peninsula, despite warnings from President Jayewardene that such an act would be considered an infringement of Sri Lankan sovereignty. India initially attempted to send the supplies by sea. When the Sri Lankan navy intercepted and turned back the Indian flotilla, Indian air force jets dropped 25 tons of food and other relief supplies over Jaffna. Amidst rumors of a possible Indian military intervention, a nervous Jayewardene indicated to India that his government was willing to work out a political solution to the conflict. As proof of sincerity, the Sri Lankan government terminated the military operations in Jaffna and released a large number of Tamil detainees from prison.

This prepared the way for renewed Indian diplomatic efforts that eventually led to the signing of the **Indo–Sri Lankan Accord** in 1987. Given the level of animosity between the Sri Lankan government and the Sri Lankan Tamil insurgent groups (especially the LTTE) and the long history of failed negotiations, New Delhi brought considerable pressure on both sides to accept the terms of the accord. The accord comprised six key provisions. First, it recognized the unity, sovereignty, and territorial integrity of Sri Lanka, thereby "eliminating Tamil claims for a sovereign state (Eelam) and averting the threat of an Indian invasion."[47] Second, it recognized Sri Lanka as a multiethnic and multilingual plural society composed of Sinhalese, Tamils, Moors, Malays, and Burghers. Third, although the northern and eastern provinces of Sri Lanka were recognized as "areas of historical habitation of Sri Lankan Tamil speaking peoples," the accord also recognized the territorial rights of other groups that lived in this territory. Fourth, the accord provided for the temporary merger of the northern and eastern provinces as a single administrative unit after the newly created provincial council elections were completed by the end of 1987; the permanency of this merger was to be determined by a referendum to be held within a year. Fifth, it provided for the cessation of hostilities, the surrender of arms by the Sri Lankan Tamil insurgent groups, and the return of the Sri Lankan security forces to the barracks; it also provided for a general amnesty to all political detainees and the repeal of the Prevention of Terrorism Act and other emergency laws. Last, India agreed to be the guarantor of the accord and promised to provide military assistance as and when requested by Colombo to implement the various provisions of the accord.[48] The Indo–Sri Lankan Accord also served to protect India's security interests. Through letters exchanged between the Indian prime minister and the Sri Lankan president, India sought and received three important guarantees from Sri Lanka, including the following:

- There will be an early understanding between the two countries about the employment of foreign military and intelligence personnel, with a view to ensuring that such presence will not prejudice Indo–Sri Lankan relations.

- The port of Trincomalee will not be made available for military use by any country in a manner prejudicial to India's interests, and India and Sri Lanka will jointly undertake the restoration and operation of the oil tank farm at Trincomalee.
- Any broadcasting facilities in Sri Lanka to foreign organizations will be reviewed to ensure that such facilities are not used for any military or intelligence purposes.[49]

The Indo–Sri Lankan Accord came as a huge disappointment to the Sri Lankan Tamil insurgent groups and to extremist-nationalist elements within the Sri Lankan political establishment. The insurgent groups were upset that the accord did not grant the right of national self-determination to the Sri Lankan Tamil people. None of the Sri Lankan Tamil political parties and insurgent organizations happened to be cosignatories to the accord, so they were not technically and legally bound by its provisions. Extremist-nationalist Sinhalese politicians and segments within the Sri Lankan military also had serious reservations about it. Given these oppositions, the Indo–Sri Lankan Accord was ineffective from the beginning. Yet clause 6 of the Annexure to the Accord committed an **Indian Peace-Keeping Force (IPKF)** to Sri Lanka to help implement the accord, although the accord itself was ambiguous about the IPKF's specific role. A day after the accord was signed, 8,000 IPKF troops entered Sri Lanka. Because the force was not supposed to engage in military action, the maxim of concentration of force was ignored, and it brought in no heavy weaponry. Within a few months of its induction, the IPKF became bogged down. In violation of the accord, the LTTE refused to surrender weapons and ammunition to the IPKF, and the Sri Lankan government continued to colonize traditional Tamil areas in the eastern province by resettling Sinhalese families there. This soon led to a renewal of hostilities between the LTTE insurgents and the Sri Lankan security forces.

The IPKF was criticized by all quarters in Sri Lanka for failing to restrain the combatants and protect civilian lives and property. Stung and humiliated by the criticisms, Prime Minister Rajiv Gandhi ordered the IPKF to crack down on anyone violating the terms of the accord. Consequently, from November 1987 to December 1989, the IPKF became embroiled in the ethnic violence in Sri Lanka, which it was incapable of effectively halting for a variety of reasons. First, the IPKF's preparation for a large-scale military action in Sri Lanka was grossly inadequate. For instance, the IPKF lacked reliable intelligence on the military strength of the various Sri Lankan Tamil insurgent groups, which prevented it from calculating accurately the strength of the forces it required for the task. Consequently, the Indian peace keepers were often surprised to find how powerful an enemy the LTTE was, and this greatly increased their losses.[50] Second, the success of counterinsurgency operations against modern-day insurgents depends to a great extent on the degree of support the troops receive from the local population. However, by the time the IPKF received orders to engage the LTTE and the Sri Lankan forces, it had clearly alienated both the Tamil and Sinhalese communities, which undermined its operational effectiveness. Third, the IPKF had to function under certain tactical and logistical restrictions because the Indian government did not want to appear insensitive to its own Tamil supporters by cracking down brutally on the LTTE. As a result, the IPKF could not use heavy weapons, tanks, and aircraft against the LTTE, thereby reducing its battlefield capabilities and increasing its casualties. And fourth, the IPKF's failure in the battlefield drew criticism from all sides that affected its morale. Units in the field were dejected because of the very high casualty rates they suffered. Officers in Sri Lanka were critical of the military top brass for being insensitive to their problems. The military top brass criticized the Indian government for imposing restrictions on the IPKF that reduced its fighting capability. On their part, Indian government officials criticized the IPKF for failing to wipe out what they deemed a handful of insurgents. The Sri Lankan government also criticized the IPKF whenever its operations bogged down or failed.

With the IPKF stymied, opposition to the accord in Sri Lanka gathered momentum. Interested in scoring political points against the ruling UNP government, the opposition Sri Lanka Freedom Party (SLFP) openly criticized the accord as violating Sri Lanka's sovereignty. More disturbing was the revival of militant Sinhalese nationalism under the Janatha Vimukthi Peramuna (JVP), or the People's Revolutionary Front, which was anti-India and anti-accord in orientation.[51] Within a short period, the JVP unleashed a reign of terror, assassinating ruling UNP members that it considered traitors to the Sinhalese cause and massacring Tamil and Indian civilians as reprisals for LTTE killing of Sinhalese civilians. The JVP-led terrorist campaign received support from the Buddhist monastic order and from opposition political parties. Some of Jayewardene's UNP colleagues who were opposed to the accord also provided support to the JVP, mainly as a ploy to put pressure on President Jayewardene to call for the withdrawal of the IPKF from Sri Lanka. By the early 1990s, this complex conflict opened a new front, with violent clashes between Sri Lankan Tamils and Muslims in the eastern province.[52]

The IPKF's failure to disarm the LTTE and prevent violent clashes demonstrated why regional powers are poor international third-party managers of ethnic conflicts. Regional powers are often distrusted by the warring parties, as was evident in Sri Lanka, where the Tamils and the Sinhalese not only did not trust each other but also did not trust India. New Delhi's offer of good offices to resolve the ethnic conflict after providing covert partisan support to the Sri Lankan Tamils only helped to sharpen both sides' suspicion that India had its own vested interests in the matter and was hardly sincere in helping the parties find a fair solution. When the adversaries distrust the third party, it may also adversely affect the peace process because the adversaries lack a positive attitude toward a peace agreement. When India urged negotiations between the Tamils and the Sinhalese, it gradually became clear that the disputants had agreed to talk to each other, not because they believed that such talks would resolve the dispute but because they were in no position to antagonize India. Hence, while they negotiated, they also prepared for war. Furthermore, in their haste to find a solution, regional powers often do not take the time to understand the basic nature of the dispute, which may undermine their role. This was evident when the Indian government did not recognize the most important factors in its dealings with the Sri Lankan government and the LTTE: the Sinhalese unwillingness to share power meaningfully with the Sri Lankan Tamils and the LTTE's uncompromising demand for Eelam. The Indians also did not fully appreciate the difficulty of convincing the adversaries that they needed to commit to the peace process. For instance, President Jayewardene's faction-ridden cabinet included prominent hard-liners, which reduced the government's ability to offer meaningful concessions to the Sri Lankan Tamils; by the mid-1980s, the Tamil nationalist movement had clearly been taken over by extremist groups such as the LTTE, which was steadfast in its demand for Eelam. Yet in its eagerness to reach a deal, India continued to recognize the moderate TULF as the prominent insurgent group because it was more likely to accept a compromise peace agreement. It was not surprising, therefore, that the LTTE lost faith in the peace process and came to regard India and the moderate Tamil groups as traitors to the Tamil cause.

## THE ETHNIC CIVIL WAR IN THE 1990s

Under pressure from its own citizens and the Sri Lankan government, New Delhi finally withdrew the IPKF from Sri Lanka in March 1990. Once the IPKF was gone, the LTTE quickly consolidated its position in the northeastern province, thereby demonstrating the support and popularity that the Tigers enjoyed among the Sri Lankan Tamil population. The Sri Lankan government attempted to counter the LTTE's gains by annulling the merger of the northern and eastern provinces. This led to the resumption of serious fighting in the north and east. In the south, the JVP insurrection assumed even bloodier proportions. The government responded by organizing death squads that killed thousands of youths and students belonging to or sympathizing with the JVP, including the organization's leader, Rohana Wijeweera, and his immediate followers.

In 1993, President Premadasa (who had taken over from Jayawardene in 1988) was assassinated by an LTTE suicide bomber. In the presidential election that followed in 1994, Chandrika Bandaranaike Kumaratunga of the People's Alliance won by a comfortable margin. In 1995, the Kumaratunga government entered into a ceasefire agreement with the LTTE and promised to come up with a set of new proposals for the devolution of power. After waiting for three months for the new proposals, the LTTE finally repudiated the ceasefire agreement. As fighting between the LTTE and the Sri Lankan military once again intensified, President Kumaratunga's new peace proposals (released in August 1995) had no takers and, in frustration, she endorsed the military's plan to launch a massive operation (code-named **Operation Riviresa**) to reestablish government control over the northern Jaffna Peninsula, the main LTTE stronghold.[53] By mid-1996, the Sri Lankan military had recaptured most of the Jaffna Peninsula, a great achievement for the Sri Lankan government and a major setback for the LTTE. The LTTE, however, was far from being completely wiped out. After lying low for a while and regrouping, the LTTE retaliated through a series of spectacular terrorist attacks on civilian and military targets.

Colombo responded to these LTTE attacks through another forceful counterinsurgency operation (code-named **Operation Jayasikuru**) designed to (1) establish a secure land corridor between Jaffna and the rest of Sri Lanka, (2) clear the northern jungles of the Wanni district, and (3) gain full control of the upper sectors of the eastern province. But despite launching repeated offensives, the Sri Lankan military failed to gain full control of Jaffna and suffered heavy casualties at the hands of the LTTE in the process, which led to large-scale desertions from its ranks.[54]

By the late 1990s, the LTTE had regained much lost ground. Although it had failed to recapture Jaffna City from the Sri Lankan military, it effectively ruled a wide belt of territory bordered by Kalmunai and Vannankulam in the far northwest and northeast, Kokkilai in the east, Vavuniya in the south, and Chirunaatkulam in the west. The LTTE had also augmented its military strength by procuring both basic and advanced combat weapons from foreign sources, paid for from funds raised by the Sri Lankan Tamil diaspora in North America, western Europe, and the Australasia region. The LTTE further appeared to be having no major problem in recruiting new cadres, and the total strength of the group was estimated to be between 8,000 to 12,000 well-armed and well-trained soldiers. The LTTE seemed capable of striking almost at will, as borne out by several terrorist strikes, the most spectacular being the attack on a Buddhist holy shrine in Kandy. The LTTE also showed no signs of giving up the demand for a separate Tamil state.

The LTTE's obduracy, potency, and ruthlessness, however, were major factors in undermining the organization's international image. Although, in general, international sympathy and support for the Sri Lankan Tamils in their just struggle remained intact, international opinion in the late 1990s came to regard the LTTE as the main obstacle to peace in Sri Lanka. This international sentiment was most evident in India's attitude toward the LTTE. After the humiliating withdrawal of the IPKF from Sri Lanka in early 1990, New Delhi had adopted a hands-off approach toward Sri Lanka's ethnic conflict. The assassination of former Prime Minister Rajiv Gandhi in 1991 at the hands of an LTTE suicide bomber, however, raised India's ire toward the organization. In the aftermath of Gandhi's assassination, the Indian government, over the objection of the Tamil parties in Tamil Nadu, classified the LTTE as a terrorist organization and launched a massive manhunt to nab Prabhakaran and other key LTTE leaders. The Indian government also publicly blamed the LTTE for prolonging the ethnic conflict in Sri Lanka and resolved to strengthen the Sri Lankan government's hands in its fight with the Tamil Tigers. The Chennai High Court hearing the Rajiv Gandhi assassination case issued death sentences for the captured suspects, all of whom were known to be LTTE cadres and working under direct orders from Prabhakaran. These revelations by the Indian government led to a significant public mood swing in India (including Tamil Nadu) against the LTTE and its stated goal of Eelam. The Indian military, too, nursed a deep resentment against the LTTE, mainly for its brutal attacks on Indian soldiers serving in the IPKF in Sri Lanka.

India's hostility toward the LTTE rubbed off on other major international actors. For instance, when the Sri Lankan military launched Operation Riviresa, the Sri Lankan government was surprised to find widespread international support for its position.[55] Then, after the Sri Lankan military captured Jaffna and forced the LTTE to withdraw to the east, few tears were shed internationally for the LTTE's military defeat, even though the LTTE's public relations office in London tried hard to project the Sri Lankan military offensive as genocide of the Tamil people. The reasons for this international apathy were obvious. The LTTE was widely regarded as a terrorist organization involved in various kinds of criminal activities, such as narcotics trafficking and arms smuggling, to finance its campaign of terror.[56] The LTTE was also condemned internationally for indiscriminately killing civilians, for torturing and mutilating captured enemy soldiers, and for using children and women as frontline combatants.[57] The LTTE's policy of assassinating key political leaders further revolted and upset the international community and earned the organization the reputation of a ruthless criminal gang.

## THE NORWAY-FACILITATED PEACE PROCESS

Throughout the 1990s, the ethnic conflict in Sri Lanka showed all the signs of a classic dirty war. Because of the heavy destruction and suffering that this conflict caused, there was widespread international support for Norway's initiative in early 2000 to facilitate peace negotiations between the Sri Lankan government and the

LTTE. The key player in the facilitation process was Erik Solheim, special adviser to Norway's foreign minister and previously the leader of the Norwegian Socialist Left Party. In 2000, Solheim held discussions with Prabhakaran regarding the framework for a ceasefire agreement leading to negotiations. Later that year, Prabhakaran and Solheim had another meeting, which resulted in the LTTE agreeing to a unilateral ceasefire.

Nothing much came of this unilateral ceasefire. In April 2001, immediately after the LTTE had ended its unilateral ceasefire, the Sri Lankan military launched a major offensive (code-named Rod of Fire) in an effort to recapture the strategic Elephant Pass, a causeway that links the Jaffna Peninsula to the south mainland. For the Sri Lankan military, control of the Elephant Pass was vital for providing needed supplies to almost 35,000 trapped soldiers in Jaffna City and the surrounding areas through a more reliable land corridor. A fierce battle raged for almost four days. The Tamil Tigers put up a strong resistance, and the Sri Lankan forces suffered heavy casualties.[58] The LTTE followed this military victory by attacking the international airport in Colombo and destroying half the fleet of Air Lanka, the national carrier, and eight military planes.[59] The government retaliated by carrying out air strikes against LTTE positions in the north. The prospects for peace negotiations appeared bleak.

Parliamentary elections in Sri Lanka at the end of 2001 resulted in a change of government and a realignment of political forces in the country. The opposition United National Front (UNF), led by Ranil Wickremesinghe, replaced the People's Alliance as the largest group in parliament and formed the new government. With the formation of the UNF government, hopes were raised that Norway-facilitated peace negotiations between the LTTE and the Sri Lankan government would be revived. As a prelude to Norway-facilitated peace talks, the LTTE and the Sri Lankan government agreed to observe a month-long ceasefire starting on December 24, 2001 (the ceasefire was subsequently extended). The government also lifted a ban on goods destined for areas under LTTE control.

Several key developments made it increasingly difficult for the LTTE to say no to Norway-facilitated peace talks with the Sri Lankan government. First, the 2001 elections brought in a new government in Colombo and, with it, a new willingness to negotiate with the LTTE. Prime Minister Wickremesinghe had long indicated his desire to deal directly with the Tamil Tigers and favored the creation of an interim administration for the Tamil-majority northeastern province in which the LTTE would have a major role. Such a stance was different from the Kumaratunga policy, which favored constitutional change to give the northeastern province more autonomy and have it accepted by the moderate Tamil parties and (hopefully) a militarily humbled LTTE. Wickremesinghe was also in favor of lifting the ban on the LTTE, the Tamil Tigers' main demand for participating in the peace talks.

Second, as a result of the new political alignments brought about by the 2001 elections, the Tamil Tigers found new political clout in Colombo. The Tamil National Alliance (TNA), a conglomeration of four Tamil parties that had, in the past, been victims of LTTE-sponsored violence but now backed the position that the Tamil Tigers, would represent the Sri Lankan Tamils in negotiations with the government. For the first time in Sri Lanka's political history, the LTTE had something akin to a political wing, with seats in parliament.[60] This would definitely strengthen the Tamil Tigers' hands at the negotiating table.

Third, it was becoming increasingly difficult for the LTTE to sustain a high level of fund-raising in western countries, especially in the aftermath of the 9/11 terrorist attacks and the subsequent U.S.-led global war on terror. Most of the key western states from which the Tamil Tigers had previously raised vast amounts of funds, such as the United States, the United Kingdom, and Canada, had already designated the LTTE as a terrorist organization and tightened their law enforcement machinery, which made it difficult for the Tamil Tigers to sustain their fund-raising activities.[61] This in turn may have had a detrimental effect on the LTTE's military preparedness and fighting capabilities. The LTTE's reputation of being a ruthless terrorist group that had massacred thousands of innocent civilians; of showing no interest in negotiated peace; and of being involved in smuggling, gun running, and drug trafficking further tarnished its international image and created difficulties in fund-raising, especially after 9/11.[62]

Fourth, there were clear indications that the Sri Lankan military was actively seeking weapons and counterinsurgency training from several sources. After their Elephant Pass defeat at the hands of the Tamil Tigers in 2001, the Sri Lankan military turned toward Israel for weapons and counterinsurgency training. Full diplomatic ties between Sri Lanka and Israel were quickly established, and Israeli military officers and advisers arrived in Sri Lanka with a large quantity of weapons. These weapons were subsequently used by a more confident Sri Lankan military in battles against the Tamil Tigers. The Sri Lankan defense budget also increased to around US$1 billion in the aftermath of 9/11, and there were growing signs that the Sri Lankan government was actively trying to secure military supplies and training from India, China, the United Kingdom, and the United States.[63] The LTTE thus faced the future prospect of being challenged by a better-trained and better-equipped Sri Lankan military that was backed politically by powerful allies.

Fifth, the Tamil Tigers were reported to be suffering from war fatigue and were facing problems in recruiting new personnel to sustain their military campaign. Although the LTTE had won spectacular victories against the Sri Lankan military in 2000 and 2001, it had suffered heavy casualties in the process. Being war weary, the LTTE had failed to recapture Jaffna City from an expensively rearmed Sri Lankan army. Sri Lankan military observers, as well as independent media and nongovernmental organization (NGO) sources, also reported that recruitment difficulties had forced the LTTE to replace fighters lost in battle with women and young children.[64]

From Colombo's viewpoint, negotiation rather than confrontation with the LTTE was also advantageous for several reasons. First, in the post-9/11 world, for reasons mentioned above, the LTTE was clearly under pressure to move away from its steadfast demand for a separate Tamil state to be achieved through armed struggle. Press reports also suggested that Prabhakaran might be willing to drop the demand for a separate state in favor of greater autonomy in the northeast region.[65] Second, in the aftermath of 9/11, world opinion had clearly turned against groups that employed terrorism, regardless of the justness of their cause. The Sri Lankan government received pledges of support from many different quarters in its war against the LTTE. Because almost no country of significance within the international community (especially neighboring India, with its population of almost 80 million fellow Tamils) supported the LTTE's demand for a separate state, the Sri Lankan government's position was further strengthened for negotiations with the Tamil Tigers. Third, creation of a stable and lasting peace was crucial for the economic regeneration and recovery of Sri Lanka. As an island economy, Sri Lanka is heavily dependent on external trade and tourism. Throughout the nineties, as the civil war continued to cause havoc, its gross domestic product (GDP) growth was badly affected. Since the late nineties, however, Sri Lanka's economy had started to revive, mainly as a result of the economic liberalization policies of the government. Consequently, GDP growth increased from 4.3 percent in 1999 to 7.4 percent by 2000. Experts forecast a far higher growth rate if peace could be achieved on the island. And fourth, Prime Minister Wickremesinghe represented a new generation of political leadership in Sri Lanka that was less concerned with ethno-religious nationalism and zero-sum military conflict and more interested in peace and prosperity in the context of globalization and market liberalization.[66] Unencumbered by past failures in the decades-long ethnic conflict, Wickremesinghe was in a position to take bold decisions to achieve peace.

## Peace Negotiations

After months of separate talks with representatives of the Sri Lankan government and the LTTE, Norwegian facilitators were able to procure an indefinite ceasefire agreement between the two sides in February 2002.[67] The signing of the agreement was followed by a visit to Jaffna by Prime Minister Wickremesinghe. This was the first visit to the Jaffna Peninsula by a Sri Lankan government leader since 1982. Wickremesinghe's message to the people of Jaffna seemed sincere and raised hopes for peace among the local population. Providing a further impetus to peace following the prime minister's visit to Jaffna, the Sri Lankan Muslim Congress (SLMC) declared that it was willing to enter into a "sincere dialogue" with the LTTE regarding Muslim problems in the northeastern province. Reciprocating the SLMC's gesture, the LTTE admitted that the Muslims had suffered severely at its hands and apologized for committing such ethnic cleansing; it further recognized the Sri Lankan Muslim people's "unique cultural identity" and pledged to address Muslim concerns and apprehensions.[68]

On April 10, 2002, LTTE chief Prabhakaran came out of his jungle hideout to hold a press conference—his first in more than a decade—with the national and international media in Kilinochchi, in northern Sri Lanka. Flanked by the LTTE's chief negotiator and political strategist, Anton Balasingham; the head of the LTTE's political section, Thamil Chelvan; and two of his top commanders, Prabhakaran fielded questions from more than 200 journalists for more than two and half hours. After indicating that he was pleased with the onset of the peace process and thanking Prime Minister Wickremesinghe for his bold actions, Prabhakaran pledged that the LTTE was "sincerely and seriously committed to peace." He pointed out, however, that "the right conditions have not arisen for the LTTE to abandon the policy of an independent statehood." He stressed that, for any solution to Sri Lanka's ethnic conflict to be acceptable to the LTTE, it must incorporate three fundamentals— Tamil homeland, Tamil nationality, and Tamil right to self-determination—and that "once these fundamentals are accepted or a political solution is put forward by Sri Lanka recognizing these three fundamentals and if our people are satisfied with the framework of a solution that recognizes these core issues, then we will consider giving up the demand for Eelam."[69] Balasingham further expanded the LTTE's understanding of self-determination: "We mean the right of people to decide their own political destiny—it can also apply to autonomy and self-governance. If autonomy and self-governance is given to our people, we can say that internal self-determination is to some extent met. But if the Sri Lankan government rejects our demand for autonomy and self-governance and continues with repression, then as a last resort we will opt for secession—that also comes under self-determination."[70] Both Prabhakaran and Balasingham noted in their press conference that, because the Wickremesinghe government was politically weak and not in a position to offer an acceptable permanent solution, it had accepted the LTTE's suggestion to create an **interim self-governing authority (ISGA)** for the northeastern province to give time to prepare the people for a permanent solution.[71]

On the eve of the much anticipated peace talks, scheduled to be held in Thailand, two key developments took place that augured well for future peace. First, realizing that the LTTE might become the de facto ruler of the northeastern province, the SLMC struck a deal with the Tamil Tigers. The Muslims accepted the de facto authority of the LTTE in the northeast; in return, the LTTE pledged that it would immediately stop the harassment of and extortions from Muslims and return paddy fields taken forcibly from Muslim farmers. The two sides also agreed to appoint a joint committee to facilitate the return of 100,000 displaced Muslims who were expelled from Jaffna and the northern mainland by the LTTE almost twelve years prior. The LTTE also accepted the SLMC as the sole representative of the Muslims in the northeastern province and agreed on its participation in the talks about the interim administration to be held in Thailand.[72] Second, the leader of the Indian Tamils, Armugam Thondaman, pledged to support the LTTE in its quest for self-determination. Thondaman was a senior cabinet minister and leader of the Ceylon Workers Congress (CWC). He had met Prabhakaran after the LTTE leader's infamous press conference, and in that meeting, the CWC and the LTTE had agreed to "work together for the resolution of the Tamil national question."[73]

The peace talks in Thailand were delayed, however, because several snags developed. Like President Kumaratunga, the Wickremesinghe government seemed to have suddenly developed apprehensions about the proposed ISGA in the northeastern province. In a speech to the European Parliament in 2002, Prime Minister Wickremesinghe stressed that the unity of Sri Lanka was nonnegotiable and remarked that, while the LTTE wanted priority to be given to the setting up of an interim administration in the northeast, his government believed that the issue of the ISGA should be linked to core political issues. President Kumaratunga held almost identical views based on her apprehension that the formation of an LTTE-controlled interim administration in the northeast would, over time, become automatically entrenched as the final solution and a precursor to a de facto separate Tamil state; she shared her apprehensions with the visiting Norwegian deputy foreign minister and made it clear that she expected the ISGA to be linked to a final political solution to the conflict.[74] Prime Minister Wickremesinghe also categorically denied that his government had given any blanket assurance to the LTTE that an interim administration under the Tamil Tigers' sole control would soon be established in the northeastern province. He further rejected the concept of a Tamil homeland within the country; instead, he reiterated the concept of a single Sri Lankan homeland incorporating all communities.[75] He even indicated that his government had no plans to repeal the Prevention of Terrorism Act, which gave sweeping detention powers to the police and armed forces against the Tamil insurgents, and expected the LTTE to respect human rights and democratic norms.[76]

Sensing that the earlier optimism about the peace talks was fast eroding, Norwegian facilitators went into overdrive to try and convince the LTTE and the Sri Lankan government to open face-to-face talks. The Norwegian initiatives finally succeeded, and a first round of face-to-face peace talks between representatives of the LTTE and the Sri Lankan government was held in Sattahip, Thailand, in September 2002. At the end of the three-day talks, the chief negotiator and political strategist of the LTTE, Balasingham, clarified that the LTTE was ready to accept "autonomy and self-governance" in northeastern Sri Lanka, the details of which could be worked out if both parties first agreed to a particular political system for the whole country. On his part, the head of the government delegation, Gamini Lakshman Peiris, stressed that the LTTE's political aspirations could be fulfilled "within one country."[77] The two sides agreed to meet again shortly for further talks and decided to set up a joint task force for humanitarian reconstructive activities.

Another round of talks between the Sri Lankan government and the LTTE was held in Oslo in December 2002. The most crucial outcome of this round of negotiations was the agreement in principle by both sides to develop a federal political system in Sri Lanka that would give the Sri Lankan Tamils "internal self-determination" in the Tamil-dominated areas of the northeast. Norway's special envoy to Sri Lanka's peace process termed this agreement as a "major step" but warned that a long and bumpy road must be traveled before a final solution could be agreed upon: "They have decided what sort of house they want to build. They want to build a house with a federal structure within a united Sri Lanka. The decision to raise this house takes a long time."[78] The end of the Oslo round of talks further provided an opportunity as well as a stiff challenge to the peace negotiators to come up with a viable method of political power sharing that could be discussed at future meetings. G. L. Peiris, head of the Sri Lankan government delegation, cautioned that the Oslo decision to explore a "federal model" was just the outer perimeter of a complex conflict resolution model and that the more contentious issues of "division of power" and "human rights" would be taken up for discussion at the next round.[79]

## Suspension of Peace Talks

Between December 2002 and April 2003, representatives of the LTTE and the Sri Lankan government held several rounds of Norway-facilitated peace talks aimed at resolving the decades-old ethnic conflict. However, the slowness of the complex negotiations, coupled with contradictory signals emanating from both sides, subjected the peace process to severe strain by mid-2003. Throughout the peace talks, the LTTE had continued to rebuild its military strength and war preparedness, and for this purpose it (especially the Sea Tigers) often violated the terms of the ceasefire agreement.[80] It had also started recruiting heavily, and its cadre strength was reported to have shot up to around 16,000 during the peace talks. The LTTE steadfastly refused to reduce its military strength until a final political settlement was reached, continued to commit atrocities against other minorities and anyone who dared to oppose it, and refused to categorically rule out the option of territorial secession and the creation of a sovereign and independent Tamil state. The Sri Lankan military also took this time to conduct a massive recruitment drive to replace a large number of deserters and soldiers killed in the battlefield. The military drew up plans for large-scale modernization of the armed forces and for building a well-trained and technologically savvy fighting force. Toward this end, Colombo requested that New Delhi provide weapons and training to its military forces.[81]

President Kumaratunga had also developed apprehensions regarding the nature of the concessions made to the LTTE by the UNF government and felt that, by utilizing the ceasefire agreement and the subsequent peace talks, the LTTE had already set up a de facto independent Tamil state in the northeastern province of Sri Lanka.[82] Her concern was shared by her party, the SLFP, and allies such as the JVP, which strongly criticized any concession made to the LTTE by the Sri Lankan government. In addition, there were significant levels of opposition to the peace talks from Sinhalese ultranationalists and religious leaders. From the very beginning of the peace process, the Sinhalese-Buddhist clergy had vehemently opposed the concessions being granted to the Tamils and argued that the peace process would undermine Sri Lanka's status as an exclusive state-protected and state-promoted Buddhist state.

Finally, key foreign governments as well as major donors had developed serious reservations about the behavior of the LTTE and the overall direction of the peace process. For instance, the National Democratic Alliance government in India, led by Atal Bihari Vajpayee, made it clear that any solution to Sri Lanka's ethnic conflict must ensure principles of democracy, pluralism, and human rights. India voiced its concern for the way the LTTE treated other Tamil political parties, members of minority and majority communities in Sri Lanka, and captive government soldiers. Another serious issue was the extradition of the LTTE chief, Prabhakaran, a key figure implicated in the Rajiv Gandhi assassination case.[83] Some of India's concerns were shared by the United States.[84] Sri Lanka's main donors and aid providers also developed skepticism about the peace process and stressed that only rapid progress in the peace talks would give the two sides a significant advantage at the June 2003 donor conference in Tokyo.[85]

In April 2003, the LTTE abruptly suspended the peace talks on the grounds that the resettlement of displaced people would not be possible until the Sri Lankan army relocated from the high-security zones in Jaffna City. Regaining Jaffna City, either by force or through negotiations, had been high on the LTTE's agenda since it lost control of that area in December 1995. In April 2000, when it recaptured the Elephant Pass, it had come close, but it could not take Jaffna City mainly because its military resources had been stretched thin. Some observers believed that the LTTE's decision to suspend peace talks was also a tactical ploy to win major concessions from the government, such as recognition of the Sea Tigers as a de facto naval unit.

Intense diplomatic efforts were once again undertaken by the Norwegian deputy foreign minister, Vidar HelgesenTokyo's special envoy, Yassushi Akashi and Oslo's special envoy, Erik Solheim, to bring the Tamil Tigers back on board the peace process and to convince them to attend the donors' conference in Tokyo. But on May 1, 2003, the Tamil Tigers escalated their brinkmanship by rejecting the government's offer to deescalate the crisis and by relocating Sri Lankan soldiers guarding Jaffna City to its outskirts. The government was unwilling to concede any more because it feared that any further relocation of the soldiers would mean the loss of state control over Jaffna City, which the LTTE wanted to retake desperately. The impasse thus continued, which raised fears of a return to the days of full-scale war.[86]

## Political Turmoil and Its Impact on Peace Talks

Although the Norwegian facilitators prevailed upon the LTTE and the Sri Lankan government not to return to the days of war, from late 2003 to early 2004, serious doubts developed regarding the continued viability and relevance of the peace process. Frustrated and angered by what she perceived as the appeasement of the

LTTE and the de facto partitioning of the country by the Wickremesinghe government's peace concessions, President Kumaratunga evoked the executive presidency's enormous powers to declare a state of emergency in the country in November 2003, under which she suspended the parliament and took over control of the ministries of defense, the interior, and the media from the government.[87] She also directed her party, the SLFP, to explore the possibility of forming an electoral and political alliance with the JVP, thereby fuelling speculation that she intended to shortly call for fresh parliamentary elections. The SLFP–JVP alliance was formed in January 2004, with the two parties agreeing to form a combined front, the United People's Freedom Alliance (UPFA). In early 2004, President Kumaratunga dissolved parliament and called fresh elections.

The dismissal of the UNF government and the formation of the UPFA was an ominous development for the peace process mainly because the UPFA's position regarding the peace process differed significantly from that of the Wickremesinghe government's. For instance, unlike the UNF, the UPFA publicly declared that it did not recognize the LTTE as the sole representative of the Tamil people and hence preferred to hold discussions with all stakeholders, including relevant Tamil political parties and civil society groups, to find an acceptable solution to the country's ethnic conflict. The UPFA also criticized the Norway-facilitated peace process for "taking an undesirable turn" and for setting out a path for a separate state. Rejecting the federal model favored by the LTTE and the UNF, the UPFA made it clear that it preferred a peace process aimed toward decentralization and devolution of power within a unitary structure.[88] The UPFA further blamed the LTTE for its repeated and provocative violations of the ceasefire agreement and for not negotiating in good faith by continuing to recruit soldiers and stockpile weapons. Finally, the inauguration of the Tamil Eelam police headquarters in Kilinochchi by LTTE chief Prabhakaran in 2003, was a clear indication to the UPFA that, regardless of what it had said earlier, the LTTE was gradually trying to put in place all the trappings of a quasi-state in the northeastern province.[89] The JVP's propaganda secretary even went so far as to suggest that, with the collapse of the UNF government, the ceasefire agreement was no longer in effect and warned that "the people must not be afraid that the war is coming back."[90] In addition to these pronouncements, the UPFA declared that, if it came to power after the parliamentary elections, it would abolish the executive presidency and reconvert Sri Lanka into a full parliamentary democracy.[91] Not surprisingly, the LTTE categorically refused to participate in any peace talks with the UPFA; Balasingham noted in an interview: "Our organization will not enter into negotiations with anyone who does not recognize the LTTE as the sole and authentic representative of the Tamil people."[92] He further warned that the formation of the UPFA signaled the coming together of Sinhala chauvinistic forces that reject the Tamils' legitimate territorial rights in the northeast and have no intention of sharing power with the Tamils; hence, dangerous consequences would arise if the UPFA were voted into power.

Close on the heels of the formation of the UPFA, reports circulated of a split between the LTTE's main organization, led by Prabhakaran and based in Kilinochchi in the northern Wanni region, and its eastern unit, led by Muralitharan, alias **Colonel Karuna**, and based in the eastern Batticaloa-Amparai district. The reasons for the north–east split within the LTTE are still shrouded in mystery, although many have speculated about its causes. For instance, some in the media suggested that the split was triggered by a demand from the LTTE's northern leaders that Karuna send 1,000 of his combat troops to the Wanni, which Karuna refused on the grounds that redeployment of his forces would weaken the LTTE in the vulnerable eastern districts. It was also reported that the eastern wing of the LTTE had been harboring a grievance that leaders from the north, particularly from Jaffna, were monopolizing the leadership positions within the organization, while the bulk of the actual fighting with the Sri Lankan forces was conducted by soldiers from the east. Karuna was further reported to be upset at the condescending treatment of the eastern Tamils by the LTTE's northern leadership. He was said to have complained that funds collected by the LTTE abroad had almost entirely been spent in the Wanni and Jaffna, and none had reached the Batticaloa-Amparai area; moreover, not one out of the thirty-odd divisions of the LTTE's administrative setup was headed by someone from Batticaloa-Amparai. Another area of disagreement between the northern and eastern leadership was alleged to be the overtures that the LTTE made toward the Muslims in eastern Sri Lanka. The LTTE's eastern leadership was reportedly upset by Prabhakaran's soft line toward the SLMC at a time when clashes between members of the two communities were a regular feature in the eastern region, and Muslim youth were said to be forming anti-LTTE "Osama suicide squads" to hit back.[93] A final theory suspected Indian and U.S. complicity behind the split within the LTTE.[94]

Regardless of its causes, the split introduced uncertainty into the peace process by undermining the LTTE's political standing and bargaining power at the negotiating table. For instance, the LTTE's claim to being the sole representative of Sri Lankan Tamils was badly dented by Karuna's revolt. Karuna's claim that the LTTE represented North Eelam while he and his forces (numbering around 6,000) represented South Eelam largely negated the LTTE's long-standing position that the northeastern province formed the historic homeland of the Sri Lankan Tamil people. Additionally, Karuna's attempts to obtain official recognition of his unit from the Sri Lankan government and the Norwegian facilitators did not bode well for the LTTE.

In an exercise in damage control, Prabhakaran expelled Karuna from the organization and ordered a large number of his forces to quietly move into the eastern region from their positions in the north. Given the LTTE's past history in dealing with insubordination within its ranks, it was predictable that Prabhakaran would attempt to crush Karuna's revolt. And although Prabhakaran's forces surprisingly met with little resistance (most of Karuna's fighters meekly surrendered, and Karuna himself fled the region), the potential for Karuna to play the role of a spoiler in any future peace negotiation remained strong, provided he retained his popularity among the Tamil population of eastern Sri Lanka and received political and military support from the Sri Lankan government willing to use him as a counterweight to the LTTE.[95]

## TSUNAMI DISASTER AND THE DISPUTE OVER RELIEF AND RECONSTRUCTION

The 2004 parliamentary elections drastically altered the political landscape in Sri Lanka again. The UPFA emerged as the single largest party (105 seats) in a parliament with a total strength of 225 and formed the new government under Mahinda

Rajapakse. The election results indicated a strong ethnic polarization in Sri Lanka, which cast a shadow over the peace process. The UPFA government was critical of Norway's mediation, refused to recognize the LTTE as the sole representative of the Tamil people, and rejected the "federal model" that had been agreed to in principle earlier.[96]

In December 2004, Sri Lanka suffered a major tragedy when a giant tsunami, which also devastated northern Indonesia, southern Thailand, and parts of southeastern India, hit the northern and eastern parts of the island and caused massive destruction and loss of life. As international humanitarian and relief aid poured in, a tussle developed between the Sri Lankan government and the LTTE over aid allocation and distribution. The LTTE accused the government of being less than generous to the Tamil-speaking areas of the northeast, which made reconstruction work difficult. On its part, the Sri Lankan government refused to form a joint LTTE–government mechanism (as suggested by the LTTE and facilitator Norway) for reconstruction work as long as LTTE paramilitaries continued to operate in the northeast. Both sides refused to budge from their respective positions and preferred to take their case to the international community.[97]

The bad blood that developed between the LTTE and the Sri Lankan government over tsunami aid distribution and reconstruction work eventually took its toll on the Norway-facilitated peace process. The first sign of trouble came when the Sri Lankan foreign minister, Lakshman Kadirgamar, was assassinated in 2005 by an unidentified sniper.[98] Although the LTTE denied any role in the assassination, Sinhalese-Buddhist opinion was vehemently critical of the organization and put enormous pressure on the government to pull out of the peace process. In this tense climate, Sri Lanka held a fresh presidential election, which was won by the UPFA's candidate, the hard-liner Mahinda Rajapakse. In his election manifesto, Rajapakse had made it clear that he supported a unitary rather than a federal polity in Sri Lanka.[99] Rajapakse had also been a strong critic of the Norway-facilitated peace process and in the past had advocated a "military solution" to Sri Lanka's decades-old ethnic conflict.[100]

## ENDGAME: BACK TO WAR AND THE LTTE'S DESTRUCTION

As expected, the inauguration of Mahinda Rajapakse as Sri Lankan president drove the final nail in the coffin of peace negotiations and signaled a return to full-scale civil war in the north and east. Ironically, however, given what was to come, it was the LTTE that landed the first major blow. In a spectacular land-mine attack in the northern Jaffna Peninsula in late 2005, the LTTE executed eleven government soldiers and a policeman—this was the biggest Tiger attack since the signing of the CFA in 2002.[101] The government's military response was swift and harsh, and over the next few months massacres were committed by both sides. As the death toll climbed and thousands of civilians started fleeing the combat zones, international condemnation of the LTTE spread. The U.S. government, for example, called the LTTE a "reprehensible terrorist group" and mainly blamed it for the resumption of civil war in Sri Lanka.[102] Canada also labeled the LTTE a "terrorist group."[103]

From the beginning of 2006, major confrontations between the LTTE and the Sri Lankan military became a daily occurrence. A series of major sea battles took place between the Sea Tigers and the Sri Lankan navy; in support of its naval forces, the Sri Lankan air force also resorted to aerial bombardment of Tamil areas.[104] In retaliation, the LTTE carried out suicide terrorist attacks against the Sri Lankan army headquarters in Colombo, killing several people and seriously wounding the head of the army.[105] Violence also broke out between the LTTE and the Karuna faction, which was being used by the Sri Lankan military against the Tigers. Communal violence between Tamils and Sinhalese/Muslims was also reported from the east. Violence was also directed at the international truce monitors belonging to the Sri Lanka Monitoring Mission (SLMM).[106] In this climate of spiraling violence, human rights abuses were committed by all sides. For example, while the LTTE was accused of intimidating and targeting foreign truce monitors, especially those who were European Union (EU) nationals, the Sri Lankan armed forces were criticized by human rights groups such as Amnesty International for killing unarmed Tamil civilians, including children, in the Jaffna Peninsula and seventeen aid workers in the eastern town of Muttur.[107]

In 2006, major clashes flared up in the Jaffna Peninsula in the north, in Batticaloa in the east, and around the Trincomalee port in the northeast.[108] A major confrontation between the Sri Lankan navy and the Sea Tigers took place near Trincomalee Harbor.[109] By the end of the year, the Sri Lankan military, with unofficial help from Colonel Karuna's fighters, was able to retake control over almost the entire eastern province from the LTTE.

In early 2007, the Tigers avenged the military setbacks they had suffered by carrying out a series of daring air strikes on Sri Lankan air force bases and on two oil-storage facilities located in the Colombo airport. The advent of the Air Tigers (albeit consisting of only a few light aircrafts) once again demonstrated the Tigers' resourcefulness. It also added a new dynamic to the conflict, that is, the LTTE's acquired capacity to expand the conflict out of the northeast by striking deep within Sinhalese-controlled areas.

The increased threat perception from the LTTE played into the hands of the Sri Lankan government. Although President Rajapakse continued to pay lip service to the importance of holding peace talks, in diplomatic circles the Sri Lankan government made the case that only a "decisive war" with the LTTE would open up the possibility of a final resolution of Sri Lanka's decades-old ethnic conflict. Having joined the American-led global "war on terror" and having received international sympathy and support, Colombo felt emboldened that, it could win a decisive military victory over the LTTE and once and for all smash the power and influence of the organization, which would then allow it to negotiate the terms of peace with more moderate Sri Lankan Tamil political parties and groups (see Box 7.1).

With tacit support from the Indian National Congress (I)–led United Progressive Alliance (UPA) government in India, Sri Lanka launched a full-scale military offensive to retake the northern province and the entire Jaffna Peninsula from the LTTE. A series of intense battles took place between the Sri Lankan military and the LTTE in 2007 and 2008 in which the LTTE suffered serious losses. By December 2008, the Sri Lankan military had fought its way up to the doorsteps of Kilinochchi, the northern town in the Wanni region that served as the LTTE's main administrative center and capital of the quasi–Ealam state that the LTTE had set up.

In early January 2009, after a series of fierce battles with the LTTE fighters involving helicopter gunships, jet fighters and intense hand-to-hand combat, the

## BOX 7.1

## Theorizing the Linkage Between the Tamil–Sinhalese Conflict in Sri Lanka and Its International Dimension

*Complementary Perspectives from Comparative Politics and International Relations*

**1. Domestic factors**

Primordial racial, religious, and ethnic cleavages and ancient hatred

British colonial policy and interethnic competition and conflict

Postindependence internal colonialism and discrimination against ethnic minorities

Demonstration effect of the liberation of Bangladesh

**2. International factors**

Initial covert partisan involvement of regional powers (India and other foreign states)

Role of diaspora behind armed conflict

Strong impact of national self-determination principles on secessionist struggle

Globalization and its impact on operational aspects of armed conflict

Generation of refugees, internally displaced persons, and child soldiers

Guns-for-drugs syndrome

**3. Conflict resolution**

Coercive diplomacy, signing of peace accord, and the limitations of mediation

Appeal of military solution to both parties at different stages of the conflict

Tilt in military balance of power to government side

Tilt in international diplomatic support to government side

Sri Lankan military was able to recapture the towns of Kilinochchi and Paranthan.[110] The Sri Lankan military followed up with a major ground, air, and sea assault on the strategic Elephant Pass, the gateway to the Jaffna Peninsula.[111] After regaining control of Kilinochchi in the Wanni region and the Jaffna Peninsula, the Sri Lankan military turned its attention to Mullaittivu, the last remaining LTTE stronghold on the east coast, which served as the Tigers' military headquarters.[112]

Over the next few months, the Sri Lankan government pressed on with its military campaign against the LTTE. Fierce fighting was reported around the Mullaittivu area. The Sri Lankan military resorted to intense shelling and aerial bombardment of the area under the LTTE's control. The LTTE tried to break the stranglehold by launching repeated suicide attacks against the advancing army columns. Caught in this intense crossfire were around 200,000 Tamil civilians. Some reports suggested that the Tamil civilian population was being used by the LTTE as a "human shield" against the advancing Sri Lankan forces, and that LTTE soldiers were under orders to shoot any civilians who tried to escape.[113] Human rights groups, the UN, and several Western states also accused the Sri Lankan military of causing mass civilian fatalities through indiscriminate and intense shelling and aerial bombardment of LTTE-controlled areas.[114]

By the beginning of May 2009, the Sri Lankan forces had managed to corner the last remaining soldiers and the top leaders of the LTTE to a small strip of land in the northeast corner of Sri Lanka and cut-off their main escape routes through land and sea. A fierce final battle now ensued and lasted for about two weeks. The battle eventually ended with the complete massacre of most of the remaining LTTE soldiers and the group's top leadership, including Prabhakaran and his entire family.[115] With the death of Prabhakaran and his top aides and the complete destruction of the LTTE fighting machine, one of the world's longest running ethnic dirty war has finally come to an end.

## Conclusion

The LTTE's military defeat raises two important questions: why did the LTTE lose and what impact would the LTTE's defeat have on the Tamil–Sinhalese ethnic conflict in Sri Lanka? Regarding the first question, five factors may have been particularly important. First, it is quite clear that Prabhakaran made a series of tactical blunders (e.g., attacking the IPKF, assassinating Rajiv Gandhi and several top Sri Lankan and Tamil politicians, using child soldiers, etc.) that left the LTTE short of friends and sympathy internationally. Second, by making unreasonable demands of the Wickremesinghe government and by taking advantage of peace negotiations to put in place the trappings of a quasi–Tamil state, the LTTE showed clearly that it was not really interested in accepting anything short of a sovereign Tamil state; this, in turn, allowed a hardline and ultranationalist Sri Lankan government under Rajapakse, fully committed to a decisive military showdown with the LTTE, to take power in Colombo. Third, Karuna's defection was a body blow to the LTTE and greatly reduced its fighting capacity in the East, which allowed the Sri Lankan military to concentrate its entire resources to the North. Fourth, in a post-9/11 world, the LTTE's capacity to raise funds and procure weapons was drastically reduced, which adversely affected its fighting capability. By contrast, the Sri Lankan government was able to carry out a major modernization of its armed forces with support from China, India, Israel, US, UK and the European Union.[116] Finally, the LTTE's popularity among the Tamil masses in Sri Lanka had gradually declined over the years. This could have adversely affected the LTTE's ability to recruit new soldiers from among the Sri Lankan Tamil population.

The second question concerns the eventual resolution of Tamil–Sinhalese ethnic conflict in a post-LTTE era. In this regard, the UPA government in India has made it clear to Colombo that it considers the destruction of the LTTE as a separate issue from the plight of the Sri Lankan Tamils in Sri Lanka. Hence, while Colombo can expect New Delhi's support and cooperation on the first issue, in a post-LTTE environment it has to ensure that Tamils in Sri Lanka would be treated justly and without any discrimination and intimidation.[117] Other prominent international actors such as the United States, European Union, United Kingdom, Germany, Russia, China, Japan, and the UN are also likely to take an approach similar to India's regarding Sri Lanka's ethnic conflict. The post-LTTE environment in Sri Lankan politics is therefore likely to remain dogged by challenges of nation-building, reconstruction and reconciliation.

## Discussion Questions

1. What are the main characteristics of a dirty war? Are they more prone to becoming internationalized? What impact do they have on international security?

2. For many years, Sri Lanka was considered to be a model of stable multiethnic democracy. Why and how did it emerge as an example of a brutal and protracted ethnic war?

3. Discuss the reasons for the failure of India's conflict resolution attempts in Sri Lanka. What lessons can be learned about ethnic conflict resolution from India's failed attempt?

4. Explain the reasons for the turbulent nature of the peace process initiated in Oslo in 2002. How have electoral politics in Sri Lanka affected the process? How have divisions within the Tamil leadership affected the process?

5. Why did the Norway-facilitated peace process fail in Sri Lanka? Which side is most responsible for the collapse of the peace talks?

6. Why did the Sri Lankan government under President Rajapakse decide to seek a military solution to Sri Lanka's ethnic conflict? Will the Tamil–Sinhalese conflict be resolved following the military defeat of the LTTE?

## Key Terms

all-party conference
*bhikkhus*
Burghers
Colonel Karuna
counterinsurgency
   operations
dirty wars
50:50 formula
Indian Doctrine of
   Regional Security
Indian Peace Keeping
   Force (IPKF)

Indian Tamils
Indo–Sri Lankan Accord
interim self-governing
   authority (ISGA)
Liberation Tigers of Tamil
   Eelam (LTTE)
Malays
Moors
Operation Jayasikuru
Operation Riviresa
Parthasarathy Formula

Research and Analysis
   Wing (RAW)
Sinhalese
Soulbury Commission
Sri Lankan Tamils
*Swabasha* movement
Tamil Eelam
Veddhas

## Notes

1. The Moors are descendents of the ancient Arab traders that used to visit Sri Lanka before the advent of the Europeans. They practice Islam, speak mostly Tamil, and are concentrated in the major trading centers such as Colombo and in the east of the island. The Moors living in the trading centers are usually wealthy and literate, whereas those living in the east are economically backward with a low literacy level. The Burghers are of mixed European and Sri Lankan descent. They are mostly Christians and speak English. They are mainly concentrated in Colombo and are economically prosperous. The

Malays are descended from the Malay traders and guards brought to the island during the colonial periods. The Veddhas are the descendants of the aboriginal tribes of ancient Sri Lanka and their numbers have been greatly reduced over the years because many of them have been absorbed into the Sinhalese race. The remaining Veddhas continue to rely on hunting for their food and live under extreme primitive conditions in the forests of eastern Sri Lanka.

2. Ministry of Finance and Planning, *Statistical Pocketbook of the Democratic Socialist Republic of Sri Lanka—1998* (Colombo: Department of Census and Statistics, 1998), pp. 9–26.

3. K. de Silva, *Sri Lanka: Ethnic Conflict, Management and Resolution* (Kandy: International Center for Ethnic Studies, 1996), p. 4.

4. Bruce Matthews, "The Situation in Jaffna—And How It Came About," *The Round Table,* 290, April 1984, pp. 188–204.

5. Shelton U. Kodikara, "Communalism and Political Modernization in Ceylon," *Modern Ceylon Studies,* 4, no. 3, January 1970, pp. 94–114.

6. Chelvadurai Manogaran, *Ethnic Conflict and Reconciliation in Sri Lanka* (Honolulu: University of Hawaii Press, 1987), p. 24.

7. Ibid., p. 2.

8. Robert Kearney, *Communalism and Language in the Politics of Ceylon* (Durham, N.C.: Duke University Press, 1967), p. 16.

9. For details of the British colonial government's education policy in Sri Lanka, see H. A. Wyndham, *Native Education* (London: Oxford University Press, 1933).

10. Kearney, *Communalism and Language in the Politics of Ceylon,* p. 56–57.

11. The 1953 census revealed that while the Sri Lankan Tamils constituted only 12.8 percent of the total population (compared with the Sinhalese, at 79.2 percent), they dominated various government jobs and professions in the following manner: 30 percent—Ceylon administrative service, 50 percent—clerical services (including postal, railway, hospitals, and customs), 60 percent—professions (engineers, doctors, lecturers), 40 percent—armed forces, and 40 percent—labor forces. 1953 Census data obtained from Rajesh Kadian, *India's Sri Lanka Fiasco: Peacekeepers at War* (New Delhi: Vision Books, 1990), p. 57.

12. This was done because the Sri Lankan Tamils and the Sinhalese were alike in rejecting plantation labor as a way of life. The Sinhalese peasants, in particular, were reluctant to give up their casual schedule of rice cultivation for the low-paid and strictly regulated work on the plantations. The Sri Lankan Tamils, on their part, utilized their proficiency in the English language and sought jobs in the public service and the professions.

13. Kearney, *Communalism and Language in the Politics of Ceylon,* p. 59.

14. Kearney, *Communalism and Language in the Politics of Ceylon,* p. 16.

15. Ibid.

16. S. Arasaratnam, "Nationalism in Sri Lanka and the Tamils," in Michael Roberts, ed., *Collective Identities, Nationalism, and Protest in Modern Sri Lanka* (Colombo: Marga Institute, 1979), p. 502.

17. Manogaran, *Ethnic Conflict and Reconciliation in Sri Lanka,* p. 32.

18. This constitution remained in force until 1972, when the United Front coalition government of Shirimavo

Bandaranaike introduced a new constitution that replaced the post of governor general with a president. The name of the country was also changed from Ceylon to Sri Lanka. In 1978, the UNP government led by Jayewardene introduced another constitution that created a presidential form of government with Prime Minister Jayewardene becoming the first executive president of Sri Lanka for a six-year term.

19. Under the Citizenship Act of 1948, Indian Tamils could no longer become citizens of Sri Lanka by virtue of their birth on the island and had to prove three or more generations of paternal ancestry to become citizens by descent. It was almost impossible for most Indian Tamils to provide such proof. As a result, they were made stateless. Similarly, the Indian and Pakistani Residents (Citizenship) Act of 1949 and the Ceylon Parliamentary Elections Amendment Act of 1949 also disenfranchised most of the Indian Tamils who had participated in the country's general elections since 1931. The total outcome of all three acts was that about 975,000 Indian Tamils were rendered stateless.

20. In the initial years after independence, the Sri Lankan government recognized both Sinhalese and Tamil as official languages of Sri Lanka. In 1956, the Sri Lanka Freedom Party (SLFP)–led government under SWRD. Bandaranaike passed the Official Language Act, which made Sinhalese the sole official language of Sri Lanka. The act granted no concessions to the Sri Lankan Tamils, the national minority, with regard to the use of the Tamil language for education, employment, and administrative purposes. Faced with a massive Tamil protest and mounting ethnic tension, the government passed the Tamil Language Act of 1958 to provide for the "reasonable use" of Tamil in education, administration, and public service examinations in the northern and eastern provinces. The implementation of the act was, however, minimal.

21. Under this plan, for admission purposes in higher educational institutions, the marks obtained by Tamil students were weighted downward against marks obtained by Sinhalese students.

22. Because the Tamils have always claimed the northern and eastern provinces to be their traditional homeland based on the fact that they constitute a numerical majority in these areas, the Sinhalese-dominated governments of independent Sri Lanka started the deliberate colonization of these provinces by resettling large numbers of Sinhalese families from the south and west. The purpose behind this policy was twofold. First, by changing the population ratio between Tamils and Sinhalese, the Sri Lankan government sought to eliminate any Tamil territorial claims over the northern and eastern provinces; and second, because election results reflected a clear polarization of politics (Sinhalese parties and Tamil parties won clear victories in their respective areas), a changed population ratio was sure to provide Sinhalese political parties a greater degree of control over traditional Tamil areas.

23. Brian Senewiratne, "The Problems of Sri Lanka," in Kalim Bahabur, ed., *South Asia in Transition: Conflicts and Tensions* (New Delhi: Patriot Publishers, 1986), p. 237.

24. Robert N. Kearney, "Ethnic Conflict and the Tamil Separatist Movement

in Sri Lanka," *Asian Survey,* 25, no. 9, September 1985, p. 902.

25. Ibid., p. 903.
26. Senewiratne, "The Problems of Sri Lanka," p. 237.
27. Kearney, "Ethnic Conflict and the Tamil Separatist Movement in Sri Lanka," p. 905.
28. Under the 1978 constitution, the president was to be elected by direct popular vote. Therefore, a candidate sympathetic to the minorities could hope to win by combining minority votes with a large minority of Sinhalese votes. Parliament was to be elected by proportional representation. Hence, Sinhalese parties now needed to form alliances with minority parties in order to form governments.
29. James Manor, "Sri Lanka: Explaining the Disaster," *The World Today,* November 1983, p. 452.
30. For an excellent account of the 1983 anti-Tamil riots in Sri Lanka and the role played by government agencies and personnel, see Manor, "Sri Lanka: Explaining the Disaster," pp. 450–459.
31. Kearney, "Ethnic Conflict and the Tamil Separatist Movement in Sri Lanka," p. 906.
32. Karthigesu Sivathamby, "The Sri Lankan Tamil Question: Socio-Economic and Ideological Issues," *Bulletin of Peace Proposals,* 18, no. 4, 1987, p. 634.
33. Urmila Phadnis and Rajat Ganguly, *Ethnicity and Nation-building in South Asia,* rev. ed. (New Delhi; London; Thousand Oaks, Calif.: Sage Publications, 2001), pp. 326–333.
34. P. Venkateshwar Rao, "Ethnic Conflict in Sri Lanka: India's Role and Perception," *Asian Survey,* 28, no. 4, April 1988, p. 425.
35. Ibid.
36. Ibid.

37. Kadian, *India's Sri Lanka Fiasco,* p. 67.
38. Victor Ostrovsky and Claire Hoy, *By Way of Deception* (New York: St. Martin's Press, 1990), pp. 67–69 and 127–131; and P. Seneviratne, "The Mossad Factor in Government Repression," in Kalim Bahadur, ed., *South Asia in Transition: Conflicts and Tensions* (New Delhi: Patriot Publishers, 1986), pp. 288–294.
39. Kadian, *India's Sri Lanka Fiasco,* pp. 98–109.
40. *The Hindustan Times,* July 24, 1983.
41. For details, see *India Today,* August 31, 1983, pp. 14–15.
42. Robert L. Hardgrave, Jr., *India Under Pressure: Prospects for Political Stability* (Boulder, Colo.: Westview Press, 1984), p. 167.
43. Kadian, *India's Sri Lanka Fiasco,* p. 92.
44. Ibid., pp. 93–94.
45. Shelton U. Kodikara, "International Dimensions of Ethnic Conflict in Sri Lanka: Involvement of India and Non-State Actors," *Bulletin of Peace Proposals,* 18, no. 4, 1987, p. 647.
46. Ibid.
47. Ralph R. Premdas and S. W. R. de A. Samarasinghe, "Sri Lanka's Ethnic Conflict: The Indo-Lanka Peace Accord," *Asian Survey,* 28, no. 6, June 1988, p. 678.
48. Kumar Rupesinghe, "Ethnic Conflicts in South Asia: The Case of Sri Lanka and the Indian Peace-keeping Force (IPKF)," *Journal of Peace Research,* 25, no. 4, 1988, p. 346.
49. Ibid.
50. At the time of induction, the IPKF comprised only 8,000 men; in the next two years, its strength was increased to more than 100,000 men, but even this number proved to be inadequate.
51. Shelton U. Kodikara, "The Continuing Crisis in Sri Lanka: The

JVP, the Indian Troops, and Tamil Politics," *Asian Survey,* 29, no. 7, July 1989, p. 717.

52. Manik de Silva, "Communal Bloodbath," *Far Eastern Economic Review,* August 30, 1990, p. 19.

53. O. N. Mehrotra, "Ethnic Strife in Sri Lanka," *Strategic Analysis,* 21, no. 10, January 1998, p. 1519.

54. Peter Chalk, "The Liberation Tigers of Tamil Eelam Insurgency in Sri Lanka," in Rajat Ganguly and Ian Macduff, eds., *Ethnic Conflict and Secessionism in South and Southeast Asia: Causes, Dynamics, Solutions* (New Delhi; London; Thousand Oaks, Calif.: Sage Publications, 2003), pp. 133–156.

55. Nirupama Subramanian, "Fight to the Finish," *India Today,* November 30, 1995, pp. 38–43; Howard B. Schaffer, "Sri Lanka in 1995: A Difficult and Disappointing Year," *Asian Survey,* 36, no. 2, February 1996, pp. 216–223.

56. Walter Jayawardhana, "Guns for Drugs," *Sunday,* November 4, 1990, p. 82.

57. See Guy Goodwin-Gill and Ilene Cohn, *Child Soldiers: The Role of Children in Armed Conflict* (Oxford, England: Clarendon Press, 1994), pp. 31, 40; Graca Machel, *The Impact of Armed Conflict on Children* (New York: United Nations, 1997); and "Sri Lanka's Under Age War," *Economist,* August 5, 1995.

58. "Tiger Teeth," *Economist,* May 5, 2001, p. 35.

59. "The Tigers Pounce," *Economist,* July 28, 2001, p. 42.

60. "A Vote for Peace?" *Economist,* December 8, 2001, p. 39.

61. "Hitting the Tigers in Their Pockets," *Economist,* March 10, 2001, p. 38; "The Wounded Tigers," *Economist,* January 12, 2002, p. 39.

62. O. P. Verma, "LTTE-Dawood-ISI Ring in Smuggling," *Deccan Herald* (Online), January 4, 2002.

63. "The Growing Cost of War," *Economist,* July 15, 2000, p. 40.

64. "Tiger Tamed?" *Economist,* December 2, 2000, p. 43.

65. "Sri Lanka Seeks Unconditional Talks," *The Times of India* (Online), December 17, 2001.

66. Farah Mihlar Ahmed, "Economic Growth a Priority, Says Lanka PM," *The Times of India* (Online), January 22, 2002.

67. Catherine Philp, "Sri Lanka Agrees to Ceasefire with Tigers," *The Times* (London), February 22, 2002, p. 22.

68. Nirupama Subramanian, "Ready for Talks with LTTE: Muslim Leader," *The Hindu* (Online), April 8, 2002.

69. "Pirapaharan Commits to Peace, Self-Determination," *Tamil Guardian* (Online), April 10, 2002.

70. Ibid.

71. "The Prime Minister and President of Tamil Eelam," *Outlook* (Online), April 10, 2002.

72. Nirupama Subramanian, "Muslims Strike Deal with LTTE," *The Hindu* (Online), April 15, 2002.

73. Nirupama Subramanian, "Thondaman to Work with LTTE," *The Hindu* (Online), April 16, 2002.

74. Nirupama Subramanian, "Ranil, Chandrika Speak in Same Voice," *The Hindu* (Online), May 30, 2002.

75. K. Venkataramanan, "No Assurances on Interim Administration to LTTE: Ranil," *Hindustan Times* (Online), May 13, 2002.

76. "Lankan Government Says It Has No Plans to Repeal POTA," *The Times of India* (Online), May 9, 2002.

77. V. S. Sambandan, "Separation Only if Autonomy Is Denied: LTTE," *The Hindu* (Online), September 19, 2002.

78. V. S. Sambandan, "Colombo, LTTE Agree on Federal Structure," *The Hindu* (Online), December 6, 2002.

79. V. S. Sambandan, "Peace Negotiators Face Uphill Task," *The Hindu* (Online), December 10, 2002.

80. See Nirupama Subramanian, "Chandrika Questions Release of Flotilla," *The Hindu* (Online), May 2, 2002; Farah Mihlar Ahmed, "Norwegian Official to Probe Lanka Sea Battle," *The Times of India* (Online), May 2, 2002; and Nirupama Subramanian, "Wickremesinghe Plays Down Clash," *The Hindu* (Online), May 3, 2002.

81. Nirupama Subramaniam, "India May Train Sri Lankan Troops," *The Hindu* (Online), June 17, 2003.

82. Amit Baruah, "LTTE Has Set up de-facto State," *The Hindu* (Online), April 12, 2003.

83. V. S. Sambandan, "India Adds Clause for Resolution of Sri Lanka Conflict," *The Hindu* (Online), December 10, 2002.

84. V. S. Sambandan, "LTTE Pursuing Violent, Separatist Agenda: US," *The Hindu* (Online), April 25, 2003.

85. "Lanka, Tamil Rebels Must Show Results at Peace Talks," *The Times of India,* April 10, 2003.

86. V. S. Sambandan, "Efforts to Defuse Stalemate in Sri Lanka," *The Hindu* (Online), May 5, 2003.

87. David Rohde, "Sri Lankan President Declares a State of Emergency," *The New York Times* (Online), November 6, 2003.

88. P. K. Balachanddran, "Chandrika Says She Would Work for Peace if Voted to Power," *Hindustan Times* (Online), February 28, 2004.

89. P. K. Balachanddran, "Inauguration of 'Eelam Police' HQ Considered Significant," *Hindustan Times* (Online), September 9, 2003.

90. V. S. Sambandan, "Peace Process: Chandrika Seeks Clear Mandate in Poll," *The Hindu* (Online), February 17, 2004.

91. "Kumaratunga's Political Alliance Says It Will Abolish Presidency," *Hindustan Times* (Online), March 17, 2004.

92. P. K. Balachanddran, "LTTE Says It Will Not Talk to Chandrika–JVP Alliance," *Hindustan Times* (Online), January 21, 2004.

93. See "Osama Squads to Fight the LTTE," *The Times of India* (Online), August 19, 2003; P. K. Balachanddran, "Prabhakaran Undisputed Leader, Says LTTE's Eastern Wing," *Hindustan Times* (Online), March 4, 2004, and "LTTE Row Creates a Powder Keg," *Hindustan Times* (Online), March 8, 2004.

94. P. K. Balachanddran, "Pro-LTTE Tamils Suspect India's Hand in Karuna's Revolt," *Hindustan Times* (Online), March 18, 2004.

95. V. S. Sambandan, "Exploitation of 'dissent' Will Cause Irreparable Damage: Balasingham," *The Hindu* (Online), March 18, 2004, and "LTTE to 'Get Rid of Karuna'," *The Hindu* (Online), 26 March 2004.

96. P. K. Balachanddran, "Chandrika Says She Would Work for Peace if Voted to Power," *Hindustan Times* (Online), February 28, 2004.

97. P. K. Balachanddran, "Lankan Government, LTTE Take Their Fight to Global Arena," *Hindustan Times* (Online), April 18, 2005.

98. "Sri Lankan Foreign Minister Shot Dead, Rebels Blamed," *Express India* (Online), August 13, 2005.

99. P. K. Balachanddran, "Rajapakse for Unitary Constitution," *Hindustan Times* (Online), October 18, 2005.

100. "Hawk Named as Sri Lanka Premier," *BBC News* (Online), November 21, 2005.

101. "War Fear Grips Lanka as Tigers Kill 11 Soldiers," *The Telegraph* (Online), 27 December 2005.

102. P. K. Balachanddran, "LTTE is 'Reprehensible', Says US," *Hindustan Times* (Online), January 23, 2006.

103. "Canada Labels LTTE a Terrorist Organization," *The Hindu* (Online), April 11, 2006.

104. "Dozens Dead in Sri Lanka Clashes," *BBC News* (Online), May 11, 2006.

105. "Bomb Attack on Sri Lanka Army HQ," *BBC News* (Online), April 25, 2006.

106. P. K. Balachanddran, "LTTE Warns Nordic Truce Monitors," *Hindustan Times* (Online), May 12, 2006.

107. "LTTE Wants EU Monitors to Go, Says Sri Lanka," *Hindustan Times* (Online), August 9, 2006; "Sri Lanka 'Must Probe' Killings," *BBC News* (Online), May 17, 2005; "Sri Lanka Blamed for Aid Deaths," *CNN.com,* August 30, 2006.

108. "Deadly Clashes Flare in Sri Lanka," *BBC News* (Online), August 12, 2006.

109. "Sri Lanka Sea Battle 'Kills 70'," *BBC News* (Online), September 25, 2006.

110. Rhys Blakely, "Sri Lankan Troops Enter Tamil Tigers Stronghold of Kilinochchi," *The Times* (Online), January 2, 2009.

111. T. V. Sriram, "Lankan Troops Seize Last LTTE-Held Area, Take Full Control of Jaffna," *Hindustan Times* (Online), January 14, 2009.

112. "Lankan Troops Enter Key Town en Route to Mullaittivu," *The Hindu* (Online), January 4, 2009.

113. See Somini Sengupta, "Boat to Safety is Death Trap to Sri Lankans," *The New York Times*, May 6, 2009.

114. See Thomas Fuller, "Sri Lanka Rejects 'Lectures' from Western Countries," *The New York Times*, May 1, 2009; "U.N. Council Sees No Need to Punish Sri Lanka," *The New York Times*, April 30, 2009; "Sri Lanka Must Understand Consequences for Its Actions: Brown," *The Hindu*, May 18, 2009.

115. Robert Bosleigh, "Claims of Massacre as Tamil Tiger Leaders Die," *The Times*, May 19, 2009; Sutirtho Patranobis, "Prabhakaran & Son Killed," *Hindustan Times*, May 18, 2009.

116. See Amit Baruah and Sutirtho Patranobis, "Scripting the Endgame," *Hindustan Times*, May 19, 2009; Sutirtho Patranobis and Amit Baruah, "The 'General' Who Ran Out of Moves," *Hindustan Times*, May 18, 2009; Jeremy Page, "Chinese Support Crucial to Sri Lankan Victory over Tamils," *The Times*, May 16, 2009; Jeremy Page, "Britain Sold weapons to Help Sri Lankan Army Defeat Tamil Tigers," *The Times*, June 2, 2009.

117. M. R. Narayan Swamy, "In Victory, Show Magnanimity," *Hindustan Times*, May 19, 2009.

# CHAPTER 8

# Weak States and Ethnic Conflict: State Collapse and Reconstruction in Africa

## INTRODUCTION

Much of today's ethnic conflict can be found in the developing world, particularly on the vast continents of Africa and Asia. The large number of communal groups living here, combined with the artificial nature of state borders drawn by European colonial powers, has furnished hothouse conditions for ethnic competition. Within the developing world, Africa accounts for a large proportion of conflicts based on ethnicity, kinship, religion, and other identity markers.

Studying cases from Africa is important for several reasons. The continent is rich in terms of ethnic diversity, but it also has many weak central governments. In addition, state boundaries are arbitrary and, more than in the rest of the world, are not congruent with patterns of ethnic settlement. Ian Lustick observed that "[a]fter more than thirty years of independence . . . the hegemonic status of the belief that African borders are immutable, and thereby excluded from calculations about how Africans can respond to the exigencies of their existence, appears to be breaking down." As a result, "Africa faces, among its other woes, the possibility of cascading patterns of fragmentation and attachment."[1]

Examining what happens when states fragment can help us understand the role played by ethnicity in this process as well as the part played by international actors. As we have seen time and again, international actors are reluctant to recognize the validity of ethno-secessionists' arguments and prefer status-quo arrangements. The statist bias of the international system allows for no exceptions even when (1) the states that are fragmenting are insignificant, located on the periphery of the global economy and the state system; and (2) the movements attacking the state often have justifiable historical grievances, land claims, victimization histories, and other moral claims.

The one notable case in Africa of a recent successful secession was Eritrea's independence from Ethiopia in 1993. A large part of the explanation for this lies in the collapse two years earlier of the Soviet Union, which had secured Ethiopia as a military and political ally beginning in 1977. When the Soviet Union ceased to exist, so did authoritarian Ethiopia.[2] But in many African states today, both borders and central governments continue to come under attack. The Darfur conflict in Sudan—Africa's largest country in terms of surface area—has been recognized by the international community as a humanitarian tragedy. Another large country on the continent, the Democratic Republic of Congo (previously Zaire), has also succumbed to the malaise of weak central authority. But a third, South Africa, has surprised observers by constructing a strong state with widespread legitimacy.

This chapter focuses on ethnic conflicts in large but weak African states—Congo in Central Africa and Sudan in northeast Africa—as well as on a strong, large state—South Africa. Our analysis begins with the notorious case of massive genocide carried out in a compact and weak state with high population density—Rwanda in Central Africa.

The case studies of unsettled African states can shed light on the part played by external intervention in exacerbating or resolving ethnic conflicts. A hypothesis to be tested is that intervention by forces from the economically and militarily more powerful first world should have a much greater chance of success in regions where warring parties possess fewer resources. We also wish to know whether outside intervention to manage ethnic-related conflicts in seemingly hopeless collapsed states is even likely. Or are external parties complicit in these conflicts because they manipulate them to maintain control over valuable natural resources that the world needs?

## WEAK STATES

**Weak states** or unsettled states may be charitable descriptions for what William Zartman has bluntly termed state collapse, a widespread phenomenon across Africa. "Current state collapse—in the Third World, but also in the former Soviet Union and in Eastern Europe—is not a matter of civilizational decay. . . . Nor is the process merely an organic characteristic of growth and decay, a life cycle in the rise and fall of nations."[3] For Zartman, state collapse entails the loss of a multiplicity of functions:

> As the decision-making center of government, the state is paralyzed and inoperative: laws are not made, order is not preserved, and societal cohesion is not enhanced. As a symbol of identity, it has lost its power of conferring a name on its people and a meaning to their social action. As a territory, it is no longer assured security and provisionment by a central sovereign organization. As the authoritative political institution, it has lost its legitimacy, which is therefore up for grabs, and so has lost its right to command and conduct public affairs. As a system of socioeconomic organization, its functional balance of inputs and outputs is destroyed; it no longer receives supports from nor exercises controls over its people, and it no longer is even the target of demands, because its people know that it is incapable of providing supplies.[4]

State collapse, like the related notion of unsettled states, may not simply be a by-product of ethno-nationalism; it may represent a factor promoting a retreat into ethnic identities. This was the case in Rwanda in the mid-1990s and much of neighboring Congo after that.

When anticolonial struggles succeeded in forging independent states in much of Africa beginning in the late 1950s, it appeared that a honeymoon period would arise during which various ethnicities in new countries would put off disagreements in the interests of state. In practice, however, separatist movements appeared simultaneously with the independence of the first African colonies. Given the widely perceived illegitimacy of colonially demarcated borders, the power vacuum created by the withdrawal of European powers, and the precarious existence of nascent independent states, this appeared to be a propitious time for breakaway movements to be successful.

The most significant bids were made in the Congo and Nigeria.[5] Key ethnic groups located in Katanga and **Biafra**, respectively, sought to break away from the new states that had been constructed—often designed in such a way as to safeguard the economic interests of the departing colonial powers. Their failed efforts to achieve statehood owed much to the role played by international actors (the United Nations [UN] in the Congo, multinational oil companies in Nigeria) that resolved to maintain the territorial integrity of fragmenting states. For the UN, which was strongly backed by the United States, secession of Katanga would have set a dangerous precedent for the rest of postcolonial Africa. For the oil companies involved in the region at the time—and subsequently in other parts of Africa for natural resource companies (usually headquartered in the United States or the European Union) having stakes in diamond, gold, rubber, petroleum, phosphate, magnesium, or other mineral enterprises—political stability represented a requirement for doing business. It is striking, then, that "ethnic" conflicts in Africa, fought fifty years apart, appear to display a local character but, on closer examination, have commonalities anchored in the global economy.

## Central Africa

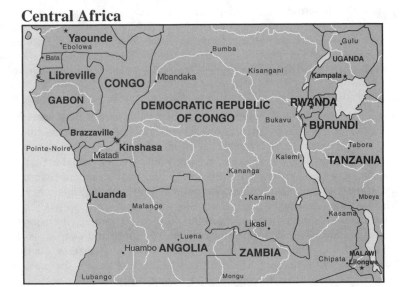

# WEAK STATES, POLITICIZED IDENTITIES IN CENTRAL AFRICA

In few other places is the view that ancient hatreds account for mass killings more accepted as an explanation than in Rwanda and Burundi in the 1990s. Markers distinguishing Hutu and Tutsi identities are believed to be so fixed, and their hatred for each other is taken as such a given, that observers saw the mass killings in Central Africa in the 1990s as almost inevitable. Yet, in Central Africa, as in many other parts of the world, ethnic identities are often not so much acquisitions inherited at birth but ascriptions engendered by the need to anchor artificial states in collective identities.

Arguably, we are dealing with three interlocking cases of ethnic violence and state disintegration in Central Africa: the mass killings in Rwanda and Burundi in the mid-1990s were followed shortly afterward by the spread of ethnic rivalries to neighboring Congo (then called Zaire). Ethnic divisions were a necessary condition for mass violence but alone, we contend, they do not furnish an adequate explanation for why genocidal acts were committed, nor why the attempt to kill off a state, Congo, should have been attempted. It is important to examine some of the background conditions. Chief among these is that in order to prop up colonial governments and maintain centralized rule, colonizers used divide-and-rule tactics, thereby politicizing preexisting ethnic divisions and privileging one group over others. "Ethnic" conflicts in Central Africa can be construed, therefore, as the ethnicization of a struggle for power and a battle over natural resources.

## The Colonial Legacy and Hutu–Tutsi Rivalry

One specialist summarized the complex historical sources of identity among peoples from Central Africa as follows: "A woman living in central Africa drew her identity from where she was born, from her lineage and in-laws, and from her wealth. Tribal or ethnic identity was rarely important in everyday life and could change as people moved over vast areas in pursuit of trade or new lands. Conflicts were more often within tribal categories than between them, as people fought over sources of water, farmland, or grazing rights."[6]

John Bowen, author of this passage, was describing Rwanda, site of large-scale massacres between April and July 1994. He acknowledged that in some districts of the country, ethnic identities have more salience (northern Rwanda) than in others (southern Rwanda). He nevertheless contended that "it was the colonial powers, and the independent states succeeding them, which declared that each and every person had an 'ethnic identity' that determined his or her place within the colony or the postcolonial system." European powers had recognized for a long time the importance of securing allies from among the native population. The prerequisite for fomenting ethnic schism, and therefore divide-and-rule tactics, was cultivating ethnic markers among groups. To be sure, before German colonialists arrived in 1899, the **Tutsis**, representing about 15 percent of the population, ruled over the majority Hutu population. When Belgium took over the protectorate after World War I, it extended Tutsi domination by favoring this ethnic group over others.

Colonial powers thus politicized ethnicity. Both "in Rwanda and Burundi, German and Belgian colonizers admired the taller people called Tutsis, who formed a small minority in both colonies. The Belgians gave the Tutsis privileged access to education and jobs and even instituted a minimum height requirement for entrance to college." The Tutsi minority was thus groomed as the traditional ruling class in the region. The irony was that "**Hutus** and Tutsis had intermarried to such an extent that they were not easily distinguished physically (nor are they today)."[7] The two groups share the same language and customs in Rwanda, just as they share another language and other customs in Burundi. Hutus are set off from each other by clan and regional affiliations, just as Tutsis are. They are not unified communities whose only fault line is Hutu–Tutsi. The high population density of the region should, if anything, make ethnic "boundaries" even less fixed.

For René Lemarchand, "it is the interplay between ethnic realities and their subjective reconstruction (or manipulation) by political entrepreneurs that lies at the root of the Hutu–Tutsi conflict."[8] Making ethnic categories salient in the first place, and inflating and politicizing their significance, serve to disguise the struggle over the more fundamental matters of power and resources. The introduction of ethnic identity cards by the Belgian administration in 1931—dividing the Central African population into Hutu, Tutsi, or Twa—was a first step in the process of politicizing ethnicity.

Following World War II, both Burundi and Rwanda became United Nations trust territories. Both became independent in 1962. In Burundi, a military-controlled government headed by Tutsis was to wield power until 1993. Although Hutus formed the majority ethnic group, a succession of Hutu political leaders who strove for public office was systematically killed by the army. In 1972, a wider Hutu rebellion broke out; it was crushed by the Tutsi army, leading to the death of some 200,000 Hutus. A similar though smaller-scale ethnic massacre had occurred in 1965, and another was to take place in 1988. Finally in 1993, Burundi, following South Africa's lead, embarked on a democratic transition and a Hutu was elected president. But the experiment was short lived: in October of the same year, he was assassinated by Tutsi extremists, triggering a new civil war between the two ethnic groups. Again the Tutsi-dominated army killed tens of thousands of Hutus. In an illustration of stimulus-response dynamics, his assassination was the catalyst for revenge by Hutu extremists—but it was carried out on Tutsis in neighboring Rwanda.

Rwanda's president, Juvénal Habyarimana, a Hutu, had first taken power in 1973. Over two decades of rule, he was pressured by Hutu extremists in his government to take more repressive measures against Tutsis. Well supplied with military equipment by France, which wanted to ensure that power in the ethnically divided country remained centralized, Habyarimana had few incentives to pursue a policy of political accommodation. France conveniently ignored the increasing human rights abuses committed by the Rwandan government until it was too late to stop a more generalized armed conflict.

The trigger for the mass slaughter in Rwanda was the death of President Habyarimana and his counterpart—the second elected Hutu president of Burundi—in a suspicious plane crash in April 1994. A tribunal in France blamed Tutsi rebels for firing the missile that shot down the jet. In the late 1980s, a disgruntled Tutsi rebel group, the **Rwandan Patriotic Front (RPF)**, led by Paul Kagame, had been formed in neighboring Uganda. (As we will see over and over again in this chapter, ethnic movements in the African conflicts we describe had an uncanny knack for adopting names for their organizations suggesting broad political and national consensus—which is precisely what they did not stand for.) RPF leader Kagame denied involvement in the assassination of two Central African Hutu presidents and instead claimed that it was a Hutu ploy to legitimate planned genocidal actions against Tutsis. An even less credible hypothesis was that in trying to supplant France's influence in Central Africa, the Clinton administration had ordered the killings of pro-French Hutu politicians.

The assassination of three elected Hutu leaders in six months in Central Africa led to the rapid mobilization of Hutu soldiers. Formed into a loose militia group that became known as the *Interahamwe*, they were incited to slaughter their ethnic "Other." Between April and July 1994, over half a million Tutsis were massacred; some historians claim this 100-day period of killing represents the swiftest genocide in history. " 'The [Hutu] extremists' aim,' stated Africa Rights, 'was for the entire Hutu populace to participate in the killing. That way, the blood of genocide would stain everybody.' "[9] The murderous Hutu reprisals contributed to the next cycle of ethnic violence: by fall 2004, the RPF had retaken all of Rwanda; had in turn killed hundreds of thousands of Hutus, some as a result of diseases like cholera and dysentery; and had forced another 2 million to flee to nearby countries. Because many took refuge in eastern Congo, the RPF had a ready-made pretext—settling accounts with Hutu militias—for launching an incursion into that country in 1996. Kagame soon became president of the country, banned opposition parties, had himself re-elected in a way that invited comparisons to Robert Mugabe in Zimbabwe, and made it a crime to deny the RFP-authored version of the genocide.

In Burundi, a civil war continued between Tutsi and Hutu militias until 2005. Its toll was over 300,000 dead. Hutu militias operated from bases in northern Tanzania to attack Tutsi-led Burundi government forces. The government agreed to peace-keeping talks with rebel forces, but a series of ceasefires were breached. Finally, agreement was reached on a presidential election. Held in 2005, it resulted in the coming to power of a moderate Hutu. Nevertheless, Burundi's political stability was possible only if it was accompanied by peace in Rwanda and Congo.

As in South Africa, Burundi and Rwanda faced political transitions in the early 1990s that could have been seized to promote democratization. Unlike South Africa, however, the two Central African states ended with "aborted transitions" because of a lack of clarity in the transition bargain, a failure of leadership, an obstructionist attitude by opposition forces, and the lack of support for the transition by military forces.[10] Authoritarian governments masked the existence of divided societies. There was no charismatic leader like Nelson Mandela to breach differences, nor was there the political will on the part of key ethnic actors to do so.

## International Involvement in Rwanda and Burundi

According to Stephen Stedman, "Africa's conflicts have prompted six different subregional, continental, and international responses, including military support or intervention to aid one side; peace enforcement, to impose a settlement on the warring parties; humanitarian intervention, to ameliorate the effects of war; mediation, to bring conflicts to a negotiated end; preventive diplomacy, to keep incipient conflicts from becoming violent; and regional institution-building, to manage conflicts."[11]

Third parties were involved in the Central African conflict well before it had spiraled into genocidal violence. The RPF, which had recruited Tutsi refugees who had fled from Rwanda to Uganda, first attacked the Habyarimana regime in 1990. But it was beaten back by Rwandan government forces with military assistance from Belgium, France, and Zaire. Outside military intervention was a fact well before the genocidal events took place.

The Rwanda conflict spread contagionlike across the border to Burundi. It raised the fear that "similar violence could erupt and provide opportunities for leaders to learn the costs and benefits of violence and the likely responses of the international community."[12] Contagion also shaped the international response to ethnic conflict in that country. Aware of the Rwandan tragedy of 1994, President Clinton called for "all Burundians to reject extremism and resolve their differences peacefully." But the United States opted not to exercise preventive diplomacy in Burundi and limited involvement to humanitarian efforts—economic assistance, medical help, and food deliveries channeled through the International Red Cross and other nongovernmental organizations (NGOs).

During the worst of the massacres in mid-1994, few western countries were willing to recognize the fact of genocide in Rwanda. International institutions were equally guilty: the UN Security Council refused to describe what was happening in Rwanda as genocide, referring cryptically instead to "acts" of genocide. This let the UN off the hook because the violence fell outside the scope of the 1948 Convention on the Prevention and Punishment of the Crime of Genocide. As late as 1998, the UN Security Council continued to condemn violence in the country, appealed for a cease-fire, and called for the punishment of those responsible for the massacres. But the UN proved ineffective in ending mass slaughter or mediating a resolution to the killings.

UN rejection of the use of peace-enforcement measures was most clearly exemplified in the inattention given to the plea by the Canadian commander of a small contingent of UN peace keepers in Rwanda (United Nations Assistance Mission for Rwanda [UNAMIR] established in August 1993) for immediate reinforcements. General Romeo Dallaire realized that preparations for mass killings were under way, but his superiors in the UN secretary general's office in New York were unresponsive, and the United States appeared to be stonewalling as well.[13] After ten of its peace keepers were killed in fighting with Hutu militias, Belgium pulled its peace keepers out of Rwanda altogether, thereby effectively destroying the UN mission. In turn, nearby French forces did nothing to close down the Hutu radio station that was broadcasting detailed plans for the massacre of Tutsis.

One third party that had the capability to make a difference and prevent genocide was the United States. But the Clinton administration was still smarting from the peace-keeping debacle suffered in Somalia in October 1993. Firefights involving U.S. troops and Somali warlords and their militias claimed twenty-nine American lives. The lesson drawn from this misadventure became known as the "Mogadishu line:" when peace keepers are forced to become combatants, there is cause to end the military mission. President Clinton had no desire to become caught up again in a complex ethnic conflict in a weak African state. Spiraling ethnic conflicts in Europe—in the Balkans—were enough of a challenge to his divided foreign policy team. This is not to say that the United States played no role in Rwanda. The U.S. ambassador to Rwanda after the genocide had been perpetrated claimed that the United States lent support to the RPF to regain power from Hutu extremists, then to attack Hutu camps in eastern Congo.[14]

It took several years for efforts at peace and reconciliation in Rwanda and Burundi to take shape. One option that was ruled out was the creation of two ethnically defined new states replacing Rwanda and Burundi, to be called Uhutu and Tutsiland. Such a resolution of the conflict (resembling the way the 1995 Dayton agreement reorganized Bosnia Herzegovina, which we discuss in the next chapter) would have required extensive ethnic resettlement and further demarcation of peoples whose identity was not that dissimilar.

**BOX 8.1**

**Theorizing the Linkage Between Ethnic Conflicts and Outside Involvement in Rwanda**

*Complementary Perspectives from Comparative Politics and International Relations*

### Hutu Versus Tutsi Conflict in Rwanda

**1. Domestic factors**

Weak state

Hutu political grievances

Tutsi military domination in Hutu-majority state

**2. International factors**

Demonstration effect of Burundi ethnic conflict

Tacit Belgian and French support for Hutu-led government

Tutsi kin in neighboring states (Burundi, Congo, Uganda)

**3. Conflict resolution**

Negligible third-party mediation, preventive diplomacy, or peace enforcement

Alleged unsuitability of international law (1948 Convention on the Prevention and Punishment of Genocide)

International institutions' role in creating transitional justice regimes after mass killings ended

The most significant measures taken in the aftermath of the conflicts were the work of external actors (Box 8.1). A United Nations International Criminal Tribunal for Rwanda was set up to try war crimes. In 1998, a former Rwandan prime minister was convicted for inciting the 1994 genocide and sentenced to life imprisonment. In 2008, the mastermind behind the genocide, a chief of staff in Rwanda's defense ministry in 1994, was jailed for life on charges of genocide, crimes against humanity, and war crimes. He, together with two other army officers who also were sentenced to life terms, were found guilty of conducting an "organized military operation" that killed hundreds of thousands of Tutsis.

Another judicial institution set up by international actors, modeled loosely on South Africa's Truth and Reconciliation Commission, was the Rwandan National Unity and Reconciliation Commission. Its mission was to identify the perpetrators of the mass killings of Tutsis. Under a system called *gacaca*, named after traditional village courts, the commission authorized the release of nearly all of the estimated 150,000 prisoners into the custody of local judges responsible for the districts where the crimes were committed. Perpetrators were to be classified under a four-tier system of punishment: the masterminds, those who killed in the hundreds, those who killed dozens, and those who provided information on where Tutsis could be found.

Although sentencing guidelines were unclear, as under South Africa's commission, punishment was deliberately not intended to fit the crime. Thus, in Rwanda, people who killed a dozen or fewer people could be sentenced to community service. As unjust as this appeared, it marked a departure from earlier practice where, as one official put it, "in the previous regime, if you killed you were glorified. The culture of hate has been so institutionalized in our system." It also represented a starting point for the RPF-dominated Rwandan government headed by Kagame (the first Tutsi president in independent Rwanda's history, elected in 2000 by a transitional parliament) to refute charges that it was bent on revenge against the Hutus. It is a "very imperfect system to deal with an impossible situation."[15]

In the case of Burundi, South Africa again played a part in the peace-making process. Former president Mandela mediated peace talks among various Tutsi and Hutu groups. In 2000, President Clinton's visit to several African states included a stop in Arusha, Tanzania, to preside over a peace-signing ceremony. The prestige of both Mandela and Clinton was crucial, therefore, in achieving the breakthrough that officially put an end to seven years of bloody conflict, though violence was to continue, at a lower level, in subsequent years.

## WORLD WAR IN THE DEMOCRATIC REPUBLIC OF CONGO

The conflict in Congo has been called **Africa's first world war** by one western aid agency, a term echoed by former U.S. Secretary of State Madeleine Albright.[16] While the exact reasons why various outside countries have become involved differ, it seems clear that Congo has become the site of an international battle over natural resources. A UN panel in 2001 said as much when it condemned the plunder of gems and minerals (copper, tin, cassiterite) by external parties; eighty-five companies, including American, Belgian, British, and German ones, were included on a "list of shame"—breaching Organization for Economic Cooperation and Development (OECD) standards and countenancing human rights abuses so as to make profits from the collapsed Congo state.[17] Not surprisingly, international arms dealers have gained considerably from the conflict. Weapons deliveries have come from former Soviet bloc states as well as the United States, which has also provided military training for some groups.

It should not be surprising, then, that the character of the Congo war has been interpreted in various ways. "The wars of 1996–1997 and 1998–2002 were civil wars, according to some. They were international wars designed to overthrow a dictatorship, according to others. They represent a continuation of Rwanda's Hutu–Tutsi conflict, pursued on Congo soil, for still others. They were resource wars, according to an abundant literature. The intervention of Congo's neighbors, Rwanda and Uganda in particular, were acts of self-defense. These neighbors were pawns of great powers from outside the continent."[18] The periodization of the war is itself subject to disagreement.

The so-called first civil war in Congo in 1996–1997 is easier to categorize than the armed clashes that followed. It can be regarded as a prime example of **conflict contagion**, spreading from Rwanda and Burundi. In particular, Congo's eastern region (referred to as Kivu), became a military theatre for Hutu–Tutsi battles. Capitalizing on the terminal illness of long-ruling Zairean dictator Joseph Mobutu Sese Seko, in 1996 the Tutsi-dominated RPF attacked Hutu refugee camps inside Zaire, claiming that the *Interahamwe* militia had taken refuge there. Soon, however, the RPF joined forces with Zairean rebel groups, and in 1997, deposed the corrupt Mobutu regime, in power for thirty-two years. The new government was headed by Laurent Kabila, who immediately renamed Zaire the Democratic Republic of Congo (DRC). For a time, he cooperated with RPF forces: A UN team of investigators seeking to discover the fate of thousands of Hutu refugees in Congo who may have been victims of Tutsi reprisal killings was harassed by the Kabila regime in spring 1998.

## Democratic Republic of the Congo

*Source*: Courtesy of the University of Texas Libraries, The University of Texas at Austin.

Within a year, cooperation between the new regime in Congo and the Tutsis collapsed. Many Congolese insisted that Kabila prove that he had not become a mere puppet of the RPF. Conversely, the RPF leadership accused him of promoting dictatorship and corruption and of harboring the *Interahamwe*, who, it alleged, were preparing to invade Rwanda. Kabila responded by ordering the expulsion of Rwandan and ethnic Tutsi soldiers located in the east of his country, even though they had helped bring him to power. These troops resisted and, together with Ugandan-based rebel groups, instead launched an offensive. They captured the country's third largest city, Kisangani, and moved close to the capital, Kinshasa. Kabila's regime survived only because a group of southern African countries—Angola, Namibia, and Zimbabwe, together with Chad—sent troops to keep the country from falling apart. In radio broadcasts, the Congolese president now inveighed against the Tutsis, saying that they should be wiped out "before they make slaves of us."

Africa specialist Ali Mazrui had written that "if Zaire can avoid collapsing into chaos in the near future, it will be one of the major actors in Africa in the twenty-first century, taking Burundi and Rwanda under its wing."[19] Remarkably, by 1998, it appeared that Tutsi-ruled Rwanda had taken vast Zaire under its wing. What had started off as mass killings orchestrated by ethnic entrepreneurs in Rwanda had become transformed into a battle for control among many African states for the continent's third largest country—one the size of all of western Europe.

A report prepared in 2000 by Amnesty International described the way that the Congolese people had become the primary victims of the civil war that had also attracted external involvement. There had been

> a catalogue of human rights abuses and suffering that the people of the DRC have been subjected to since August 1998 by forces whose foreign and Congolese political and military leaders claim to be fighting for security or sovereignty. In reality, many of the leaders are involved in a fight for political and economic control of the DRC. Amnesty International has concluded that these leaders are perpetrating, ordering or condoning atrocities on a large and systematic scale, and deliberately violating people's individual and collective right to security and sovereignty.[20]

Renewed armed conflict broke out in 1998, sparking the so-called second civil war that lasted until 2003. The war encompassed tribal conflicts, rival ethnic militias, and gang warfare—often with neighboring countries supporting opposing sides.[21] An estimated 5.5 million people perished from war-related causes. The majority were women, children, and the elderly, who died of starvation or disease. Over 1 million people had been driven from their homes, and a large proportion of these were beyond the reach of humanitarian organizations. Another half a million had fled the country.

African states involved in the Congo conflict were implicated in many human rights abuses. Here is a case in point: while the official pretext given for the deployment of a 20,000-strong Tutsi-controlled Rwandan army in eastern Congo was to secure the border from *Interahamwe* attacks, the reality was that it had taken control of Congolese diamond mines and other mineral resources. A follow-up UN panel report in 2003 cited Burundi and Uganda as being involved in developing slave-labor to more quickly and cheaply loot coltan Columbite-tantalite—an indispensable component in computer-based technology, including cell phones, stereos, and DVDs. Multinational corporations were inevitably drawn in as well. An Amnesty International report from 2005 listed companies from Britain, the United States, South Africa, Israel, and eastern Europe as sellers of large quantities of arms to rebel militias.

Human rights abuses were to be expected in a lawless state. The assassination of Laurent Kabila in 2001 was a further blow to the establishment of a stable DRC. His successor was his son, Joseph Kabila, who set up a transitional government based on power sharing, and made some inroads in limiting the second civil war. Often this required "striking deals with the devil"—for example, appointing rebel warlords who headed ethnic militias ("ethnic self-defense groups" was the name they preferred) but who were accused of mass killings and rape, to top government and national army positions. This cooptation process was widened in 2007 when combatants loyal to eastern Congo rebel leader Nkunda were integrated into the national army in a process called **mixage**. However, many continued to commit human rights abuses, even in their new uniforms.

A step toward the reconstruction of the DRC state was the adoption by referendum in late 2005 of a constitution that established a democratic presidential republic. The elections the next year were won by sitting president Kabila and his political movement. His main challenger was Jean-Pierre Bemba, one of Congo's richest men and the head of a militia group; he was subsequently arrested by the International Criminal Court for human rights abuses. After the election result was announced, some of his supporters rioted in the capital. Peace-keeping forces from the **MONUC** (Mission de l'Organisation des Nations Unies en République démocratique du Congo) [United Nations Organization Mission in the Democratic Republic of the Congo] had to intervene to stop the disturbances from spreading. This was one of the first important actions taken by MONUC, whose strength within two years was to reach 17,000, making it the United Nations' largest peace-keeping mission in the world.

## The Ethnic-Foreign Nexus in Eastern Congo

During this second civil war, much of the fighting, killing, and population displacement centered on the northeastern and eastern regions of Congo where local militias, backed by their respective foreign allies, were based. The complex international alliance system the war spawned—it is hard to think of it as a civil war—was summarized by one scholar this way: "Kabila allied himself with Zimbabwe, Angola, and Namibia (and to a certain extent with Chad, Libya, and Sudan). Facing them were Rwanda and Uganda (along with Burundi, to a certain extent) and the rebel groups these countries supported."[22]

The outcome of the five-year war was the division of the country into three separate zones. The northern third of the country was dominated by the Ugandan army and its Congolese ally, the Movement for the Liberation of Congo (MLC). The zone in the east was controlled by Tutsi-dominated Rwandan forces and their Congolese supporters. The remaining third of the country was all that the Congolese government forces and their foreign allies had authority over.

**THE ITURI CONFLICT.** The DRC's greatest success was in regaining a measure of central government control over the resource-rich **Ituri District** in northeastern Congo. By 2008, most armed groups operating there had been disarmed and demobilized. Observers from MONUC provided tactical support for the conflict resolution process. The United Nations Development Corporation and other international development agencies had set up offices in Ituri. To be sure, long-term stability was far from guaranteed. Among factors that could produce a reversion to instability were the return of large numbers of refugees to the district; the uncertain future of demobilized soldiers; the proliferation of small arms; a rise in interethnic tensions as disputes over land broke out afresh; and, of course, control over gold and diamond mines and markets.

Let us begin with the ethnic dimension. Initially it was driven by competing Hema and Lendu claims on land and grazing rights, but there were few signs that it would lead to armed conflict. Belgian colonial rule had favored the Hema, and a *modus vivendi* between the two groups was established under Mobutu's regime. But as central authority imploded after his death, Lendu began to fear that their land rights would be eroded by increased Hema ambitions.

Outside actors soon became involved. Contagion from the conflict in Rwanda and Burundi inclined the Lendu and Hema to adopt Hutu and Tutsi identifications, respectively. Although there were no objective grounds for doing so, the salience of ethnic and linguistic identity in Central Africa had been raised by the Rwandan genocide. The practical consequence of remaking ethnic identity was military support from outside the country. Thus, by the late 1990s, the Hutu militia *Interahamwe* had sided with the Lendu umbrella organization, the Nationalist and Integrationist Front (NIF), while it opportunistically pillaged the district's natural resources to finance its own military buildup. In turn, Tutsi-dominated Rwandan forces moved into Ituri to support their new, socially constructed "ethnic kin" and the movement that embodied it, the Hema-dominated Union of Congolese Patriots (UCP). One of the leaders of the UCP, Thomas Lubanga, earned the distinction in 2006 of being the first person ever arrested under an International Criminal Court warrant; the war crime charge was "conscripting and enlisting children under the age of fifteen years and using them to participate actively in hostilities." Tutsi militias, like Hutu ones, exploited the resource-rich district—for example, by exporting gold illegally—and transferred some of the revenue to Rwanda to finance the modernization of its national army.[23]

Northeast Congo borders both Uganda and Sudan, where long-running civil and ethnic strife has occurred. As the Mobutu regime entered its final days, Uganda—and Rwanda—moved forces into the region to help overthrow the ailing dictator. But in 1998, Mobutu's successor, Laurent Kabila, turned on both neighboring countries: he dismissed all Tutsi ministers from his government and demanded that Rwandan and Ugandan forces leave the DRC, accusing them of pillaging and looting the country's resources. Neither country complied. In the case of Uganda, support was thrown behind an anti-Kabila rebel group called the Movement for the Liberation of Congo (MLC), headed by Jean-Pierre Bemba. Following democratic elections in 2006 won by Joseph Kabila, the Uganda-backed MLC became Congo's official opposition party and Bemba, runner-up in the presidential election, was appointed vice president. But fighting on the streets of Congo's capital, Kinshasha, between supporters of the rivals, and continued warfare in northeast Congo between government forces and the MLC, made the Kabila–Bemba alliance untenable. As Uganda's influence in the DRC waned, Bemba fled the country in 2007. A year later, he was arrested in Belgium on an International Criminal Court warrant for war crimes and preparations got under way for his trial. While he had been in command of his rebel force, Bemba had even been accused of presiding over acts of cannibalism of his enemies.[24]

Ugandan forces had come under international pressure to withdraw from the Ituri District. Human Rights Watch charged the forces of acting as "both arsonist and fireman" in Ituri: "During its four years occupying the northeastern DRC, the Ugandan army claimed to be a peacemaker in a region torn by ethnic strife. In reality, the Ugandan army provoked political confusion and created insecurity in areas under its control. From its initial involvement in a land dispute between the Hema and Lendu, the Ugandan army more often aggravated than calmed ethnic and political hostilities."[25] In 2003, most Ugandan government forces withdrew, reportedly taking with them some $10 million in gold.

The DRC took Uganda to the International Court of Justice (ICJ) for what it viewed as an illegal occupation, human rights abuses, and exploitation of the region's natural resources. The ICJ's ruling in 2005 sided with the DRC: Uganda had violated Congo's sovereignty by invading it; by providing military, logistical, and financial backing of the MLC rebels; by carrying out human rights abuses, including killings, torture, and deployment of child soldiers; and by looting of gold, diamonds and silver. The ICJ ordered Uganda to "make reparation for the injury caused"—the sum was to be negotiated between the two states, but the DRC had demanded that $10 billion be paid in compensation. International law is rarely able to enforce sanctions applied to a country, and forcing Uganda to pay reparations seems unlikely in the near future. Similar judgments are pending elsewhere in the world, and the best that can be expected is a set of political settlements and tradeoffs by the governments that are parties to a dispute—not payouts.

When Uganda withdrew its forces in 2003, the resulting power vacuum prompted UN Secretary General Kofi Annan to call for a multinational force to be deployed to Ituri District that would reinforce a skeletal MONUC mission there. In 2003, the Security Council authorized the deployment of an Interim Emergency Multinational Force (IEMF), and France was put in charge. Within three years, UN peace-making operations, together with Congolese government cooptation of some of the top rebel commanders for service in the national army, had reduced violence in Ituri.

There is another aspect to the DRC–Uganda confrontation in Ituri that only indirectly involves a state-to-state conflict. Since 1987, a religious Christian sect organized around the Acholi ethnic group has been active in northern Uganda. The Lord's Resistance Army (LRA), led by Joseph Kony, a self-described "voice of God," has fought to establish a theocracy in Uganda and in adjacent parts of the DRC and Sudan. Over the last two decades, some of Africa's worst human rights abuses, which include barbaric killings, mutilation, kidnappings, and enslavement, have been attributed to the LRA. Uganda government forces have pressed offensives against the LRA in the north of the country as well as in neighboring Congo. The LRA has accused the Ugandan government of using the pretext of an LRA presence in Congo (which it denies) to maintain Ugandan forces in the resource-rich region. During Christmas celebrations in 2008, several hundred Catholics were butchered by the LRA in a village in northeastern Congo. The LRA's home base appeared now to be in northeast Congo, although its fighters were active in four other neighboring states. Not surprisingly, in 2009 the DRC army joined with Ugandan and Sudanese forces to hunt down LRA militia units.

The northeastern border of the DRC with Uganda and Sudan has represented an ethnic powder keg. Overlapping ethnic, religious, and civil conflict in one country has appeared inevitably to spill over into another. One country's confrontation between government and rebel armies swiftly becomes the entire region's dispute.

**CONFLICT IN KIVU.** Compared to Ituri, the DRC central government has had less success in regaining authority over its eastern region. Battles continued into 2009 in the Kivu provinces of eastern Congo, pitting the DRC national army against rebel forces made up of Congolese Tutsis and rebel soldiers from eastern Congo who had previously served in the Congolese national army.

The commander of the Tutsi-dominated National Congress for the Defense of the People (CNDP) was Laurent Nkunda, a charismatic military strategist who simultaneously earned the admiration of many western officials for being a strongman in a weak state, and the condemnation of Human Rights Watch for being a war criminal guilty of repeated atrocities. In 2009, the International Criminal Court continued its investigation of war crimes charges against him, beginning with massacres carried out under his command in 2002 in the eastern Congo city of Kisangani (formerly known as Stanleyville), as well as in other areas captured by his forces.

But Nkunda seemed to have apologists in the West. Claiming to be a Seventh Day Adventist minister and enjoying close ties with American Pentecostal groups, the Tutsi commander also controlled much of eastern Congo's natural resources, including coltan and tin ore. Multinational electronic corporations, among others, were reluctant to offend him, and Anglo-American media coverage had generally presented a positive view of him. In late 2008, one American journalist described how Nkunda cultivated the image of a statesman-in-waiting but warned that "beneath the veneer lies a ruthlessness of a piece with Congo's unbroken history of brutality."[26] Indeed, by 2008, the CNDP's military successes in Kivu had persuaded him that his forces could even bring down Kabila's government in Kinshasha, a thousand miles away.

The reputation of the military coalition opposing Nkunda was as tarnished. Government forces were repeatedly accused of ransacking and raping in towns they entered. In 2008, they took the eastern city of Goma and pillaged it, allegedly in the presence of UN peace keepers who did nothing to stop it. MONUC's armed forces—over half of whom are South Asian (Bangladeshi, Indian, and Pakistani)— took part in the government offensive, raising questions about its peace-keeping role and neutrality. Worse, there were accusations leveled at MONUC units of sexual abuse of civilians. Finally, MONUC was blamed for not acting to arrest Nkunda, whose whereabouts they knew.

Arguably the most unsavory militia in eastern Congo, and ally of the Congolese army, was one organized by Hutu extremists. Called the Les Forces Démocratiques de Libération du Rwanda [Democratic Liberation Forces of Rwanda (FDLR)], many members had been implicated in the 1994 genocide in Rwanda and had fled to eastern Congo. The DRC–*Interahamwe* alliance had exacerbated relations between the DRC and Rwanda, and the FDLR's presence in eastern Congo continued to create tension. It had not renounced its political aim of returning to power in Rwanda. In the interim, the FDLR continued to be well armed and controlled access to precious minerals in Kivu like cassiterite, coltan, and gold. Moreover, in 2009 "with the rebel group deeply implanted in the forests and mountains of DR Congo, those weapons are also used to extort taxes and minerals from local diggers and traders, reaping profits worth millions of dollars a year."[27]

The repeated military failures of government forces in eastern Congo appeared to leave president Kabila with one option—to negotiate with Nkunda and his Rwandan allies. An important breakthrough was recorded in late 2008 with an agreement between the Rwandan and DRC governments to disband the FDLR militia. Nkunda had long insisted that it was this notorious group of Hutu extremists that had compelled his rebel army to widen its control over north Kivu. The DRC government's commitment to disband the FDLR seemed to reflect the shift in the balance of military power in east Congo toward Nkunda's forces. But a wild card factor turned out to be senior officers in the CNDP who turned against Nkunda in early 2009, declared an end to the hostilities, and joined the Congolese army. The appeal of mixage and the incentives it provided—exchanging the position of a rebel commander for a senior post in the national army—seemed to be growing as a conflict resolution mechanism. As for Nkunda, a joint Congolese-Rwandan operation launched to track down Rwandan Hutu militiamen operating in the DRC captured the rebel leader in January 2009. The pro-Tutsi warlord was reportedly being held in Rwanda and it was uncertain that he would be extradited to the DRC, which had issued an international arrest warrant for him.

The increasing presence of MONUC troops in eastern Congo seemed to be Congo's best hope for regaining influence over all parts of the country, including the eastern breakaway region. Congo took heart from a UN panel's formal charge in 2008 against the Rwandan government that it had engaged in blatant military involvement on the DRC's territory. Rwandan authorities denied the charge and described the report as "a calculated move to shift blame away" from Congo and the international community, "both of whom have failed to resolve the conflict." The paradox was that international resolution of conflicts in the DRC had to be based on a condemnation of outside countries' interference in internal Congolese affairs.

## International Mediation in the Congo Conflict

Conflict in the Congo became internationalized in three distinct ways: (1) the Tutsis who had routed the Hutus in Rwanda and Burundi seemed intent on building an empire, and ethnic Tutsi leaders of Rwanda were seen as the masterminds of a Tutsi imperial project that would take control of the weak or even collapsed states of the region; (2) the number of African countries with a stake in the region had increased and caused frictions elsewhere on the continent, for example, between Rwanda and Uganda for control of Kisangani, and between a neutral South Africa and a pro-Kabila Zimbabwe; and (3) transnational warlord actions exploited ethnic differences for the benefit of militia leaders, as in the case of Nkunda in Kivu. Often these leaders were politically—and sometimes even ethnically—agnostic and had no deep commitments to any cause.

Hope for a resolution of the Congo conflict had risen with the signing of a ceasefire agreement in Lusaka, Zambia, in 1999. The principal international parties to the conflict—Congo, Angola, Uganda, Rwanda, Namibia, and Zimbabwe—accepted the accord, as did the anti-Kabila rebel groups operating inside Congo and who controlled about one-third of the country. In 2000, the UN Security Council authorized deployment of a 5,000-strong peace-keeping force, but fighting in eastern Congo continued. Later that year, the five foreign African armies present in the Congo met in Maputo, Mozambique, under the leadership of South African President Thabo Mbeki, and pledged to pull their forces from the DRC (the various rebel groups operating within the Congo did not participate). The withdrawals were to be supervised and monitored by MONUC. But it took several years before the international community gave this U.N. force sufficient authority, personnel, and equipment to deal with the crisis.

In 2004, to stem the tide of regional violence and instability, the United States helped launch the so-called tripartite process. Its institutional form was the Tripartite Plus Joint Commission, which included the DRC, Rwanda, Uganda, and Burundi. Its missions were to encourage cooperation among these countries as well as to enhance regional security. In 2005, a summit of the **African Union**, the successor to the Organization of African Unity, promised to help the DRC disarm militias operating in the country. In 2007, a bilateral agreement between the DRC and Rwanda resulted in the Nairobi communiqué—a joint commitment to resolve the presence of the FDLR in eastern Congo.

In early 2008, the government of the DRC signed a ceasefire agreement with twenty-two armed groups in the eastern town of Goma. It followed the government's failed offensive in eastern Congo a few months earlier. The United States actively encouraged rebel forces to accept the Goma agreement, and it offered the

**BOX 8.2**

**Theorizing the Linkage Between Ethnic Conflicts and Outside Involvement in Congo**

*Complementary Perspectives from Comparative Politics and International Relations*

**Central Government Versus Regional/Ethnic Militias in Congo**

**1. Domestic factors**

Fragmenting state

Ethnic and linguistic diversity

Instrumentalist use of ethnic identities to create militias

Extensive natural resources

**2. International factors**

Contagion of conflicts in Rwanda and Burundi

Third-party military interventions of multiple African states

Economic interests of multinational corporations

**3. Conflict resolution**

Diplomatic initiatives by select African states (especially South Africa)

Expanding peace-keeping role of UN Mission in Congo

International Criminal Court threat to indict rebel leaders

---

DRC government support for its peace initiative for eastern Congo. Called the Amani program, its strategy for restoring peace in the region was through demobilization and reintegration of all the armed groups into the national army.

Since 1997, Congo has veered from being a consolidated to a weak, to a fragmented, and even to a collapsed state—and then back in the reverse direction. The combination of a weak central government, regional ethnic militias, foreign armies, abundant natural resources, and the presence of multinational corporations have made reconstructing the DRC a daunting task (see Box 8.2). The political stakes in this large African state are high, turning any losers into potential rebel groups. To complicate matters further, the number of stakeholders is high too.

## THE DARFUR CONFLICT: A CLASH OF CIVILIZATIONS?

The Darfur region in western Sudan captured the world's attention in 2005 when it was poised on the brink of a purportedly ethnically driven humanitarian catastrophe. A quarter of a million people had died as a result of war, famine, and disease. According to the World Health Organization, about 20 percent of the deaths were attributable to direct violence and 80 percent to drought-related diarrhea. Close to 2 million other people had been displaced; a quarter of a million had become refugees in neighboring Chad. The inability of international aid agencies to deliver food and medical supplies to the region, largely the result of the Khartoum government's obstructionist policies, heightened global concern. In the West, sympathy for the beleaguered Christian community in the country spread quickly as news about the conflict became better known.

# Sudan

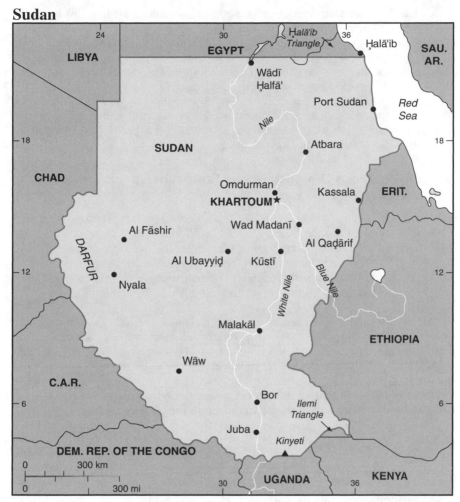

*Source*: Courtesy of the University of Texas Libraries, The University of Texas at Austin.

The origins of the conflict can be found in the devastating famine that affected Sudan in 1987, which in turn was caused partly by a process of desertification of arable lands. The three provinces composing Darfur are largely inhospitable; they range from the sand desert of the eastern Sahara in the north to the barren savannah in the south. Even though life is difficult to support in the region, about 6 million people inhabit the area, mostly crowded in the mountainous central district. A demographic explosion had doubled the population in a twenty-year period. Thus, the battle to control fertile lands is central to the conflict.

Other underlying causes of conflict include economic underdevelopment, widespread illiteracy, and poor infrastructure. The existence of a weak Sudanese state unable to exercise authority over much of the country created an opportunity structure for local political actors to fill the vacuum. The discovery of large oilfields in western and southern Sudan, especially in 2005, led to heightened outside interest in the region, especially on the part of Chinese corporations. Even as the humanitarian crisis in Darfur deepened, Sudan experienced an investment boom led by French, German, Swiss, and Middle Eastern companies alongside Chinese ones. Drilling for oil was risky, however, as long as armed conflict was taking place in Darfur. The Sudanese government's scorched-earth strategy against Darfur rebels was prompted by the desire to accelerate stability so that multinationals could invest safely. A struggle over energy sources was also integral to the conflict.

Yet other explanations are grounded in a more general and even apocalyptic view. The Darfur conflict has been constructed in racial and ethnic terms as one between Arabs and Africans. It is even seen as a clash of civilizations—a battlefront in the worldwide Arab-led *jihad* against infidels.

## The Ethno-religious Dimension: Muslim Arabs Versus Animist Africans

Racial, ethnic, and religious divisions had been behind Sudan's long-running civil war that had raged before the Darfur conflict broke out. It had pitted the northern and southern halves of the country against each other in an armed struggle that had begun in 1955.[28] Southern Sudan is inhabited by African ethnic groups, most of which practice different forms of Christianity or **animism**—a belief in the existence of spirits in humans and objects. The north is dominated by Muslim groups and is culturally Arabic (though less so in Darfur).

For decades, different military and political movements in southern Sudan fought for political autonomy. They reportedly received military assistance from Ethiopia, Somalia, and Uganda. The United States too, was said to have shipped military equipment to southern Sudanese rebels in the 1990s, hoping they would overthrow the regime of Omar al-Bashir, a general who took power in a military coup in 1989. The United States placed Sudan on the list of nations sponsoring terrorism as early as 1993, shortly after bin Laden had moved to the country.

The lengthy war was waged mainly in the south. Up to 2 million civilians were killed—making it one of the deadliest conflicts since World War II. Twice as many southerners became refugees across Sudan and in neighboring countries. Rape was used as a strategy of deracination of non-Arab groups. Hundreds of thousands of southerners were put into slavery in the country. The international community, led by the United Nations, expressed increasing horror at the war's toll. After the 2001 terrorist attacks on the United States, pressure mounted on al-Bashir to distance himself from Islamic fundamentalism.

As the conflict in Darfur began to escalate, al-Bashir reached an agreement with south Sudanese rebels that became formalized in 2005. Its main provisions called for political autonomy to be granted to the south for six years, after which—that is, in 2011—the south would hold a referendum on whether it wished to secede from Sudan (the provision resembled the 1996 Khasavyurt Accord concluded between Russia and Chechnya but which was subsequently nullified by the 1999 Russian invasion). The armed forces of the two sides would be merged if southerners elected to stay in Sudan. Oil revenues from oilfields in the south would be split evenly between the Khartoum and southern governments. Thirty percent of central government posts were to be allotted to southern leaders; the president of the government of south Sudan became the first vice president of the Sudanese national government.

A contentious aspect of the 2005 accord was the status of Sharia law. It was agreed that Islamic law would govern in the north, though a separate controversy erupted over whether it should be enforced in the capital, where there was significant religious diversity. The accord left it to southern Sudan's assembly to decide if Sharia law would apply in that region. The interim constitution adopted for southern Sudan was ambiguous on the subject. While "legislation applicable to Southern Sudan should be derived from the sources of consensus, customs and values of the people of Southern Sudan," it could be argued that Islamic law should "be applied in the South since religion is part of the customs of some people."[29]

If the north–south conflict had ended—or at least was put on hold—clashes along similar ethno-religious and racial lines were becoming more frequent in Darfur. They had first erupted into large-scale fighting in the two years that followed the 1987 famine. One side was the Fur, a nominally Sunni Muslim ethnic group whose members widely practice animism. Until Britain conquered their territory and abolished the sultanate in 1916, they had ruled themselves and had successfully resisted **arabization**. In the 1987–1989 war, mostly agrarian Fur were attacked by groups of nomadic Arabs who wanted their land. The Sudanese government had no overt role in this conflict.

One analysis underscored the vicious nature of the strife, seemingly reflecting the primordial animosity of the groups toward each other. The conflict

> was marked by indiscriminate killing and mass slaughter on both sides. The language of genocide was first employed in that conflict. The Fur representative at the May 1989 reconciliation conference in El Fasher pointed to their adversaries and claimed that "the aim is a total holocaust and no less than the complete annihilation of the Fur people and all things Fur." In response the Arab representative traced the origin of the conflict to "the end of the '70s when . . . the Arabs were depicted as foreigners who should be evicted from this area of Dar Fur."[30]

This conflict was subsiding when al-Bashir took power and, for the next twenty years, ruled over a fragmented state. Sudan was racked by regional conflicts, between the north and the south, then in Darfur. Were al-Bashir's policies responsible for the spread and escalation of ethnically anchored conflicts? The International Criminal Court (ICC) seemed to think so. In 2008, it determined that he had played a pivotal role in fanning these conflicts by promoting ethnic and racial polarization. Al-Bashir had categorized the tribes politically aligned with him as Arabs, those opposed as *Zurga*—slang for "dirty blacks." His stated aim was a *Zurga*-free Sudan. The principal "African" groups in western Sudan were the Fur, Masalit, and Zaghawas.

In 2008, the ICC prosecutor charged al-Bashir with genocide, crimes against humanity, and war crimes during his reign. But according to a specialist on the region, the Sudanese president had not invented the wheel—or in this case, Sudan's racial categories. "The racialization of identities in Darfur has its roots in the British colonial period. As early as the late 1920s, the British tried to organize two confederations in Darfur: one Arab, the other black (*Zurga*). Racialized identities were incorporated into the census and provided the frame for government policy. It is not out of the blue that the two sides in the 1987–1989 civil war described themselves as Arab and *Zurga*."[31]

Racialization of identities in Darfur is connected to racism. "In terms of skin color, everybody is black. But the various forms of Sudanese cultural racism distinguish '*zurug*' from 'Arab,' even if the skin has the same color."[32] To complicate matters further, linguistic divisions are crosscutting, so that some of the African tribes have lost their native language and replaced it with Arabic.

Successive ethnic conflicts in Darfur entailed a fight over land, but they could not be reduced solely to ethnic divisions.

> The land-grabbing has been a consequence of three different, if related, causes. The first is the colonial system, which reorganized Darfur as a series of tribal homelands, designating the largest for settled peasant tribes and none for fully nomadic tribes. The second is environmental degradation: according to the United Nations Environment Program, the Sahara expanded by 100 kilometers in four decades; this process reached a critical point in the mid-1980s, pushing all tribes of North Darfur, Arab and non-Arab, farther south, onto more fertile Fur and Masalit lands. This in turn led to a conflict between tribes with home-lands and those without them. The imperative of sheer survival explains in part the unprecedented brutality of the violence in every successive war since 1987–1989. The third cause came last: the brutal counterinsurgency unleashed by the Bashir regime in 2003–2004 in response to an insurgency backed up by peasant tribes.[33]

Another ethnic group involved in the Darfur conflict is the Masalit, who, like the Fur, are a non-Arab Muslim tribe living along the Sudan-Chad border. The policy of arabization first launched by the Sudanese government in the 1970s had hardened the identities of its non-Arab targets, whether black Muslim groups in the south, which assumed an African identity, or the Fur and Masalit in the west, which rebelled against the government's arabization measures. Following a revolt in 2003, the majority of Masalit, one of the poorest groups in the area, were driven from their homes over the next three years. Many ended up in refugee camps in Chad, which a newly created militia of Arab nomads attacked in cross-border raids.

The Zaghawa (who call themselves Beri) were the third African Muslim group of Darfur targeted by Sudanese arabization policy. A dominant ethnicity in neighboring Chad and more devout Muslims than the animist-influenced Fur and Masalit, most of Darfur's Zaghawa were forced to flee their homes and take refuge in camps on the other side of the border.

The conflict between tribes of African farmers and Arab nomads deepened in 2003 when Fur, Masalit, and Zaghawa leaders organized two rebel groups, the Sudan Liberation Army/Movement (SLA/M) and the Justice and Equality Movement (JEM). The chief grievances they articulated were economic marginalization (therefore reactive ethnicity) and political ostracism within the Arab-ruled state. They also demanded Sudanese government action to stop the attacks carried out by nomadic Arab militia, which had been driven onto African farmlands by desertification and drought.[34]

In reality, the Arab militia appeared to have been a creation of the government of Sudan. Especially after the 2003 rebellion, which featured armed clashes between government troops and the SLA/M and JEM, al-Bashir decided to construct a third party having Darfur credentials—a loose alliance of nomadic Arab militias on horses and camels. Supplied and backed by the Sudanese army, the so-called *Janjaweed* ("devils on horseback") developed into a fearsome militia made up of Arab speakers from Darfur and neighboring Chad.[35] The SLA/M and

JEM self-defense groups proved no match for the combination of Sudanese armed forces—which unleashed air attacks on the African tribes' villages—and riders on horseback storming out of the desert (though often their chiefs arrive at a battle scene in Land Rovers). A Human Rights Watch report in 2004 graphically captured the clashes:

> The government and its *Janjaweed* allies have killed thousands of Fur, Masalit, and Zaghawa—often in cold blood—raped women, and destroyed villages, food stocks and other supplies essential to the civilian population. They have driven more than one million civilians, mostly farmers, into camps and settlements in Darfur where they live on the very edge of survival, hostage to *Janjaweed* abuses. More than one million others have fled to neighboring Chad but the vast majority of war victims remain trapped in Darfur.[36]

The Sudanese government repeatedly denied that it provided material support to the militia, and it construed the *Janjaweed* as a spontaneously formed local counterinsurgency opposed to the African groups' revolt. But in 2008, the pretense was dropped when a militia leader was appointed as minister in al-Bashir's government.

Ecological, economic, and political factors helped spawn the fierce clashes of 2003 and those thereafter, but we should not downplay the part played by race, ethnicity, and religion. The *Janjaweed* were a product of Arab nomads' lengthy battle with black farmers, and in the first decade of the new century, they "cashed in on their strategic positions as agents of the Sudanese government . . . to vent their racial/ethnic anger and hatred on rival African communities with whom they have clashed for decades over economic resources and ethnic/racial differences."[37] Although Muslims themselves, they went after the Islamic symbols of the black tribes in Darfur, desecrating their Qur'ans, destroying their mosques, killing their imams.[38] The only logical explanation for the intrareligious killing appears to be of an Arab racism that discriminates against black Muslims. The overall silence of the Islamic Middle East states on the Darfur tragedy is significant.

## Outside Actors in Sudan

Darfur may represent Exhibit A of the ethnic conflicts that became internationalized. Two global powers in particular have had major stakes in the region, China and the United States, and both involve oil. China's largest overseas oil project has been in western Sudan, where its main energy company extracts crude oil and pumps it through a Chinese-made pipeline to the Red Sea, where tankers then transport it to China's industrial centers. Its rapid industrial growth had made China desperate for energy, and it was prepared to invest in pariah states like Sudan, as well as Angola and Iran, because the West was reluctant to do so.

In return, China became the Sudanese government's largest supplier of arms. Despite a United Nations embargo on supplying weapons to the country, China, together with Russia, provided the Khartoum government with significant military equipment. China's shipments included everything from machine guns and rocket-propelled grenades to tanks, helicopters, and jets. In addition, for Khartoum, "China is in a lucrative partnership that delivers billions of dollars in investment, oil revenue and weapons—as well as diplomatic protection—to a government accused by the United States of genocide in Darfur and cited by human rights groups for systematically massacring civilians and chasing them off ancestral lands to clear oil-producing areas."[39]

The United States has oil stakes in the region as well. Chevron and Exxon operate in oilfields next door, in Chad, and from there use a pipeline to send crude to a Cameroon port on the Atlantic coast. They would like to be able to drill in Darfur, which could become possible if Sudanese government troops were driven out and Chinese contracts nullified. The Bush administration backed the SLA/M forces in Darfur; President Bush even welcomed a top rebel commander in the White House in 2006. Simultaneously, his administration launched an effective propaganda attack accusing the *Janjaweed* of perpetrating genocide and encouraging international military intervention in the area.

The European Union (EU) was more circumspect about trying to resolve a humanitarian crisis through military intervention. It gave higher priority to preventive diplomacy as a tool. France in particular has extensive interests in this part of Africa. It has a military presence in and provides assistance to two countries next to Darfur, the Central African Republic and Chad, to which some of the Darfur fighting spread. In 2008, a rebellion—backed by the Sudanese government—aimed at overthrowing Chad's president (a Zaghawa) was defeated when president Sarkozy declared his intention to deploy French troops while also encouraging the Darfur-based Zarghawa group JEM to stop the Chad rebels. He himself visited Chad shortly after the coup attempt failed. To bring peace to the area, Sarkozy endorsed the UN Security Council's mandate for deployment of a European Union Force (EUFOR Chad/CAR), made up mostly of French forces, in eastern Chad and the northeast Central African Republic.

In 2004, the UN Security Council also mandated a peace-keeping force for Darfur. It began as a small African Union Mission in Sudan (AMIS), whose task was to protect civilian life. But even when it reached 7,000 in number of troops, it proved ineffective, in large part due to obstruction by the Sudanese government, which labeled it a group of foreign invaders. In response, in 2007, the UN established a new force called the **African Union–United Nations Hybrid Operation in Darfur (UNAMID)**, which was accepted by Khartoum. The plan was for it to reach 26,000 in number, making it the largest UN peace-keeping force in the world. But by the end of 2008, it was half that strength, had been fired upon by Sudanese government forces, and had proved incapable of protecting civilians (see Box 8.3).

The job of assisting the victims of the conflict in Darfur fell to humanitarian agencies. By 2009, Darfur had become the site of the largest humanitarian operation in the world, with about 17,000 aid workers (94 percent of whom are Sudanese) working for eighty-five international aid organizations and sixteen UN agencies.[40] Yet this vast humanitarian network was able to reach at best 65 percent of the people affected by the strife. As with UNAMID, attacks on humanitarian workers, often by government forces, were commonplace.

Military offensives by Sudanese military and *Janjaweed* militia in 2008 had made Darfur a more violent place than ever. Toward the end of that year, al-Bashir offered an unconditional ceasefire to fighting in Darfur, but it seemed a last-ditch attempt to stall the International Criminal Court's case against him. Indeed, in March 2009 the ICC prosecutor issued an international arrest warrant for him, making al-Bashir the first sitting head of state to be indicted for war crimes. The charges included war crimes and crimes against humanity, but not genocide. To issue an international arrest warrant for a sitting political leader is extraordinary enough, but in al-Bashir's case it was even

## BOX 8.3
## Theorizing the Linkage Between Ethnic Conflicts and Outside Involvement in Sudan

*Complementary Perspectives from Comparative Politics and International Relations*

### Sudanese Central Government Versus Darfur Ethnic Rebel Groups

**1. Domestic factors**

Fragmented state

Primordial racial and ethnic categories

Overlapping religious cleavage between Muslims and Christians/animists

Government arabization policies

Oil fields

**2. International factors**

Great power interests of China and the United States

Interests of energy corporations

Illegal arms deliveries from third parties

Spillover of conflict to neighboring Chad

Support of Arab states for Sudan's government

**3. Conflict resolution**

Ineffectiveness of African Union/UN missions in Darfur

Inability to operationalize international norm of humanitarian assistance to civilians affected by war

International Criminal Court indictment of the president of Sudan

more exceptional because of the global economic interests and external political actors who stood to lose with his conviction. The Sudanese leader's indictment was opposed by China, Russia, the African Union, the League of Arab States, and the Non-Aligned Movement. Emboldened by such widespread support and charging the ICC with neocolonialism, a defiant al-Bashir responded to the ICC indictment with an international tour of his regional allies which included Eritrea, Egypt, Qatar, Saudi Arabia. It was hard not to see a clash of civilizations over the indictment, as over the entire Darfur tragedy.

## KEEPING THE STATE STRONG: SOUTH AFRICA

Transitions from authoritarianism do not always go smoothly, as seen in the cases of the former Soviet Union and Yugoslavia. When South Africa emerged out of the oppressive apartheid regime, pessimists believed that the country would be riveted by racial and ethnic strife, weak state structures, and uncompromising political leadership. This forecast has largely proved incorrect. How, then, were ethnic rivalries defused and central authorities given legitimacy in the new South Africa—without the help of external actors?

The collapse of the Soviet bloc in the USSR and that of white-ruled South Africa occurred within two years of each other. The existence of an empire furnishes an obvious point of comparison: "The South African state formed in 1910 was a British empire in microcosm and, without apartheid, was always likely to show the same fissiparous tendencies of the Russian empire without communism."

# South Africa

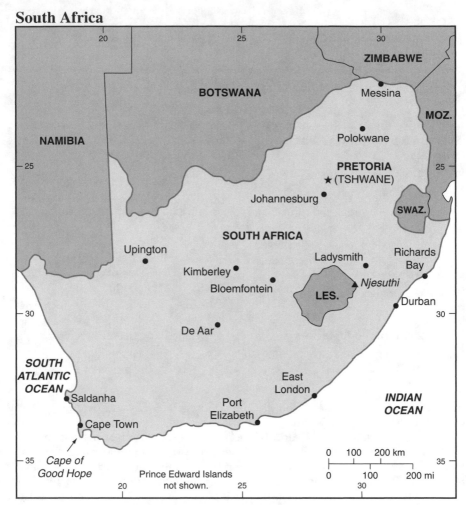

*Source:* Courtesy of the University of Texas Libraries, The University of Texas at Austin.

The consequence in each case was that "[e]thnic politics, so long obscured or concealed, suddenly mattered a great deal."[41]

## Transition from Apartheid

Few political systems, anywhere, have ever been based so profoundly on racial and ethnic categories as that of South Africa under **apartheid**. The assumption was that the country's various black tribes would eventually mature into nations, like Afrikaans and English-speaking whites had done. Until then, the different black groups were to live in designated tribal homelands (or language areas) and townships even though, as a result of wars, uprooting, and relocation, few of them really had an ancestral home. Critics of apartheid argued that ethnicity was an outdated concept and was used in South Africa only to create divisions.

The transition from apartheid to black majority rule in the early 1990s represented a struggle for power among the country's black peoples, who made up about 75 percent of the total population (whites represented 14 percent; mixed race, or coloreds, nearly 9 percent; and Indians 2.5 percent). When President F. W. de Klerk announced his initiative for democratic reform, it was to the **African National Congress (ANC)** and its imprisoned leader, Nelson Mandela, that he turned. Privileged by the overture, ANC leaders—most of whom belonged to the Xhosa group—refused to include a representative of the Zulus—a historic, large, and influential nation in South Africa since the times of King Shaka in the early nineteenth century.

Even before the democratic breakthrough, one African specialist stressed how Xhosa and Zulu "occupy polar positions on some key questions of ethnic identity, ideology, organizational affiliation, leadership preferences, and strategic inclinations." More than that, "one of these groups is significantly overrepresented and the other underrepresented in the leading extraparliamentary opposition organizations."[42] This classic grievance has mobilized many a secessionist movement, and there was reason to believe that a new democratic South Africa's first challenge would be to manage the threat of separatism.

What, then, were the supposed differences between the two groups? The languages they speak are related and, as with the other seven African languages given official constitutional status (along with Afrikaans and English), belong to the Bantu group. Of South Africa's population of about 45 million, more than one-fifth is Zulu (over 9 million) compared with about 7 million Xhosas (many of whom also speak English). Zulus are concentrated in South Africa's most populous province, KwaZulu-Natal, and Xhosas have settled near the Cape. For one observer, the most important difference between the groups was that they had different political cultures. "The Xhosa-speakers of the Cape were the most politically aware Africans in the country, having grown up within a relatively liberal environment in which a qualified franchise had long been available. . . . Zulu-speakers were conservative, even parochial, by comparison."[43] At the time that the Union of South Africa was created in 1910, there were already 12,000 blacks and coloreds registered as voters in the Cape, but only a handful in Natal. The implication was that Zulus lagged behind Xhosa in democratic culture. For Xhosas, it seemed natural, therefore, that they should constitute the core group in the new democracy.

The shift from white minority to black majority rule entailed many changes, above all, constitutional ones. The 1996 constitution (which came into effect in 1997) began with a preamble asserting that South Africa "belongs to all who live in it"—a choice of an unproblematic identity and marking a stark contrast to the apartheid system. It formally established nine non-ethnically-defined provinces, all of which had black majority populations, except for the Western Cape. The constitution acknowledged the institution of traditional indigenous leaders and recognized the principle of self-determination for all groups within the country. But its commitment to an inclusive democracy did not go so far as to embrace federalism. Whereas provincial legislatures were elected, the chief executives of provinces were appointed by the central government. Provinces' powers were enumerated while the central government had both designated powers as well as residual ones not specified by the constitution. The constitution precluded any asymmetrical arrangement that would give special status to the Zulus.[44] Clearly, the specter of federal systems collapsing or under strain in various parts of the world in the early 1990s influenced how the new South African system was designed.

Political reform meant that the tribal homelands had to be dismantled. These tribal homelands, including the semiautonomous kingdom of KwaZulu, had been set up under the 1953 Bantu Authorities Act to "train" the Bantu for self-government while moving them away from white-populated areas and denying them citizenship. An "independent" KwaZulu proclaimed in 1972 consisted of forty-four pockets of land on both sides of the Tugela river—a "polka-dot state," in the words of Mangosuthu Buthelezi, head of the Zulu nationalist organization **Inkatha**, originally a cultural organization for Zulus set up in the 1920s. It was a fraction of the size of Shaka's kingdom but, nevertheless, the Inkatha Freedom Party (IFP) made use of the bantustan to monopolize government.

Black majority rule in South Africa eliminated the homelands and, with them, fiefdoms of power and patronage established by homeland rulers. When South Africa's first general election was scheduled for 1994, Inkatha, having lost its privileged status in KwaZulu, threatened to boycott it. The threat deepened the rupture between the ANC, led by Mandela, and Inkatha, headed by Buthelezi. Although it would be oversimplifying to describe the ANC as a multiethnic movement and Inkatha as a Zulu one, it is also true that, in the 1994 election, Inkatha invoked the grand history of the Zulus while the ANC emphasized the future that all blacks in South Africa would build together.

The two groups had pursued different strategies under apartheid. The ANC waged an armed struggle against the government in the hope of making South Africa ungovernable. Inkatha concentrated its efforts on a negotiated solution. After the democratic transition, Inkatha allied itself with opponents of change, ranging from bantustan leaders to representatives of the white Afrikaaner right. This discredited Inkatha more than did the ANC's acceptance of Soviet and Cuban backing and its inclusion of communist leaders within its ranks during the antiapartheid struggle.

In the 1994 election, the ANC–Inkatha rivalry was transformed into violent clashes between black groups. Many black townships in KwaZulu-Natal became war zones, where Inkatha organized anti-ANC rallies. ANC officials, in turn, portrayed Buthelezi as a Zulu nationalist who was undermining the construction of a new South Africa. For one historian, he "was a mass of paradoxes, a Christian who honored African tradition and an avowed democrat who yet clearly distrusted the ballot. Urbane and charming, with connections in the boardrooms of Western corporations, he could, in a moment, turn from avuncularity to the language of tribal war."[45]

Inkatha leaders did not see Mandela as the conquering hero depicted in the West. To be sure, shortly after his release from prison in 1990, after serving twenty-seven years, Mandela visited Durban to quell political violence and was hailed by tens of thousands of Zulus. He had still not met Buthelezi but apparently agreed to make concessions to the Zulus: There would be formal recognition of KwaZulu and its king in the new constitution. One scholar observed, however, "[t]o recognize nationalism below the level of an inclusive Black nationalism is to run afoul of an important South African taboo."[46]

Mandela fudged and agreed in principle that Inkatha leaders could seek international mediation over the province's status at some later date. This promise was empty because it was obvious that black South Africans would be deciding their future on their own, without outside involvement. One South African newspaper even praised Mandela for his duplicity: "It is almost reassuring to note among the blemishes on his track record the reneging on solemn promises made to the Inkatha Freedom Party before the previous elections to invite foreign mediation in the problem of endemic violence in KwaZulu-Natal."[47]

The results of the 1994 elections produced the expected victory for the ANC. Mandela was appointed by the legislature to become the country's first black president. But Inkatha did not fare poorly: despite organizing its campaign at the last minute, it gained 11 percent of the vote nationwide, winning forty-three seats compared with 252 by the ANC and eighty-two by the Nationalists. This entitled it to three of twenty-seven cabinet posts. Inkatha entered into a power-sharing agreement with the ANC, and Buthelezi was appointed to the cabinet. As for the election to the KwaZulu-Natal legislature, Inkatha defeated the ANC handily by a 50 percent to 32 percent margin.

## Ethnicity, State Building, and the International System

Shortly after the 1994 elections, Buthelezi withdrew from South Africa's Constitutional Assembly, which was responsible for drafting a new constitution. He accused Mandela of failing to honor the promise of allowing for international mediation of the question of federalism. By this point, Mandela had begun an all-out campaign in favor of a single South African identity. He preached national reconciliation and sought an end to political violence. In 1996, he achieved success on both fronts as the Truth and Reconciliation Commission was established under the leadership of Archbishop Desmond Tutu (the commission's work was concluded in 2001). Political violence ended abruptly at that time (see Box 8.4).

In 1999, just prior to South Africa's second free election, the quarrel between the ANC and Inkatha was patched up. An estimated 12,000 people had been killed in clashes between rival supporters since 1985, and the new accord established a code of conduct for the election and even envisaged a joint election rally involving the ANC's Mbeki (who had succeeded Mandela) and Chief Buthelezi. Although the rally never took place, for the first time, each party was able to campaign in some of the strongholds of the other in KwaZulu-Natal.

---

**BOX 8.4**

**Theorizing the Linkage Between Ethnic Diversity and Outside Interest in South Africa**

*Complementary Perspectives from Comparative Politics and International Relations*

### Xhosa Versus Zulu Political Competition

#### 1. Domestic factors

Legitimacy of the postapartheid state

Recognition of political pluralism

Quality of transition leadership

Transitional justice regime

African National Congress as all-South Africa party

#### 2. International factors

Demonstration effect of failure of federal system (the Soviet Union, Czechoslovakia and Yugoslavia)

Demonstration effect of tragedy of ethnocracies (Balkans)

#### 3. Conflict resolution

International backing for South Africa's political transition

Inkatha itself was being transformed in the process of South African democratization. Its new logo was a family of elephants symbolizing "unity in diversity."[48] Its campaign program now stressed a pan–South African program and accused the ANC of having "no answers for the future." It claimed that South Africa was "deeply troubled. By unemployment. By crime. By poverty. By disease. By corruption. By a breakdown in the social fabric. By a lack of discipline. By a lack of respect for others. By indolence. In key respects, South Africa is not being governed properly and is becoming, and has at times already become, ungovernable." In sum, "life is getting rougher and tougher for all South Africans," and Buthelezi exhorted: "If the government of the day can't cope, then it is time to change the government. It's time for a government that will make South Africa governable. It's time for the IFP."[49]

The ANC's overwhelming victory nationwide in 1999 was tempered by its one regional loss—in KwaZulu-Natal to Inkatha. The ANC won 66 percent of the national vote and was one seat short of a two-thirds legislative majority. Inkatha, which had placed second in 1994, obtained 9 percent of the vote (and thirty-four seats), behind the 10 percent (thirty-eight seats) registered by the Democratic Party (formerly the Progressive Party, which had been the lone parliamentary voice opposing apartheid). Even with the poorer performance, Buthelezi and two IFP colleagues were appointed to Mbeki's cabinet. In the KwaZulu-Natal provincial election, the IFP edged out the ANC by 41 to 40 percent.

The ANC's message proclaiming a single new South African identity received even greater backing in the 2004 election. It captured 70 percent of the vote (and 279 of the 400 seats); Inkatha was down to 7 percent (twenty-eight seats). More surprising was that, for the first time, the ANC defeated Inkatha on its home turf: in the KwaZulu-Natal legislative election, the ANC got 47 percent of the vote (and thirty-eight seats) compared with the IFP's 37 percent (thirty seats). Even as the ANC tactfully offered a power-sharing agreement to Inkatha in the province, Buthelezi accused the ANC of seeking to create a single-party state across South Africa. That appeared to be the logical result of a policy underscoring South African unity.

It was ironic, then, that the ANC itself became increasingly disunified. At a party convention in 2007, Jacob Zuma was elected head of the party over Mbeki. Two years earlier, Zuma had been charged with both corruption and rape, charges viewed by many as politically motivated to stop his bid for the ANC leadership; they were subsequently dropped. It was even alleged that Mbeki had attempted to have them reinstated, but he was subsequently cleared by a court of meddling in the Zuma affair.

A more populist and leftist politician than Mbeki, Zuma made the redistribution of South Africa's wealth to favor the poor one of his priorities. He scared some in his own party with the militaristic theme of his personal anthem, *Umshini wami* ("Bring me my machine gun"). But it did not in any way symbolize his policy on ethnic groups: Zuma himself was a Zulu who had joined the ANC in 1959 and had risen to become the highest Zulu figure in the party. He was popular in KwaZulu-Natal and seemed poised to sap Inkatha's electoral strength even further in the 2009 elections.

The political divide created by Zuma's election to the ANC leadership resulted in the setting up of a new South African political party. In late 2008, the Congress of the People (COPE) was established by disaffected ANC members unhappy with Zuma. Led by Mosiuoa Lekota, its platform supported a free-market economy as well as multiracial governance. Inkatha head Buthelezi welcomed COPE's formation on the grounds that it would end one-party domination in South Africa. But the South African Communist Party and the Congress of South African

Trade Unions condemned the splinter party and suggested it amounted to political suicide by the ANC.

That warning proved to be unjustified. The Zuma-led ANC captured two-thirds of the vote in the April 2009 parliamentary election and won 264 seats—just shy of a two-thirds majority in the 400-seat national assembly and only slightly down on its 2004 showing. Helen Zille's Democratic Alliance finished second with a 17 percent share of the electorate and 67 seats. It also wrested control of the Western Cape legislature, based in Cape Town, from the ANC. The province has a sizeable white population, is one of the economically better off parts of the country, and is home to a thriving tourist industry.

Lekota's much-touted ANC-splinter party COPE was repudiated at the polls, taking just 7 percent of the vote and 30 seats. Inkatha's ranks were reduced to just 18 seats. In the KwaZulu provincial legislature, it also won only 18 seats, compared to 51 for the ANC and 7 for the Democratic Alliance. Zuma had delivered the Zulu vote to the ANC.

Two weeks after the election, the National Assembly elected Zuma as South Africa's president. The more radical, egalitarian, populist platform that he had embraced may have suggested that the ANC was becoming a more left-wing party. But early in his presidency, Zuma struck a moderate tone and avoided both the politics of class and that of ethnicity.

South Africa has consolidated its democracy with no real outside support: it is a remarkable achievement of the diverse peoples that make up the once-troubled country. The international standing of Mandela certainly gave him leverage in promoting ethnic harmony in the country. But without this advantage, Mbeki also succeeded in keeping the ethnic peace, even though in other respects, for example, the UN's Human Development Index, South Africa was doing poorly. Political transitions in multiethnic states, then, do not always lead to weak states and ethnic strife.

## Conclusion

We have considered the relations between ethnic groups in central, northeastern, and South Africa. There are also other complicated disputes based on ethnic lines on the continent: in Angola, Ivory Coast, Sierra Leone, Nigeria, Somalia, and Kenya. Mazrui has argued that the UN can make a bigger difference in Africa, where the stakes in human lives is high, than elsewhere: "Even its 'failed' enterprise in Somalia probably saved more lives than its 'success story' in Cambodia."[50] Yet it was precisely during the terms of two African secretaries general of the UN, Boutros-Boutros Ghali and Kofi Annan, that so many ethnicized wars broke out in Africa and could not be contained. Mazrui echoed the position of many policymakers, including those in the United States, that "Africans must establish an African peace enforced by Africans."[51] But neither in Congo nor Sudan was it effective.

In contrast, other analysts have taken a more sanguine view and have pointed to fading support for a global humanitarian agenda. "Given the half-hearted response to the horrors of Rwanda, it is not too farfetched to think that humanitarian issues are becoming more theater than reality for most of the developed world."[52] Outside parties are most likely to intervene in ethnicized conflicts when their own national interests can be advanced. Selfless commitment to the international mediation of such conflicts, no matter how horrific they may be, remains a rare occurrence in contemporary international politics.

## Discussion Questions

1. What are the characteristics of weak states? How do ethno-nationalist groups exploit the weakness of central authorities to advance their own political autonomy? Are these dynamics limited to states in Africa?

2. Do ethnic identities alone explain the atrocities committed by Hutus and Tutsis against each other in Rwanda and Burundi in the 1990s? Which third parties were in a position to make a difference and limit the conflict at an early stage?

3. How did Congo become the battleground for Hutu–Tutsi clashes? Which other part of the DRC became ethnically divided and drew in outside states? Discuss how ethnic and political divisions overlapped.

4. Is the war in Darfur better explained as a racial rather than ethnic or religious conflict? Why have the world's great powers played a part in a conflict set in a remote part of the Sahara?

5. How did postapartheid South Africa construct national unity out of a multinational state? Explain why South Africa did not need external assistance to promote unity.

## Key Terms

African National Congress (ANC)
African Union
African Union–UN Hybrid Operation in Darfur (UNAMID)
Africa's first world war
animism
apartheid
arabization
Biafra

conflict contagion
Hutus
Inkatha
*Interahamwe*
Ituri District
*Janjaweed*
MONUC (Mission de l'Organisation des Nations Unies en République démocratique du

Congo) [United Nations Organization Mission in the Democratic Republic of the Congo]
mixage
Rwandan Patriotic Front (RPF)
Tutsis
weak states

## Notes

1. Ian S. Lustick, *Unsettled States, Disputed Lands: Britain and Ireland, France and Algeria, Israel and the West Bank–Gaza* (Ithaca, N.Y.: Cornell University Press, 1993), p. 442.

2. The case of Eritrea's breakaway from Ethiopia was included in the first three editions of *Understanding Ethnic Conflict*. For this edition, we focus attention instead on current ethnic clashes in Africa, notably Darfur in Sudan.

3. I. William Zartman, "Introduction: Posing the Problem of State Collapse," in Zartman, ed., *Collapsed States: The Disintegration and Restoration of Legitimate Authority* (Boulder, Colo.: Lynne Rienner, 1995), p. 1.

4. Ibid., p. 5.

5. On the Congo, Nigeria, and other cases of "subnationalism," see Victor A. Olorunsola, ed., *The Politics of Cultural Sub-Nationalism in Africa: Africa and the Problem of "One*

*State, Many Nationalisms"* (Garden City, N.Y.: Anchor Books, 1972). For a study before decolonialization, see Thomas Hodgkin, *Nationalism in Colonial Africa* (New York: New York University Press, 1957). For one after "indigenization," see Timothy K. Welliver, ed., *African Nationalism and Independence* (Hamden, Conn.: Garland Publishing, 1993).

6. John R. Bowen, "The Myth of Global Ethnic Conflict," *Journal of Democracy,* 7, no. 4 (October 1996), p. 6.

7. Ibid., p. 6.

8. René Lemarchand, "Managing Transitional Anarchies: Rwanda, Burundi, and South Africa in Comparative Perspective," *Journal of Modern African Studies,* 32, no. 4 (December 1994), p. 588.

9. Jack Snyder and Karen Ballentine, "Nationalism and the Marketplace of Ideas," *International Security,* 21, no. 2 (Fall 1996), p. 32.

10. Ibid.

11. Stephen John Stedman, "Conflict and Conciliation in Sub-Saharan Africa," in Michael E. Brown, ed., *The International Dimensions of Internal Conflict* (Boston, Mass.: MIT Press, 1996), p. 249.

12. Stedman, "Conflict and Conciliation," p. 248.

13. An excellent account of the tragedy is Philip Gourevitch, *We Wish to Inform You That Tomorrow We Will Be Killed with Our Families: Stories from Rwanda* (New York: Picador Books, 1999).

14. Robert E. Gribbon, *In the Aftermath of Genocide: The U.S. Role in Rwanda* (New York: iUniverse, 2005).

15. John Donnelly, "After Helping to Bury Rwanda's Dead, a Peacekeeper Confronts the Killers," *Boston Globe* (October 14, 2000).

16. Oxfam, "No End in Sight" (August 6, 2001), www.oxfam.org.uk.

17. "Report of the Panel of Experts on the Illegal Exploitation of Natural Resources and Other Forms of Wealth of the Democratic Republic of the Congo," United Nations Security Council (April 12, 2001; October 28, 2003).

18. Thomas Turner, *The Congo Wars: Conflict, Myth and Reality* (London: Zed Books, 2007), p. 8.

19. Ali A. Mazrui, "The New Dynamics of Security: The United Nations and Africa," *World Policy Journal,* 13, no. 2 (Summer 1996), p. 39.

20. Amnesty International, "The Democratic Republic of Congo: Killing Human Decency" (May 31, 2000), www.amnesty.org.

21. John F. Clark, *The African Stakes of the Congo War* (Harmondsworth, Middlesex: Palgrave Macmillan, 2004).

22. Gregory S. Gordon, "An American Marshall Plan: Changing U.S. Policy to Promote the Rule of Law and Prevent Mass Atrocity in the Democratic Republic of Congo," paper presented at the International Peace Research Association Annual Meeting, University of Leuven, Belgium (July 15–19, 2008), pp. 8–9.

23. Kristin Drake, "Gold and Ethnic Conflict in the Ituri Region of the Democratic Republic of the Congo," *Inventory of Conflict and Environment Case Studies,* 173 (May 2006), at http://www.american.edu/ted/ice/ituri.htm.

24. See Johan Pottier, "Rights Violations, Rumour, and Rhetoric: Making Sense of Cannibalism in Mambasa, Ituri (Democratic Republic of Congo)," *Journal of the Royal Anthropological Institute,* 13, no. 4 (2007), . 825-843.

25. Henry Wasswa, "Will Uganda Pay Up for Congo Occupation?" Global Policy Forum (July 26, 2007), at http://www.globalpolicy.org/

intljustice/icj/2007/0726uganda-payup.htm.

26. Lydia Polgreen, "Congo Warlord Linked to Abuses Seeks Bigger Stage," *New York Times* (19 December 2008).

27. "From Rebel-held Congo to Beer Can," *BBC News* (April 9, 2009), at http://news.bbc.co.uk/2/hi/africa/7991479.stm. Accessed May 26, 2009.

28. See the analysis by Robert O. Collins, *Civil Wars and Revolution in the Sudan: Essays on the Sudan, Southern Sudan and Darfur, 1962–2004* (Los Angeles: Tsehai Publishers, 2005).

29. "Islamic Law Can Still Be Applied in South Sudan," *Juba Post* (September 29, 2007).

30. Mahmood Mamdani, "The New Humanitarian Order," *The Nation* (September 29, 2008). At http://www.thenation.com/doc/20080929/mamdani

31. Ibid.

32. Gérard Prunier, *Darfur: The Ambiguous Genocide* (Ithaca, N.Y.: Cornell University Press, 2005), p. 4.

33. Mamdani, "The New Humanitarian Order."

34. Julie Flint and Alex De Wall, *Darfur: A Short History of a Long War* (London: Zed Books, 2008).

35. Brian Steidle and Gretchen Steidle Wallace, *The Devil Came on Horseback* (New York: Public Affairs Books, 2007).

36. Human Rights Watch, "Sudan: New Darfur Documents," (July 19, 2004), at http://www.hrw.org/en/news/2004/07/19/sudan-new-darfur-documents.

37. David J. Francis, *Civil Militia: Africa's Intractable Security Menace?* (London: Ashgate, 2005), p. 145.

38. Human Rights Watch, "Q & A: Crisis in Darfur" (April 25, 2008), at http://www.hrw.org/en/news/2008/04/25/q-crisis-darfur.

39. Peter S. Goodman, "China Invests Heavily in Sudan's Oil Industry," *Washington Post* (December 23, 2004).

40. "The Current Situation in Darfur: October 2008," Oxfam America, at http://www.oxfamamerica.org/whatwedo/emergencies/sudan/current_situation

41. Stephen Taylor, *Shaka's Children: A History of the Zulu People* (London: HarperCollins, 1995), p. 339. See also Donald R. Morris, *The Washing of the Spears* (New York: Da Capo Press, 1998).

42. Donald L. Horowitz, *A Democratic South Africa: Constitutional Engineering in a Divided Society* (New York: Oxford University Press, 1991), p. 61.

43. Taylor, *Shaka's Children,* p. 299.

44. See Gerrit Viljoen and Francois Venter, "A Culture of Negotiation: The Politics of Inclusion in South Africa," *Harvard International Review,* 17, no. 4 (Fall 1995), p. 80.

45. Taylor, *Shaka's Children,* p. 2.

46. Horowitz, *A Democratic South Africa,* p. 130.

47. André Brink, "Mandela: A Tiger for Our Time," *Johannesburg Mail and Guardian* (June 4, 1999).

48. See the Inkatha website: www.ifp.org.za.

49. Cited by www.ifp.org.za/emanifesto.htm

50. Mazrui, "The New Dynamics of Security," p. 38.

51. Mazrui, "The New Dynamics of Security," p. 40.

52. Barry Buzan and Gerald Segal, "The Rise of 'Lite' Powers: A Strategy for the Postmodern State," *World Policy Journal,* 13, no. 3, Fall 1996, p. 7. See also Michael Ignatieff, *The Warriors' Honor: Ethnic War and the Modern Conscience* (New York: Owl Books, 1998).

# CHAPTER 9

# Western Military Intervention and Ethno-Religious Conflicts: Iraq, Afghanistan, and Former Yugoslavia

## INTRODUCTION

Beginning in the 1990s and continuing to the present, political leaders in western states have claimed that nationalism in various parts of the world—invariably they had the economically less developed countries in mind—had destabilized international politics. Conflicts in Africa, the Middle East, South Asia, the former Soviet republics, and the Balkans have been explained as products of the pathology of nationalism. As Tom Nairn had put it, anticommunist demonology was replaced by the "Devil of Nationalism. . . . Armageddon has been replaced by the ethnic Abyss."[1]

It is ironic that nationalism has been identified as the scourge of the contemporary international system. After all, at the end of World Wars I and II, national self-determination was held up as the panacea for the ills of the world system. Many central European nations obtained statehood in 1918, and colonies large and small became independent from 1947 onward.

There are many reasons why impediments to the construction of a peaceful, democratic world order have less to do with nationalism than with traditional balance-of-power concerns. Mass poverty in many parts of the world has produced organized and anomic political violence, and even political terrorism. Over a decade of globalization, beginning in the 1990s, only widened the gap between the advanced economies and poor countries—by an additional 2 percent. Fragmentation of central authority has brought about state collapse and the emergence of **gangster states**—breakaway enclaves rich in a natural resource and run by warlords. The clash of modernity with tradition in many Muslim-majority countries is said to lead to a clash of civilizations, although some scholars who have examined the results of world values surveys say the clash has more to do with *eros* than *demos*—contrasting attitudes toward gender equality and sexual emancipation than democracy.[2] Whatever its main cause, a cultural fault line has exacerbated the fractious nature of international politics. Nationalist conflicts have usually followed from, rather than preceded, these problems.

And yet the West has played a part in fanning the nationalism it has roundly condemned. This chapter contends that the most significant cases of western military intervention since the end of the cold war—in Iraq, Afghanistan, and Yugoslavia—have actually led to the increased salience of ethnic and religious divisions in these countries.[3] The U.S. invasion of Iraq in 2003 led almost immediately to the rise of hitherto dormant ethnic and religious movements, most of which are now fueled by militant anti-Americanism. Following U.S. military intervention in Afghanistan in 2001, the importance of the country's ethnic and regional warlords to consolidating central authority increased. In the Balkans in the 1990s, military intervention led by the North American Treaty Organization (NATO) seemed, for a time, only to accelerate Serb efforts at ethnic cleansing. Greater Serb ambitions were subsequently dashed by the creation of independent states in Bosnia and Kosovo—two shaky countries carved out of historic Serb lands—but only an uneasy ethnic peace prevails in much of the region.

There is an ironic "domestic" twist to U.S. interventions in Iraq and Afghanistan—President Bush's enmeshment in **nation building**. As a presidential candidate in 2000, he vowed not to get involved in this tricky business. During a campaign debate with Democrat presidential candidate Al Gore at Wake Forest University in 2000, Bush pledged he would "absolutely not" engage in nation building. Yet after faulting Clinton for involving the United States in nation building in Yugoslavia, Bush has followed suit in several countries, including postintervention Iraq and Afghanistan.[4]

Nation building entails everything from ensuring public safety and providing running water for citizens to creating national institutions that become the focus of identification for citizens in a society. The Bush administration's nation-building efforts between 2001 and 2008 included constitution writing; forging coalitions; and hammering out accords with ethnic, regional, and religious leaders to construct viable governments. In support of this political wheeling and dealing, the U.S. military had to provide public safety, water, and electricity in war-torn countries. That raised some serious problems, as scholar Amitai Etzioni noted: "nation-building—however defined—by foreign powers can rarely be accomplished and tends to be very costly, not merely in economic resources and those of political capital, but also in human lives."[5]

Another implication was attached to Bush's foreign policy *volte-face*. If the United States was to effect regime change in authoritarian states in the name of democratization, it had to be accompanied invariably by nation building. So was regime change really worth the risks involved? For one specialist on international law, the answer was elusive. Conceding that "[r]egime change may seem necessary even when the conditions are not propitious, the costs are unknowable but likely to be high, and durable international support is uncertain." Michael Reisman nevertheless warned: "let the strongest and best-intentioned government contemplating or being pressed to undertake regime change remember that not everything noble is lawful; not everything noble and lawful is feasible; and not everything noble, lawful, and feasible is wise."[6]

It is important to examine, then, the impact of U.S.-led western military interventions, designed to trigger regime change, on a country's preexisting ethnic and religious cleavages. What preintervention calculations (if any) were made about the political weight of these divisions? What unintended "ethnic" consequences followed from military interventions? Was the sustained post–cold war effort to marginalize ethno-nationalist and -sectarian movements sidetracked by interventions that unintentionally made them more salient to political struggles? Has the result been to make communal contenders and militant sects (see Chapter 1) more central to postintervention politics?

## THE U.S. OCCUPATION OF IRAQ

Even before the U.S.-led attacks on Iraq in 1991 and 2003, Iraq's modern history was as problematic as its early history was glorious. Under the Abbasid caliphate, ninth-century Baghdad was the world's center of learning. Poetry, the arts and sciences, and intellectual debate flourished, profoundly shaping the world around it. Today's Iraqi Sunnis regard themselves as heirs to that golden age of Arab-Islamic civilization.

### Iraq

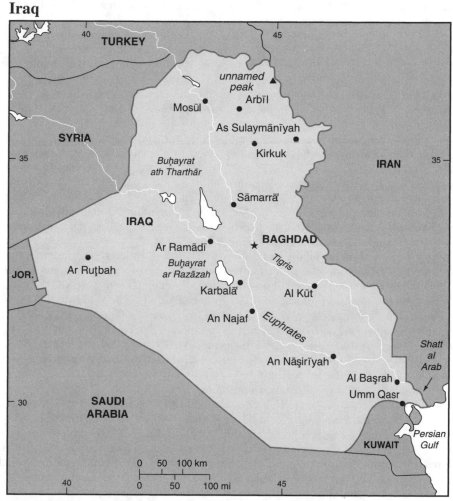

*Source:* Courtesy of the University of Texas Libraries, The University of Texas at Austin.

But the rebirth of Iraq in the twentieth century was anything but illustrious. During World War I, Britain had encouraged the revolt of Arab peoples against the German-allied Ottoman empire that governed their lands. With the collapse of that empire after the war, British forces occupied much of these territories. In 1922, European powers agreed on a settlement for the Middle East: the Ottoman sultanate was to be dissolved and its lands in the Middle East were to be partitioned among Britain, France, and Turkey. Britain obtained a League of Nations' mandate to administer Iraq, an artificially constructed state: "Kurdish, Sunni, Shi'ite, and Jewish populations had been combined into a new Mesopotamian country named Iraq, under the rule of an Arabian prince."[7] Instead of appointing a government representing Iraqi nationalists, the British established a monarchy under King Faisal, brother of Jordan's king El Amir Abdullah. King Faisal had helped the British cause by taking part in the Arab revolt against the Turkmen. Iraq became formally independent in 1932 and was proclaimed a republic in 1958 after one of a series of military coups. The last of these, in 1968, brought the Arab nationalist Baath party, of which Saddam Hussein was a member, to power.[8]

Iraq's political instability—and indeed that of the entire region—can be traced back to the post–World War I period. For historian David Fromkin, the settlement of 1922 "is at the very heart of current wars, conflicts, and politics in the Middle East, for the questions that Kitchener, Lloyd George, and Churchill opened up are even now being contested by force of arms, year after year, in the ruined streets of Beirut, along the banks of the slow-moving Tigris–Euphrates, and by the waters of the Biblical Jordan."[9]

In 1979, Saddam became supreme Iraqi leader, and a year later, he launched a surprise attack on Iran, which was weakened by the overthrow of the shah and the volatility of its new leader, Shia Ayatollah Khomeini. Saddam's objective was to capture the Shat al-Arab waterway leading to the Arabian Gulf, but the attack turned into an eight-year-long inconclusive war that left hundreds of thousands of Iraqis and Iranians dead. In 1988, as the war with Iran was ending, Saddam's regime, fearing unrest in the northern Kurdish provinces, attacked the Iraqi city of Halabja, using poison gas to kill thousands of Kurds.

Undeterred by his failure in Iran, in 1990, Saddam ordered his army to invade oil-rich Kuwait and annex it as Iraq's nineteenth province—a move immensely popular among Iraqi Sunnis as well as Shias, whose religious kin were discriminated against by the Kuwaiti political elite. A broad coalition of forces led by the United States drove the Iraqis out during the Gulf War of January–February 1991. The UN Security Council ordered Iraq to scrap all weapons of mass destruction and long-range missiles and to allow regular inspections by international verification teams. A no-fly zone over northern Iraq was also implemented; Saddam's air force was no longer able to strike targets in the rebellious Kurdish provinces.

From its creation in 1920, Iraq constituted a complex ethnic and religious society. Its arbitrarily drawn colonial-era borders and the presence of diverse ethnic and religious communities always made national unity problematic. In terms of its ethnic makeup, the country is close to 80 percent Arab, with Kurds and Turkmen representing the largest minorities. Iraq is divided up differently in religious terms. **Shia Muslims** represent about 60 percent of the population, and **Sunni Muslims** (which include Kurds and Turkmen) account for about 35 percent (by contrast, more than 80 percent of the Muslim population worldwide belongs to the Sunni branch).[10] Iraq also has tiny minorities of Assyrians, Chaldean Christians, Jews, and Bedouins.

Despite these ethno-religious divisions, since its founding, Iraq had been a relatively successful multicultural—even cosmopolitan—society with a secular-oriented state.[11] From the monarchy through Saddam's dictatorship, the government controlled religious teaching and institutions. Islam remained the official state religion after the Baath party coup in 1968, even though the new ruling elite sought to reduce its political and social reach. For most Iraqi Shias, religion is central to their lives, so the secularizing Baath policy began to widen the divide between the two communities. An Iraqi identity based on Sunni Islam was strengthened after the 1979 Shia Iranian Revolution and subsequent Iran–Iraq War; as in most other Arab states, Sunni Arabs in Iraq have traditionally comprised the country's ruling elite. In 1999, one of Saddam's cousins was implicated in the assassination of Shia Ayatollah Mohammed Sadiq al-Sadr and in the execution of hundreds of Shias in Basra who had taken part in an uprising sparked by the killing. Relations between the two groups deteriorated.

Iraqi Shias are religiously linked with Iran's predominantly Shia population, although ethnically they differ: the first are mainly Arabs, the second Persians. Some of the religion's most important holy sites are located in southern Iraq. Saddam's regime discriminated against Shias while exploiting their large population. For example, while Shias constituted 80 percent of the ranks of Saddam's army, they made up only 20 percent of the officer corps.

Kurds account for more than 15 percent of the Iraqi population. A non-Arab Sunni group with a distinct language (related to Persian) and culture, they had been promised their own independent state by the Treaty of Sèvres in 1920. Instead of a state, however, the Kurdish population, which numbers more than 25 million, was scattered across four countries—Iran, Syria, Turkey, and Iraq. They have been described as the world's largest nonstate nation. Kurdish separatist movements in Iraq, as well as Turkey, have proved tenacious over the years.

After Arabs and Kurds, the Turkmen are the third largest nationality group in Iraq. Sharing close cultural and linguistic links with Turkey, their population has been estimated at anywhere from 2 to 10 percent and is concentrated in northern and central Iraq, including the city of Kirkuk. Otherwise political rivals, Turkmen, like Kurds, were targets of the Baath policy of arabization. The methods used against them ranged from forced assimilation to dispersion and ethnic cleansing, to populating their regions with Arabs. Kurds and Turkmen claim that they were the primary victims of human rights abuses by Saddam's dictatorship, although Shias also incurred the wrath of his Sunni-based regime, especially after their U.S.-encouraged uprising following the 1991 Gulf War was crushed.

## Toppling a Dictator, Creating a Weak State

Much speculation has surrounded the decision attributed to President Bush, Vice President Dick Cheney, and Defense Secretary Donald Rumsfeld to order an invasion of Iraq in 2003, which was to inject the U.S. military into Iraqi politics for the next eight years. A status-of-forces agreement in 2008 between the U.S. and Iraqi governments allowed American forces to remain in the country until the end of 2011, although President Obama promised to draw down troops earlier.

Bush's motives have come under questioning: theories range from his desire to avenge Saddam's assassination plot against his father to the existence of a business partnership—based primarily on oil—between the house of Bush and the house of Saud. The president seemed convinced that Iraq had something to do with the terrorist attacks of 9/11, and in June 2002, at West Point, he presented his new defense doctrine emphasizing preemption: the United States had to strike first against another state to prevent the growth of a potential threat. The claim that Saddam was in possession of weapons of mass destruction was considered reason enough to trigger a preemptive strike.

The United States and Britain lobbied for international support for an invasion of Iraq. Only two other members of the UN Security Council—Spain and Bulgaria—were willing to back a U.S.–U.K. resolution (nine votes were needed), so Bush decided not to call for a vote on the resolution. With the approval of Congress, the president launched the attack on Baghdad on March 19, 2003. Just over two weeks later, U.S. troops entered the capital while British forces captured Basra. On May 1, 2003, Bush announced the end of major combat operations. In fact, the war was really just beginning.

UN Secretary General Kofi Annan had pressed for the establishment of the UN Assistance Mission in Iraq (UNAMI) to try to show that the United Nations was still relevant even in a western-occupied Iraq. But a suicide bombing in August 2003 destroyed its headquarters in Baghdad and killed the UN's special representative. This was a key event marking the process of transforming the war into a direct conflict between the Iraqi resistance—usually described in the West as the insurgency—and Anglo-American forces, with international organizations becoming bystanders.

Iraq was placed under the rule of the Coalition Provisional Authority (CPA), headed by U.S. administrator Paul Bremer. In 2003, he appointed an interim governing council of twenty-five Iraqis, but retained final authority for himself. In May 2004, the CPA transferred "sovereignty" to an interim Iraqi government. Iyad Allawi, a Shia neurologist with ties to the U.S. Central Intelligence Agency (CIA), was designated prime minister.

Until the U.S. occupation, the Sunni–Shia division in Iraq was primarily a political and economic—not religious—struggle over the distribution of wealth and political power. But American military rule radicalized Iraqi Sunni militants, helped Shia groups coalesce and take power in much of southern Iraq, attracted thousands of **jihadists** ("religious warriors") from other Islamic countries, and allowed al-Qaeda groups to penetrate the country. These developments were consistent with predictions made in two classified reports prepared for President Bush in January 2003 by the National Intelligence Council. The reports warned that a U.S. invasion would increase support for political Islam while fermenting violent internal conflict.[12]

It is difficult to gauge the degree of cooperation these disparate groups engaged in. The concept of *fitnah* ("civil strife") was regularly invoked by Iraqi clerics to warn against creating divisions within Islam, as had occurred in earlier times. In spring 2004, both Iraqi Shias and Sunnis launched coordinated attacks against American troops in Baghdad and other areas. As one sheikh in Najaf preached, "We will all stand now in the face of our enemies who seek to divide us. . . . The occupiers are creating the problem between Shiites and Sunni. It is the same old conspiracy, divide and conquer."[13]

Up to 2008, the anti-American insurgency was strongest in the so-called Sunni triangle around Baghdad. Sunnis had lost most from Saddam's overthrow, so it was predictable that they became the spearhead of anti-American attacks. "The strongly nationalist Sunni part of the insurgency took on a more Islamist and sectarian profile from 2006, with al-Qaeda in Iraq (AQI) becoming one of its deadliest elements."

Nevertheless, al-Qaeda and its allied groups never made up more than 15 percent of the insurgency, and foreign fighters another 5 percent.[14] A particularly radical Sunni political movement was the Association of Muslim Scholars (*Ulemas*). It denounced "the terrible crime" committed by the United States and exhorted all Iraqis to "join forces to expel the occupying forces."

Major fighting against coalition forces also occurred in other areas, including the largely Shia-populated southern provinces. One of the most virulent Iraqi leaders opposing the United States was Shia cleric Moqtada al-Sadr. A few months after the invasion, he established a militia group, the Mehdi army, to defend Shia religious sites in Najaf. Al-Sadr organized several revolts in the holy city against U.S. forces (which classified him an outlaw). The battles ended in 2004 after mediation by senior Iraqi Shia cleric Grand Ayatollah Ali al-Husseini al-Sistani, who nevertheless refused to meet with any American representative during the five years of American occupation, whose legal status changed with the status-of-forces agreement that came into force in January 2009. In general, Shia leaders "sought to avoid accusations similar to those leveled against them after 1991, namely that they constitute a fifth column within Iraq and are collaborators with Western powers."[15]

Shia leaders were unsuccessful in dispelling this impression. The result was that "[s]ince early 2006 the Sunni-dominated insurgency had become increasingly intertwined with Sunni sectarianism directed at Shias perceived as being pro-MNF-I [Multinational Force in Iraq led by the U.S.], pro-government or pro-Iranian."[16] To be sure, the Iraqi national army and much of the police force (especially in southern cities like Basra) were made up largely of Shia recruits, thereby convincing Sunnis that Iraqi security forces were masterminding sectarian violence.

It was just a matter of time before Shia militias, including the Mehdi army and those associated with the Iraqi government, adopted increasingly sectarian anti-Sunni orientations. The principal Shia groups had become major stakeholders in the government and had largely ceased targeting the MNF-I by 2007. They now directed their attention to fighting Sunnis. But new splinter Shia groups, along with radical elements in the Mehdi army, emerged that year and decided their main targets would not be Sunni militias, the MNF-I, or Iraqi security forces, but government-affiliated fellow Shia organizations, like the Islamic Supreme Council of Iraq, that appeared to be a new Iranian-backed political establishment. Shia groups were now fighting each other, with some of the most brutal killing occurring in Basra.

Sectarian violence had exploded not long after the U.S. invasion. It began with isolated events, such as the killing in 2003 of a top Shia cleric in Najaf. Sunni mosques were targeted in reprisal attacks, and the spiral continued until the Golden Mosque in Samarra, a Shia shrine, was bombed in 2006. In many of these cases, Islamic extremists (denounced as *Wahabbis*) were the perpetrators. In 2006, at the height of sectarian conflict, the number of internally displaced persons tripled to nearly 700,000.

Even as sectarian strife increased, the U.S. military remained a prime target of Iraqi insurgents. Since the 2003 invasion up until the beginning of 2009, over 4,200 American soldiers had been killed and another 30,000 wounded in hostilities. In each of the years from 2004 to 2007, about 900 American soldiers were killed. But the number plunged to just over 300 in 2008. The reduction was due to a much-publicized "surge" in U.S. troop strength that year, accompanied by a new strategy of paying Sunni insurgents off to become self-defense militias protecting their communities against outsiders (both al-Qaeda groups as well as Shia militia).

The *Sahwa,* or Awakening Councils, acted as local patrol units and were headed by Sunni tribal leaders. Funded by the U.S. military—the 100,000-strong Sons of Iraq militia were paid $300 a month to fight al-Qaeda, and not fight the U.S. military. They themselves became targets of Shia insurgents, of government security forces controlled by Shia leaders deeply suspicious of a rebirth of Sunni power—as well as of fellow Sunnis whose priority remained to drive the occupying forces out of Iraq. As part of an effort to recentralize power, beginning in 2008, Prime Minister al-Maliki's government sought to take over the *Sahwa,* which it viewed sometimes as Sunni militias, sometimes as criminal gangs.

Another axis of conflict pitted Iraqi security forces, including army units and the police, against the Sunni resistance. These forces were considered proxies of the American military because the latter helped finance, train, and arm them. According to Iraqi government figures, nearly 8,000 had been killed over the four-year period from 2005 to 2008. In 2008, hundreds of Awakening Council members and a few of the tribal leaders were killed because of their association with the U.S. military.

Civilian casualties in Iraq have been much higher than combatant ones. Iraq Body Count, a human rights organization that keeps track of killings of civilians by U.S.-led coalition forces, Iraqi militias, and unknown perpetrators, also noted a downward trend. In 2006, the peak year, approximately 26,000 Iraqis had been killed; the total fell to about 24,000 for 2007 and only 9,000 for 2008. It was believed that the overall civilian toll since the 2003 U.S. invasion reached 100,000 in early 2009. It is impossible to tell with any accuracy which forces accounted for most of the killings of civilians; indeed, three-quarters of civilian deaths had no identifiable perpetrator. So the question whether outside occupation forces or Iraqi sectarian militias were deadliest cannot be answered. Iraq Body Count reported that "[m]ost frequently identifiable are civilian killings caused by coalition military or those who violently oppose them (17 percent of all deaths in 2006–2008)." But being able to identify military combatants as the perpetrators in 17 percent of all civilian deaths does not provide a full picture. To this has to be added, for example, the U.S. military's use of airstrikes—the most frequent cause of civilian deaths, as late as in 2009, by coalition forces. Less easy to identify perpetrators were the many cases where bombs were placed in cars and in marketplaces with the aim of not only killing occupation forces but also with the aim of killing Iraqi civilians.

Determining with any accuracy what proportion of all remaining civilian deaths was attributable to sectarian violence was impossible. According to Iraq Body Count, killings in Iraq were tied, one way or another, to foreign military occupation: "examination of these data leaves little doubt that an irreducible portion of the violence that remains in Iraq is associated with the continuing presence of coalition military forces in the country."[17] By contrast, in his 2007 report to the U.S. Congress, General David Petraeus, commander of U.S. forces in Iraq, claimed that the surge had actually reduced ethno-sectarian violence. Since reaching their peak in December 2006, deaths across Iraq were down 55 percent and 80 percent in Baghdad.[18] However, during the 2007 surge, the number of internally displaced people had nearly doubled, going from close to 700,000 to over 1,200,000. If sectarian violence had dropped, it had much to do with the "sectarian cleansing" that had forced people living in mixed communities to abandon their homes and take refuge in safer mono-sectarian areas.

If the Bush administration had been aware of the risks involved in creating a power vacuum in Baghdad and a weak Iraqi state, and the ethno-sectarian consequences that followed, it did not ever acknowledge them. The mantra to the end was that sectarian violence had broken out spontaneously, that it was the result of the ancient curse of Sunni–Shia animosity, and that U.S. forces were taking part in a humanitarian intervention seeking to save Iraqis from each other. None of this formed part of the stated mission of the 2003 invasion.

## The Domestic and International Impact of Ethno-sectarian Cleavages

At the end of 2004, Jordan's King Abdullah—an ally of the West—accused Shias in Iran of meddling in postinvasion Iraq and seeking to create a so-called **Shia Crescent**. This crescent would stretch from central Afghanistan through Iran—the center of the project—and Iraq to Syria and Lebanon. A region hitherto dominated by Sunnis would, King Abdullah warned, fall under the influence of Islamic Iranian fundamentalists. This specter of Shia fundamentalism was nothing new. Ever since the 1979 Iranian revolution, most Sunni-led Arab states feared the expansion of Shia influence, even though ethnic differences separate Persian Iranians from Arab Shias. Not surprisingly, the leaders of these states were lukewarm about the election of Mahmoud Ahmadinejad, viewed as a Shia conservative, to the Iranian presidency in 2005.

The Shias' rise to power in Baghdad has added to the specter of a Shia Crescent, but it may not end there. The minority Shias of Saudi Arabia, Kuwait, and the United Arab Emirates, along with the majority in Bahrain, may make bids for power in their states, too. The Saudi regime was under particular threat as it battled a low-intensity insurgency of its own. The House of Saud was dominated by the conservative *Wahabbi* sect of Islam that regards Shias as heretics. Not surprisingly, Shias would welcome the fall of the Saudi regime. Because all these states rank among the world's largest oil producers, the establishment of Shia-dominated regimes would represent a major shift in the global balance of power, one the United States had not planned for.

Noam Chomsky, long-time critic of U.S. wars beginning with Vietnam, sketched what a Shia-controlled Iraq might involve: "The first thing they'll do is reestablish relations with Iran. . . . The next thing that might happen is that a Shia-controlled, more or less democratic Iraq might stir up feelings in the Shia areas of Saudi Arabia, which happen to be right nearby and which happen to be where all the oil is. So you might find what in Washington must be the ultimate nightmare—a Shia region which controls most of the world's oil and is independent."[19]

For a time, the Bush administration seemed blithe about this scenario. It emphasized instead the need for staying true to procedural democracy: any increase in the political power of Shias had to be legitimized through the ballot box. The 2005 election in Iraq for a 275-member constituent assembly, which was to choose interim leaders and write a new constitution, went ahead even as it sparked a wave of political violence.[20] Many outside observers warned that, under these conditions, a representative assembly could not be chosen. The Kremlin, for example, inveighed that no one could question the legitimacy of elections in Chechnya if those in Iraq were being treated seriously.

Even as an exercise in electoral democracy, the Iraqi election was flawed. Voters cast ballots for parties rather than individual candidates. Not all candidates' names on the party slates had even been disclosed before the ballot, so voters did not know who they were electing. Voter registration was based on a popular

Saddam-era enrollment list for food rationing. When heads of households collected their 2005 ration cards from distribution centers around Iraq, voter registration clerks confirmed their family members' eligibility for voting. Many of the people who went to the polls apparently feared that they would lose their entitlement if they did not cast their ballot.

The official results were announced a week later than planned, heightening suspicions of voter tampering. Many Shias, in particular, became convinced that their hopes for building an Islamic state—through the ballot box—had been scuttled. The official results claimed that turnout had been 58 percent, just 3 percent less than the closely contested 2004 U.S. presidential election between Bush and John Kerry (which itself had marked the highest U.S. turnout since 1968).

The United Iraqi Alliance, a predominantly Shia coalition with ties to Iran, won 48 percent of the vote (and 140 assembly seats)—less than the two-thirds that it had expected (which had been based on the assumption—a correct one as events showed—that most Sunnis would boycott the poll). The alliance was endorsed by Ayatollah Ali al-Sistani, whose writ carried the force of law for devout Iraqi Shias. Its unimpressive electoral showing deprived it of the ability to craft a new constitution that would incorporate Islamic law. The Vietnam War–era mantra for some in the United States—that if voting could change things, elections would be made illegal—now resonated among Iraqi Shias.

The next strongest electoral performance was by the Kurdish Alliance List, which won 26 percent (seventy-five seats), but it was primarily a regional movement, so it became the hegemonic force in northern Iraq. Its mandate was to transfer as much authority as possible from Baghdad to the Kurdish region. The secular-oriented Iraqi List of interim prime minister Allawi received 14 percent (forty seats). The best result the United States could realistically have hoped for was a three-bloc checks-and-balances assembly in which Islamists, secular Arabs, and Kurds had to make deals with each other. That was exactly what happened in 2005.

The sectarian cleavages in the country were exposed when turnout in the various provinces was analyzed. The overwhelming proportions of voters were Shias and Kurds. In the nine mainly Shia southern provinces, turnout ranged from 61 to 75 percent. In the three predominantly Kurdish northern provinces, turnout averaged 85 percent. Nearly independent for fourteen years (following the 1991 Gulf War) and supported heavily by the United States, Kurds had an added incentive for casting a ballot: they were also voting for a separate parliament for the self-governing region.

The situation was very different in four Sunni-majority provinces, where turnout was miniscule and Sunni Arab parties won just a fraction of the vote. For example, Sunni turnout was 2 percent in Anbar, west of Baghdad, which was soon to become an al-Qaeda stronghold, and in Saddam's native province of Salahaddin (which has a substantial Shia minority), turnout was 29 percent, indicating that few eligible Sunnis voted.

The election result meant that Kurdish leader Jahal Talabani became president. Alliance leader Ibrahim al-Jaafari became the country's prime minister, although Ahmed Chalabi, the notorious exile leader whose volatile relationship with the United States included persuading the Bush administration to invade Iraq, had also contested the post.

Such a confessional model of power sharing (consociational in Lijphart's terminology; see Chapter 1) had not had staying power in Lebanon, which had been shaken by civil war in 1958 and collapsed during the fifteen-year civil war from 1975 to 1990. An Iraq with a Kurdish president or Kurdish de facto state in the north incurred the suspicion of nearly all Arab governments, as well as of Turkey, which has faced a long-running secessionist threat from its Kurdish minority.

At the end of 2005, Iraqis were again called to vote for a new parliament. The results were not much different from the constituent assembly election. The United Iraqi Alliance, the Shia slate, won 128 of the National Assembly's 275 seats—again just short of a majority. The Kurdish Alliance gained fifty-three seats and was the alliance's obvious coalition partner in government. Feeling they had shot themselves in the foot by boycotting the last election, Sunni leaders encouraged voting this time around, and two Sunni blocs combined for fifty-five seats. The results accurately reflected Iraq's religious and ethnic cleavages. The secular party contesting the election captured only twenty-five seats.

Elections did little to resolve spreading violence across the country and may have exacerbated it by identifying political winners and losers. At his trial and in his last testament before being hanged at the end of 2006, Saddam Hussein condemned the U.S. divide-and-rule strategy that had set off a civil war. Many leading Shia and Sunni clerics, including al-Sadr, echoed Saddam's view, even though they despised him.

The United States engineered the selection in 2006 of a Shia, Nouri al-Maliki, as prime minister. But when he reached an agreement with the Mehdi army to keep U.S. forces out of Sadr City in Baghdad, it appeared that the United States had become trapped by Iraq's volatile system of ethno-sectarian alliances. American strategists had apparently failed in any divide-and-rule game plan that they may have initially crafted. At the same time, it was too late "to reverse the damage they have already done to themselves by having built up a Shiite state and army." Starting a "war against all" in Iraq, as one senior U.S. military expert summed up the option of having simultaneously to battle Sunni insurgents, al-Qaeda, and the Mehdi army—with the military forces at al-Maliki's disposal an unreliable ally—would be "a blunder of Hitlerian proportions."[21] The Bush administration did not commit it.

For a time. it appeared that managed partition of Iraq had become the preferred U.S. scenario. But the establishment of Shia, Kurd, and Sunni regions was likely to create as many risks as benefits for the United States.[22] The Iraqi parliament could not agree on even devolution of power, fearing it could lead to a definitive breakup of the country. De facto Kurdish autonomy became a model for Shias in Basra (where three-quarters of Iraqi oil is produced) to aim for and in late 2008, demonstrations were organized to support a referendum on the issue. Prime Minister al-Maliki declared that he would not intervene in such referendums as long as they did not weaken the federal government.

In mid-2006, al-Maliki had put forward what was called a national reconciliation plan in an attempt to lure armed groups into the political process. According to one security expert, "the plan represented al-Maliki's commitment to the new constitution and his political will and determination to embrace national unity, engage in negotiations with armed groups, and to offer amnesty."[23] Although it had greater symbolic than practical importance, the initiative reflected an undertaking by the prime minister at the height of sectarian strife to keep Iraq intact and not let it disintegrate. This was at a time when the Bush administration was wavering about how best to reconfigure Iraq. A notable supporter of the partition solution was Democratic senator Joe Biden, Dick Cheney's successor as vice president.

The United States had locked itself into a catch-22 position. It seemed that it was damned if it did leave Iraq and damned if it didn't, damned if it tried to partition Iraq and damned if it tried to keep it together. The countervailing imperatives were captured by Larry Diamond, a democracy promotion emissary appointed by Secretary of State Condoleeza Rice who subsequently quit his job in frustration: "only military occupation in some form can fill the vacuum left behind when a state has collapsed and a country is in or at the edge of chaos and civil war." He continued: "While fending off total chaos, however, the presence of these forces is also a constant stimulus to insurgency. Until foreign forces are fully withdrawn from its soil, Iraq will never truly be at peace."[24]

In 2009, the U.S. military withdrew its forces from Iraqi cities and formally handed over control to Iraqi government security forces of the Green Zone—the fortress-like enclave in Baghdad that had symbolized foreign rule of the country. Throughout 2008, the United States had been handing over provinces to Iraqi forces. Combat and killing had continued on the streets of Iraqi cities, but the many political, paramilitary, and criminal factions energized by the U.S. invasion began to lose some of their purpose and direction. A journalist summarized the zeitgeist of the endgame: "civil war was always too tidy a term for it. The entropy, for now at least, has run its course. So have many of the forces the United States so dangerously unleashed with its 2003 invasion, turning Iraq into an atomized, fractured land seized by a paroxysm of brutality. In that Iraq, the Americans were the final arbiter and, as a result, deprived anything they left behind of legitimacy."[25]

Whether Iranian-supported political forces would encounter a legitimacy deficit in postoccupation Iraq was to become the next important question to address (see Box 9.1). Prime minister al-Maliki became a regular visitor to Teheran beginning in 2006, and although he referred to both sides' respect for the international principle of noninterference in a country's internal affairs, closer military ties were cemented. In 2009, the Iraqi leader did his part to curtail interference in his neighbor's affairs by disbanding the main armed Iranian opposition group, the People's Mujahedeen Organization of Iran (PMOI), which had been operating out of Iraq. By contrast, Iran had so many surrogates in Iraq's governing circles, religious establishment, and military groupings that diffusion of its interests to its Arab neighbor was all but guaranteed.

Provincial elections early in 2009 strengthened al-Maliki's hand. His State of Law coalition beat out other Shia parties in southern Shia-dominated Iraq. For example, it took 37 percent of the vote in Basra, and slightly more in Baghdad. In turn, Sunni parties regained power in many Sunni areas, though in vast, restless Anbar province the election produced a stalemate. If that was the good news—that al-Maliki was becoming strongman of Iraq and the country's geopolitical map now more accurately reflected ethno-sectarian divides—the bad news was that violence across the country— including assassination attempts of newly elected officials—had not abated even as President Obama spurred U.S. forces to disengage. The new game plan was not working: "The transition from insurgency to politics to governance—a key to stabilizing the country after six years of war—has proved to be anything but steady and sure."[26] We are inevitably drawn to the conclusion that conflict resolution efforts without the involvement of Iraq's Arab neighbors or of Iran offer bleak prospects for success.

---

**BOX 9.1**

**Theorizing the Linkage Between Ethnic Conflicts and Outside Involvement in Iraq**

---

*Complementary Perspectives from Comparative Politics and International Relations*

**Iraqi Central Government Versus Ethno-Sectarian Groups**

**1. Domestic factors**

Colonial state borders

Lack of sovereignty after 2003 invasion

Preexisting ethnic, sectarian, and regional cleavages

Oil fields

**2. International factors**

U.S.-led military intervention justified as democracy promotion

Iranian support for Iraqi Shias (sectarian kin)

Appearance of al-Qaeda after 2003 invasion

**3. Conflict resolution**

Marginalization of international organizations and their mediation efforts

Phased handover of responsibility for security to Iraqi government forces

---

# EXPANDING AFGHANISTAN'S WARS THROUGH INTERVENTION

Afghanistan is a tribal Islamic society that has been wracked by internal wars since 1973, when its king, Mohammed Zahir Shah, was overthrown. The Soviet invasion of 1979 and Soviet withdrawal in 1988 (although an Afghan communist government survived for another three years), the rise of the Taliban in 1995, and the U.S. military intervention in late 2001 are other key junctures in the country's recent history. U.S. President Obama is committed to stamping out a Taliban insurgency and hunting down al-Qaeda terrorists allied to it operating along the border with Pakistan, but it is difficult to predict when Afghanistan's conflicts will come to an end.

The country is home to about fifty distinct ethnic groups, although four account for close to 90 percent of the population. Unlike Iraq, Afghanistan is a mountainous country, so its terrain facilitates the separation of its many ethnic groups; however, ancient trade routes running through the country have brought the different groups into contact with each other. The autocratic centralized state that first appeared in the nineteenth century reinforced communal divisions because individual ethnic groups had no reason to identify with a remote central government.[27]

The **Pashtuns** represent the largest ethnicity. A Sunni Muslim group with a well-formed collective identity, they account for close to 40 percent of the population. Historically, they have served as the country's ruling elite, and Afghanistan's "national" identity (such as it is) has largely been borrowed from the Pashtuns. The group can be subdivided into Durrani and Ghilzai, although there are about thirty

## Afghanistan

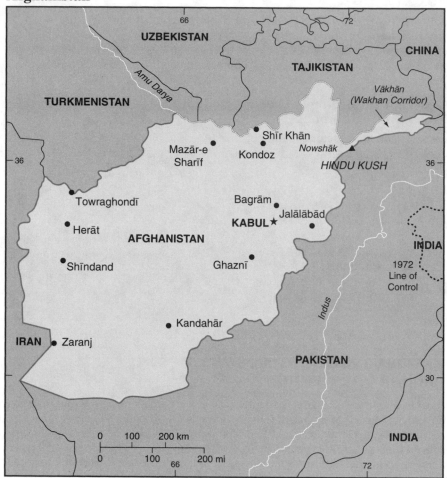

tribes that, in turn, are made up of clans and lineages. About 10 million Pashtuns also live in the neighboring North-West Frontier Province (NWFP) of Pakistan. Afghanistan, then, is a frontier state: "at the crossroads as well as at the frontiers of ancient empire-building in the region; it was both a gateway to foreign armies as well as a source of invasions."[28]

When Afghanistan declared its independence from Britain in 1919 following the third Anglo–Afghan war, Durrani Pashtuns became the political elite for the next six decades. The Soviet invasion of 1979 led other ethnic groups to coalesce around tribal warlords and fight the Russians, so Soviet military intervention actually accentuated ethnic differences and galvanized them into separate political and military entities.

The Sunni Tajiks represent one-quarter of the population, but they comprise a much higher proportion of urban dwellers. Speaking Dari, a language related to Persian, they have often been overrepresented in state administration even when Pashtuns have ruled the country.

The Shia Hazaras, who also speak Dari, make up 20 percent of the population and are among the country's poorest people. Turkic-speaking Uzbeks make up 6 percent and have also been politically influential. Baluchis living on both sides of the border with Iran also play a key part in Afghan politics. The most politically consequential case of ethnic kin spilling over the country's borders, however, is the Pashtuns.

## Ethnicity, Warlords, and Internal Conflict

Despite historical arguments claiming that the country's many ethnic, regional, economic, and political cleavages are crosscutting and do not overlap, ethnicity has counted more than any other factor when it has come to organizing security and political structures. Examples from the recent past bear this out. The legendary anti-Soviet commander Ahmad Shah Masud organized an almost exclusively Tajik army (with some Uzbeks) in his native Panjshir Valley in the north. Abdul Haq, one of only a few anti-Soviet Pashtun warlords who did not become an Islamist, opposed the fundamentalist Taliban regime but wanted to co-opt its moderate elements in a future government. He therefore criticized the U.S. bombing campaign against Afghanistan in 2001 for radicalizing Taliban moderates. Masud, who had received substantial logistical support from Russia and Iran, was assassinated two days before the attacks of 9/11, presumably by the Taliban, though weeks later, almost all of his lieutenants were on the CIA's payroll. In turn, Haq was captured and hanged by the Taliban a few weeks after the United States began bombing the country.

When Soviet forces withdrew in 1988, the new Afghan government was based on the predominantly Tajik movement *Jami'at-i Islami,* headed by Burhanuddin Rabbani, who became Afghanistan's president. A Pashtun backlash followed: the Taliban, made up largely of fundamentalist Pashtuns, seized power in Kabul in 1996 with substantial assistance from Pakistan and Saudi Arabia.[29] To be sure, warlords had frequently adopted tactical shifts in their political and even ethnic loyalties. Gulbuddin Hekmatyar was head of a group of fundamentalist Sunni Muslim Pashtuns who helped bring an end to the Soviet occupation of Afghanistan. Not content with the modest role he was given in the subsequent Afghan government, he proclaimed himself an Islamist opposed to any foreign influence in the country. The artillery attacks on Kabul that his forces unleashed in 1994 killed more than 25,000 civilians and alienated him from most Afghans. In 2003, he was the target of a failed U.S.-planned assassination attempt, which served to revive his standing in the country.

The ethnic balance in the military has always been a source of contention in Afghan politics. Under the monarchy, the majority of army officers were Pashtun. During the pro-Soviet governments of the 1980s, the number of non-Pashtun military— especially Tajiks and Hazaras—increased. By the early 1990s, Tajiks had become overrepresented in the army. Not surprisingly, when a new national government was constructed after the defeat of the Taliban in late 2001, Pashtuns, who had dominated Taliban ranks, feared they would again become subordinate to Tajiks. As with Soviet military intervention in 1979, American involvement after 2001 had to strike a balance between contending ethnic interests if a viable national government was to emerge.

But ethnicity's role in Afghanistan cannot be reduced to a two- or three-party struggle for power. During the battle against Soviet occupation in the 1980s, Pashtun groups living in the south and east began to fragment as rival local commanders, each with their own support bases, vied with each other. The extensive involvement of the CIA, as well as of Pakistan's intelligence agency, the Inter-Services Intelligence (ISI)—often at odds with each other in their support of rival commanders—further split the Pashtuns.[30] The arrival of Arab *jihadists* in the region (including Osama bin Laden) also evoked mixed Pashtun reactions, some welcoming such "international" help for the anti-Soviet cause, others engaging in anti-Arab rhetoric.

The relationship between Pashtuns and *jihadists* was an uneasy tactical alliance aimed at defeating Soviet forces. When they succeeded in this task, their alliance had to be redefined. After Pashtun seminarians, backed by Pakistan, swept northward through the country and established the Taliban regime, the Arab-Afghans—that is, Arab fighters from Middle Eastern countries who had come to Afghanistan to assist in the war against Soviet forces—sought to exploit the opportunity. Political as well as personal ties were cemented between supreme Taliban leader Mullah Mohammed Omar and bin Laden. bin Laden was given permission to organize training camps for Islamic fundamentalists bent on overthrowing pro-American Arab regimes, such as Saudi Arabia, and driving the United States out of the Arabian Gulf.

How did Afghanistan's powerful warlords react when the Taliban took over the country? Most offered little resistance and fled into northern Afghanistan, Central Asia, and Iran. They remained there until after the terrorist attacks on the United States of September 2001, when the CIA got in touch with them to discuss setting up a military alliance targeting the Taliban government.

In Afghanistan, warlords, ethnicity, and regions are interconnected. One observer summarized the dynamics: "Currently, warlordism is part of the complex distribution of regional and subregional power. Local conditions vary widely with the individual commander. Their legitimacy resides primarily in their ethnic and tribal affiliations. Commanders are supported largely for the critical funds they provide to their ethnic group or tribe."[31]

Installing a new national government for post-Taliban Afghanistan constituted a tricky challenge, given the complex ethnic, regional, and warlord makeup of the country. In December 2001, delegates at UN-sponsored talks in Germany reached the **Bonn Agreement** on creating an Afghan government that would represent a broad range of ethnic groups and regions. At its head would be a Pashtun, Hamid Karzai, who had been handpicked by the United States. He belonged to the same clan as former king Zahir Shah, with whom he retained links.

The transfer of power from Northern Alliance leader Rabbani to Karzai took place at the end of 2001. A Pashtun was now a prowestern leader of Afghanistan, and the three power ministries—defense, interior (security), and foreign policy—went to members of the Tajik *Shura-i Nazar-i Shamali* ("Supervisory Council of the North") party. The following year, the king returned to Kabul from Italy after thirty years in exile and summoned an emergency *Loya Jirga* ("grand assembly")—a centuries-old forum unique to Afghanistan in which tribal elders traditionally come together to resolve common problems. Over 80 percent of participants backed Karzai as the country's head of state. The king was given the honorary title of "father of the nation" and died in 2007, as last Afghan monarch.

Many Pashtuns soon came to believe that Karzai had sold out to Panjshiri Tajiks (Masud's former power base). He became the target of a number of assassination bids—by members of the Taliban and opposing Afghan warlords—and he was wounded by a U.S. "friendly fire" missile attack. After becoming president, he had to be guarded by American security forces rather than Afghan ones. Security in the country remained precarious for years thereafter. Already in 2004, the international nongovernmental organization Médecins sans Frontières (Doctors Without Borders) left Afghanistan—an unprecedented move for this resilient group—when some of its workers were killed while delivering humanitarian assistance.

Karzai tried many different strategies to rein in the warlords. He launched attacks against the home bases of a few of them, especially in the north and west. During his presidency, the national army grew to 75,000, enough to pose a threat to any warlord. Karzai exploited battles between them in western Afghanistan to remove a troublesome warlord-governor in Herat. The Afghan president co-opted several by giving them government positions, especially in the run-up to the 2004 presidential election. He also "normalized" their roles, making them into "security chiefs." An example was Abdul Rashid Dostum, former communist general in command of a northern militia who abruptly switched sides in 1990, helping bring down the communist government the next year. Ten years later, his forces helped defeat the Taliban. Karzai had named Dostum deputy defense minister for northern Afghanistan, but in 2003 he was reassigned to Kabul to become presidential adviser on security issues.

The most convincing reason why Karzai had little choice but to establish a *modus vivendi* with the warlords was that the United States wanted it that way. As one writer in *Foreign Affairs* suggested, instead of disarming the militias the United States was trying to use them to attack Taliban and al-Qaeda remnants. The author concluded: "If Washington really wants to help, it must abandon its policy of working with the warlords and factional leaders of the Northern Alliance."[32]

To survive politically, Karzai could *not* be an even-handed broker. His alliance with the Tajik movement, *Shura-i Nazar,* became the lynchpin of his presidency, and in some ways, he became a hostage to it. His vice president was a younger brother of Tajik warlord Masud. His first defense minister was another powerful Tajik, Muhammad Qasim Fahim, whose militia controlled the northeast of the country as well as parts of Kabul. In 2002, thirty-seven of the thirty-eight generals appointed by Fahim were Tajiks, as were 40 percent of troops in the new national army, compared to 37 percent Pashtuns.[33] When Karzai reshuffled leading officials in the defense ministry and brought in more Pashtuns in 2003, it was in response to a UN threat to suspend a major financial package—a multimillion-dollar program aimed at the disarmament, demobilization, and reintegration of 100,000 armed Afghanis serving in independent militias.

The Bonn process was intended to offset Tajik control of security forces with Pashtun oversight of financial institutions. In theory a good idea, the arrangement did not make much of a difference to the power balance because regional commanders had, for some time, developed private sources of funding. Revenue from opium was the most important. Along the Pakistani border, smuggling and arms trafficking were also important sources of cash. Pashtun commanders even controlled road tolls along the highways leading to Pakistan and Iran.

In 2004, another *Loya Jirga* was convened to enact a new constitution for the country.[34] The Islamic Republic of Afghanistan—the official name of the country—constitutionally recognizes fourteen ethnic groups as constituting the Afghan nation. The constitution identifies two official national languages—Pashto and Dari—as well as six regional languages (including Uzbek and Turkmen). While in the spirit of South Africa's inclusive 1997 constitution, its Afghan counterpart has had few practical consequences. As in South Africa and Iraq, the question of adopting a federal system came up (the Federal Republic of Germany favored such a change). But Karzai, backed by the United States, rejected the move, claiming that, as one American commentator put it, it "would have opened the entire apparatus of state to 'colonization' by clans."[35]

For the Bush administration, the most celebrated "success" in post-Taliban Afghanistan was the holding of a presidential election in 2004, after it had been postponed several times out of security concerns. Karzai called the election at the urging of the United States and against the advice of the UN. The election's credibility was questioned on many grounds. Karzai's one campaign trip outside Kabul was aborted when his helicopter came under fire; other candidates did not even attempt to campaign. While twenty-three candidates, including several regional warlords, entered the race, a handful pulled out, fueling speculation that they had been paid off not to oppose U.S.-backed Karzai.

On election day, fourteen of the remaining fifteen challengers to Karzai called for a boycott when it was discovered that ink used to mark the fingers of those who voted was washable; these voters could return several times to cast ballots. Powerful American ambassador Zalmay Khalilzad, who soon after took up the same post in Bagdad, immediately met with opposition candidates and pressured them to end the boycott. The reported turnout was 84 percent (some cynics expressed surprise it was not over 100 percent). Karzai won 55 percent, just enough to avoid a runoff. In some parts of the country, he lagged far behind the respective region's "native son," underscoring persisting regional and ethnic cleavages. Despite the hollowness of his election triumph and the perception of many Afghans that he was as an ineffective leader, Karzai announced his intention to seek a second term in 2009.

## International Intervention, Renewed Combat

Within a month after the 9/11 attacks, the Bush administration declared that a Taliban–*jihadist* alliance had provided al-Qaeda with the conditions needed to organize the terrorist strikes from positions in Afghan territory. President Bush announced that the United States was going to war in Afghanistan in order to eliminate the Taliban and al-Qaeda. The United Nations Security Council never formally authorized the military intervention, but that may not have been required if the attack was construed as an action of collective self-defense, which would be in keeping with Article 51 of the UN Charter.

Together with Britain, in October 2001, the United States launched a military campaign against Taliban and al-Qaeda forces. There is evidence that plans to invade Afghanistan and eliminate al Qaeda had actually been finalized before the 9/11 terrorist attacks.[36] To overthrow the Taliban regime required superiority in ground forces, which required troops experienced in fighting in the mountainous terrain. So the United States turned to the warlords. A deal was quickly reached (thanks largely to the extensive contacts the CIA had established years earlier) and, led by American special operation forces, the warlord militias launched an offensive against the Taliban.[37]

Key to U.S. war strategy was the **Northern Alliance**, which had first been cobbled together with Russia's help in 1998. It included regional militia leaders Masud, Hekmatyar, Rabbani, and Dostum. By November 2001, the Northern

Alliance had captured the northern city of Mazar-e-Sharif, and a few days later, Kabul fell. The Taliban's home city of Kandahar fell in December, but some of the important battles that would determine whether all major U.S. political objectives would be achieved lay ahead. U.S.-led forces looking for Omar, bin Laden, and his deputy Ayman al-Zawahiri encountered stiff resistance near Jalalabad in eastern Afghanistan. Relentless bombing of the Tora Bora mountain range did not succeed in killing the al-Qaeda leadership.

Routing the Taliban in 2001 proved surprisingly easy; eliminating al-Qaeda structures turned out to be much more difficult. The U.S. decision to employ Afghan militias produced a quick victory, and kept American casualties very low. However, it also allowed leading Taliban and al-Qaeda leaders to escape—because they bribed the warlords to let them get away. Over the next several years, U.S. special forces operating along the Pakistani border recorded few successes in eliminating al-Qaeda. A Taliban war of attrition in the south and east simmered, taking a small but steady toll on American and allied forces. From 2007 onward, there were signs the Taliban was ready to launch a new offensive.

The United States prodded the Pakistani government, headed by President Pervez Musharraf, to use his military to go after the Islamists who regularly took refuge in Pashtun villages on the Pakistani side of the border. But Pashtun solidarity only increased with the expanding American military presence. Civilian casualties grew as missiles launched from unmanned CIA-operated drone aircraft regularly struck innocent people. By 2007, elements of the Pakistani government were even implicated in pro-Taliban activity.

In 2001, the UN had approved the establishment of a NATO-led security and development mission for Afghanistan. Known as the **International Security Assistance Force (ISAF)**, it represented NATO's first ever operational mission outside Europe. In 2003, it was composed of 10,000 soldiers from more than thirty countries. By early 2009, its troop strength reached 50,000, recruited from twenty-six NATO members, ten partners, and five other countries. While the U.S. contribution to ISAF was 20,000 troops—there were 12,000 other American combatants under direct U.S. command in Afghanistan—President Obama pledged an additional 30,000 when Afghanistan replaced Iraq as the top overseas U.S. security concern. Britain furnished 8,000 soldiers, and Canada, France, and Germany around 3,000 each. Most of these were based under NATO-ISAF command in the south.

The original "3-D" doctrine of Canada's military contingent—defense, development, and diplomacy—was overhauled to include offensive combat operations. Canadian and ISAF casualties were particularly high in the provinces of Helmand and Kandahar, and in 2009 at least 20,000 additional American troops were infused into the area. U.S. forces had primarily been operating out of bases in eastern areas of the country. New runways were constructed at Bagram and Kandahar airports as well as at smaller airfields close to the Pakistan border. Small units of military and civilian officers, known as provincial reconstruction teams, were also deployed throughout the country. The 150 deaths the U.S. military sustained in Afghanistan in 2008 exceeded the number in Iraq, and with increased combat operations planned, casualties figures were likely to go higher.

In early 2007, experts had estimated that approximately one-half of Afghanistan was not secure. Despite an increase in the number of ISAF and U.S. troops, by early 2009, the situation had worsened: one think tank estimated that 72 percent of Afghanistan had a permanent Taliban presence.[38] Warlord armies had not been disarmed. With the fall of the Taliban (which in its last year in government had made systematic efforts to eradicate the poppy crop), the opium trade boomed again and became a multibillion-dollar business. Some studies suggested that 75 percent of all opium in the world was now produced in Afghanistan. The expanded drug trade directly benefited regional leaders. Once again, the United States was caught in a catch-22 scenario: it was damned if it did not attempt to destroy the poppy fields, but it was damned if it did because it would further impoverish Afghan's rural population.

The Taliban and the regional warlords retained their foreign backers. Karzai's government was helpless, by and large, to prevent a continued flow of cash and weapons arriving from Pakistan, Iran, and Islamist groups in Turkey, Uzbekistan, and even Russia. The first UN Afghanistan Human Development Report explained why limited progress had been recorded in converting external interference into constructive engagement: "The involvement of Afghanistan's neighbors seems to be aimed as much at maintaining options in case of renewed conflict as it does at contributing to peace-building and reconstruction."[39]

In particular, disagreement arose between President Karzai and the Bush administration over the respective roles of Iran and Pakistan in Afghanistan. The Afghan leader refuted U.S. charges that Iran was supporting Islamists in his country. Washington had accused the Iranian government of shipping weapons furnished by the Chinese to the Taliban. But Iran, in 2001 had supported its Shia ally, the Hazaras, who made up part of the Northern Alliance Karzai emphasized, therefore, that "[t]he two Iranian and Afghan nations are close to each other due to their bonds and commonalities, they belong to the same house and they will live alongside each other for good." At a meeting with President Bush at Camp David in 2007, Karzai claimed Iran had been "a helper and a solution," as well as "a supporter of Afghanistan in the peace process that we have and the fight against terror, and the fight against narcotics in Afghanistan."[40]

Conversely, Karzai was more outspoken about Pakistani interference in his country than Washington was (see Box 9.2). He accused the Musharraf government of helping train, supply, and dispatch Islamic militants to Afghanistan. In his view, Islamic schools (or *madrasa*) in Pakistan also preached fundamentalism and encouraged followers to fight alongside the Taliban in Afghanistan. The Bush administration was more circumspect in its criticism of the Pakistani leader, offering the generic complaint that he was not doing enough in the war on terrorism. Pakistan itself, under Musharraf, expressed little sympathy for Karzai. In addition to its wish to support its Pashtun kin across the border, "Pakistan has argued that politically fragmented, anarchical, and unfriendly Afghanistan would menace Pakistan's security environment."[41] In 2008, elections for a successor to Musharraf, who had resigned under domestic and Western pressure, brought Asif Ali Zardari to the presidency. He became more committed to stamping out the Taliban presence in Pakistan, but the risk was that the Afghan war would spill over into Pakistan.

Other disagreements arose between Karzai, facing reelection in 2009, and the outgoing Bush administration. Washington accused him of obstructing poppy crop aerial eradication efforts and of protecting Pashtun drug lords and poppy farmers in southern Afghanistan, where his political base lay. In turn, Karzai demanded a fixed timeline for the pullout of foreign troops from Afghanistan.

## BOX 9.2
## Theorizing the Linkage Between Ethnic Conflicts and Outside Involvement in Afghanistan

*Complementary Perspectives from Comparative Politics and International Relations*

### Afghan Government Versus Ethnic Groups and Warlords

**1. Domestic factors**

Primordial ethnic and linguistic cleavages

Warlord tradition and weak central authority

Islamic fundamentalism

Frontier state

**2. International factors**

Pashtun kin in Pakistan

Presence of Afghan Arabs and al-Qaeda

U.S.-led military intervention justified as collective self-defense

**3. Conflict resolution**

Conversion of ISAF mission from peace keeping to combat operations

Recognition of importance of development to resolution of conflict

---

He contended that if no deadline were set, a sovereign Afghanistan had the right to negotiate an end date for the presence of coalition forces. He also appealed to President Obama to end air strikes by U.S. warplanes, which killed civilians, as well as house searches by ground forces. Karzai also offered protection for Taliban leaders, including Mullah Omar, if they would agree to peace talks with the Afghan government. The United States, by contrast, had offered a high bounty for Omar's capture. The Afghan president declared that if the United States disagreed with his proposal for negotiations with the Taliban, they could either leave the country or remove him.

In sum, President Karzai began to emphasize a pan-Afghan agenda even as the Taliban's grip on the country tightened. His quarrel with the United States intensified as the Obama administration took office, deployed more American troops to Afghanistan, and promised an Iraq-like surge—with mounting U.S. casualities a likely prospect. At home, Karzai's choice as vice-presidential running mate of Tajik warlord Qasim Fahim, his first defense minister who had come to be despised by Western officials, Afghan citizens, and the Taliban alike for a brutal past and newfound wealth, proved highly unpopular. At the same time Karzai entered into negotiations with President Bush's former ambassador to Kabul, Afghan-born Zalmay Khalilzad. The talks were intended to give the U.S. diplomat a key, possibly allpowerful (if unelected) role in Afghanistan's government. All the while, the issue of whether to negotiate with moderate Taliban leaders or not created a separate political cleavage. Western involvement in the country seemed bound only to deepen as the country's divisions widened.

## WARS IN A DISINTEGRATING YUGOSLAVIA

It was in the Balkans in the 1990s that the major players in world politics first imposed their postbipolar *realpolitik* in the resolution of a regional conflict. The West faced a Balkans dilemma: how to manage Yugoslavia's breakup while not allowing the pieces to fall in a way that Serbia, Russia's close ally, would benefit. Disagreements between the West and Russia about Yugoslavia's postcommunist future were largely a carryover from Yugoslavia's border status in the cold war when it had been a battleground in the clash between Soviet communist and western liberal ideologies.

Most Russian leaders saw it this way. An article published in a leading Russian newspaper in 1994, before NATO took military action in Bosnia, stated: "By its very nature, because of its intrinsic genetic code, NATO has been, and is now and will continue to be designed exclusively for the military–political containment of the USSR and now Russia. Whereas in the past it was a matter of containing Soviet expansion, now the tasks that have been set up are the perpetuation of the breakup of the Soviet Union, weakening Moscow's military–political position and bringing its foreign and military policies under Western control."[42]

So while ethnic conflicts in the Balkans were nothing new, neither was great-power rivalry. For centuries, nationalism in the region has been inextricably linked to shifting balances of power and spheres of influence. The supposed unique brutality of Balkan wars also needs to be put into context: "raping, looting and aimless

## The Balkans

games with death have always accompanied war. An explanation of this requires the psychology of war rather than the political or cultural analysis of the ethnic groups of former Yugoslavia."[43]

The way that socialist Yugoslavia broke up, then, should be explained in terms of great-power rivalry. When it started disintegrating in 1990, it did not inevitably have to fall apart into those "national" pieces that ultimately received international recognition. From the outset, Serbia, the most powerful nation in Yugoslavia and Russia's historical ally, did not desire Yugoslavia's breakup. But under its nationalist leader, Slobodan Milosevic, it was willing to accept the breakup if a Greater Serbia could be constructed out of the remnants of the disintegrating federation. Milosevic was prepared to employ ethnic cleansing, if necessary, as a way of achieving this goal. As one observer noted, "[t]he role of Slobodan Milosevic as an individual was critical to the persistence of the *ancien regime* in Serbia. He had created around himself a highly personal web of *extrainstitutional* political, economic, and coercive power (*sultanism*). The personalized nature of politics with an oligarchic power-clique clustering around Milosevic was replicated in areas such as the **Republika Srpska** where local hierarchical elites flourished."[44]

After nearly a decade of war that had varied from low-intensity to all-out conflict, the last of the nationalist Balkan leaders left office. In 2000, Alija Izetbegovic, president of the Bosnian Muslim part of Bosnia Herzegovina, announced his resignation after nine years in power. He had been wartime leader of a nation that had suffered more than any other in the Balkan conflicts. His Islamist policies—even if moderate—were now out of step with the norms being promoted in the postwar Balkans: ethnic reconciliation, inclusionary approaches to citizenship, multiethnic harmony. These values were given greater emphasis with the passing from the political stage of two other ethno-nationalist leaders: Franjo Tudjman, president of Croatia, who died in 1999, and Milosevic, Yugoslav president, who resigned after an election defeat less than two weeks before Izetbegovic's departure. Within a year, the three main signatories to the **Dayton Accords** peace agreement of 1995, which tried to map peace for the region, were off the political stage. Ironically, without the peace plan participants around, peace now had a better chance to take root.

The turning point in Balkan politics was October 2000, when a popular revolution finally put an end to eleven years of rule by Serb strongman Milosevic. This popular uprising was to serve as a model for triggering political change in the former Soviet republics of Georgia in 2003 (the so-called Rose Revolution) and Ukraine in 2004 (the Orange Revolution). Opposition candidate Vojislav Kostunica had won the presidential election ten days earlier, but Milosevic, who had led Yugoslavia to defeat in four wars in the 1990s, was not about to allow the ballot box to end his political career. It took several days of mass demonstrations and the takeover of the parliament building in Belgrade—with the police standing aside—for the nationalist leader to admit defeat.

Yugoslav electors, the political establishment, and the security apparatus had been enticed with pledges of massive western economic assistance if they turned their support away from Milosevic. The presidential election had become a contest between two visions: in one, a rump Yugoslavia was integrated into Europe; in the other, it underwent further decay and disintegration. The muscle of the West in pressing its strategic vision in the Balkans prevailed with Kostunica's win.[45]

Whether Yugoslavia had ever been little more than an idea, an artificial creation, an imagined community, or a natural primordial community bringing together southern Slav peoples into a common political structure has sparked considerable debate. In an enlightening study of Yugoslavia, Andrew Wachtel pointed out that "the Yugoslav national idea was much more similar to the Italian or the German than it was to national concepts created on the basis of political expediency, like the Soviet, or geographical accident, like many postcolonialist African variants."[46]

Serbs, Croatians, and Bosnian Muslims speak the same basic language, although in writing the same word, Serbs use the Cyrillic alphabet, and Croatians and Bosnians use the Latin one. Slovenes speak a closely related language. Ethnic markers are no more distinct among these peoples than language. Interethnic marriages were commonplace in the socialist Yugoslav federation. However, these groups have experienced very different histories and profess different religions, thus forming the basis for different identities.

The first successful union of the south Slav peoples came only in the twentieth century, in the aftermath of World War I. In the vacuum created by the collapse of the Habsburg and Ottoman empires, a kingdom of Serbs, Croats, and Slovenes was established. In 1929, its name was changed to the Kingdom of Yugoslavia. Eventually falling under a Serb-dominated royal dictatorship, the country became the scene of some of the worst atrocities and partisan fighting during World War II. In 1945, the communist insurgency led by Marshal Josip Broz Tito succeeded in capturing power. The Socialist Federal Republic of Yugoslavia (SFRY) was established and survived without serious ethnic conflicts until 1991–1992, when five successor states based on the former constituent republics became independent. The name Yugoslavia was initially retained by the Serb republic. In 2006, after Montenegro voted for independence, the Serb state changed its name to just that.

When democratic revolutions broke out across eastern Europe in 1989, the upheaval in Yugoslavia took the form of nationalist competition between the constituent republics. As William Pfaff contended, "The troubles caused throughout the Balkans and Southeastern Europe at the beginning of the 1990s . . . have not resulted from external threats but from the anxieties caused by the existence of national or ethnic minorities in countries where other communities are dominant. In each of these countries, the minority is perceived as a threat to the integrity of the host nation, producing a hostility which reinforces the insecurity of the minority."[47] The Serbs were the group that formed a majority in one Yugoslav republic but the largest minority in most of the other republics. Their historical rallying cry was, "Serbia will either be united or it will perish."

In 1990, Slovenes overwhelmingly approved independence in a referendum. Quickly, Croatia announced that it would follow suit. The leader of Bosnia, Izetbegovic, realized that his republic was likely to become the main victim of the spiraling tide of nationalism among the peoples of Yugoslavia: as a multiethnic state with a large Serb minority, it would represent an obvious target for Serb nationalist leader Milosevic. Then–U.S. ambassador to Yugoslavia Warren Zimmerman interpreted disintegration the following way: "The breakup of Yugoslavia is a classic example of nationalism from the top down—a manipulated nationalism in a region where peace has historically prevailed more than war and in which a quarter of the population were in mixed marriages. The manipulators condoned and even provoked local ethnic violence in order to engender animosities that could then be magnified by the press, leading to further violence."[48]

A Serb political sociologist placed greater emphasis on the reciprocal fears of peoples who were traumatized by their version of World War II history: "The vicious cycle of self-fulfilling ethnic prophecies created a highly irrational dynamic in the Yugoslav body politic, reinforcing national self-identifications until the outbreak of the war made the process practically irreversible."[49] Another Balkans observer put it more grandly: "Socialist Yugoslavia was always a Tower of Babel whose builders not only spoke different languages, but talked past each other. In many ways, the diverse peoples of socialist Yugoslavia failed to comprehend each other's cultures."[50]

Serb nationalists were aware of the obstacles that faced them in Slovenia and Croatia. That did not stop them from launching preemptive wars, one (in Slovenia) unsuccessful from the start, the other (in the border regions of Croatia) successful for a time. With regard to Bosnia Herzegovina, they were convinced that the annexation of most of its territory entailed few political or military risks.

The position taken by international actors on Yugoslavia's breakup was crucial in determining the sequence of events. In 1991, four republics of Yugoslavia asked the European Community (later called the European Union) to recognize their independence; Croatia and Slovenia were granted such recognition, Bosnia Herzegovina and Macedonia were told to get their house in order first. Izetbegovic realized that proclaiming Bosnia's independence entailed the risk of precipitating a war, but the alternative was to do nothing and risk Serb domination. In a referendum on Bosnian independence held in 1992, 64 percent of Muslims and Croats voted in favor of a Bosnian state. The vast majority of the 1.3 million Serbs in Bosnia boycotted the poll. A few days after the referendum, even before Bosnian independence was officially proclaimed, Bosnian Serb ultranationalist Radovan Karadzic announced the creation of a Serb republic—Republika Srpska—that laid claim to more than 70 percent of Bosnia's territory. A Bosnian Serb army, supplied by and partially under the command of the Yugoslav national army, was established, and a Bosnian Serb parliament and government, located in the outskirts of Sarajevo (in Pale), were set up. The West's decision to delay recognizing the Muslim government was the pretext Milosevic needed to throw his support behind Karadzic; he was certain that, in time, the Bosnian Serb republic would become part of a Greater Serbia.

In 1992, Serb paramilitary units began to commit atrocities against Muslims in Bosnia that had not been witnessed in Europe since World War II. The barbarism was deliberately chosen to destroy the very identity of the victims. As Pfaff wrote, "This was the rationale for the systematic rape of Muslim women: doing so desecrated and 'ruined' them."[51] Another preferred strategy of the Serb forces in Bosnia was to blockade Muslim-held towns, set up heavy artillery positions on hills overlooking them, and shell the trapped population randomly. Sarajevo, the capital, did not fall to the Serbs when they resorted to this strategy. The fact that the UN had designated it and other Bosnian towns as safe havens made the Serbs think twice about a full-scale attack.

That was not the case with **Srebrenica** in July 1995, also designated as a safe haven and protected by a small, poorly prepared Dutch contingent. The Bosnian Serb army led by General Ratko Mladic decided to call the UN's bluff. The town was overrun, and mass executions of its civilian population followed. More than 10,000 Muslim men were killed and unknown numbers of women were brutalized.[52] Video footage released around the tenth anniversary of the Srebrenica massacre provided graphic proof of Serb atrocities—a shock to many average Serbs who had been living in denial. By this stage in the war, 200,000 people, mainly Muslims, had lost their lives. With the Srebrenica massacre and the humiliation it brought on the UN, the West was finally ready to act.

About the same time, a power grab by Serbs had begun in Kosovo—one of two provinces (the other was Vojvodina) within Serbia. Milosevic eliminated its autonomous status and began to suppress its Albanian cultural institutions—the province was 90 percent ethnically Albanian. The response of ethnic Albanian legislators was to proclaim a **Republic of Kosovo** in 1991 following a hastily organized referendum in the province. Only neighboring Albania recognized the new state and its government; at this time, it seemed unlikely that outside actors in western Europe would become involved.

For the rest of the decade, Milosevic sought to tighten his rule in Kosovo. Ethnic Albanians, or Kosovars, suffered increasing discrimination, and the number of killings and beatings rose. By 1996, a shadowy resistance organization, the **Kosovo Liberation Army (KLA)**, had emerged. Disowned by the mainstream Albanian leadership in the capital, Pristina, the KLA staged bombings and attacks on Serb police officers, local officials, and Serb refugees—as well as on "domestic traitors," Albanians who were regarded as Serb collaborators. By late 1997, the KLA had gained footholds in many parts of western Kosovo.

In 1998, Kosovars went to the polls to elect a president and parliament for the province, but Serb authorities declared the election illegal. That month, Serb police torched several Kosovar villages, putting the province on the brink of war. According to a Balkans specialist, "Analysts in Belgrade speculated that Milosevic's decision to launch the offensive in Kosovo may have been influenced by the desire to 'create a psychology and illusion of acute threat' which would open up new political options and possibilities."[53] That same month, the UN Security Council adopted Resolution 1160, condemning the excessive use of force by the Serb police against civilians in Kosovo. Not surprisingly, in a referendum held the following month, 95 percent of Serbs voted against international mediation in Kosovo. But a year later, the conflict had escalated to the point where not mediation but NATO military intervention had to be employed to quell unrest in the province. Throughout spring 1999, U.S. warplanes, with support from other air forces, pounded military targets in Kosovo and Serbia, forcing Milosevic to withdraw his troops from Kosovo.

It was in mid-1999 that the first large protests calling for the overthrow of Milosevic were held in Yugoslav cities. Some of the protesters were from among the estimated 150,000 Serbian refugees that the UN refugee agency reported had flooded into Serbia from Kosovo. Serbia was already burdened by the influx of 500,000 refugees fleeing earlier conflicts in Bosnia, Croatia, and Slovenia. Only about 100,000 Serbs were left in Kosovo, and few of these could move around safely in the face of ethnic Albanian paramilitary groups.

Was the Christian–Muslim divide part of the political problem in Kosovo? It is difficult to maintain that it was not and, indeed, it was central to the conflicts we examined in this chapter, as well as those in Chapter 5. As one authority on religion and politics summarized, "An unmistakable pattern exists among the cases of post-communist separatist conflict of Muslims and Christians pitted against each other. In the most well-known cases it has been Muslim groups seeking independence from a majority Christian state, such as Bosnia, Kosovo, and Chechnya, but in the two cases from the post-communist world where Christian minorities have existed within Muslim territories—Republika Srpska and Nagorno-Karabakh—they, too, have sought separatism, and the result has been just as bloody."[54]

## International Responses in Bosnia and Kosovo

The West's cautious reaction to the cycle of conflicts in former Yugoslavia was tacit acknowledgment of the complex history of the Balkans. Diplomatic measures were uncoordinated and halfhearted. In 1991, U.S. secretary of state James Baker sought to mediate the brewing conflict but failed to persuade Milosevic to agree on new constitutional arrangements. Zimmerman wrote of the Baker visit: "Never was a green light given or implied to Milosevic or the army to invade the seceding republics. . . . But was there a red light? Not as such because the United States had given no consideration to using force to stop a Serbian/JNA [Yugoslav National Army] attack on Slovenia or Croatia."[55] It was just a few days after Baker's failed mission that Slovenia and Croatia declared their independence.

Also in summer 1991, the European Community (EC) and the United Nations combined their efforts to put an end to fighting in Croatia. They made it clear that

## Kosovo

*Source*: Courtesy of the University of Texas Libraries, The University of Texas at Austin.

the West would not recognize the independence of any of the Yugoslav republics until they had defined their relationships with each other. But under German prodding, the EC decided to extend formal recognition to the breakaway Yugoslav republics in December 1991 if they met certain conditions concerning human and minority rights and territorial claims against other republics.

The decision to offer automatic recognition of statehood to the constituent parts of the Yugoslav federal system—depending on their resolving border disputes and pledging to observe human rights—was made in the last month of the Soviet Union's existence. The contingent recognition of Yugoslav republics as states was part of a grander design, therefore, for dealing with the breakup of the communist bloc. To the West, the policy of diplomatic recognition represented the line of least resistance and was the only orderly way to handle an expected proliferation of claims for sovereignty. But the policy was also at odds with the prevailing international normative regime that discriminated against secessionism. In trying to reconcile conflicting principles, the EC decision was, in the end, the worst possible one. The recognition of only Croatia and Slovenia in December 1991 while dissembling on Bosnia Herzegovina and Macedonia led directly to the war in the Balkans that Europe was trying to avoid.

Hypocrisy may also explain the West's position on Yugoslavia. The universal values that were said to be lacking in the Balkans, such as national self-determination, were of no more than instrumental interest to the West. Croatian writer Dubravka Ugresic captured the dissembling:

> They claimed that Yugoslavia was a gigantic lie. The Great Manipulators and their well-equipped teams began to take the gigantic lie apart. . . .
> They threw ideological formulae out of the dictionary ('brotherhood and unity,' 'socialism,' 'titoism,' etc.) and took down the old symbols (hammer and sickle, red star, Yugoslav flag, national anthem, and Tito's busts). The Great Manipulators and their teams created a new dictionary of ideological formulae: 'democracy,' 'national sovereignty,' 'euro-peanization,' etc. The Great Manipulators had taken apart the old system and built a new one of identical parts.[56]

The United States began moving toward an interventionist role in the Bosnian conflict in late summer 1995, shortly after the Srebrenica massacre. The vacillation by the Clinton administration and its European allies could no longer be justified, and one high-level mediator in the Balkan war told the U.S. administration "to piss or get off the pot."[57] President Clinton was prodded into taking action by the election in 1995 of a more interventionist-oriented French president, Jacques Chirac. The new leader had threatened to withdraw his country's 4,000 peace keepers in Bosnia—the largest national contingent in the 23,000-strong UN mission—if the West refused to use military force to stop Serb aggression. Reversing the humiliations suffered by French and UN peacekeepers became a matter of national honor for the conservative French leader. He supported reinforcement of UN safe havens and was instrumental in creating a 10,000-member rapid reaction force. Its first major deployment was on Mount Igman, a strategic site south of the Bosnian capital of Sarajevo, overlooking a road used to bring in supply convoys.

For a long time, most NATO members had shied away from the use of punitive air strikes against Serb positions, fearing it would lead to Serb reprisals (as it did in the case of Srebrenica) or even to the spread of terrorism to western Europe.

The **Contact Group on Bosnia**, consisting of the United States, England, France, Germany, and Russia, was split on the issue of prolonging economic sanctions against Serbia. The British, French, Dutch, and Canadians sent in peace keepers, while the United States refused to deploy ground forces. Peace keepers were regularly held hostage by the Serbs whenever action was contemplated against them. The rapid deployment force organized in 1995 was partly to counter this by carrying out rescue and evacuation missions under the command of the United Nations Protection Force (UNPROFOR). But it was also to deliver food supplies to starving, besieged Muslim enclaves.

After more than three years of war in the Balkans, the Clinton administration reached the conclusion that the nationalist conflict had become internationalized: ethnic kin from one country—Serbia—had begun intervening to support their brethren in neighboring states—Bosnia Herzegovina and the Krajina part of Croatia. The United States therefore gave the green light to the Croatian army to retake Serb-occupied lands in Krajina. In addition, under the auspices of NATO, the United States began pinpoint bombing of Bosnian Serb military positions.

A few years later, the West's response to the escalation of hostilities in Kosovo was quicker than in Bosnia. Already in 1995 U.S. policymakers had wanted Kosovo to be included in peace negotiations held in Dayton to end the Balkans wars. But it was not. As a result, "[t]he Kosovars were not pleased that they had been summarily excluded from the Dayton Accords. To them, this exclusion was nothing less than tacit approval of Milosevic's goals in the region."[58] This assessment shared a paranoiac view of supposed western machinations in the region as that held by Serbs. But the Kosovars were proved wrong: the West would not abandon them.

In 1998, clashes on the Kosovo–Albanian border between the Yugoslav army and the KLA raised fears that an all-out Balkan war would spill over to Albania and Macedonia. U.S. ambassador to the UN Richard Holbrooke met with KLA commanders in a Kosovo village, giving added legitimacy to the anti-Serb organization. Shortly after, the Serbs launched a month-long offensive against ethnically Albanian regions. As the plight of Kosovar refugees displaced by Serb actions worsened, calls for NATO intervention increased. In September, the **UN High Commissioner for Refugees (UNHCR)** reported that up to 200,000 civilians had been displaced within Kosovo since fighting began in February. UN secretary general Kofi Annan stressed that NATO would have to obtain a Security Council mandate for any military intervention. But in September, the Security Council (with China abstaining) passed **Resolution 1199**, which demanded a cessation of hostilities in Kosovo and cautioned that "additional measures to maintain or restore peace and stability in the region" might be considered. Almost immediately thereafter, NATO took the first formal steps toward military intervention by approving two contingency operation plans, one for air strikes and the other for monitoring and maintaining any ceasefire agreement reached.

In response, Milosevic resorted to his tried tactic of stalling while increasing Serb forces in Kosovo. In January 1999, the bodies of forth-five people were discovered in the village of Racak; the Yugoslav army was blamed for the massacre. Under pressure from the contact group, Serb and ethnic Albanian leaders agreed to participate in peace talks, which were held the next month in France. Three co-mediators representing the United States, the European Union, and the Russian Federation took part. U.S. secretary of state Madeleine Albright—the most vociferous advocate in the Clinton administration of western intervention to stop Milosevic—arrived for the final days of the **Rambouillet talks**. The Kosovar delegation accepted the political accord, but the Serbs objected to its military annex, which authorized a NATO-led peace-keeping force in Kosovo. Despite considerable U.S. diplomatic pressure on Milosevic to accept the interim political accord, when talks resumed in Paris in March 1999, the Serb delegation rejected even its earlier positions at Rambouillet and walked out.

The day after the Paris peace talks collapsed, Yugoslav armed units launched an offensive in Kosovo, driving thousands of ethnic Albanians out of their villages and executing many. President Clinton warned that the dangers of acting were now outweighed by the risks of failing to act, and he referred to both the imminent humanitarian tragedy and the *realpolitik* calculus of "risks that the conflict will involve and destabilize neighboring nations."[59] In late March 1999, NATO launched air strikes on military targets in Yugoslavia. One month later, Yugoslavia formally filed a lawsuit at the International Court of Justice against ten NATO countries, accusing them of genocide.

The Yugoslav army offensive in Kosovo continued as the air strikes began, leading to the flight of hundreds of thousands of Albanians to neighboring Albania and Macedonia. The UN High Commissioner for Refugees estimated that over half a million Kosovars had fled to other countries shortly after NATO bombing started.

In May, a meeting of the G7 foreign ministers, plus Russia's, adopted the following principles as the basis for a political solution to the Kosovo crisis: (1) an immediate and verifiable end of violence and repression in Kosovo; (2) withdrawal from Kosovo of military, police, and paramilitary forces; (3) deployment in Kosovo of effective international civil and security presences, endorsed and adopted by the United Nations; (4) establishment of an interim administration for Kosovo to be decided by the Security Council of the United Nations; (5) the safe and free return of all refugees and displaced persons and unimpeded access to Kosovo by humanitarian aid organizations; (6) a political process toward the establishment of an interim political framework agreement providing for a substantial self-government for Kosovo, taking full account of the Rambouillet accords and the principles of the sovereignty and territorial integrity of the Federal Republic of Yugoslavia; (7) the demilitarization of the KLA; and (8) a comprehensive approach to the economic development and stabilization of the crisis region.

After two months of punishing NATO bombing, Milosevic finally capitulated and accepted these principles. The Serb military began to withdraw from Kosovo, and NATO secretary general Solana ordered a suspension of the bombing campaign, declaring that "the air campaign achieved every one of its goals."[60] The UN Security Council ratified the peace agreement: Its **Resolution 1244** included assertions "reaffirming the commitment of all Member States to the sovereignty and territorial integrity of the Federal Republic of Yugoslavia and the other States of the region. . . . Reaffirming the call in previous resolutions for substantial autonomy and meaningful self-administration for Kosovo."[61]

## Third-Party Mediation and Peace Keeping

Bombing campaigns against the Serb military in both Bosnia and Kosovo quickly attained their objectives. In the case of the 1995 Bosnian conflict, once a ceasefire had been agreed upon, the United States insisted on immediate negotiations among representatives of the Muslim, Croatian, and Serbian groups in Bosnia. These talks took place outside Dayton, Ohio, and the agreement was signed in Paris. It granted 51 percent of Bosnian territory to a Muslim–Croat federation; the remaining 49 percent (roughly corresponding to the balance of power on the ground) was to go to the Republika Srpska.

The idea behind the contrived territorial division was to establish a soft partition of Bosnia to begin with; political and ethnic integration would be encouraged once the situation was stabilized. The agreement provided for the return of refugees to their former homes, and it precluded people indicted as war criminals by **The Hague War Crimes Tribunal** from taking part in Bosnian politics. A special force was set up for peace-making duties in Bosnia, and in late 1995, a 60,000-strong NATO **Implementation Force (IFOR)**, one-third of which were U.S. soldiers, began to move into Bosnia.

The most important challenge facing IFOR was how to promote the construction of a multiethnic Bosnia so soon after war and ethnic cleansing had polarized its communities. The only group that embraced the notion of a *Bosniak* people composed of different ethnicities was the Bosnian Muslim political elite. The Serb half of the Bosnian state remained firmly under the control of Serb nationalists. One optimistic development was the return of many refugees to their former homes: the number of citizens reclaiming their old homes in areas belonging to the rival ethnic group doubled each year between 1996 and 2000. This encouraging sign allowed IFOR (now known as **Stabilization Force [SFOR]**) to reduce its size by one-third, to 20,000.

President Clinton's National Security Affairs adviser Anthony Lake explained why the United States had to be involved in the Balkans in the 1990s: "The conflict in Bosnia deserves American engagement. It is a vast humanitarian tragedy; it is driven by ethnic barbarism; it stemmed from aggression against an independent state; it lies alongside the established and emerging market democracies of Europe and can all too easily explode into a wider Balkan conflict."[62]

Many of these same conditions existed when the Kosovo conflict ignited in 1999. The success of U.S.-led NATO air attacks in driving Serb forces out of the province opened the way for the establishment of a UN-backed international **Kosovo Force (KFOR)**. It was made up of about 45,000 soldiers from NATO countries, with Britain providing the largest contingent (13,000 troops) and France, Germany, the United States, and Italy sending between 5,000 and 8,000 each. The proposal for a separate Russian-controlled sector was turned down, although a separate agreement concluded by Russian and U.S. leaders authorized about 3,000 Russian troops to take part in KFOR. In all, soldiers from thirty-nine countries were represented in KFOR.

UN Resolution 1244 created the **UN Interim Administration Mission in Kosovo (UNMIK)**, which served as a transitional administration. The first operation of its kind, UNMIK brought together four "pillars" (or missions) under UN leadership: (1) humanitarian assistance, led by the Office of the UN High Commissioner for Refugees; (2) civil administration, under UNMIK itself; (3) democratization and institution building, led by the Organization for Security and Cooperation in Europe; and (4) economic development, managed by the European Union.[63]

UNMIK was entrusted, then, with the ambitious mission of developing democratic institutions in Kosovo and laying the foundations for longer-term social and economic reconstruction, even as the urgent phase of humanitarian assistance and emergency relief was taking place. Compared to the more modest agendas of other

UN missions, UNMIK's far-reaching objectives were, in retrospect, a telltale sign that Kosovo was being singled out for special treatment; indeed, in 2008, Kosovo independence was declared and most NATO countries quickly recognized it.

As Serb forces pulled out of the province in mid-1999, KFOR took over control of its security. The next step was to obtain an agreement from Hashim Thaci, KLA political head and prime minister of the self-proclaimed provisional government of Kosovo, for demilitarization of his ethnic Albanian military organization. While offering KLA leaders "special consideration" in a future administration, UNMIK turned down its request to have itself immediately transformed into a national guard.

Talks sponsored by UNMIK between the Serb government and KLA leaders on Kosovo's status continued into 2007 without a breakthrough. Moderate Serb leader Kostunica strongly opposed any loss of Serb sovereignty over Kosovo, which is regarded as the cradle of Serb civilization. By contrast, ethnic Albanians, who make up 90 percent of the province's population of 2 million, were unwilling to accept any status short of independence. Ethnic tensions between the Serb minority living in the north and the ascendant Albanians remained high. Indeed, according to the United Nations, about 220,000 non-Albanian Kosovars, fearing ethnic violence, had become refugees in neighboring Serbia and Montenegro.

In early 2007, Martti Ahtisaari, former president of Finland and UN envoy to the province, announced a plan for determining Kosovo's final status. While the plan made no mention of either Serb sovereignty or Kosovo independence, its practical effect was to create statehood for Kosovo, subject to international supervision. Final status provisions included Kosovo's right to apply for membership of international organizations, like the UN, but its preclusion from seeking a merger with Albania. Its territorial integrity would be enforced, and Serb areas would not be allowed to split off and join Serbia, as some Serb nationalist leaders threatened to do. The Serb language and Serb Orthodox Church would be given constitutional protection in Kosovo, and all non-Albanians would be guaranteed positions in government, the civil service, and the security forces.

The Ahtisaari plan had to be approved by the UN Security Council. While the United States and most EU states now backed Kosovo statehood, Russia voiced strong objections to what it viewed as further partitioning of its former sphere of influence and a weakening of Serbia, its closest ally in the Balkans (see Box 9.3).

A year earlier, in 2006, Serbia had lost another of its provinces. Montenegro had voted to sever its union with Serbia, which had been created in 1992 following socialist Yugoslavia's demise. With a smaller population (620,000) than Kosovo and greater ethnic and religious overlap between Serbs and Montenegrins—the majority of the country's population speaks Serb and belongs to the Serb Orthodox Church—Montenegro's statehood was less contentious.

The proposal advanced by Ahtisaari—he was to be awarded the Nobel Peace Prize later in 2008—on Kosovo's final status provided the framework for an EU–U.S. agreement. Ignoring Russia's objections, it led in February 2008 to the Kosovo legislature's approval of what appeared to be a unilateral declaration of independence. Quickly, the United States and twenty-two of the twenty-seven EU states extended recognition. But Russia and much of the rest of the world were concerned about both the morality and legality of the process. Those who objected claimed that Kosovo was being rewarded for its ethnic cleansing of Serbs and that, unlike

---

**BOX 9.3**

**Theorizing the Linkage Between Ethnic Conflicts and Outside Involvement in Bosnia and Kosovo**

---

*Complementary Perspectives from Comparative Politics and International Relations*

**Serbia Versus Bosniaks and Kosovars**

**1. Domestic factors**

Disintegrating federal state

Balkan multinationalism and multi-confessionalism

Great Serb nationalism

**2. International factors**

Domino effect: independence of one state engenders another's

Ethnic kin as majority or minority group in most states

U.S.–EU effort to shut Russia out of the Balkans

**3. Conflict resolution**

Military intervention to back humanitarian missions in both Bosnia and Kosovo

Military intervention and mediation for *realpolitik* purposes in Kosovo

EU as biased power broker in the Balkans

EU membership as incentive for Serbia to drop regional ambitions

Lack of international consensus on diplomatic recognition of Kosovo

---

Bosnia, it exemplified a uninational rather than multinational state. Some KLA leaders had been charged with war crimes by The Hague Tribunal on Yugoslavia. Serbs living in northern Kosovo continued to face harassment and intimidation by Kosovar authorities.

As for its legality, in October 2008, Serbia won a bid in the United Nations to have the International Court of Justice (ICJ) review the manner in which Kosovo declared its independence. In the UN General Assembly vote, seventy-seven countries sided with Serbia, just six voted against it (including the United States), and seventy-six abstained (including most EU members). The ICJ has often mediated border disputes between countries, but a request from the UN for a legal ruling is exceptional. Many UN members, facing separatist threats of their own, had been alarmed by the haste with which the EU and the United States had proceeded. Their skepticism was reflected in the fact that, at the end of 2008, only forty-eight countries had recognized Kosovo; 144 had not. Many were genuinely waiting to hear the ICJ's nonbinding legal opinion.

The role of the United States and the EU in engineering the breakup of, first, socialist Yugoslavia and, then, the Serb federation had been decisive. The day after Kostunica was sworn in as president in 2000, the EU lifted economic sanctions against Serbia and offered $2 billion in aid to help rebuild the country. EU foreign ministers also agreed to end the oil embargo on Serbia imposed during the Kosovo war. In 2001, Serb police arrested Milosevic just before a U.S.-imposed deadline for Serbia to qualify for aid expired. In 2008, they arrested a wanted

Bosnian Serb fugitive, Radovan Karadzic, and turned him over to The Hague Tribunal to face war crime charges. This coincided with a meeting of EU foreign ministers who were to discuss EU–Serb relations. Shortly after Serbs reelected pro-western Boris Tadić as president in 2008 (he was first elected in 2004), the EU signed a Stability and Association Agreement (SAA)—the precursor to full accession talks—with Serbia.

Kosovo independence has remained the main sticking point in the Balkans. Most Serb politicians agree that recognizing Kosovar statehood would be too high a price to pay as a condition for EU accession. Tadić emphasized that Kosovo should join the EU, but as an integral part of Serbia. Other international consequences were linked to Kosovo. Russia's defeat of the Georgian military in August 2008 led to declarations of independence of two of Georgia's breakaway regions: Abkhazia and South Ossetia. While western backers of Kosovo saw no analogy between the cases, those who sympathized with Russia did. Elsewhere, the uneasy ethnic equilibrium in Bosnia was tied to Kosovo's status: if Serbs lost Kosovo, then some Serb nationalists would feel justified in pushing for Republika Srpska's separation from Bosnia.

The West had succeeded in rebalkanizing the Balkans. Had this been its intention? Writing about Kosovo, security expert Michael MccGwire cautioned: "one suspects that much of the moralistic rhetoric, the demonizing, the claim to be pioneering a foreign policy based on values as well as interests, was a form of denial."[64] In other words, Kosovo was not about values but about interests. It was in the strategic interests of the United States and western Europe to rebalkanize Yugoslavia to weaken Russia's influence. The main gravedigger of Yugoslavia was the West. Whether its balkanization policy has left the peninsula more secure and stable remains an open question.

## Conclusion

The balance sheet seems clear. Whether in a coalition with other western states or not, U.S. military interventions have deepened rather than weakened ethnic and religious divisions in a country. Intervention in Yugoslavia combined good intentions with self-interest. Intervention in Afghanistan was for self-protection, as well as for undermining the growth of Islamism. Intervention in Iraq was because the United States thought it could. Whatever the purpose, the outcome aggravated ethnic and religious competition and usually led to an explosion of violent conflict.

## Discussion Questions

1. Outline the principal ethnic and religious divisions in Iraq. Did Saddam Hussein play the "ethnic card" to divide and rule his country? Did the United States play the ethnic card to divide the insurgency?

2. Which ethnic communities have benefited from the 2003 U.S. invasion of Iraq? Which have lost political influence? Was this shift in the ethnic balance of power an objective of American military intervention in the country?

3. How have Afghanistan's regional and ethnic warlords maintained their power under the Karzai government? Have international organizations in the country been able to affect their position?

4. What are the Pashtuns' grievances in Afghanistan? Are Pashtuns the principal reason for the spillover of violence across the Afghanistan–Pakistan border?

5. Explain why the West intervened quickly in Kosovo. Was an "imminent humanitarian tragedy" the most important consideration? Assess whether UNMIK was an impartial third party in Kosovo.

6. What are the international ramifications of Kosovo's declaration of independence? Evaluate both the moral and legal objections to diplomatic recognition of this breakaway state.

## Key Terms

Bonn Agreement
Contact Group on Bosnia
Dayton Accords
gangster states
The Hague War Crimes
    Tribunal
Implementation Force
    (IFOR)
International Security
    Assistance Force (ISAF)
Islamists
*jihadists*

Kosovo Liberation Army
    (KLA)
Kosovo Force (KFOR)
*Loya Jirga*
Montenegro
nation building
Northern Alliance
Pashtuns
Rambouillet talks
Republic of Kosovo
Republika Srpska
Resolution 1199

Resolution 1244
Shia Crescent
Shia Muslims
Stabilization Force [SFOR]
Srebrenica
Sunni Muslims
UN High Commissioner for
    Refugees (UNHCR)
UN Interim Administration
    Mission in Kosovo
    (UNMIK)

## Notes

1. Tom Nairn, *Faces of Nationalism: Janus Revisited* (London: Verso, 1997), p. 61. He referred to issues of *The New Statesman* (June 1, 1990) and *Time* (August 6, 1990), which had cover stories titled "Nationalities on the Loose" and "Nationalism: Old Demon," respectively.

2. Ronald Inglehart and Pippa Norris, "The True Clash of Civilizations," *Foreign Policy* (March/April 2003), pp. 63–70.

3. For a review essay, see Patricia Owens, "Theorizing Military Intervention," *International Affairs,* 80, no. 2 (March 2004), pp. 355–365.

4. Nation- and state-building are closely related. For an overview, see Robert I. Rotberg, ed., *State Failure and State Weakness in a Time of Terror* (Washington, D.C.: Brookings Institution Press, 2003).

5. Amitai Etzioni, "A Self-Restrained Approach to Nation-Building by Foreign Powers," *International Affairs,* 80, no. 1 (January 2004), p. 1.

6. W. Michael Reisman, "Why Regime Change Is (Almost Always) a Bad Idea," *American Journal of International Law,* 98, no. 3 (July 2004), p. 525.

7. Davie Fromkin, *A Peace to End All Peace: The Fall of the Ottoman Empire and the Creation of the Modern Middle East* (New York: Owl Books, 2001), p. 528.

8. See the review article by Marion Farouk-Sluglett and Peter Sluglett, "The Historiography of Modern Iraq," *American Historical Review*, 96, no. 5 (December 1991), pp. 1408–1421.

9. Fromkin, *A Peace to End All Peace*, p. 565.

10. The differences are rooted in history. Sunni Islam accepts the legitimacy of the order of succession of the first four caliphs (supreme religious authority) after the Prophet Muhammad. Therefore, it is the heir to the early central Islamic state. Shias reject the first three caliphs as usurpers.

11. See Edmund A. Ghareeb, *Historical Dictionary of Iraq* (Lanham, Md.: Scarecrow Press, 2004).

12. "Prewar Assessment on Iraq Saw Chance of Strong Division," *New York Times* (September 28, 2004).

13. Dan Murphy, "On Edge, Shiites and Sunnis in Iraq Try to Talk it Out," *Christian Science Monitor* (January 6, 2004).

14. Stockholm International Peace Research Institute, *SIPRI Yearbook 2008: Armaments, Disarmament, and International Security* (New York: Oxford University Press, 2008), pp.46–47.

15. Yitrzhak Nakash, "The Shi'ites and the Future of Iraq," *Foreign Affairs*, 82, no. 4 (July/August 2003), p. 24.

16. Ibid., p.47.

17. "Post-Surge Violence: Its Extent and Nature," Iraq Body Count (28 December 2008), at http://www.iraqbodycount.org/analysis/numbers/surge-2008/

18. David H. Petraeus, "Report to Congress on the Situation in Iraq," (September 10–11, 2007).

19. Democracy Now, "Noam Chomsky: U.S. Might Face 'Ultimate Nightmare' in Middle East Where Shi'ites Control Most of World's Oil" February 9, 2005, http://www.democracynow.org.

20. Jamal Benomar, "Constitution-Making after Conflict: Lessons for Iraq," *Journal of Democracy*, 15, no. 2 (April 2004), pp. 81–95.

21. "Bush's Three-Front Blunder," *Asia Times* (January 31, 2007), at http://www.atimes.com/atimes/middle_east/ia31ak01.html.

22. Liam Anderson and Gareth Stansfield, *The Future of Iraq: Dictatorship, Democracy, or Division?* (New York: Palgrave, 2004).

23. Anthony H. Cordesman (with Emma R. Davies), *Iraq's Insurgency and the Road to Civil Conflict* (Westport, Conn.: Greenwood, 2008), p.321.

24. Larry Diamond, "Lessons from Iraq," *Journal of Democracy*, 16, no. 1 (January 2005), pp. 17, 23. See also his *Squandered Victory: The American Occupation and Bungled Effort to Bring Democracy to Iraq* (New York: Henry Holt, 2005).

25. Anthony Shadid, "In Iraq, the Day After," *Washington Post* (January 2, 2009).

26. "Election Results Spur Threats and Infighting in Iraq," *New York Times* (February 10, 2009).

27. Nazif M. Shahrani, "War, Factionalism, and the State in Afghanistan," *American Anthropologist*, 104, no. 3 (2002), pp. 715–721.

28. Rasul Bakhsh Rais, *Recovering the Frontier State: War, Ethnicity, and State in Afghanistan* (Lanham, Md.: Rowman and Littlefield, 2008), p. 6.

29. For an excellent account of this period, see Ahmed Rashid, *Taliban* (New Haven, Conn.: Yale University Press, 2001).

30. The complex relationship betweenthe CIA and Inter Services

Intelligence Service, on the one hand, and rival warlords and their militias in Afghanistan, on the other, is described in Steve Coll, *Ghost Wars: The Secret History of the CIA, Afghanistan, and bin Laden, from the Soviet Invasion to September 10, 2001* (New York: Penguin, 2004).

31. Riphenburg, "Ethnicity and Civil Society in Contemporary Afghanistan," p. 47.

32. Kathy Gannon, "Afghanistan Unbound," *Foreign Affairs,* 83, no. 3 (May/June 2004), p. 44.

33. Carol J. Riphenburg, "Ethnicity and Civil Society in Contemporary Afghanistan," *Middle East Journal,* 59, no. 1 (Winter 2005), p. 43.

34. Barnett R. Rubin, "Crafting a Constitution for Afghanistan," *Journal of Democracy,* 15, no. 3 (July 2004), pp. 5–19.

35. S. Frederick Starr, "Silk Road to Success," *National Interest,* no. 78 (Winter 2004/05), pp. 68–69.

36. "U.S. Sought Attack on al Qaeda: White House Given Plans Says Before Sept. 11," MSNBC (May 16, 2002), at http://www.msnbc.msn.com/id/4587368/.

37. Stephen Biddle, "Afghanistan and the Future of Warfare," *Foreign Affairs,* 82, no. 2 (March/April 2003), pp. 31–46.

38. International Council on Security and Development, "Taliban in 72 percent of Afghanistan" *NewsDaily* (December 8, 2008), at http://www.newsdaily.com/news/international_council_on_security_and_development/.

39. UNDP, *Afghanistan National Human Development Report 2004,* at http://hdr.undp.org/en/reports/nationalreports/asiathepacific/afghanistan/Afghanistan_2004_en.pdf.

40. "Karzai's Iran Reference Raises Eyebrows at Camp David," *Canada.com* (August 6, 2007), at http://www.canada.com/topics/news/world/story.html?id=c5d07911-605b-4a4a-becb-8768009974b3.

41. Rais, *Recovering the Frontier State,* p. 188.

42. Vladislav Chernov, "Moscow Should Think Carefully," *Nezavisimaia gazeta,* February 23, 1994. Quoted in Ilya Prizel, *National Identity and Foreign Policy: Nationalism and Leadership in Poland, Russia, and Ukraine* (Cambridge, England: Cambridge University Press, 1998), p. 263.

43. Gertjan Dijkink, *National Identity and Geopolitical Visions: Maps of Pride and Pain* (London: Routledge, 1996), p. 118.

44. Robert Thomas, *The Politics of Serbia in the 1990s* (New York: Columbia University Press, 1999), p. 424.

45. See Michael Parenti, *To Kill a Nation: The Attack on Yugoslavia* (New York: Verso Books, 2002).

46. Andrew Baruch Wachtel, *Making a Nation, Breaking a Nation: Literature and Cultural Politics in Yugoslavia* (Stanford, Calif.: Stanford University Press, 1998), p. 228.

47. William Pfaff, *The Wrath of Nations: Civilization and the Furies of Nationalism* (New York: Touchstone Books, 1993), pp. 199–200.

48. Warren Zimmerman, "The Last Ambassador: A Memoir of the Collapse of Yugoslavia," *Foreign Affairs,* 74, no. 2, (March/April 1995), p. 12.

49. Veljko Vujacic, "Historical Legacies, Nationalist Mobilization, and Political Outcomes in Russia and Serbia: A Weberian View," *Theory and Society,* 25 (1996), p. 786.

50. Sabrina Petra Ramet, Balkan Babel, *The Disintegration of Yugoslavia from the Death of Tito to the War for Kosovo,* 3rd. ed. (Boulder, Colo.: Westview Press, 1999), p. 329.

51. Pfaff, *The Wrath of Nations*, p. 229.
52. See Slavenka Drakulic, *S.: A Novel from the Balkans* (New York: Viking Penguin, 1999).
53. Robert Thomas, *The Politics of Serbia in the 1990s* (New York: Columbia University Press, 1999), p. 414.
54. Christopher Marsh, "The Religious Dimension of Post-Communist 'Ethnic' Conflict," *Nationalities Papers*, 35, no. 5 (November 2007), p. 826.
55. Drakulic, *S.: A Novel from the Balkans*, pp. 11–12.
56. Dubravka Ugresic, *Kultura lazi [antipoliticki eseji]*. Zagreb, 1996, p. 50. Quoted in Wachtel, *Making a Nation, Breaking a Nation*, p. 231.
57. Glenny, "Heading Off War in the Southern Balkans," p. 100.
58. Greg Campbell, *The Road to Kosovo: A Balkan Diary* (Boulder, Colo.: Westview Press, 1999), p. 154.
59. "Statement by President Clinton on Kosovo," *New York Times* (March 25, 1999).
60. Javier Solana, "NATO's Success in Kosovo," *Foreign Affairs*, 78, no. 6 (November–December 1999), p. 118.
61. "UN Resolution on Kosovo: Full Text," *BBC News* (June 17, 1999). Also see United Nations, "Resolution 1244 (1999)," at http:// www. un.org/Docs/scres/1999/99sc1244. htm.
62. Anthony Lake, "From Containment to Enlargement: Current Foreign Policy Debates in Perspective," *Vital Speeches*, 60, no. 1 (October 15, 1993), p. 13.
63. United Nations, "What is UNMIK?" at http://www.un.org/peace/kosovo/pages/unmik12.html.
64. Michael MccGwire, "Why Did We Bomb Belgrade?" *International Affairs*, 76, no. 1 (January 2000), p. 23.

# CHAPTER 10

# To Intervene or Not to Intervene?

## STUDYING POST–COLD WAR POLICY MAKING

A decade into the new millennium, international politics continues to be punctuated by nationalist and religious strife. Whether they surface in the Middle East, Africa, South Asia, or eastern Europe, ethnic and religious fault lines may lead to armed conflict within a country, followed by some degree of outside intervention. In some cases, external intervention in support of an ethnic or religious community precedes the breakout of violence. The internationalization of hitherto localized ethnic or religious conflicts has become commonplace. More often than not, international organizations such as the United Nations (UN) have initiated diplomatic efforts to try to manage such disputes, although not always with success. The United States has at times stepped in, too—even using overwhelming military force—but over the past decade it has resolved few countries' conflicts for them.

The **postmodern dilemma**, brought on by a kaleidoscopic world of changing identities, alliances, and affiliations, has been trenchantly captured by Moroccan writer Fatima Mernissi: "Our fin-de-siècle era resembles the apocalypse. Boundaries and standards seem to be disappearing. Interior space is scarcely distinguishable from exterior."[1]

An illustration is the 2005 London public transport suicide attacks, which were carried out by four United Kingdom citizens, all of whom were Muslims. Two were born in Britain of Pakistani descent, the third was born in Pakistan, and the fourth was born in Jamaica. Such kaleidoscopic identities in a globalized world are no longer surprising. Defining the role that a state should play under such conditions requires fresh thinking. Using past experience, precedent, analogies, and axioms to formulate foreign policy decisions is of limited value because the distinction between interior and exterior political space has been fading, and boundaries are increasingly permeable. This is a challenge to both international organizations like the UN and to powerful third-party actors like the United States. Yet decisions to intervene in ethnic and religious conflicts seem at times to display unawareness of how the blurring of national borders may shape the conflict resolution process.

Our case studies have revealed the many efforts made by the United Nations to mediate conflicts and, most important, to place peace keepers on the ground. Invariably UN-brokered peace processes are limited to the particular country in which a conflict has taken place. This reflects the persistent statist bias of the international system. But as we have found, many conflicts—in Afghanistan, Congo, Darfur, Kosovo—are regional in nature and have spilled across state boundaries. For peace keeping to be successful, a regional approach is required—something that UN conflict resolution structures are not designed to carry out.

The vacuum can be filled by regional and global powers that, in the process of resolving a conflict, may wish to tilt it in a way favorable to themselves. Examples are the United States in the Middle East, Russia in the Caucasus, and India in Sri Lanka and more broadly in South Asia. These powers have the military capability to broker—and at times impose—a regional solution on the ethnic and religious strife raging in a particular state. Great-power conflict resolution methods may appear to have the greatest chance of success, but as we see in the case of U.S. entanglement in Iraqi ethno-sectarian conflict, or Russian and then American intervention in Afghanistan's warlord politics, they can also galvanize opposition because of perceptions of the great power as the intervener, invader, and occupier. Vast military capabilities and regionwide programs for resolving conflicts do not guarantee peaceful outcomes.

No country has assumed a greater responsibility for shaping the contemporary international system than the United States. Whether a conflict in a faraway corner of the world (for example, Darfur in the Sudan) becomes an international crisis or is left to fester has depended largely on the U.S. response to it. That response, in turn, is framed by U.S. national interests; moral arguments are usually of secondary importance, even if in public discourse they may have pride of place. Multiple U.S. efforts to resolve conflicts abroad—whether through use of overwhelming force or through appeal to irresistible doctrines (democracy, freedom, human rights)—have become associated with the notion of ***Pax Americana***. That is, they are conflict resolution outcomes that embody American principles but also American interests. Few regions of the world have wanted a resolution of their conflicts to reflect an "American peace."

Given this blowback against U.S. internationalism,[2] the quandary facing a new American administration is when to choose intervention to manage a conflict in line with U.S. national interests, and when to opt for **isolationism**, where the United States stays out because it believes that it has more to lose than gain by intervening. The interventionist–isolationist debate has been central to U.S. foreign policy making for some time. But it is a question that also confronts international organizations that have the power to affect ethnic and religious conflicts. A "United Nations peace" can also muster opposition, as we have seen in the case of the Sudanese government's accusation that UN peace-keeping forces in the country were foreign invaders.

What, then, are legitimate reasons for international intervention in an ethnic conflict and what are legitimate grounds for staying out, even though a humanitarian catastrophe may be in the making? In the cases we presented in this book, which responses to ethnic conflict have worked and which have not?

# RATIONALES FOR INTERVENTION

No hard-and-fast rules exist for deciding when to intervene in a conflict. Nor is it obvious which means should be used—hard power (military and economic strength to subdue adversaries), soft power (diplomacy and consensus building reflecting "the ability to get what you want through attraction rather than coercion"),[3] or sticky power (the universal appeal of a cultural model, from hip American pop culture to "Cool Britannia").[4] U.S. secretary of state Hillary Clinton has identified **smart power** as her preferred method—complementing military and economic might with diplomacy for the purpose of investing in the global good. According to a Democratic-leaning think tank, smart power means "providing things people and governments in all quarters of the world want but cannot attain in the absence of American leadership."[5]

In answer to the question, Should the United States act unilaterally or as leader of a multinational coalition? smart power opts firmly for the latter. "The United States can work through treaties, alliances, and multilateral organizations—so-called norms-based internationalism. Formal agreements and global norms provide the United States with the standing capacity to act in conjunction with allies at the times we need them most. This approach served the United States well in the Cold War and should be the bedrock of our internationalism going forward."[6] Smart power embraces a return to a longstanding values-based approach to dealing with global conflicts—liberal internationalism.

## Promoting Liberal Internationalism

**Liberal internationalism** calls for an international order to be founded on the ideas of human rights, tolerance, and democracy. From its founding charter, the United Nations' mission essentially reflects liberal internationalism. American presidents as different as Bill Clinton and George W. Bush agreed on these three ideas, though the Bush administration's willingness to use coercive means as part of **democracy promotion**—spreading democratic values, procedures, and institutions around the world—gave democracy a bad name. Democracy promotion is a praiseworthy idea, but when invoked to justify unilateral military intervention—a *Pax Americana* imposed on a target state—it becomes tarnished.

Humanitarian intervention, too, is widely praised as an objective but can produce unintended negative consequences. When undertaken by nonpartisan nongovernmental organizations (NGOs) such as the International Red Cross and Médecins sans Frontières (Doctors Without Borders), it is difficult to criticize. But humanitarian intervention rarely occurs without political complications. A tragic example was the U.S. effort (as part of a UN mission from 1993 to 1995) to bring humanitarian relief to famine-affected Somalia. Several Somali warlords turned against the U.S. presence and a score of American troops were killed before President Clinton pulled the plug on the operation. As we noted, the U.S. refusal to act preemptively in Rwanda's ethnic conflict a short time later was in large part explained by the failure of humanitarian intervention in Somalia.

We can suggest, then, that humanitarian interventions—the standard-bearer of liberal internationalism for the past three decades—is a praiseworthy but problematic project: "The 'client' affected by disaster and emergency is too often sacrificed to the interest of that other 'client,' the donor. The voice of the Samaritan remains subdued, uncertain about the consequences of providing assistance . . . humanitarianism is increasingly rudderless."[7]

## Preempting Security Threats

Democracy promotion is not just a moral ideal but is inextricably linked to national and international security. The justification for preemptive U.S. attacks on Afghanistan in 2001 and Iraq in 2003 was based on the belief that democratization of those countries would enhance the security of the western world. The attacks were portrayed as combining the prosecution of a preventive war with exercises in nation building, ethno-sectarian reconciliation, security stabilization, institutional engineering, and socioeconomic modernization. For the critics of U.S. foreign policy under President Bush, those were a lot of good intentions that masked ugly realities.

But what actions should be taken when the converse situation occurs—states collapse, democratization comes to a halt, and civil conflicts (usually ethnic) break out? Does a great power decide on preemption if it sees a security threat to itself caused by the resulting instability? A seminal study of ethnic conflict, *Pandaemonium,* began with the proposition that "[i]f international politics consists largely, not of a Manichean struggle of right versus wrong, but of impossibly competing ethnic identities and mutually incompatible dreams of national self-determination, might this not reinforce American disenchantment, not just with the supposed New World Order, but with all involvement in a hopelessly benighted world?"[8]

Let us consider two examples of devilishly complex threats. In his analysis of Africa's recent politics, Robert Kaplan described "the withering away of central governments, the rise of tribal and regional domains, the unchecked spread of disease, and the growing pervasiveness of war. West Africa is reverting to the Africa of the Victorian atlas. It consists now of a series of coastal trading posts . . . and an interior that, owing to violence, volatility, and disease, is again becoming, as Graham Greene once observed, 'blank' and 'unexplored.' " In what way can this "coming anarchy" affect the United States? For Kaplan, "Africa suggests what war, borders, and ethnic politics will be like a few decades hence."[9] Economic growth could help prevent this spiral of violence and poverty, but possibly an even more important factor is financially viable and administratively competent governments.[10] The global financial crisis that began in 2008 has made the economic viability and incorruptible governance of poor countries with ethnic divisions more improbable.

The second example involves the "*jihad* archipelago"—Southeast Asia. Large Muslim populations live in the Philippines, Indonesia, Thailand, Malaysia, and Singapore. Radical Islamic organizations have appeared more often in these countries, and terrorist acts and plots have multiplied. A Southeast Asian specialist cautioned, "The region's fight to hold true to its vision of Islam and to honor its own ethnic and cultural traditions while embracing economic and social modernization is an epic struggle of our time and one in which the West has a deep interest."[11] The threats to international security that emanate from this ethno-religious archipelago are considerable.

Are there practical guidelines that can indicate when and how intervention should be used to meet such threats? One specialist on security policy believed that military intervention made sense only when it was carried out with consequence. Whether multilateral (through the UN) or unilateral (the United States), it should be characterized by **imperial impartiality**.

If outsiders such as the United States or the United Nations are faced with demands for peace in wars where passions have not burned out, they can avoid the costs and risks that go with entanglement by refusing the mandate—staying aloof and letting the locals fight it out. Or they can jump in and help one of the contenders defeat the other. But will their impartiality bring warring sides to the peace table better than the effects of exhaustion caused by prolonged carnage? Not a gentle, restrained impartiality but an active, harsh impartiality that overpowers both sides: an imperial impartiality.[12]

For it to be effective, then, military preemption of security threats should be coupled with an imperial form of conflict resolution. This was the way that the United States managed Serb threats in the Balkans—air strikes to begin with, a Dayton peace accord, in which Serbia effectively had to capitulate to the West, to end with. It remains unclear whether this case exemplifies a lasting peace or not. A thick line separates an imposed conflict outcome that is likely to be contested for years from an indigenous, "homegrown" one in which the spirit of constitutionalism—as in Canada and South Africa—becomes infectious for parties to the dispute.

## Prosecuting a Just War

The use of military force against a selected target, including against groups accused of carrying out genocidal actions, ethnic and religious cleansing, or persecution of minorities, involves something beyond a mere a security threat. NATO's air strikes on Serb positions in Bosnia in 1995 were justified in terms of the principle of a **just war**. The war on terror announced by the Bush administration in 2003 to explain the attack on the Taliban government in Afghanistan made recourse to the just war doctrine. Russia's invasion of Georgia in 2008 was built as a just war against a political leader who had become a war criminal because of his unprovoked shelling of South Ossetian civilians. These examples of *coercing another nation into peace* reveal the contradictory nature of the just war principle.

Let us take a step back and ask, Should intervention in ethnic conflicts be *required* of third parties when the conditions for fighting a just war have been met? Ethically, this seems a desirable imperative, but *realpolitik* makes no allowances for it. While there is no unanimity about what principles make up the "justice of war theory," the most commonly cited ones include having just cause, being declared by a recognized authority, possessing right intention, having a reasonable chance of success, and ensuring that the means used be proportional to the end sought. A necessary if insufficient cause is to fight to redress a wrong that has been suffered. Another provision frequently invoked is that "A war can only be considered just if both its cause and conduct are just."[13]

Assessing the justice of a cause is oftentimes difficult, but gauging just conduct in a war is easier because of the host of international conventions on warfare that have been concluded. Use of some new military technologies, however, has raised ethical issues about the conduct of war. For example, flying unmanned airplanes (like Predators in Afghanistan) that release Hellfire missiles on targets identified in an operations center in faraway Nevada has produced many civilian deaths as well as killing a number of key terrorist leaders. Such warfare has been described as

"War Lite," "immaculate coercion," and even "humanitarian bombing" because of the well-intentioned objectives that are identified. To date, only U.S. military and intelligence agencies have employed such techniques of warfare. If the collateral damages (civilian casualties) that result are high, does that in itself disqualify the war from being a just one? It is difficult to say.

Let us consider whether a just war requires that it be conducted not unilaterally, but by a coalition of countries sharing a common cause and grievance. This question is pertinent to determining the justice of military interventions that the United States under the Bush administration launched. An important reason why a majority of security experts believe that military intervention in Yugoslavia was just, but in Iraq it was not, has precisely to do with the juxtaposition of **unilateralism** with **multilateralism**. When America acted on its own, the response of international public—and even elite—opinion was to regard such action as *sui generis,* unjust. When it worked in concert with others—including other major powers—this expanded consensus convinced people that military action is just. In the case of managing ethnic conflict, as in former Yugoslavia, multilateralism has been the more common form of action and generally enjoys widespread support. By contrast, in those cases where unilateral intervention has been carried out, as in Iraq, skepticism arises about whether the intervener has acted impartially.

There are also cases where an absence of *any* action has occurred. The most tragic example is Rwanda in 1994, when ethnic conflict ran its course with no external parties having the will (powerful western states) or the capability (the UN or any pan-African organization) to intervene. In an era of economic and political globalization populated with a host of transnational actors (terrorist groups among them), an international consensus in favor of isolationism is difficult to understand. Indeed, China and Russia made a statement that they preferred intervention to isolationism when they staged their first ever joint military exercise. Dubbed "Peace Mission 2005," the war games focused on the invasion of an imaginary country wracked by ethnic conflict and terrorism. But even relatively low-key, small-scale action to dampen ethnic strife can be significant. The impact of the International Criminal Court's investigations into possible war crimes committed by government leaders (as in Sudan) and rebel commanders (as in Congo) can produce surprisingly positive results, such as an offer to end support for ethnic hostilities in return for not being served with an International Criminal Court (ICC) indictment.

Not intervening in cases where a humanitarian catastrophe is unfolding furnishes an example of **unjust nonwar**. Genocide in Rwanda while third-party actors slept is the clearest recent case we have of this phenomenon. But Darfur's protracted humanitarian tragedy, during which potential peace makers had nightmares but failed to act decisively, is another example. The helplessness of Palestinians in Gaza, caught between Hamas militants and the Israeli military in early 2009, suggests that third-party nonintervention in a humanitarian disaster can be the result of diplomatic deadlock between powers having the ability to shape conflict resolution. As with Darfur, disagreement among great powers about what to do can produce paralysis. It is easy to assert that the outcome—further suffering on the part of innocent victims caught in the crossfire of rival nationalist forces—is unjust. But it is more difficult to identify the party responsible for the injustice.

## Promoting Functional Integration

Some advocates of liberal internationalism are convinced that national interests do not have to figure as the main rationale for international activism; helping promote a closer-knit world is reason enough. The argument is that the processes of **functionalism**, which bring about greater integration and interdependence between states through transnational institutions, interactions, and values, deserve support. There have been several resounding post–World War II success stories involving functional processes. After 1945, liberal internationalism was institutionalized through the United Nations system; the Bretton Woods monetary arrangements; the General Agreement on Tariffs and Trade (GATT), the precursor to the World Trade Organization (WTO); and NATO. The functionalist approach adopted to spur economic and political integration in western Europe, then in all parts of the continent, produced the European Union success story. It can be seen as an instrument of preemptive diplomacy—laying out incentives for nations to cooperate rather than fight with each other.

Functionalism entails multilateralism because it is a joint effort to attain a specific objective. Functionalist incentives can serve to defuse ethnic tensions or to encourage a country to adopt multinational norms by offering access to markets, economic assistance, and membership in a supranational organization like the European Union. Let us cite an example of functionalist success. An ethnic schism in Ukraine in 2004 (reflected in polarized voting in a presidential election and subsequent rival mass demonstrations) was managed by holding up the prospect of both close cooperation with Russia *and* deeper integration into European structures. In sum, "[t]he international community can, through multilateral institutions and nongovernmental organizations, help the new democracies create institutions and pass legislation to protect minorities."[14]

In a study of the "real world order" of the 1990s, two political scientists singled out the experience of democratic countries in carving out "zones of peace"—areas characterized by "freedom from military dangers to national survival and the political impossibility of wars with other democracies."[15] Democracies should intervene to reduce hostilities in the "zones of turmoil." To be sure, in seeking a resolution to the wars in former Yugoslavia, many principles dear to the democratic world conflicted with each other: "preventing ethnic conflict, self-determination, preservation of national borders and stability of government, support for democracy, encouragement of negotiated solutions for conflict, prevention or punishment of aggression, neutrality, or preserving or restoring peace."[16] It is significant, nevertheless, that the long-term objective was to promote integration of all Balkan nations (including Serbia) around a democratic consensus. The same ideals have been held out for Sri Lanka, Afghanistan, and Iraq, and they have in great measure been realized in South Africa.

Optimists envisioning a future with reduced ethnic and religious strife believe strongly in the power of functionalist integration. Pessimists, in contrast, stress the ineluctable pull of fragmentation. Historian John Lewis Gaddis theorized that "the problems we will confront in the post–Cold War world are more likely to arise from competing *processes*—integrationist versus fragmentationist—than from the kinds of competing *ideological visions* that dominated the Cold War."[17] While the integrationist agenda made notable progress in the decade following the end of the Cold War, it was stalled by the fractious international politics that resulted from the 2001 terrorist attacks and the war on terror that the United States pursued in response.

A global financial crisis, an antiglobalization backlash, the return of protectionism in advanced economies, and individual spoilers (such as nationalists in eastern Europe and ethnic warlords in resource-rich areas of the developing world) have combined to give the momentum back to the forces of fragmentation.

## Conclusion

Intervention in other countries' disputes is most credible when it is aimed at furthering the principles most of the world's peoples cherish—human rights, justice, peace, ethnic and religious harmony, self-determination. The problem is that, even in the best of circumstances, interventionism, whether by an international organization or a great power, is likely to be suspect. It will be perceived as serving the third party's interests more than reflecting its stated public aim—conflict resolution. Demilitarizing intervention is always desirable (hence the preference for UN peace-keeping forces), but it is not always realistic. Whether they consist of UN peace-keeping missions; European and African Union initiatives; third-party mediation efforts by the like of Norway (in Sri Lanka), Finland (in Kosovo), South Africa (in Congo), or Canada (in Afghanistan); or great-power military actions of the United States, China, and Russia, there will always be some degree of skepticism about the impartiality of the intervener.

The challenge for both the foreign policy makers in individual countries and the peace-making executives in leading international organizations is simple: how to engage in an internationalism that serves the interests of the community of nations while not being unduly shaped by the balance of power in the world today (which still tilts toward European as well as American interests). In no area is this challenge more put to the test than in dealing with ethnic and religious forms of nationalism. At a minimum, these policy makers should at least heed the injunction of Hippocrates, written in *Epidemics* more than 2,000 years ago: "make a habit of two things—to help, or at least to do no harm." But they should try to be more ambitious than this: deadly ethnic and religious conflicts should have no place in an international system that has otherwise kept the global peace since 1945.

## Discussion Questions

1. Describe the importance of democracy promotion after the cold war. Why was it a controversial policy? Does using smart power avoid controversies?
2. What reasons are commonly given by third parties for intervening in ethnic and religious conflicts? Which of these appears the most persuasive?
3. What form would the ideal method of conflict prevention and conflict resolution take? Preferably, who would carry it out?

## Key Terms

democracy promotion
functionalism
imperial impartiality
isolationism

just war
liberal internationalism
multilateralism
*Pax Americana*

postmodern dilemma
smart power
unilateralism
unjust nonwar

# Notes

1. Fatima Mernissi, *Islam and Democracy: Fear of the Modern World* (New York: Addison-Wesley, 1992), p. 8.
2. Chalmers Johnson, *Blowback: The Costs and Consequences of American Empire* (New York: Owl Books, 2001).
3. See Joseph S. Nye, *Soft Power: The Means to Success in World Politics* (New York: Public Affairs, 2005).
4. The classic study is Benjamin R. Barber, *Jihad vs. McWorld* (New York: Random House, 1996).
5. Hillary Clinton's idea is taken from "A Smarter, More Secure America," the 2007 report of the Commission on Smart Power, Center for Strategic and International Studies, Washington, D.C. The commission cochairs were Richard Armitage and Joseph Nye. See http://www.csis.org/media/csis/pubs/071 106_csissmartpowerreport.pdf. Nye also published an academic treatment of the subject; see Joseph Nye, *The Powers to Lead: Soft, Hard, and Smart* (New York: Oxford University Press, 2008).
6. "A Smarter, More Secure America," p. 27.
7. Randolph C. Kent, "International Humanitarian Crises: Two Decades Before and Two Decades Beyond," *International Affairs*, 80, no. 5 (October 2004), pp. 867–868.
8. Adam Roberts, "Foreword," in Daniel Patrick Moynihan, *Pandaemonium: Ethnicity in International Politics* (New York: Oxford University Press, 1994), p. x.
9. Robert D. Kaplan, "The Coming Anarchy: How Scarcity, Crime, Overpopulation, Tribalism, and Disease Are Rapidly Destroying the Social Fabric of Our Planet," *The Atlantic*, 273, no. 2 (February 1994). A global analysis is Kaplan's *The Coming Anarchy: Shattering the Dreams of the Post–Cold War* (New York: Random House, 2000).
10. James D. Fearon and David D. Laitin, "Ethnicity, Insurgency, and Civil War," *American Political Science Review*, 97, no. 1 (February 2003), p. 88.
11. Greg Sheridan, "Jihad Archipelago," *National Interest*, 78 (Winter 2004–2005), p. 80.
12. Richard K. Betts, "The Delusion of Impartial Intervention," *Foreign Affairs*, 73, no. 6, November/December 1994, pp. 28–29.
13. Neta C. Crawford, "Just War Theory and the U.S. Counterterror War," *Perspectives on Politics*, 1, no. 1 (March 2003), p. 20.
14. Charles A. Kupchan, "Conclusion," in Kupchan, ed., *Nationalism and Nationalities in the New Europe* (Ithaca, N.Y.: Cornell University Press, 1995), p. 187.
15. Max Singer and Aaron Wildavsky, *The Real World Order: Zones of Peace/Zones of Turmoil* (Chatham, N.J.: Chatham House Publishers, 1993), p. 23.
16. Ibid., p. 163.
17. John Lewis Gaddis, *The United States and the End of the Cold War: Implications, Reconsiderations, Provocations* (New York: Oxford University Press, 1992), p. 201. Emphasis added.

# SELECTED BIBLIOGRAPHY

Adeney, Katharine. *Federalism and Ethnic Conflict Regulation in India and Pakistan*. Basingstoke, UK: Palgrave Macmillan, 2007.

Addison, Tony. *Rebuilding Post-Conflict Africa: Reconstruction and Reform*. Helsinki: UNU/WIDER, 1998.

Alexander, Yonah, and Robert A. Friedlander (eds.). *Self-Determination: National, Regional, and Global Dimensions*. Boulder, Colo.: Westview Press, 1980.

Ali, Tariq. *The Clash of Fundamentalisms: Crusades, Jihads, and Modernity*. London: Verso, 2002.

Allen, Beverly. *Rape Warfare: Hidden Genocide in Bosnia-Herzegovina and Croatia*. Minneapolis, Minn.: University of Minnesota Press, 1996.

Alter, Peter. *Nationalism*. London: Edward Arnold, 1989.

Amalrik, Andrei. *Will the Soviet Union Survive Until 1984?* New York: Harper and Row, 1970.

Anderson, Benedict. *Imagined Communities: Reflections on the Origin and Spread of Nationalism*. New York: Verso, 1993.

Azar, Edward E., and John W. Burton (eds.). *International Conflict Resolution*. Boulder, Colo.: Lynne Rienner, 1986.

Bahadur, Kalim (ed.). *South Asia in Transition: Conflicts and Tensions*. New Delhi: Patriot Publishers, 1986.

Bailey, Sydney D. *How Wars End: The United Nations and the Termination of Armed Conflict, 1946–1964*. Oxford, England: Clarendon Press, 1982.

Banac, Ivo. *The National Question in Yugoslavia: Origins, History, Politics*. Ithaca, N.Y.: Cornell University Press, 1993.

Barker, Ernest. *National Character and the Factors in Its Formation*. London: Metheun, 1927.

Barkey, Karen, and Mark von Hagen (eds.). *After Empire: Multiethnic Societies and Nation-Building. The Soviet Union and the Russian, Ottoman, and Habsburg Empires*. Boulder, Colo.: Westview Press, 1997.

Barth, Frederick. *Ethnic Groups and Boundaries: The Social Organization of Cultural Differences*. London: Allen and Unwin, 1970.

Beiner, Ronald (ed.). *Theorizing Nationalism*. Albany, N.Y.: SUNY Press, 1999.

Bertelsen, Judy S. (ed.). *Nonstate Nations in International Politics: Comparative System Analyses*. New York: Praeger, 1977.

Billig, Michael. *Banal Nationalism*. London: Sage Publications, 1997.

Birch, Anthony H. *Nationalism and National Integration*. London: Unwin Hyman, 1989.

Brass, Paul R. *Ethnicity and Nationalism: Theory and Comparison*. Newbury Park, Calif.: Sage Publications, 1991.

Bremmer, Ian, and Ray Taras (eds.). *New States, New Politics: Building the Post-Soviet Nations*. New York: Cambridge University Press, 1997.

Breuilly, John. *Nationalism and the State*. Chicago, Ill.: University of Chicago Press, 1994.

Brown, Michael E. (ed.). *Ethnic Conflict and International Security*. Princeton, N.J.: Princeton University Press, 1993.

Brown, Michael E., and Sumit Ganguly (eds.). *Government Policies and Ethnic Relations in Asia and the Pacific*. Cambridge, Mass.: MIT Press, 1997.

Brubaker, Rogers. *Ethnicity without Groups*. Cambridge, Mass.: Harvard University Press, 2004.

———. *Nationalism Reframed: Nationhood and the National Question in the New Europe*. Cambridge, England: Cambridge University Press, 1996.

Buchanan, Allen. *Secession: The Morality of Political Divorce from Fort Sumter to*

*Lithuania and Quebec.* Boulder, Colo.: Westview Press, 1991.

Buchheit, Lee C. *Secession: The Legitimacy of Self-Determination.* New Haven, Conn.: Yale University Press, 1978.

Caplan, Richard, and John Feffer (eds.). *Europe's New Nationalism: States and Minorities in Conflict.* New York: Oxford University Press, 1996.

Carens, Joseph H. (ed.). *Is Quebec Nationalism Just? Perspectives from Anglophone Canada.* Montreal: McGill–Queen's University Press, 1995.

Carment, David, and Patrick James (eds.). *Wars in the Midst of Peace: The International Politics of Ethnic Conflict.* Pittsburgh, Pa.: University of Pittsburgh Press, 1997.

———. *Peace in the Midst of Wars: Preventing and Managing International Ethnic Conflicts.* Columbia: University of South Carolina Press, 1998.

Carr, Edward Hallett. *Nationalism and After.* London: Macmillan, 1945.

Catherwood, Christopher. *Why the Nations Rage: Killing in the Name of God.* Lanham, Md.: Rowman and Littlefield, 2002.

Chandler, David. *Empire in Denial: The Politics of State-building.* London: Pluto Press, 2006.

Chazan, Naomi (ed.). *Irredentism and International Politics.* Boulder, Colo.: Lynne Rienner, 1991.

Cobban, Alfred. *The Nation State and National Self-Determination.* London: Collins, 1969.

Collier, Paul, V.L. Elliott, Havard Hegre, Anke Hoeffler, Marta Reynal-Querol, and Nicholas Sambanis. *Breaking the Conflict Trap: Civil War and Development Policy.* Washington, D.C.: The World Bank and Oxford University Press, 2003.

———. *Natural Resources and Violent Conflict: Options and Actions,* Washington, D.C.: The World Bank, 2003.

Collier, Paul, and Nicholas Sambanis (eds.). *Understanding Civil Wars: Evidence and Analysis,* Vols. I and II, Washington, D.C.: The World Bank, 2005.

Colton, Timothy, and Robert Legvold. *After the Soviet Union: From Empire to Nations.* New York: W.W. Norton, 1992.

Connor, Walker. *Ethnonationalism: The Quest for Understanding.* Princeton, N.J.: Princeton University Press, 1994.

Conquest, Robert (ed.). *The Last Empire: Nationality and the Soviet Future.* Stanford, Calif.: Hoover Institution Press, 1986.

Crocker, Chester A. *Lashing the Dogs of War.* Washington, D.C.: United States Institute of Peace Press, 2006.

Crocker, Chester A., Fen Osler Hampson, and Pamela Aall (eds.). *Grasping the Nettle: Analyzing Cases of Intractable Conflict.* Washington, D.C.: United States Institute of Peace Press, 2005.

———. *Managing Global Chaos: Sources of and Responses to International Conflict.* Washington, D.C.: United States Institute of Peace Press, 1996.

Crosston, Matthew. *Shadow Separatism: Implications for Democratic Consolidation.* Aldershot, UK: Ashgate, 2004.

Dahbour, Omar, and Micheline R. Ishay (eds.). *The Nationalism Reader.* Atlantic Highlands, N.J.: Humanities Press, 1995.

Dallaire, Romeo. *Shake Hands with the Devil: The Failure of Humanity in Rwanda.* New York: Avalon, 2004.

de Silva, K. M. and S. W. R. de A. Samarasinghe (eds.). *Peace Accords and Ethnic Conflict.* New York: Pinter, 1993.

Deutsch, Karl W. *Nationalism and Social Communication.* Cambridge, Mass.: MIT Press, 1953.

Deutsch, Karl W., and William Foltz (eds.), *Nation-Building.* New York: Atherton Press, 1963.

Diamond, Larry, and Marc F. Plattner (eds.). *Nationalism, Ethnic Conflict, and Democracy.* Baltimore, Md.: Johns Hopkins University Press, 1994.

Doob, Leonard W. *Patriotism and Nationalism: Their Psychological Foundations.* New Haven, Conn.: Yale University Press, 1964.

Doyle, Michael W. *Empires.* Ithaca, N.Y.: Cornell University Press, 1986.

Doyle, Michael W., and Nicholas Sambanis. *Making War and Building Peace: United Nations Peace Operations.* Princeton, N.J.: Princeton University Press, 2006.

Dunlop, John. *The Rise of Russia and the Fall of the Soviet Empire.* Princeton, N.J.: Princeton University Press, 1993.

Earle, Robert L., and John D. Wirth. *Identities in North America: The Search for Community.* Stanford, Calif.: Stanford University Press, 1995.

Eckstein, Harry (ed.). *Internal War: Problems and Approaches.* New York: Free Press, 1964.

Eley, Geof, and Ronald G. Suny (eds.). *Becoming National.* New York: Oxford University Press, 1996.

Enloe, Cynthia H. *Ethnic Conflict and Political Development.* Boston, Mass.: Little Brown, 1973.

Eriksen, Thomas H. *Ethnicity and Nationalism: Anthropological Perspectives.* London: Pluto Press, 1993.

Eriksen, Thomas H. *Ethnicity and Nationalism: Anthropological Perspectives.* London: Pluto Press, 2002.

Esman, Milton J. *Ethnic Politics.* Ithaca, N.Y.: Cornell University Press, 1994.

Esman, Milton J., and Ronald J. Herring (eds.). *Carrots, Sticks and Ethnic Conflict: Rethinking Development Assistance.* Ann Arbor: University of Michigan Press, 2003.

Esman, Milton J., and Shibley Telhami (eds.). *International Organizations and Ethnic Conflict.* Ithaca, N.Y.: Cornell University Press, 1995.

Falk, Richard A. (ed.). *The International Law of Civil War.* Baltimore, Md.: Johns Hopkins University Press, 1971.

Forsythe, David P. *Human Rights in International Relations.* Cambridge, England: Cambridge University Press, 2000.

Franck, Thomas M. *The Power of Legitimacy Among Nations.* Oxford, England: Clarendon Press, 1990.

Gagnon Jr., V. P. *The Myth of Ethnic War: Serbia and Croatia in the 1990s.* Ithaca, N.Y.: Cornell University Press, 2004.

Gall, Carlotta, and Thomas de Waal. *Chechnya: Calamity in the Caucasus.* New York: New York University Press, 1998.

Ganguly, Rajat. *Kin State Intervention in Ethnic Conflicts.* London: Sage, 1998.

Ganguly, Rajat, and Ian Macduff (eds.), *Ethnic Conflict and Secessionism in Asia: Causes, Dynamics, Solutions.* London: Sage, 2003.

Ganguly, Sumit. *The Crisis in Kashmir: Portents of War, Hopes of Peace.* Cambridge, England: Cambridge University Press, 1999.

Ganguly, Sumit, and Devin T. Hagerty. *Fearful Symmetry: India-Pakistan Crises in the Shadow of Nuclear Weapons.* Seattle: University of Washington Press, 2006.

Gans, Chaim. *The Limits of Nationalism.* Cambridge, England: Cambridge University Press, 2003.

Geertz, Clifford. *Old Societies and New States: The Quest for Modernity in Asia and Africa.* Glencoe, Ill.: Free Press, 1963.

Gellner, Ernest. *Conditions of Liberty: Civil Society and its Rivals.* London: Penguin, 1994.

———. *Encounters with Nationalism.* Oxford: Blackwell, 1994.

———. *Nationalism.* London: Orion Books, 1998.

———. *Nations and Nationalism.* Ithaca, N.Y.: Cornell University Press, 1983.

———. *Thought and Change.* Chicago, Ill.: University of Chicago Press, 1978.

Glazer, Nathan, and Daniel P. Moynihan (eds.). *Ethnicity: Theory and Experience.* Cambridge, Mass.: Harvard University Press, 1975.

Gleason, Gregory. *Federalism and Nationalism: The Struggle for Republican Rights in the USSR.* Boulder, Colo.: Westview Press, 1990.

Glenny, Misha. *The Fall of Yugoslavia: The Third Balkan War.* New York: Penguin Books, 1993.

Gottlieb, Gidon. *Nation Against State: A New Approach to Ethnic Conflicts and the Decline of Sovereignty.* New York:

Council on Foreign Relations Press, 1993.

Gourevitch, Philip. *We Wish to Inform You That Tomorrow We Will Be Killed with Our Families: Stories from Rwanda*. New York: Picador Books, 1999.

Grant, Ronald M., and E. Spencer Wellhofer (eds.). *Ethno-Nationalism, Multinational Corporations, and the Modern State*. Denver, Colo.: University of Denver Graduate School of International Studies, 1979.

Greenfeld, Liah. *Nationalism: Five Roads to Modernity*. Cambridge, Mass.: Harvard University Press, 1992.

Griffiths, Stephen I. *Nationalism and Ethnic Conflict: Threats to European Security*. New York: Oxford University Press, 1993.

Guelke, Adrian. *Democracy and Ethnic Conflict: Advancing Peace in Deeply Divided Societies*. Basingstoke, UK: Palgrave Macmillan, 2004.

———. *Terrorism and Global Disorder: Political Violence in the Contemporary World*. New York: I. B. Tauris, 2006.

Gurr, Ted Robert. *Minorities at Risk: A Global View of Ethnopolitical Conflicts*. Washington, D.C.: United States Institute of Peace Press, 1993.

———. *Peoples Versus States: Minorities at Risk in the New Century*. Washington, D.C.: United States Institute of Peace Press, 2000.

Gurr, Ted Robert, and Barbara Harff. *Ethnic Conflict in World Politics*. Boulder, Colo.: Westview Press, 1994.

Gwyn, Richard. *Nationalism Without Walls*. Toronto: McLelland and Stewart, 1996.

Hall, John A. (ed.). *State of the Nation: Ernest Gellner and the Theory of Nationalism*. Cambridge, England: Cambridge University Press, 1998.

Hayes, Carlton J. H. *Essays on Nationalism*. New York: Macmillan, 1926.

———. *The Historical Evolution of Modern Nationalism*. New York: R.R. Smith, 1931.

———. *Nationalism: A Religion*. New York: Macmillan, 1960.

Hechter, Michael. *Containing Nationalism*. New York: Oxford University Press, 2000.

Hedetoft, Ulf, and Mette Hjort (eds.). *Reimagining Belonging*. Minneapolis: University of Minnesota Press, 2001.

Helleiner, Eric, and Andreas Pickel (eds.). *Economic Nationalism in a Globalizing World*. Ithaca, N.Y.: Cornell University Press, 2005.

Heraclides, Alexis. *The Self-Determination of Minorities in International Politics*. London: Frank Cass, 1991.

Hertz, Frederick. *Nationality in History and Politics: A Study of the Psychology and Sociology of National Sentiment and Character*. New York: Oxford University Press, 1944.

Hobsbawm, E. J. *Nations and Nationalism Since 1780: Programme, Myth, Reality*. New York: Cambridge University Press, 1993.

Hobson, John A. *Imperialism: A Study*. Ann Arbor: University of Michigan Press, 1965.

Horowitz, Donald L. *Ethnic Groups in Conflict*. Berkeley: University of California Press, 1985.

Huntington, Samuel P. *The Clash of Civilizations and the Remaking of World Order*. New York: Simon and Schuster, 1996.

———. *Who Are We: The Challenges to America's National Identity*. New York: Simon and Schuster, 2005.

Hutchinson, John, and Anthony D. Smith (eds.). *Nationalism*. New York: Oxford University Press, 1994.

Ignatieff, Michael. *Blood and Belonging: Journeys into the New Nationalism*. New York: Farrar, Straus, and Giroux, 1993.

———. *Virtual War: Kosovo and Beyond*. New York: Henry Holt, 2000.

———. *The Warrior's Honor: Ethnic War and the Modern Conscience*. New York: Henry Holt, 1998.

Jackson, Peter, and Jan Penrose (eds.). *Constructions of Race, Place and Nation*. London: UCL Press, 1993.

Jackson, Robert H. *Quasi-States: Sovereignty, International Relations, and the Third World*. Cambridge, England: Cambridge University Press, 1990.

Juergensmeyer, Mark. *The New Cold War? Religious Nationalism Confronts the Secular State*. Berkeley: University of California Press, 1993.

———. *Terror in the Mind of God*. Berkeley: University of California Press, 2000.

Jusdanis, Gregory. *The Necessary Nation*. Princeton, N.J.: Princeton University Press, 2001.

Kadian, Rajesh. *India's Sri Lanka Fiasco: Peacekeepers at War*. New Delhi: Vision Books, 1990.

Kahler, Miles, and Barbara Walter (eds.). *Territoriality and Conflict in an Era of Globalization*. Cambridge, England: Cambridge University Press, 2006.

Kaldor, Mary. *New and Old Wars: Organized Violence in a Global Era*. Cambridge, England: Polity Press, 2006.

Kamenka, Eugene (ed.). *Nationalism: The Nature and Evolution of an Idea*. London: Edward Arnold, 1976.

Kann, Robert A. *The Multinational Empire: Nationalism and National Reform in the Habsburg Monarchy 1848–1918*, 2 vols. New York: Columbia University Press, 1950.

Kaplan, Robert D. *Balkan Ghosts: A Journey Through History*. New York: Vintage Books, 1994.

———. *The Coming Anarchy: Shattering the Dreams of the Post–Cold War*. New York: Random House, 2000.

———. *The Ends of the Earth: A Journey at the Dawn of the 21st Century*. New York: Random House, 1996.

Karklins, Rasma. *Ethnopolitics and Transition to Democracy: The Collapse of the USSR and Latvia*. Washington, D.C.: Woodrow Wilson Center Press, 1994.

Kaufman, Stuart J. *Modern Hatreds: The Symbolic Politics of Ethnic War*. Ithaca, N.Y.: Cornell University Press, 2001.

Kedourie, Elie. *Nationalism*. London: Hutchison, 1960.

Kellas, James G. *The Politics of Nationalism and Ethnicity*. London: Macmillan, 1991.

Keyes, Charles F. (ed.). *Ethnic Change*. Seattle: University of Washington Press, 1981.

King, Charles, and Neil J. Melvin (eds.). *Nations Abroad: Diaspora Politics and International Relations in the Former Soviet Union*. Boulder, Colo.: Westview Press, 1998.

Kinzer, Stephen. *Overthrow: America's Century of Regime Change from Hawaii to Iraq*. New York: Times Books, 2006.

Kodikara, Shelton U. (ed.). *South Asian Strategic Issues: Sri Lankan Perspectives*. New Delhi: Sage, 1990.

Kohn, Hans. *The Idea of Nationalism: A Study in Its Origins and Background*. New York: Collier Books, 1969.

———. *Nationalism and Realism: 1852–1879*. Princeton, N.J.: Van Nostrand, 1968.

———. *Prophets and Peoples: Studies in Nineteenth Century Nationalisms*. London: Collier Books, 1969.

Kolsto, Pal. *Political Construction Sites: Nation-Building in Russia and the Post-Soviet States*. Boulder, Colo.: Westview Press, 2000.

Krasner, Stephen D. *Sovereignty: Organized Hypocrisy*. Princeton, N.J.: Princeton University Press, 1999.

Kupchan, Charles A. (ed.). *Nationalism and Nationalities in the New Europe*. Ithaca, N.Y.: Cornell University Press, 1995.

Kymlicka, Will. *Multicultural Citizenship*. Oxford, England: Clarendon Press, 1996.

———. *Politics in the Vernacular: Nationalism, Multiculturalism, and Citizenship*. New York: Oxford University Press, 2000.

Laitin, David. *Language Repertoires and State Construction in Africa*. Cambridge, England: Cambridge University Press, 2007.

Lake, David A., and Donald Rothchild (eds.). *The International Spread of Ethnic Conflict: Fear, Diffusion, and Escalation*. Princeton, N.J.: Princeton University Press, 1998.

Laqueur, Walter. *Black Hundred: The Rise of the Extreme Right in Russia*. New York: Harper Perennial, 1994.

Lemarchand, René. *Burundi: Ethnic Conflict and Genocide*. Cambridge,

England: Cambridge University Press, 1996.

Lemco, Jonathan. *Turmoil in the Peaceable Kingdom: The Quebec Sovereignty Movement and Its Implications for Canada and the United States.* Toronto: University of Toronto Press, 1994.

Leone, Bruno (ed.). *Nationalism.* St. Paul, Minn.: Greenhaven Press, 1986.

Lieven, Anatol. *America Right or Wrong: An Anatomy of American Nationalism.* New York: Oxford University Press, 2005.

————. *Chechnya: Tombstone of Russian Power.* New Haven, Conn.: Yale University Press, 1998.

Lijphart, Arend. *Democracy in Plural Societies.* New Haven, Conn.: Yale University Press, 1977.

Little, Richard. *Intervention: External Involvement in Civil Wars.* London: Martin Robertson, 1975.

Lund, Michael S. *Preventing Violent Conflicts: A Strategy for Preventive Diplomacy.* Washington, D.C.: United States Institute of Peace Press, 1996.

Lustick, Ian S. *Unsettled States, Disputed Lands: Britain and Ireland, France and Algeria, Israel and the West Bank–Gaza.* Ithaca, N.Y.: Cornell University Press, 1993.

Malcolm, Noel. *Kosovo: A Short History.* New York: Harper Perennial, 1999.

Mann, Michael. *The Dark Side of Democracy: Explaining Ethnic Cleansing.* Cambridge, England: Cambridge University Press, 2004.

Manogaran, Chelvadurai. *Ethnic Conflict and Reconciliation in Sri Lanka.* Honolulu: University of Hawaii Press, 1987.

Mansfield, Edward D., and Jack Snyder. *Electing to Fight: Why Emerging Democracies Go to War.* Cambridge, Mass.: The MIT Press, 2007.

May, Stephen, Tariq Modood, and Judith Squires (eds.). *Ethnicity, Nationalism, and Minority Rights.* Cambridge, England: Cambridge University Press, 2004.

Mayall, James. *Nationalism and International Society.* New York: Cambridge University Press, 1990.

————. *The New Interventionism 1991–1994: United Nations Experience in Cambodia, Former Yugoslavia & Somalia.* Cambridge, England: Cambridge University Press, 1996.

Mayer, Tamar (ed.). *Gender Ironies of Nationalism: Sexing the Nation.* London: Routledge, 2000.

Melvern, Linda. *Conspiracy to Murder: The Rwandan Genocide.* London: Verso Books, 2006.

Miall, Hugh (ed.). *Minority Rights in Europe: Prospects for a Transitional Regime.* New York: Council on Foreign Relations Press, 1995.

Midlarsky, Manus I. (ed.). *The Internationalization of Communal Strife.* London: Routledge, 1992.

Miller, David. *On Nationality.* Oxford, England: Clarendon Press, 1995.

Mills, Nicolaus, and Kira Brunner (eds.). *The New Killing Fields: Massacre and the Politics of Intervention.* New York: Basic Books, 2002.

Montville, J. (ed.). *Conflict and Peacemaking in Multiethnic Societies.* Toronto: Lexington, 1990.

Motyl, Alexander J. (ed.). *Encyclopedia of Nationalism.* New York: Academic Press, 2000.

———— (ed.). *The Post–Soviet Nations: Perspectives on the Demise of the USSR.* New York: Columbia University Press, 1992.

Moynihan, Daniel Patrick. *Pandaemonium: Ethnicity in International Politics.* New York: Oxford University Press, 1994.

Nairn, Tom. *The Break-Up of Britain: Crisis and Neo-Nationalism.* London: Verso, 1981.

Neuberger, Benjamin. *National Self-Determination in Postcolonial Africa.* Boulder, Colo.: Lynne Rienner, 1986.

Niebuhr, Reinhold. *The Structure of Nations and Empires.* New York: Charles Scribner's Sons, 1959.

Nimni, Ephraim. *Marxism and Nationalism: Theoretical Origins of a Political Crisis.* Boulder, Colo.: Pluto Press, 1991.

Nincic, Djura. *The Problem of Sovereignty in the Charter and in the Practice of the*

*United Nations*. The Hague, Netherlands: Martinus Nijhoff, 1970.

Oberschall, Anthony. *Conflict and Peace Building in Divided Societies: Responses to Ethnic Violence*. London: Routledge, 2007.

O'Brien, Conor Cruise. *God Land: Reflections on Religion and Nationalism*. Cambridge, Mass.: Harvard University Press, 1988.

Ozkirimli, Umut. *Contemporary Debates on Nationalism: A Critical Engagement*. London: Palgrave, 2005.

———. *Theories of Nationalism: A Critical Introduction*. London: Palgrave, 2000.

Parekh, Bhiku. *Rethinking Multiculturalism: Cultural Diversity and Political Theory*. London: Palgrave, 2000.

Paris, Roland. *At War's End: Building Peace After Civil Conflict*. Cambridge, England: Cambridge University Press, 2004.

Pfaff, William. *The Wrath of Nations: Civilization and the Furies of Nationalism*. New York: Touchstone Books, 1993.

Phadnis, Urmila, and Rajat Ganguly. *Ethnicity and Nation-Building in South Asia*. London: Sage Publications, 2001.

Pond, Elizabeth. *Endgame in the Balkans: Regime Change, European Style*. Washington, D.C.: The Brookings Institution Press, 2006.

Ponnampalam, S. *Sri Lanka: The National Question and the Tamil Liberation Struggle*. London: Zed Books, 1983.

Poole, Ross. *Nation and Identity*. London: Routledge, 1999.

Premdas, Ralph, R., S. W. R. de A. Samarasinghe, and Alan B. Anderson (eds.), *Secessionist Movements in Comparative Perspective*. New York: St. Martin's, 1990.

Prunier, Gerard. *Darfur: The Ambiguous Genocide*. Ithaca, N.Y.: Cornell University Press, 2005.

Ramet, Sabarina P. *Balkan Babel*. Boulder, Colo.: Westview Press, 1999.

———. *Nationalism and Federalism in Yugoslavia, 1962–1991*, 2nd ed. Bloomington: University of Indiana Press, 1992.

Rezun, Miron (ed.). *Nationalism and the Breakup of an Empire: Russia and Its Periphery*. Westport, Conn.: Praeger, 1992.

Roberts, Michael (ed.). *Collective Identities, Nationalism, and Protest in Modern Sri Lanka*. Colombo, Sri Lanka: Marga Institute, 1979.

Robertson, Geoffrey. *Crimes Against Humanity: The Struggle for Global Justice*. London: Penguin Books, 1999.

Rosenau, James N. (ed.). *International Aspects of Civil Strife*. Princeton, N.J.: Princeton University Press, 1964.

——— (ed.). *Linkage Politics: Essays on the Convergence of National and International Systems*. New York: Free Press, 1969.

Rotberg, Robert I. *Worst of the Worst: Dealing with Repressive and Rogue Nations*. Washington, D.C.: The Brookings Institution Press, 2007.

Rothschild, Joseph. *Ethnopolitics: A Conceptual Framework*. New York: Columbia University Press, 1981.

Rubin, Barnett R., and Jack Snyder (eds.). *Post-Soviet Political Order: Conflict and State-Building*. London: Routledge, 1998.

Rudolph, Richard L., and David F. Good (eds.). *Nationalism and Empire: The Habsburg Monarchy and the Soviet Union*. New York: St. Martin's, 1992.

Rupesinghe, Kumar (ed.). *Negotiating Peace in Sri Lanka: Efforts, Failures, and Lessons*. London: International Alert, 1998.

Ryan, Stephen. *Ethnic Conflict and International Relations*, 2nd ed. Aldershot, England: Dartmouth, 1995.

Said, Abdul A., and Luiz R. Simmons (eds.). *Ethnicity in an International Context*. New Brunswick, N.J.: Transaction Books, 1976.

Saideman, Stephen M. *The Ties That Divide: Ethnic Politics, Foreign Policy, and International Conflict*. New York: Columbia University Press, 2001.

Saideman, Stephen M., and R. William Ayres, *For Kin or Country: Xenophobia,*

*Nationalism, and War.* New York: Columbia University Press, 2008.

Searle-White, Joshua. *The Psychology of Nationalism.* London: Palgrave, 2001.

Seers, Dudley. *The Political Economy of Nationalism.* New York: Oxford University Press, 1983.

Sen, Amartya. *Identity and Violence: The Illusion of Destiny.* New York: W.W. Norton, 2006.

Seton-Watson, Hugh. *Nations and States: An Enquiry into the Origins of Nations and the Politics of Nationalism.* Boulder, Colo.: Westview Press, 1977.

———. *The New Imperialism.* Totowa, N.J.: Rowman and Littlefield, 1971.

Shafer, Boyd C. *Faces of Nationalism.* New York: Harcourt, Brace, Jovanovich, 1972.

———. *Nationalism: Myth and Reality.* New York: Harcourt, Brace and World, 1955.

Shawcross, William. *Deliver Us from Evil: Peacekeepers, Warlords and a World of Endless Conflict.* New York: Simon and Schuster, 2000.

Shiels, Frederick L. (ed.). *Ethnic Separatism and World Politics.* Lanham, Md.: University Press of America, 1984.

Singer, P. W. *Children at War.* Berkeley: University of California Press, 2006.

Sisk, Timothy D. *Power Sharing and International Mediation in Ethnic Conflicts.* Washington, D.C.: United States Institute of Peace Press, 1996.

Smith, Anthony D. *The Ethnic Origins of Nations.* Oxford, England: Basil Blackwell, 1986.

———. *The Ethnic Revival.* Cambridge, England: Cambridge University Press, 1981.

———. *National Identity.* Reno: University of Nevada Press, 1991.

———. *Nationalism and Modernism: A Critical Survey of Recent Theories of Nations and Nationalism.* London: Routledge, 1998.

———. *Nationalism in the Twentieth Century.* New York: New York University Press, 1979.

———. *Theories of Nationalism.* New York: Holmes & Meier, 1983.

Smith, Graham (ed.). *The Nationalities Question in the Post-Soviet States.* London: Longman, 1996.

Snyder, Jack. *From Voting to Violence: Democratization and Nationalist Conflict.* New York: W.W. Norton & Company, 2000.

———. *Myths of Empire: Domestic Politics and International Ambition.* Ithaca, N.Y.: Cornell University Press, 1991.

Snyder, Louis L. *Encyclopedia of Nationalism.* New York: Paragon House, 1990.

———. *Macro-Nationalisms: A History of the Pan-Movements.* Westport, Conn.: Greenwood Press, 1984.

———. *The Meaning of Nationalism.* New Brunswick, N.J.: Rutgers University Press, 1954.

Spencer, Metta (ed.). *Separatism: Democracy and Disintegration.* Lanham, Md.: Rowman and Littlefield, 1998.

Stedman, Stephen J., Donald Rothchild, and Elizabeth Cousens (eds.). *Ending Civil Wars: The Implementation of Peace Agreements.* Boulder, Colo.: Lynne Rienner, 2002.

Stern, Jessica. *Terror in the Name of God: Why Religious Militants Kill.* New York: HarperCollins, 2003.

Strachey, John. *The End of Empire.* New York: Frederick Praeger, 1966.

Suhrke, Astri, and Lela Garner Noble (eds.). *Ethnic Conflict and International Relations.* New York: Praeger, 1977.

Sureda, A. Rigo. *The Evolution of the Right of Self-Determination: A Study of United Nations Practice.* Leiden, The Netherlands: A.W. Sijthoff, 1973.

Szporluk, Roman. *Communism and Nationalism.* New York: Oxford University Press, 1988.

Szporluk, Roman (ed.). *National Identity and Ethnicity in Russia and the New States of Eurasia.* Armonk, N.Y.: M.E. Sharpe, 1994.

Tamir, Yael. *Liberal Nationalism.* Princeton, N.J.: Princeton University Press, 1993.

Taras, Ray. *Europe Old and New: Transnationalism, Belonging, Xenophobia.* Lanham, Md.: Rowman and Littlefield, 2009.

————. *Liberal and Illiberal Nationalisms.* London: Palgrave, 2002.

Taylor, Charles. *Reconciling the Solitudes: Essays on Canadian Federalism and Nationalism.* Montreal: McGill–Queen's University Press, 1993.

Teich, Mikulas, and Roy Porter. *The National Question in Europe in Historical Context.* New York: Cambridge University Press, 1993.

Thomas, Raju G. C. (ed.). *Yugoslavia Unraveled: Sovereignty, Self-Determination, Intervention.* New York: Lexington Books, 2003.

Thomas, Robert. *The Politics of Serbia in the 1990s.* New York: Columbia University Press, 1999.

Thompson, D. L., and D. Ronen (eds.). *Ethnicity, Politics, and Development.* Boulder, Colo.: Lynne Rienner, 1986.

Tishkov, Valery. *Ethnicity, Nationalism, and Conflict in and After the Soviet Union: The Mind Aflame.* Thousand Oaks, Calif.: Sage, 1997.

Tolz, Vera. *Russia.* London: Arnold, 2001.

Touval, S., and I. William Zartman (eds.). *International Mediation in Theory and Practice.* Washington, D.C.: SAIS, 1985.

Wachtel, Andrew Baruch. *Making a Nation, Breaking a Nation: Literature and Cultural Politics in Yugoslavia.* Stanford, Calif.: Stanford University Press, 1998.

Walter, Barbara F., and Jack Snyder (eds.). *Civil Wars, Insecurity, and Intervention.* New York: Columbia University Press, 1999.

Welliver, Timothy K. (ed.). *African Nationalism and Independence.* Hamden, Conn.: Garland Publishing, 1993.

Wheeler, Nicholas J. *Saving Strangers: Humanitarian Intervention in International Society.* New York: Oxford University Press, 2003.

Wiener, Myron. *The Global Migration Crisis: Challenge to States and to Human Rights.* New York: HarperCollins, 1995.

Wimmer, Andreas. *Nationalist Exclusion and Ethnic Conflict: Shadows of Modernity.* Cambridge, England: Cambridge University Press, 2002.

Wolff, Stefan. *Ethnic Conflict: A Global Perspective.* Oxford, England: Oxford University Press, 2006.

Young, M. Crawford. *The Politics of Cultural Pluralism.* Madison: University of Wisconsin Press, 1976.

————. *The Rising Tide of Cultural Pluralism: The Nation-State at Bay?* Madison: University of Wisconsin Press, 1993.

Young, Oran. *The Intermediaries: Third Parties in International Crises.* Princeton, N.J.: Princeton University Press, 1976.

Young, Robert A. *The Secession of Quebec and the Future of Canada.* Montreal: McGill–Queen's University Press, 1995.

Zartman, I. William (ed.). *Collapsed States: The Disintegration and Restoration of Legitimate Authority.* Boulder, Colo.: Lynne Rienner, 1995.

Znaniecki, Florian. *Modern Nationalities: A Sociological Study.* Westport, Conn.: Greenwood Press, 1973.

Zwick, Peter. *National Communism.* Boulder, Colo.: Westview Press, 1983.

# GLOSSARY

**Africa's first world war** the complex ethnic conflict in Congo that has involved intervention by many other African countries.

**African National Congress (ANC)** the first African liberation movement, formed in 1912 in response to the creation of the South African Union which entrenched white minority rule, to protect the rights of blacks.

**African Union** a continental union of all African states except Morocco founded in South Africa in 2002.

**African Union–United Nations Hybrid Operation in Darfur (UNAMID)** joint African Union and United Nations peacekeeping mission to bring stability to the war-torn Darfur region of Sudan.

**Affective motives** motives for partisan external intervention in ethnic conflicts that are based more on reasons of justice, humanitarian concerns, ethnic affinity, etc., rather than narrow calculations of gains and losses and costs and benefits.

**All Party Conference** a series of meetings between the Sri Lankan government and major Tamil parties held through-out 1984 to discuss the Parthasarathy proposals.

**Animism** a belief in the existence of spirits in humans and objects.

**Apartheid** policy of racial segregation and discrimination against nonwhite people as practiced in South Africa by the white minority supremacist regimes until the early 1990s.

**Arabization** a growing cultural influence on a non-Arab area that gradually changes it into one that speaks Arabic and/or incorporates Arab culture; it also involves de-westernization and promotes the usage of Arabic.

**Arbitration** process whereby the adversaries agree to hand over the determination of a final settlement of their dispute to an external third party and commit themselves to accepting the third party's decision as legally binding and authoritative.

**Assimilation** cultural absorption of minority identity groups into the main or dominant cultural body.

**Autonomy** substantial amount of freedom short of independence.

**Bhikkhus** the Buddhist clergy in Sri Lanka.

**Biafra** an eastern region of Nigeria with many Christian peoples who fought a bitter war for independence in the late 1960s before being defeated by the Muslim-dominated Nigerian federal army.

**Bill 101** an act passed by the Quebec legislature in 1976 that made French the official language of work and education in the province. It is also known as the Charter of the French Language.

**Bloc Québécois** a Quebec nationalist party that contests Canada's federal elections while committing itself to Quebec's separation from Canada.

**Bonn Agreement** UN-sponsored talks in Germany on an Afghan government that would represent a broad range of ethnic groups and regions.

**British North America (BNA) Act** passed in 1867, it served as Canada's constitution until 1982.

**Burghers** very small ethnic minority in Sri Lanka. They are of mixed European and Sri Lankan descent, practice Christianity, and mostly speak English. They are mostly concentrated in Colombo and are economically fairly prosperous.

**Bystander apathy** suggests that the greater the number of onlookers in a situation in which a suffering or victimized person requires urgent attention and assistance, the greater will be the diffusion of responsibility.

**Cease-fire** agreement among adversaries to temporarily halt military operations against each other.

**Centrifugal tendencies** political pressures toward decentralization of, devolution in, and even secession from centralized authority.

**Chechens** an ethnic group living in the north Caucasus that has fought for separation from Russia. They became Muslims in the nineteenth century and uphold a warrior tradition.

**Child soldiers** children as soldiers.

**Colonel Karuna** a top LTTE commander from Batticaloa-Amparai district; organized a split from the main LTTE.

**Collective Security** principle enshrined in the UN Charter under Chapter VII that allows the UN members, acting collectively through the Security Council, to safeguard national and international security when breaches of peace and acts of aggression take place.

**Commonwealth of Independent States (CIS)** a loose association of 12 former Soviet republics after 1991 (the three Baltic states refused to join). It has little real power, structure, or status.

**Complex humanitarian emergency (CHE)** unimaginable levels of suffering for civilian populations caught in the crossfire of conflict.

**Complex political emergency** develops as a result of state failure and collapse.

**Confidence Building Measures (CBMs)** policies and practices that build mutual trust and confidence among adversaries.

**Conflict contagion** spread of conflicts across borders.

**Consociational democracy** a type of democratic system that favors executive power sharing and the formation of grand coalition governments, formal and informal separation of powers between the various branches of government, bicameral legislature with minority groups' representation in the upper chamber, multiple party system, elections based on proportional representation, territorial and nonterritorial federalism, and written constitution with difficult amendment procedures.

**Constitutive Theory** the act of diplomatic recognition by itself confers statehood and legal personality on a country.

**Contact Group on Bosnia** a consultative group on Bosnia in the early 1990s made up of the United States, Britain, France, Germany, and Russia.

**Constructivism** the school of thought that regards ethnic identity as a product of enduring social constructions that is the result of human actions and choices.

**Cossacks** ethnically diverse "horse guards of the Russian steppe." Used as a political term, it refers to defenders of a Great Russia.

**Council of Europe** an intergovernmental organization that includes nearly all states in Western, Central, and Eastern Europe (including Russia). It is concerned primarily with respect for human rights in member states.

**Counterinsurgency operations (COIN)** military offensive undertaken to destroy the fighting capability of underground insurgent organizations.

**Dayton Accords** these were hammered out by representatives of Bosnia-Herzegovina and Yugoslavia in November 1995 in Dayton, Ohio, under the sponsorship of the United States. These set forth a plan for Bosnia's future. It was to be divided into a Bosnian Muslim and Croatian Federation encompassing 51 percent of the country's territory, and a Republika Srpska having 49 percent. A three-person presidency (one from each of the constituent parts) was also established.

**Declaratory theory of recognition** posits that the formal recognition of statehood by outside countries is enough to bring a new state into legal existence.

**Democracy promotion** spreading democratic values, procedures, and institutions around the world.

**Demonstration effect** the powerful emulative effect that ethnic conflict in one state or region has on similar conflicts in other states and regions.

**Diaspora communities** diaspora communities are found in foreign countries, caused by population migrations.

**Dirty civil wars** deep-rooted, highly internationalized, and extremely violent civil wars with high civilian casualties and often with a history of failed negotiations, mediation, and peace agreements.

**Distinct society** the most important demand in the 1990s that Quebec asked to have recognized by the rest of Canada in return for Quebec's accession to the 1982 Canadian constitution.

**Doctrine of state sovereignty** international fundamental norm to justify survival of an existing state.

**Durham Report** named after a British governor general, it recommended responsible government for Canada while urging assimilation of French speakers into English-speaking society.

**Dynastic sovereignty** government should be based on the principle of dynastic succession of leaders.

**Effectivity principle** the legal recognition of an existing de facto situation, for example, eventual legal acceptance of a country's unilateral declaration of independence.

**Empire** a great power which, as a result of conquest and colonization, has distributed political power and economic wealth unevenly between a core nation and disadvantaged peripheral ones.

**Ethnic cleansing** a systematic and deliberate policy that aims to create ethnically homogeneous territorial spaces by killing and expelling members belonging to other ethnic groups from that territory.

**Ethnic community** a large or small group of people united by a common inherited culture, racial similarity, common religion, belief in a common history and ancestry and who exhibit a strong psychological sentiment of belonging to the group.

**Ethnic conflict** confrontation (usually violent) between ethnic groups.

**Ethnic group** large or small cultural group with a distinct language, religion, and history and that exhibits strong sentiment of separate and distinct group identity.

**Ethnic identity** identity that an individual acquires from being a member of an ethnic group.

**Ethnic kin** co-nationals of an ethnic group usually residing in a neighboring state.

**Ethnic nation** a nation based upon the spirit of the cultural community that includes, among other things, common language, religion, customs, traditions, and history.

**Ethnic political movement** a movement that attempts to represent the collective consciousness and aspirations of the entire community defined on the basis of common ethnicity.

**Ethnic solidarity** the duties and responsibilities of members toward their ethnic groups.

**Ethno-religious conflict** a clash of cultures rooted in both objective and psychological factors that fuse lineage with religious belief-system.

**Ethno-religious group** a group where ethnic and religious identities are inseparable in the making of community.

**Ethnoterrorism** use of terrorist tactics by disgruntled ethnic groups.

**Failed states** generally exhibit most or all of the following characteristics: the government's social contract with its citizens is severely weakened; the government relies mainly on force and coercion to enforce its existing authority; the government's political legitimacy is highly compromised; the government is in control of only a small fraction of the state's territory and borders; and the government's capacity to deliver public goods and services to all citizens is severely restricted, with warlords and nonstate entities having taken over most of this function.

**Facilitation** the involvement of an external third party in the negotiation process between two or more adversaries in order to help them to perceive their dispute as a "problem" that they share and over which they need to cooperate if it has to be resolved rather than as a "conflict" that divides them. In this process, the third party's role is nonhierarchical, noncoercive, and neutral (the third party does not impose a settlement on the adversaries or try to influence it in any way; the ultimate settlement must come from the adversaries themselves).

**Fifty-Fifty formula** demand made by Sri Lankan Tamils before the Soulbury Commission that 50 percent of the seats in the parliament of an independent Sri Lanka should be reserved for the Sinhalese and the remaining 50 percent for the Sri Lankan Tamils and other ethnic minorities; this proposal was rejected by the Soulbury Commission.

**Forced expulsion** the forcible removal of people belonging to a particular ethnic group from a particular territory by members of a rival group in order to create an ethnically homogeneous territorial space.

**Functionalism** bringing about greater integration between states and fostering transnational institutions, interactions, and values by focusing on carrying out specific tasks.

**Gangster states** breakaway enclaves rich in a natural resource run by warlords.

**Genocidal mass rape** sexual violence directed against women for the deliberate extermination of an ethnic group or nation.

**Genocide** a systematic program of killing and massacre aimed at the complete and total extermination of an ethnic or national group.

**Guns-for-drugs cycle** narcotics trade practiced by terrorist groups to finance their military operations.

**Hague War Crimes Tribunal** a court set up by Western states in the Netherlands to try indicted war criminals involved in the 1990s Balkan wars.

**Halfway-house states** an outbreak of ethnic conflict in a weak state, though state authority has not completely collapsed.

**Hegemonic exchange** a system of state-ethnic group relations, found usually in parts of Africa, where a quasi autonomous state and various ethnoregional interests engage, on the basis of commonly accepted procedural norms and rules, in a process of mutual accommodation.

**Homeland societies** ethnic groups that are longtime occupants of a particular territory and therefore claim an exclusive as well as a moral right to rule it.

**Hurting stalemate** a situation in a conflict where the military power of the adversaries is more or less balanced; the adversaries may then become inclined to seek a peaceful solution to their dispute as there would be little more to be gained from fighting.

**Hutus** the most populous ethnic group found in Central Africa, they have usually been governed over by the rival Tutsi group.

**Ideological theory of recognition** involves using ideological criteria, for example, that it is democratic or capitalist, to determine whether the government of a new state can pass a political eligibility test.

**Imperial impartiality** the idea that the use of force by a superpower like the United States is the best way of securing an impartial outcome in a regional conflict.

**Imperialism** see *Empire*.

**Implementation Force (IFOR)** Implementation Force for Bosnia deployed by NATO in December 1995 to carry out peacekeeping there.

**Indian doctrine of regional security** Indian assertion in the early 1980s that if a South Asian state requires external assistance to deal with serious internal conflict, then it should seek such help from within the region including from India, and that any attempt to exclude India in such circumstances would be considered an overt anti-Indian move and will not be tolerated.

**Indian Peace-Keeping Force (IPKF)** to oversee the implementation of the peace provisions in the accord to resolve ethnic conflict in Sri Lanka.

**Indian Tamils** one of the two groups of the Tamil population concentrated in the drier northern and eastern parts of Sri Lanka; originated from indentured plantation workers brought to the island by British tea planters during the nineteenth and early twentieth centuries.

**Indo–Sri Lankan Accord** agreement signed between India and Sri Lanka in July 1987 that attempted to resolve the ethnic conflict in Sri Lanka. Among other things, the accord committed an Indian Peace Keeping Force (IPKF) to Sri Lanka to oversee the implementation of the peace provisions in the accord.

**Inkatha** Zulu political and cultural organization.

**Instrumental motives** motives for partisan external intervention in ethnic conflicts that are based on narrow calculations of gains and losses and costs and benefits.

**Instrumentalism** the school of thought that regards ethnic identity as essentially a tool that is used to obtain material or instrumental gains for an ethnic group and its leaders.

**Interahamwe** former Hutu soldiers from Rwanda accused of genocide against the Tutsis. They remained a military presence in Central Africa, especially Congo, in the late 1990s.

**Interculturalism** a model in which French–Canadian society is at the center of a wheel with spokes connecting it with its minority groups.

**Interim Self Governing Authority (ISGA)** a proposal issued on October 2003 by the rebel Liberation Tigers of Tamil Eelam (LTTE) of Sri Lanka for power sharing in the north and east of Sri Lanka.

**Internal self-determination** the ability to pursue the political, economic, and cultural development of a nation within an existing state.

**Internally displaced persons (IDPs)** people who have been forced to resettle elsewhere within their own country where conditions are safer.

**International Government Organizations (IGOs)** international organizations whose members are states.

**International Nongovernmental Organizations (INGOs)** internationally-operating nongovernment organizations which are involved in transnational networks.

**International normative regime** norms, rules, procedure, and principles of behavior within the international system that govern interstate relations and membership in that system.

**International Security Assistance Force (ISAF)** established as a NATO-led security and development mission for Afghanistan; represented NATO's first ever operational mission outside Europe.

**Irredentism** claim to territory belonging to and controlled by a foreign power based on historical (territory historically belonged to claimant) and cultural (ethnic affinity of the claimant with the local population) arguments.

**Islamists** Islamic fundamentalists.

**Isolationism** a recurring idea in American foreign policy that the United States should reduce its involvement in international politics as much as possible and concentrate on domestic issues.

**Ituri District** a resource-rich district in northeastern Congo.

**Janjaweed ("devils on horseback")** a fearsome militia, supplied and backed by the Sudanese army, made up of Arab speakers from Darfur and neighboring Chad.

**Jihadists** religious warriors.

**Just war** "a war can only be considered just if both its cause and conduct are just."

**Khasavyurt Accord** signed by Russian and Chechen representatives in August 1996, it ended the 1994–1996 conflict between the sides and called for a referendum in Chechnya on its future status after a five-year interval.

**Kosovo Force (KFOR)** Kosovo Force set up by NATO in 1999 to enforce peacekeeping in the province after the NATO military campaign against Yugoslavia.

**Kosovo Liberation Army (KLA; UCK in Albanian)** a paramilitary organization of Albanian Muslims fighting against Serbia for Kosovo's independence in the 1990s. It was also involved in terrorist attacks against local Serbs.

**Kto kovo Question** a Russian expression referring to who is taking advantage of whom.

**Liberal Internationalism** the world view that shared liberal democratic values can override conflicts and bring peace and liberalism to the international system. The United States is given a special role to play in imbuing such a normative consensus.

**Liberation Tigers of Tamil Eelam (LTTE)** the most powerful Sri Lankan Tamil secessionist insurgent organization operating in Sri Lanka. It is led by the charismatic Velupillai Prabhakaran.

**Loya Jirga** Afghani grand assembly.

**Maastricht option** a form of European unification in which some powers are progressively transferred to the center while others are devolved to the regions; it can provide a way by which minorities could gain autonomy within existing states.

**Malays** very small ethnic minority in Sri Lanka. They are descended from the Malay traders and guards brought to Sri Lanka during the colonial period.

**Managed ethnic heterogeneity** a group of widely articulated conflict-mitigating doctrines, practices, principles, strategies, and agreements governing intergroup relations in heterogeneous states and providing guidelines regarding how best to respond to ethnopolitical crises and conflicts.

**Matrioshka nationalism** the nationalism of larger nations has a demonstration effect on smaller nations which advance the same claims and demands. It was used to describe why the Soviet Union disintegrated in an uncontrolled spiral of nationalisms (from the wooden brightly painted, nested matrioshka dolls).

**Mediation** the engagement of an external third party in a process of dialogue with the adversaries in an effort to narrow down their differences and eventually reach a mutually acceptable compromise solution to their dispute. In this process, the third party's role may be hierarchical, coercive, and partial or impartial (having an effect on the eventual outcome as opposed to being neutral and not having any effect on the outcome).

**Meech Lake Accord** a provisional agreement concluded in 1987 by all of Canada's leaders to allow Quebec to sign the Canadian Constitution in return for its recognition as a distinct society. It failed to win the support of the legislatures of two provinces, thereby dooming it.

**Metrocentric theory of empire-building** a great power, or metropole, seeks to expand its sphere of influence because of domestic factors such as economic ambitions or overpopulation.

**MONUC** (Mission de l'Organisation des Nations Unies en République démocratique du Congo) [United Nations Organization Mission in the Democratic Republic of the Congo] a peace-keeping force of United Nations operating in the Democratic Republic of Congo; the United Nations' largest peace-keeping mission in the world.

**Mixage** the cooptation process in which combatants loyal to Congo rebel leaders were integrated into the national army under Joseph Kabila.

**Montenegro** part of socialist Yugoslavia and then in a union with Serbia, it became an independent state in 2006.

**Moors** small ethnic minority in Sri Lanka. They are descended from early Arab traders who visited Sri Lanka and are predominantly Muslims. They mostly speak Tamil and are concentrated in the main trading centers.

**Multiethnic/multinational states** states that incorporate two or more ethnic groups or nations.

**Multilateralism** the crafting of a coalition of states so that it can act to mediate and resolve a regional conflict.

**Nation** a politicized ethnic group with well-developed statist ideas.

**National home regime** a solution to competing ethnic claims; an idea designed to reconcile the integrity and sovereignty of states; to provide a context for common nationality links for nations that are divided by state boundaries; to address their yearning for national identity; and to do so without undermining the cohesion of multinational societies.

**National self-determination** right of nations to decide their political future.

**Nationalism** one's sentiment for and loyalty to one's nation.

**Nation-building** the creation of the nation either along civic or ethnic lines.

**Nation-state** strictly speaking, an ethnic nation that is coterminous with a state; colloquially, it is used to describe multiethnic states as well.

**New world order (NWO)** naïve expectation that with the end of the cold war, a stable, secure, and more peaceful world had been created.

**Nongovernmental organizations (NGOs)** national and international organizations that encompass non-state actors such as civil society, social movements, and private voluntary organizations; many are involved in humanitarian work in trouble spots across the globe.

**North American Free Trade Association (NAFTA)** an economic association of the United States, Mexico, and Canada. An independent Quebec would hope to become a member.

**Northern Alliance** U.S. supported, Tajik-led military force.

**Occupation** as an international legal principle, it signifies the acquisition of territory that is not already a part of another state. This is no longer possible as all areas of the world are under the jurisdiction of one authority or another.

**Operation Jayasikuru** military offensive launched by Sri Lanka in 1997 against the LTTE.

**Operation Riviresa** massive military offensive launched by Sri Lanka in December 1995 to reestablish government control over the northern city of Jaffna, a main LTTE stronghold.

**Organization for Security and Co-operation in Europe (OSCE)** an intergovernmental organization consisting of more than 50 states in Western, Central, and Eastern Europe. Its main function is to promote stability within Europe and Eurasia. Peacekeeping forces are also deployed by it.

**Orphan conflicts** conflicts where the major international actors have little interest and involvement in.

**Parochialist secession** argument that the only inescapable requirement for a legitimate secessionist claim is the existence of a genuine "self" wanting to control its political destiny.

**Parthasarathy Formula** a set of peace proposals drawn up mainly at the initiative of G. Parthasarathy, Indian Prime Minister Indira Gandhi's personal envoy to Sri Lanka, to resolve the Tamil–Sinhalese conflict.

**Parti Québécois** the main nationalist party in Quebec that has been committed to Quebec's independence.

**Partisan intervention** outside intervention into an ethnic conflict that is favorable to one side in the conflict.

**Pashtuns** largest ethnic group in Afghanistan that usually has held political power.

**Patriation of the Canadian constitution** in 1982 Prime Minister Pierre-Elliot Trudeau replaced the 1867 BNA Act with a Canadian constitution that no longer required British parliamentary consent for laws passed in Canada.

**Pax Americana** a peace founded upon the U.S. national interest.

**Peace enforcement** politicodiplomatic and military operations carried out by an external third party that impose and enforce a political solution in a conflict situation either with or without the consent of the adversaries.

**Peace of Westphalia** an agreement, made in 1648, that ended the Thirty Years' War in Europe and marked the breakup of medieval Christendom and the birth of the modern sovereign state.

**Peacebuilding** long-term socioeconomic and cultural activity directed mostly at the ordinary members of the disputing parties to change their negative image, perceptions, and attitudes toward the followers of the other side.

**Peacekeeping** the physical interjection of external military forces between the forces of the disputants to keep them apart and thereby halt, however temporarily, the overt manifestation of violence in a conflict situation.

**Peacemaking** activity directed at the leaders of the disputing parties in order to encourage them to seek a peaceful settlement of their dispute.

**Péquiste** see *Parti Québécois.*

**Pericentric theory of empire-building** a great power decides to embark on expansion of its sphere of influence due to the behavior of a second, rival actor.

**Plains of Abraham** a battle fought in 1759 outside Quebec City between British and French forces. The British victory confirmed the diminished political and linguistic status of French on the North American continent.

**Policy of diffusion and encouragement** policy of providing partisan support to (usually) ethnic insurgents against the state followed by an external actor.

**Policy of isolation and suppression** policy of providing partisan support to the state against ethnic insurgents followed by an external actor.

**Political opportunity structure** the incentives, disincentives, and boundaries shaping the behavior of political, especially today ethnic, entrepreneurs.

**Politico-diplomatic support** partisan external support that may include statements of concern, support in IGOs, diplomatic pressure, etc; more difficult to measure than tangible support.

**Popular sovereignty** a belief in the political theory that government is created by and subject to the will of the people, who are the source of all political power.

**Postmodern dilemma** defining state role in a world of changing identities, alliances, and affiliations.

**Preventive diplomacy** diplomatic engagement by external third parties with the adversaries at an early state of a dispute in order to prevent the dispute from escalating to the level of a violent showdown.

**Primordialism** the school of thought that regards ethnic identity as being "naturally given."

**Principle of nonintervention** cardinal principle of international law that makes it illegal for states and other international bodies to intervene in the internal affairs of a state without its express consent.

**Principle of nonuse of force** cardinal principle of international law that makes it illegal for states and other international bodies to actually use or threaten the use of force against another state.

**Quiet Revolution** describes the modernization of Quebec's political life begun in 1960.

**Rambouillet Talks** sponsored by the Contact Group for Former Yugoslavia, they brought Serb and Albanian leaders together outside of Paris in February 1999 to try to reach a political agreement on Kosovo. The talks failed.

**Red lines of international conduct** those activities of states, groups, or individuals that are impermissible under international law, mostly because they threaten international peace and violate human rights.

**Referendum** a direct popular vote on a given issue.

**Refugees** mostly civilian victims of violent conflict.

**Relative deprivation** a situation of perceived discrepancy between value expectations and value expectancies in a society.

**Remedial secession** a scheme under which, corresponding to the various degrees of oppression faced by an ethnic group at the hands of its governing state, international law would recognize a continuum of remedies ranging from protection of individual rights, to minority rights, to secession.

**Republic of Kosovo** Albanian leaders in Kosovo proclaimed a republic distinct from Serbia in 1991. It was never recognized by any major international actors. Albanian Muslims living in Kosovo are often referred to as Kosovars to distinguish them from Serbs residing in Kosovo.

**Republika Srpska** the Serb Republic, specifically used to denote the government of Serb areas of Bosnia-Herzegovina. It was proclaimed in 1992 after a Muslim-led government in Sarajevo declared independence for all parts of Bosnia-Herzegovina.

**Research and Analysis Wing (RAW)** India's main foreign intelligence agency.

**Resolution 1199** passed by the United Nations in September 1998, it threatened military intervention in Kosovo if there was no halt to hostilities. The Resolution's aim was primarily to force Yugoslav President Slobodan Milosevic to withdraw his security forces from Kosovo.

**Resolution 1244** passed by the United Nations in June 1999. It affirmed the territorial integrity of Yugoslavia while requiring substantial autonomy for Kosovo.

**Rest of Canada (ROC)** the term used to describe the nine provinces and three territories of Canada if Quebec were to secede.

**Revolution of rising expectations** situation prevailing in the immediate postcolonial period in several developing countries where people expected that their condition would improve drastically with political independence.

**Revolution of rising frustration** a general condition of mass anger and protest in many postcolonial developing states as these states' economies began to stagnate and decline in the 1960s and 1970s.

**Rose Revolution** a populist movement that began in 2003 and succeeded in bringing a pro-Western, anti-Russian leader to power in Georgia.

**Rossiiskii** people who are either ethnic Russians or are closely related to them by ethnicity, religion, or history (through conquest).

**Ruskii** people who are ethnically great Russian and Russian Orthodox in their religious beliefs.

**Russification** the imposition of the Russian language, culture, and political system on non-Russian nations. It is a phenomenon most closely associated with the Soviet period.

**Rwandan Patriotic Front (RPF)** a Tutsi-dominated military and political organization at the center of politics in several Central African states.

**Secession** an act of separation whereby a group or region breaks away from one state to either form a new independent state or join with another state.

**Security dilemma** realist concept in the field of international relations that states that whatever a state does to protect its security makes its enemies insecure; hence, they in turn try to secure themselves. This sets into motion an upward spiral of insecurity for all.

**Shariat** Islamic legal code.

**Shia Crescent** a geopolitical term to describe a region of the Middle East where the majority population or where a strong minority in the population is Shias; it runs along the Persian Gulf.

**Shia Muslims** religious group representing about 60 percent of Iraqi population and concentrated in the south and east of the country, not far from Iran.

**Sinhalese** ethnic group that forms approximately 75 percent of the population of Sri Lanka. The Sinhalese are mostly Buddhist in religious orientation and originally migrated to Sri Lanka from India. The Sinhalese mostly inhabit the southern, western, and central parts of Sri Lanka. They mostly speak Sinhalese.

**Slavophiles** originating in a Russia-first movement in the nineteenth century (even though Slav refers to other nations, such as Czechs, Poles, and Serbs), it describes those Russian intellectuals who praise Russia's culture and are suspicious of Western influence on it.

**Smart power** developing an integrated strategy, resource base, and tool kit to achieve American objectives, drawing on both hard and soft power.

**Soulbury Commission** constitutional commission that was responsible for drafting the first postindependence constitution of Sri Lanka.

**Srebrenica** a town in Bosnia-Herzegovina that had been proclaimed by the United Nations as a safe haven during the Bosnian war. In July 1995 Serb forces took the town and executed thousands of its Muslim inhabitants. It marked a turning point in the West's policy on nonmilitary intervention in the war.

**Sri Lankan Tamils** chief ethnic minority in Sri Lanka; forms about 12 percent of the total population. The Sri Lankan Tamils are predominantly Hindu in religious orientation and originally migrated to Sri Lanka from southern India. They mostly inhabit the northern and eastern regions of Sri Lanka. They mostly speak Tamil.

**Stabilization Force (SFOR)** see *Implementation Force (IFOR)*.

**Stalinism** the totalitarian political system established by Soviet leader Joseph Stalin. Its main feature was the communist leaders' total control of all aspects of public and private life.

**State** legal concept describing a social group that occupies a defined territory and is organized under common political institutions and an effective government. The state further exercises sovereign authority within its boundaries and is recognized as sovereign by other states.

**State building** the creation of state institutions, government, and civil society.

**State collapse** total disintegration of the structure, authority, power, law, and political order within a state. See also *weak states*.

**State recognition** act by which another state acknowledges that the political entity in question possesses all the attributes of statehood.

**State reconstruction** the rebuilding of the institutions, structures, and authority of a state that has collapsed.

**Status of belligerency** indication by an external party that it regards insurgents involved in an armed internal conflict as having, though temporarily, the same status as that of states.

**Status of insurgency** indication by an external party that it regards insurgents involved in an armed internal conflict as legal contestants and not as mere lawbreakers.

**Sunni Muslims** religious group representing about 35 percent of Iraqi population. It has traditionally formed the ruling group in most Arab states.

**Superpowers** states that are usually economically and militarily the most powerful and that have vast global interests and commitments compared to other states in the international system.

**Swabasha Movement** a largely Sinhalese-dominated political movement in Sri Lanka that initially demanded that the English language be replaced in official use by vernacular languages (Sinhalese and Tamil); after independence, this demand was converted to the demand that Sinhalese, and not Tamil, should be the sole official language of Sri Lanka.

**Systemic theory of empire-building** a great power sees opportunities for expansion presented by the international system, for example, the instability of a multipolar balance of power.

**Tamil Eelam** independent Tamil state.

**Tangible support** partisan external support consisting of military, financial, material, and logistical aid.

**Titular peoples** literally, the nation after which a country or region is named

**Tutsis** an ethnic minority representing about 10 percent of the population of Burundi and Rwanda, they have constituted the traditional ruling group.

**Ummah** Arabic term for a single community of Islamic believers.

**UN High Commissioner for Refugees (UNHCR)** an agency of the United Nations based in Switzerland which is concerned with the plight of refugees worldwide. Mary Fitzgerald, former President of the Irish Republic, was High Commissioner during the crisis in Kosovo.

**UN Interim Administration Mission in Kosovo (UNMIK)** United Nations Interim Administration Mission in Kosovo. It was designed as a temporary administration for the province following NATO's campaign against Serbia in 1999.

**Unilateralism** state acting independent of international opinion.

**Union of Soviet Socialist Republics (USSR)** also known as the Soviet Union, it was the authoritarian political system that was established by Vladimir Lenin following the Great October Revolution of 1917. Russia and the areas it controlled were federated into a communist state called the USSR in 1922. The state consisted of 15 "republics" (or provinces) at the time of its collapse in December 1991.

**Unjust nonwar** failure to intervene militarily in circumstances in which it would be morally jusatifiable.

**Veddhas** descendants of the aboriginal tribes of ancient Sri Lanka whose numbers have been greatly reduced over the years. They continue to rely on hunting for their food and live under extreme primitive conditions in the forests of eastern Sri Lanka.

**Velvet divorce** the peaceful breakup of Czechoslovakia into independent Czech and Slovak states in 1993.

**War crimes** violations of widely accepted and established international laws of warfare by combatants.

**Weak states** closely related to the idea of collapsed states, the term refers to the disintegration of central political and economic authority in a country.

**"White man's burden" argument** a process whereby uncivilized nations could be introduced into civilized international society after a period of enlightened education and preparation for self-government.

# INDEX

Note: Page numbers followed by *f* and *t* indicate figures and tables respectively.